D1593564

STUDIES IN COMMONWEALTH POLITICS AND HISTORY
No. 3

General Editors: Professor W. H. MORRIS-JONES
Institute of Commonwealth Studies,
University of London

Professor DENNIS AUSTIN
Department of Government,
University of Manchester

POLITICIANS AND SOLDIERS
IN GHANA 1966–1972

Politicians and Soldiers in Ghana 1966—1972

Edited by

DENNIS AUSTIN

Victoria University of Manchester

and

ROBIN LUCKHAM

Institute of Development Studies, Sussex

FRANK CASS : LONDON

First published 1975 in Great Britain by
FRANK CASS AND COMPANY LIMITED
67 Great Russell Street, London WC1B 3BT, England

and in United States of America by
FRANK CASS AND COMPANY LIMITED
c/o International Scholarly Book Services Inc.
P.O. Box 4347, Portland, Oregon 97208

ISBN 0 7146 3049 7

Library of Congress Catalog No. 74-82840

Text set in 11 pt. Photon Times, printed by photolithography,
and bound in Great Britain at The Pitman Press, Bath

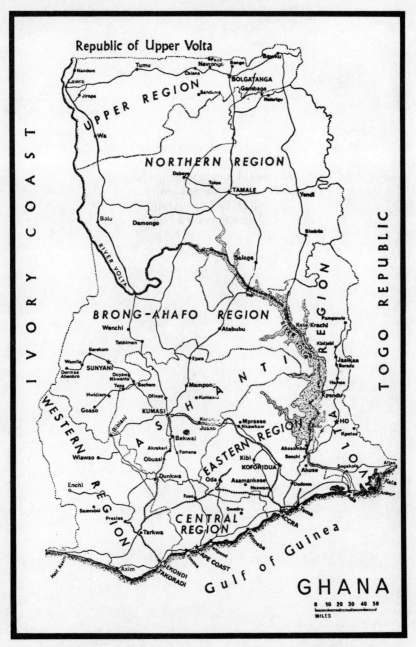

Based on a map from *Politics in Ghana* by Dennis Austin. Published by Oxford University Press under the auspices of the Royal Institute of International Affairs. Reprinted by permission of the publisher.

v

'All, all, of a piece throughout
    Thy chase had a Beast in view
Thy wars brought nothing about
    Thy lovers were all untrue.
'Tis well an Old Age is out
    And time to begin a New.'

CONTENTS

MAPS

LIST OF CONTRIBUTORS

Dennis Austin, *Victoria University of Manchester.*
Robin Luckham, *Institute of Development Studies, Sussex.*
Robert Dowse, *University of Exeter.*
J. D. Esseks, *University of Northern Illinois.*
Stephen Nkrumah, *University of Ghana.*
V. C. R. A. C. Crabbe, *High Court, Accra.*
Yaw Twumasi, *University of Ghana.*
John Dunn, *King's College, Cambridge.*
Maxwell Owusu, *University of Michigan.*
Mark Graesser, *Memorial University, Newfoundland.*
Joseph Peasah, *University of Ghana.*
Valerie Plave Bennett, *University of Boston.*

FOREWORD

Legatee of a vast empire, the Commonwealth still carries the imprint of its past. And in doing so it may be said to have a collective identity which, in a very varying degree, each of its members exhibits. This, we believe, can sustain a collective inquiry into the political history and institutions of countries which were once governed within the British Empire and we note signs of a revival of interest in this field. In recent years 'area studies' have been encouraged, but there is also a sense in which the Commonwealth is itself a region, bounded not by geography but history, and imperial history in particular. Seen thus the region cannot exclude areas into which empire overspilled as in the Sudan, or areas now outside the Commonwealth such as South Africa and Burma, or the unique case of Ireland. No account of the dilemmas which face the government of Canada or Nigeria or India—or indeed of the United Kingdom—which examines the present in relation to the past can be complete which omits some consideration of this 'imperial dimension'. Without in any sense trying to claim that there is a 'political culture' common to all Commonwealth countries it is certainly the case that some of the institutions, some part of the political life, and a certain element in the political beliefs of many Commonwealth leaders, can be said to derive from the import of institutions, practices and beliefs from Britain into its former colonies.

Nor is the Commonwealth merely a useful category of study. It is also a community of scholars, many of them teaching and writing within the growing number of universities throughout the member countries who share an interest in the consequences of imperial experience and have common traditions of study.

The present series of books is intended to express that interest and those traditions. They are presented not as a guide to the Commonwealth as a corporate entity, but as studies either in the politics and recent history of its member states or of themes which are of common interest to several of the countries concerned. Within the Commonwealth there is great variety—of geographical setting, of cultural context, of economic development and social life; they provide the challenge to comparative study, while the elements of common experience make the task manageable. A cross-nation study of administrative reforms or of legislative behaviour is both facilitated and given added meaning; so also is an examination of the external relations of one or more member states;

even a single country study, say on Guyana, is bound to throw light on problems which are echoed in Malaya and Sri Lanka. The series will bring together—and, we hope, stimulate—studies of those kinds carried out by both established and younger scholars. In doing so, it can make its distinctive contribution to an understanding of the changing contemporary world.

The present volume is fully illustrative of the intentions of the series. It examines the attempt to restore, and the failure to maintain, a parliamentary Westminster form of government in Ghana, a study in 'Commonwealth Legacies' which brings together scholars from Ghana, Britain and North America.

DENNIS AUSTIN
W. H. MORRIS-JONES

PREFACE

It is our pleasant duty to thank publicly three major institutions which gave generously of their resources to assist in bringing together contributions to the present volume: the Universities of Manchester and Ghana and the Social Science Research Council of the United Kingdom. ... The result is a study by several hands. There are ten chapters *plus* an Introduction and an Epilogue. It is a composite work. But we hope that the variety of authorship, related to a common theme, has strengthened rather than weakened the story; and that by placing at the centre of the study the 1969 election—flanked (as it were) by the two coups d'etat in 1966 and 1972—a focus has been offered for the work as a whole.

The original intention had been a little different. It was to draw together an account of the first coup and the return, via the 1969 election, to civilian rule. The first drafts were ready when the second coup occurred, whereupon the chapters were then recast in their present form and an Epilogue was added in order to take note of the full range of events between the two armed incursions. As suggested in the Introduction, these six years form an interesting bridge between the early nationalist era which ended in 1966 and the present military regime which began in 1972. The reader is also bound to note, as he moves from one to the other, a falling away of the confidence of that earlier period and a sharp anxiety over what may be the future configuration of politics. In brief, the study is now one of failure, of soldiers who failed to transfer power to political leaders, and of politicians who failed to prevent its transfer back to the military. It is a common enough theme and in no sense a singular failure. Yet the story needed to be told if only that it might stand testimony to the attempt during the latter half of the 1960s to bring politics in Ghana back within the framework of parliamentary government where it once belonged, and to the obstacles which made this so difficult a task. Nkrumah once said 'seek ye first the political kingdom'. Neither he nor his successors ever found it.

INTRODUCTION
Dennis Austin

The first coup d'état in Ghana took place in February 1966 when the army and police destroyed the Convention People's Party which had been in Office under Nkrumah since February 1951. Fifteen years of party rule had come to an end, and the soldiers began to govern by decree through a 'National Liberation Council'. Army rule was not in itself surprising: Nigeria had been brought under military control in January that year, and there was the long history of military-civilian alternation in that other post-colonial continent of Latin America. The first Ghana coup, however, was of very limited duration. For almost as soon as the members of the N.L.C. had established themselves in control, they began to talk of handing power back to a civilian government. And in August 1969, some three and a half years' later, they virtually made good their promise. A general election was held, impartially protected by the army and police. That too was hardly a unique event; but it was unusual. Freely contested and fairly conducted elections had become sufficiently rare in Africa to make the occasion worth noting, while for Ghanaians especially it was a memorable revival of earlier contests when the ballot box had put an end to colonial rule.[1] There were other precedents from the 1950s, for when the soldiers retired from politics, they did so by moving along a familiar path of retreat. They appointed Committees of Inquiry, established a Constitutional Commission, summoned a Constituent Assembly, introduced an Electoral Ordinance, and agreed to the formation of parties; then, at the end of August 1969, they held an election. The outcome was a decisive victory for the newly formed Progress Party which took office under Dr. Busia as prime minister upon the inauguration of the second Republic on 1 October. The following year, the Presidential Commission—a triumvirate of one police, and two army, officers—was dissolved and a civilian Head of State was chosen. The ballot box having thus replaced the gun, it seemed appropriate at the time, in the disturbed world of new state politics, to take comfort from the fact, and to mark the occasion with an account of the 1969 Election and of what had happened during the brief period of 'demilitarisation'.

Such was the genesis of the present volume: Ghana and the return to civilian rule. Then in January 1972, within three years of the election, a section of the army intervened again under a new commander. Col. Acheampong wrested power from Busia's government much as the earlier group of conspirators under Col. Kotoka had pulled down Nkrumah's administration. In that same year, in April, Nkrumah died in exile, while Busia remained abroad in Oxford, and a new army-constituted 'National Redemption Council' ruled in Accra. The chapters which follow this brief introduction consider these crowded, almost breathless years under different headings, but they retain as their central focus the events which preceded and followed the 1969 election. Together they cover what is likely to be seen, in retrospect, as a critical period of transition. The downfall of Nkrumah and of the C.P.P., followed by the failure of Busia and the Progress Party to govern in their stead, brought to an end the once familiar struggle between party leaders whose original strengths and weaknesses had derived a good deal from their rivalry as successors to the colonial power. Nkrumah, like Busia, was very much a hero of his time. What had mattered then was control of the nationalist party as it moved towards and through the achievement of independence in 1957. After the February coup in 1966, there began the search for a very different arrangement of power at national level—very different from the world of the dominant party or the single party—a world in which Ghana was now one of a number of states in which the army has taken its place either in the council chamber or sufficiently close to its doors to be able to impose its will from time to time on whoever rules by its favour.

At the time of the first coup, the problem was not seen in these terms. What was needed (it was assumed) was something much simpler—a return to the past, or rather to a 'reformed past'. It was believed by many, and commonly expressed in the newspapers and journals which began to reappear under the military, that democratic ways and a representative system of government could be restarted in the wake of the army once it had carried out its remedial task. What had been lost under the C.P.P. would then be regained through a new civilian government. There was need (it was said) for restraints on populist rule, under the government of laws not men within a tightly regulated constitution. Such, for example, was the argument of the Constitutional Commission and the Constituent Assembly between 1967 and 1969. The provenance of the first coup was no less simply explained as the result of the misdeeds of the former regime. The army officers were 'liberators': hence the label—'National Liberation Council'—which the soldiers attached to their rule. Nor was it difficult to understand such beliefs, or the jubilation of the crowds which, without need of curfew, celebrated Nkrumah's downfall. The former People's Party had been brushed aside with such ease that the memory of its heroic days was almost blotted out, and the quick success of the army seemed a direct measure of Nkrumah's failure. The army and police officers were able to justify their intervention therefore not only as 'inevitable' (the stock phrase of men who disguise what they want to do by arguing that it cannot be avoided), but as being in response to a popular but suppressed demand. It was demonstratively true that many Ghanaians welcomed the arrival of the soldiers and gave massive support three years later to Busia and his party as the clearest alternative to the C.P.P. The Progress vote of 876,378 in the 1969 election was more than double that for the C.P.P. during the comparable election of 1956, and the party achieved a higher proportion of the poll (59 per cent) from a much enlarged electorate. Even the loser—K. A. Gbedemah and his National Alliance of Liberals—picked up more votes than the C.P.P. had secured prior to independence. Thus was virtue rewarded with the return of parliamentary rule brought about first by the army's intervention and then by its withdrawal.

The re-entry of the army in January 1972 was more awkward to explain, except in the sense that the second coup was essentially different from the first by reason of being second. The military appetite had grown perhaps by feeding. And of course it is always the first breach of constitutionality which is the most difficult—for 'use almost can change the stamp of nature'. After the first breach is made, there is likely to be much less of an obstacle to intervention in the minds of army officers or in the institutions hastily constructed by civilian successors to the previous coup. So it was in 1972. The earlier seizure of power had been easy, the country was small, its armed forces still compact; and although the N.L.C. was uneasy in its rule between 1966 and 1969 and had had to put down a dangerous attempt by junior officers to stage a further coup in 1967, there was no parallel in Ghana to the terrible self-slaughter of the Nigerian officer corps or the horror of the Nigerian civil war. Such no doubt were among the calculations of Col. Acheampong and his colleagues in 1971–72, although in reaching the decision to intervene, they confirmed what had only been previously suspected, that when the army withdrew in 1969 it remained at the frontiers of politics and could not be prevented from crossing them again at will.

Very likely that will be the lasting effect of the two coups. And it was the final disaster of the Nkrumah regime that it gave occasion and cause for the army to act. In such a country as Ghana, where colonial government had kept the army at a distance from politics, and where (unlike Latin America) there is little other history of the state (as a state) to go by, there needed to be the dangerous combination in 1966 of grievances among the armed forces and widespread discontent with the regime to encourage the soldiers. There was (to be sure) the January coup in Nigeria, and earlier upsets in the small republics of Togo and Dahomey, but there was little evidence of 'contagion' in Ghana. And if Dr. Dowse in his opening chapter shows clearly how strong the sense of professional grievance was among the army and police, he shows too how it was brought to the point of action by the reasonable assumption that the overthrow of the C.P.P. would be generally welcomed.

One must be careful (as Dowse insists) to avoid too simple an explanation of that first coup which put an end to the colonial-nationalist era. Later chapters examine the particular grievances of the 'malcontents in uniform': but the power of the single party regime prior to its downfall is also shown. For the long shadow of the defeated party reached well beyond the line of its collapse, and much that was done by the N.L.C. and by Busia's government was carried out in some apprehension that there was substance still to the shadow. The assertion is sometimes made that by 1966 the C.P.P. had become a faded party or, at best, very poorly articulated—more head than body, and when the head was off the body quickly died. But that was not how many Ghanaians who had felt its power, saw the former regime. It had become oppressive, and its members had grossly enriched themselves at public expense; but it was not at all clear in February 1966 that the party had ceased to exist as a country-wide apparatus of control. On the contrary, it was feared by many, and supported by some, precisely because it was still powerful, and since it was also apparently irremovable, it could be argued that the army and police were needed to dislodge the party from its legally entrenched position.

There was a distinction, therefore, between the two coups. The 1966 conspirators—Kotoka, Harlley, Ocran and Afrifa—could point to the oppressive nature of the C.P.P., including its denial of free elections, in defence of the need to act forcibly, and justify their action as being the only way in which change could be brought about. They could also talk not only of reform but of withdrawal—as if what had gone wrong, like a clock which had stopped working, could be put right with a firm shake and new time-keepers—since they believed that alternative leaders were available. It seemed reasonable to assume that because the C.P.P. had ceased to excite widespread approval, there would be no difficulty in finding acceptable successors. And so it proved. The swing against the defeated regime was so strong that Busia had little trouble in winning the election, whereupon the N.L.C. was induced to transfer power to the Progress leaders, many of whom, having opposed the C.P.P., had spent several years in prison or exile or, at least, in disfavour for doing so. 'Induced' is perhaps too strong a word. A majority (but by no means all) of the members of the N.L.C. were very willing in the end to see Busia and his colleagues as successors to their rule. This is not to say that they had intervened in order to put Busia in office since they were primarily concerned with the defence (as they interpreted it) of the state, and of their own interests, against the misuse of party rule. Nor could one say of Busia that 1966 was *his* coup in the sense of *qui facit per alia facit per se:* there was no correspondence between the aims of the soldiers and the hopes of the politicians. Nevertheless, as soon as the N.L.C. gave permission for parties to appear, many of the pre-coup divisions and leaders re-appeared, including the former opposition under Busia, Victor Owusu, R. R. Amponsah and veteran politicians from the pre-C.P.P. days, represented pre-eminently by W. E. Ofori Atta; a reformed C.P.P. under Gbedemah; and individual groupings under Joe Appiah, M. K. Apaloo and others. There were, therefore, alternatives to the former regime—and they were known to exist.

No such alternative exists today, nor could it be thought to have been there in January 1972. Col. Acheampong could use the ineptitude of the Progress government as ground for his actions, since it was Busia's peculiar misfortune to offend in turn, by specific acts and general policies, those on whom the government most depended for support—the civil service, the judiciary, trade unions, market traders, cocoa farmers, the universities and, by 1971, the army itself; and the government must surely have forfeited a large measure of its popularity by its inability to arrest the worsening economic situation which ended in the massive devaluation of the Cedi a month prior to the second coup.[2] One could add to this category of disasters a certain arrogance of power and wealth. But there was still an essential difference between the former C.P.P. government and Progress Party rule which it was not easy for Acheampong and the N.R.C. to dismiss. Nkrumah had shown very clearly that he had no intention of allowing himself to be removed from power: there was an ideological presumption and very sharp legal powers to make it impossible. That could not be said categorically of Busia's administration under a constitution which its leaders had helped to devise, including the requirement of fresh elections by 1973–74. In 1966 Col. Kotoka could point to the absence of any provision for change in the light of the absurd charade of the single-party 'election' which the C.P.P. had staged in June the previous year (when every candidate was returned unopposed); but Col. Acheampong could only assert in 1972 that such a situation was likely to recur. If, therefore, the first coup was an optimistic attempt by the army to break the enforced monopoly of single party government, and to restore competitive politics to a disfranchised electorate, the second coup marked the arrival of the army as one of the permanent contenders for power. And since there was no discernible alternative to the dismissed Progress Party, Col. Acheampong could put no limit to his rule.

At this point, the reader may brush aside such distinctions by pointing to the prevalence of military rule throughout a large part of the world, and to the difficulty of resisting a determined Commander and his soldiers when they appear as an armed pressure group. The leaders of a coup may mask their demands by a cloak of reform or behind an ideology of salvation; but both in 1966 and 1972 the army officers were clearly out to ward off what they saw as threats to themselves—threats which were particularly disturbing no doubt to an army and a police force which interpreted an obligation 'to remain free from politics' as implying a reciprocal freedom to maintain their professional autonomy. Valerie Bennett shows very well how dissatisfaction over promotions, equipment, rates of pay, questions of seniority and the privileges which went with rank, played a large part in 1966 and a dominant part in 1972. Were they not simply 'armed malcontents'? There was no great sense of destiny nor any clear ideological compulsion among either the N.L.C. or N.R.C. members. In 1966, the army moved against a regime which was commonly held to be on the 'left': in 1972, it overthrew a government which was said to be on the 'right'. What was there, then, to the two coups, but the plain assertion of military interests by aggrieved officers taking advantage of the times?

Against such an argument—brought by Busia against the N.R.C. and by Nkrumah against the N.L.C. with the added charge by the former President that somewhere or other, if only one could find it, there was at work the hidden hand of the neo-colonialist—against such an argument, there is no easy reply. One can only repeat what was argued earlier, that whereas the first coup did actually lead to a free election and a renewed attempt at parliamentary rule, the second intervention—a little over two years after the Progress Party took office—offered no such hope for the foreseeable future. Thus, one could say 1972, unlike the earlier intervention by Kotoka, that worse begins and bad remains behind.

Does it matter—matter, that is, to Ghanaians? Throughout those six years they were remarkably (and favourably) responsive to each change of regime. The crowds which gathered to listen delightedly to the C.P.P. leaders at independence in 1957 actually danced in the streets to welcome Kotoka in 1966. They queued patiently in the sun to vote for Busia in 1969, but were ready again to turn to Acheampong in 1972. There was a hopeful acceptance of each turn of fate, and popular expectation rode high at least until the second coup. Of course there were many, at each turn of the wheel, who were disadvantaged since those who benefitted, individually or communally, from a particular structure of power went out of business: but there was always the possibility that their chance would come again. Fortune's wheel could turn, when those who had been displaced might, if they survived, return to benefit not only themselves, but their kinsmen and dependents. What mattered, therefore, was to survive each castle revolution. The ordinary elector waited hopefully, while those who claimed to act for him, when their time came round, did what they could to capitalise on the resources which they could offer to the new rulers. As Achebe makes his hero comment reflectively in that most political of African novels, *A Man of the People:*

> ' "Let them eat", was the people's opinion, "after all when white men used
> to do all the eating did we commit suicide?" Of course not. And where is the
> all-powerful white man today? He came, he ate and he went. But we are still
> around. The important thing then is to stay alive; if you do you will outlive
> your present annoyance. The great thing, as the old people have told us, is
> reminiscence; and only those who survive can have it. Besides, if you sur-
> vive who knows? it may be your turn to eat tomorrow. Your son may bring
> home your share.'[3]

A later chapter by Maxwell Owusu explores this notion of a political
stock exchange and its brokers. The Ghanaian world (it is argued) is essentially one of distributory politics. It embodies the values of the
market place—a political market in which allegiance is determined by
the goods on offer. And if the distributory government runs out of
benefits, the customers, if they can, will go elsewhere. It was this con-
ditional loyalty which the soldiers understood in 1966 and 1972 when
they acted not simply because they were exasperated by the treatment
they had received, but because they were reasonably sure that the party
regime had run out of the recourses needed to keep intact its network of
political alliances. Such an 'instrumentalist' view of politics—of
governments as instruments of disbursements *via* an intermediary élite
to the electorate at large—is not of course peculiar to Ghana. Clientage
and brokerage are age old. It is simply that in many independent states,
including Ghana, such trading relationships between the national
government and local centres of power may become the prime matrix of
political life. They reflect not only the poverty of trust in national institutions (whether parties or parliaments or trade-union) but the persistence of 'poliarchies'—of semi-autonomous concentrations of
power, still largely territorial, in what was once a colonial artifact. So it
came about that the military won support with the promise of a restored
world of plenty, and were excelled in 1969 when the Progress Party,
skilfully weaving together local threads of support, offered not only
superior benefits but the exercise of virtue. Then, when both
failed—both the rewards and the probity—the electorate turned
without demur (despite no longer being able to vote) to a new military
Council which in its first Budget statement, promised once again to 'end
the severe hardship and increase in the cost of living to many people'.

Such arguments do help to explain both the volatility of the electorate
during these years and the apparent triumph of hope over experience.
For many local leaders there remained the possibility that fortune might
come one's way, to the benefit of the locality as well as oneself, if only
the wheel of chance could be made to turn. Despite the earlier period of
nationalist-centred expectation, and the actual performance of the
nationalist party, the Ghanaian voter—like many bemused elec-

torates—did, it seems, retain the belief that future governments would be more rewarding and less predatory than their predecessors. Only by 1972 had hope begun to grow grey hairs in waiting: hence perhaps the somewhat tempered welcome given to Acheampong. Hope was very much alive, however, in 1969. Maxwell Owusu describes how powerfully the promise of a future Progress government acted upon the voters in his Swedru constituency, and how such hopes had been revived by the reappearance in political life of would-be party leaders who used the local support which they had been able to draw together in their areas to gain national recognition by one side or other to the election.

Other accounts suggest different explanations of Dr. Busia's victory, particularly in the constituency studies which comprise the latter half of the book. John Dunn, for example is interested in the social location of moral feeling in the Ahafo district. He describes how both Progress and N.A.L. managed to 'stitch together' a party équipe on the strength of personal obligations, traditional loyalties or ethnic ties within the constituency; and how Busia and the Progress Party emerged as clear victors not because they offered better material rewards (though they certainly did not offer *worse* than their opponents) but because they were seen as morally superior to Gbedemah's National Alliance of Liberals about which there clung the opprobrium of the former party regime. Moreover—and other contributors stress the point as one of substance—Busia's ascendancy during the election owed much to his earlier opposition to Nkrumah. He was seen not only as a man of probity and an educated leader—'the Prof'—but as the rightful alternative to the former C.P.P. It was a concept of 'ins and outs' well understood in chieftaincy disputes, and it is used to good effect by Yaw Twumasi in his general account of the election to explain why so large a proportion of the electorate turned naturally to Busia. 'Popular justification for the coup ran along lines which Busia had adumbrated in his long political career, thus giving him the image of a prophet (and) a constant refrain . . . was: "Busia said so and so . . . let us give him a chance".'

There is much, therefore, in the story of these six years which, though they bring to a close a distinct chapter of Ghanaian history, is familiar in relation to the past. In the description of the debates within the Constituent Assembly, as in the first hand account by the Electoral Commissioner, V. C. R. A. C. Crabbe, of the work of the Commission, the reader will notice that inter-play of communal loyalties and élite rivalries which has been characteristic of Ghanaian contests since the beginning of nationalist politics. What should one understand by such phrases? There has always been both an intense local patriotism, and a fierce competition between different levels of the educated community; and the subtlety of a large part of national politics has consisted of their being compounded. Perhaps a model will help? It is almost an obligation on political scientists today (and even historians are not guiltless) to present one to their readers. A stepped pyramid perhaps? Certainly it is tempting to see Ghanaian society as a broad social pyramid, levelled off at the top, on which a small though growing élite stands uneasily poised. They are an 'upper élite' of the professions, businessmen, high civil servants and, today, the military. The base is very broad—farmers and their migrant labourers, producing food for local markets or cocoa for export, and the urban poor—while above them rise the gradations of education and wealth, from the semi-educated artisan and wealthier cocoa farmer to the contractor, store-keeper, trader, teacher, and the élite group of senior civil servants, doctors, lawyers, business executives and the like. A cross section through the pyramid, therefore, at a particular echelon can be defined by wealth and occupation and, their usual concomitant, the level of education. But the main slopes of the pyramid are the ethnic solidarities—Ga, Ewe, Dagomba, Gonja, Tallensi, Akan (whether Fanti, Ashanti, Brong or Akwapim) and the other local peoples—of which Ghanaian society is composed. The structure is not of course symmetrical. Quite apart from the question of majority and minority communities (and the centre of political life has always been within the Akan majority), it is much more difficult as one moves from the southern to the northern regions to clamber to the top of this stepped pyramid. (There are many more southern Fanti, than northern Dagarti, lawyers for example.) We may still take note however of the cross-placing of, say, an educated market trader as belonging both 'hierarchically' and 'territorially' to a particular point on the pyramid. And it may be very necessary to remember (if we are talking politics) that a Police Officer who has risen through the professional hierarchy of the force, or a member of the Bar Association of wealth and social distinction, is likely still to retain something of his birth as a Ga or Fanti or Ewe. Similarly, an Ashanti railway worker is likely to have lost something of his 'tribal identity' by reason of his common interests either with others of his trade or with those of a similar economic status, whether of the same or different ethnic group.

Such conceits may have their use; but they may also mislead if used too nicely as a guide to N.R.C. rule or the 1969 election. For the gradations on the pyramid as sketched here are measured by economic standing and educational attainment, and both may vary according to location. A middle-Form IV-educated clerk of council in, say, Tumu in the far north, will have much greater sway politically than his southern counterpart. And it is not easy to place hierarchically either the army officer whose authority is his occupation, or the holder of a traditional office (at village rather than Paramount level) whose influence is not yet eroded. There are considerable difficulties, too, in talking about the

'politics of ethnic solidarity'. At first sight, there appeared a clear ethnic
pattern to the voting in 1969 if only because of the rivalry at national
level between the two party leaders—Busia (an Akan) and Gbedmah
(an Ewe) and, within the N.L.C., between Lt. General Afrifa (an Akan)
and Inspector General Harlley (an Ewe). There was a rallying of Akan
and Ewe support, therefore, between Progress and N.A.L. candidates—to the great advantage of Gbedemah in the Volta region and
to the great embarrassment of N.A.L. candidates in the five Akan-
dominated regions of Ashanti and the south. But throughout the larger
number of the 140 constituencies (as may be seen in the meticulous accounts by Dr. Graesser and Dr. Peasah) the principal source of conflict
lay in the rivalry between neighbouring towns or chiefdoms, between
immigrant 'strangers' and local residents, or between would-be party
leaders (of the same ethnic origin) who tried to bind their followers personally to their cause.

There are so many sides to the pyramid, therefore, and such uneven
divisions between the summit and the base, that one may wonder
whether the analogy is very helpful except to note the complexity of
'talking politics' in such states. One may also wonder (in Ghana in particular) how long the intensity of this local patriotism, and the grouping
of power on a personal base, will last. The writer is inclined to argue that
while 'tradition as chieftaincy' is likely to diminish (and there is clear
evidence for *that*), 'tradition as locality' will continue so long as Ghana
remains a predominantly peasant and small town society. Communal
and personal relationships are likely to persist, therefore, as the stuff of
local politics for a long time to come. Despite sharp inequalities of income and status between the powerful and the poor, Ghana still has a
long way to go towards the concept of class as a major source of conflict. Admittedly, there were notions of 'class distinction', and even
ideological differences, put about by the party leaders in 1969. There was
a good deal of loose talk in the party newspapers at the time from which
it might be thought that there were substantial social differences in
membership between the two main contenders. Dr. Busia's party was
often described, either admiringly or disparagingly, as an 'intellectuals'
party', while Gbedemah professed to stand for 'the common man'. But
such distinctions were more easily claimed than substantiated. There
was of course every sign throughout the country of a political class on
the make, but its members were obliged to cast about on all sides for
some foothold of power by appealing to local loyalties or kinship ties or
personal obligations. Similarly, at national level, in the early stages of
what Robin Luckham calls the 'politics of going back into politics'
before parties were allowed, there was a fair amount of switching by
would-be candidates from one pre-party group to another, including
attempts at a composite Third Force. Both N.A.L. and Progress could

be described (in western terms) as 'parties of the right', but in many ways there was very little at the centre or 'on the left' to appeal to, since it was an unusual (and certainly unintended) achievement of the Nkrumah period to have made socialist objectives even as an election slogan unattractive to the candidates of every party in the contest.

It did not make the election unreal: that was far from being so for the actual contestants. If the politics of class was absent from the local struggles in the constituencies and was, at best, faintly discernible in the quarrel at national level, the existence of a 'political class' of would-be politicians was very much in evidence. A striking characteristic of these years—certainly one that stands out most clearly in the writer's view—is not the persistence of territorial or personal rivalries (the exact configuration of which were very much subject to change) but the growth in number on the higher slopes of the pyramid (if the model is to be retained) of an 'educated and semi-educated political class, dominated in the 1960s by that professional and entrepreneurial minority to which all the parties in the election turned for leadership. Such a growth, in their many thousands from the middle schools, or in the remarkable increase (plotted by Robin Luckham) in the single and telling category of lawyers—from 60 in 1948 to 600 in 1969—has continued unchecked under colonial, nationalist, civilian and military regimes alike, multiplying political competition throughout the country far in excess of the small number of teachers, traders and clerks who scrambled for office under the C.P.P. More and more people were being drawn into politics. At the last election before independence under 700,000 voters went to the polls; in 1969 the number had more than doubled. Yet the local leaders who dominated the politics of the 1950s were very similar to those who reappeared in the latter half of the sixties. Of course there were changes at the top. The heroes came and went—Danquah, Nkrumah, Gbedemah, Busia; and some of their immediate followers failed to adjust to changes in the Castle or in Flagstaff House. Robin Luckham also shows the extent to which the Constituent Assembly and the 1969 parliament were drawn from a higher level of the élite than were earlier assemblies under Nkrumah; but that was primarily because of the expansion in the number and 'educational quality' of this very politically conscious group. The constituency executives of both Progress and N.A.L. contained much the same kind of local leaders as those who had once upheld the C.P.P.—some indeed were astute enough to make the transition from one regime to another. And to measure the distance between the C.P.P. and Progress is not to record any major shift in the social base of power. on the contrary. After talking to many of the local leaders of Progress and noting the weight of their electoral support, one could easily reach the conclusion that it was perhaps the kind of party which many of the early nationalists would have liked the C.P.P. to have become; and it may be that Busia and his colleagues were the kind of élite which those who had done well out of the former People's Party, and who hoped to do still better out of Progress, were now rather inclined to admire.

It is interesting to note that throughout these years there was no sign of a challenge to the dominance of this élite and its political following up and down the country. Despite the grievances of the cocoa farmers, there was no attempt to bring together a small-holders' party nor was there, despite the wretched level of urban poverty, any serious eruption of organised discontent in the large towns. There was almost a farmers' movement in Ashanti in the 1950s—until a dissatisfied section of the C.P.P. took control of its protests and produced the 'National Liberation Movement' under Dr. Busia. There was the earlier history of farmers' protests, and of 'cocoa hold-ups', under the colonial government. But still, in 1968 and 1969, the rural population, cocoa and food farmers alike, turned to (or allowed themselves to be represented by) the educated élite. They continued in this way to place an expectant trust in their educated kinsmen, and to whom else (lacking the confidence in their own ability) could they in practice turn with any comparable degree of confidence? It is in such painful choices that we can understand John Dunn's suggestion that the search behind politics in many African states—a search which can hardly be described as successful—has been not for "democracy' as such (of which at least the rural population has direct if intermittent experience in its day to day life) but representation.

This present volume is concerned primarily with the activities of this dominant political class and its leaders—including those in uniform—who claimed to speak for the interests of the population as a whole. It is not a very encouraging account. Rising in hope after 1966 it ends in frustration in 1972. Political life in Ghana does not (fortunately) run to extremes. There is no major class of extortionate landowners or landless peasants, no spectre of famine, and much less of the desperate poverty of the urban dispossessed of Asia and Latin America. One might add, too, that differences of religion and language, though they exist, do not enter directly and fanatically into political life. In many instances there is still an active family relationship, not only between the different layers of the educated community and the illiterate villager, but between political opponents. Admittedly, there was an unpleasant *Bonapartiste* flavour to Nkrumah's government in its corruption of nationalist hopes; and single party rule was harshly imposed towards the end of the first Republic until it was abruptly ended. The N.L.C. then locked up the C.P.P. leaders, just as the N.R.C. locked up the Progress party. But there has been mercifully absent from Ghana (to date) the atrocious brutality of many single-party, or military-

dominated states: no forced confessions, staged trials and the execution
of political prisoners. The twentieth century has not reached that far in
Accra. Nor has the country suffered as yet the degradation of politics to
be seen in Central and South America. To set Professor Busia and Col.
Kotoka or Col. Acheampong alongside, say, Prof. Ramon San Grau
Martin and Col. Batista in Cuba is to bring out, by contrast, the relative
decency of Ghanaian political life.[4]

What does exist in Ghana in the early 1970s is uncertainty—almost
a paralysis of political life after the rapid alternation of civil-military-
civil-military governments. Perhaps it is simply that nobody now knows
what to do, the sole achievement of the nationalist movement being the
single and dubious gift of independence? The weakness of the political
fabric has become dreadfully apparent, whether under the guise of an
imported liberalism in a 'Westminster constitution', or in the form of a
single-party, dominant-party or military-*cum*-administrative rule. What
is there now left to try? It is as if the gap between the colonial/traditional
past and the future cannot as yet be filled up or even bridged, certainly
not by a mimicry of that past or the pretence of a 'socialist ideology'.
Does the cause lie outside the country's control? There were times indeed when much of the drama of these years appeared as the politics of
theatre—of words not deeds, and rhetoric in place of politics—when
successive governments, in whatever role they cast themselves,
appeared like actors of a play in which the effective decisions were taken
off stage by others, in the cocoa markets and loan agencies of the
developed world. A shrill note of exhortation marked the last days of
Nkrumaism when it seemed, almost, as if the single party had been reduced
to its newspaper, as one may perhaps say a little unkindly of the N.R.C.
today in its reliance on the radio.[5] When Nkrumah looked back over his
years in office and the causes of his downfall, he was understandably
disposed to allot the larger share of the blame to the international world.
Neo-colonialism was the rocky shore on which the sea of nationalist
discontent beat in vain: no wonder therefore that the leader was thrown
off balance.[6] Nkrumah had tried to find new allies in the Soviet Union
and eastern Europe to reduce his dependence on western markets, and
he was overthrown. Busia tried to come to terms with the fact of
Ghana's need for external support, and he too was overthrown.
Acheampong is still in control (at the time of writing) but how fortunate
he is! For consider the country's financial position immediately prior to
and after the downfall of the Progress government.

Foreign Trade (Cedis m.)

	1971	1972
Exports	380.2	570.1
Imports	445.3	396.2
Balance of Trade	−65.1	+173.9

The difference is very great. By the end of 1972 imports were controlled, down by 11 per cent; exports were rising sharply, primarily because of higher cocoa prices which—£275 a ton in 1972 against £236 in 1971—soared to over £600 in 1973.[7] Here was wealth indeed! It meant that the country's foreign currency reserves moved from virtually zero, at the end of the Progress Government's brief period in office, to NC 98m by June 1972 in the first six months on the N.R.C.'s rule. A similar contrast before and after the 1966 coup is noted by John Esseks. It was perhaps the essential difference between the last year of party rule and the early months of military Government. The openly proclaimed shift after 1966 from 'socialism' to private enterprise had little effect on the fundamental structure of the economy. The critical distinction lay in the availability of resources. And it can hardly be omitted when looking at the uneasy politics of control in Accra. The question may be asked, therefore, whether Nkrumah might not have been able to continue in office, or whether Busia might not still be there today, had the economy been free of that crippling effect of the sudden fall in cocoa prices which took place immediately before their overthrow?

But we, too, must be careful of the note of rhetoric. For there is no unambiguous answer to such questions. It would certainly be helpful, to party leaders and soldiers alike, if the government had a more stable command of the resources of the state, and a more copious supply of such resources, than have hitherto existed: if, that is, they could meet Maxwell Owusu's requirements for 'good government'—larger rewards and more jobs. It would also be an advantage, no doubt, if Ghanaian society were less diverse and without the edge of distrust between ethnic communities. Yet these are hardly exceptional conditions. The rulers of most new (and a number of old) states have to manoeuvre as best they can in circumstances of economic scarcity and communal tension. There are societies more inveterately divided than Ghana, and poorer, whose leaders have escaped hitherto the succession of civil and military regimes so perplexing in Accra. Is the critical factor that of the impression of colonial rule, and the depth of that impression? Or is it, more simply, a matter of political skill—of a steady balance and calm nerves—there having been, during both periods of party government, under Busia as under Nkrumah, as much a failure perhaps of skill as of circumstances? Writing in 1973 so close to the events of these years, it is difficult to arrive at a clear answer, and it is surely proper (as it is certainly more prudent) to leave the reader free at this point to be able later to come down firmly, if he will, on one side or the other in the apportioning of blame for what must surely be seen, from the chapters that follow, as a marked lack of success in the government of a small West African republic.

Notes

1. Amply described in *Politics in Ghana 1946–60*, O.U.P. 1964.
2. £1 = NC 2.85 (mid-1973 rates of exchange).
3. And from the same novel, a passage which might well have been written about 1966 or 1972 in Ghana:

    Overnight everyone began to shake their heads at the excesses of the last regime, at its graft, oppression and corrupt government: newspapers, the radio, the hitherto silent intellectuals and civil servants—everybody said what a terrible lot; and it became public opinion the next morning. And these were the same people that only the other day had owned a thousand names of adulation, whom praise singers followed with song and talking-drum wherever they went. Chief Koko in particular became a thief and a murderer, while the people who had led him on—in my opinion the real culprits—took the legendary bath of the Hornbill and donned innocence.

4. The paragraph was written shortly after the 1972 coup: but by 1974 a new phenomenon could be observed. The military had begun to 'colonise' many civilian structures of authority in order to consolidate their hold. The number of officers appointed to ministerial posts, public corporations and para-statal bodies greatly exceeded the number in civilian command positions under the NLC, and the Redemption Council began to take an altogether more political view of its role, inevitably so if it was to stay in control. It was perhaps this almost CPP-like extension of (military) power which brought about the clumsy attempts, first by a small number of displaced Progress Party supporters, then by similarly disgruntled ex-CPP leaders, to stage a counter-coup in league with dissatisfied elements in the army. At the time of writing, the NRC had so far warded off two attempts, one from the 'Right', the other from the 'Left'. The ex-Progress Party attempt ended when George Ofusu Amaah (senior lecturer in law at Legon) was brought before a military tribunal, found guilty of subversion and, together with Staff Sergeant Opon Nyantakyi and six other conspirators, sentenced to death. These sombre events were repeated when John Alex Hamah, a former trade-unionist turned businessman, who had stood for election in 1969, was found guilty of trying to subvert Col. Kotei, Commander of the First Brigade in Accra. Then at the end of 1973 Imoru Ayarna, Kojo Botsio and John Tettegah, together with Owusu Boateng (a journalist) and Major Awuviri were also charged and found guilty of plotting. Ayarna, Botsio and Tettegah were sentenced to death, Owusu Boateng to twenty years imprisonment, Awuviri was acquitted. Hamah, too, was sentenced to death in a separate verdict late in December. None was executed, but during the trials ugly stories were told of torture, including the violent death of the brother of da Rocha, the former Progress Party general secretary. Perhaps it is simply that in Ghana in 1974 the military has not yet reached the conclusion that *organised* state terrorism is required?

5. See, for example, the closing articles to Col. Acheampong's two-year Budget Statement on Ghana Radio in September 1972—'[88]. We shall certainly overcome. [89] The Revolution continues unabated [90] God be with you.'

6. As in John Dunn's imagery of the revolutionary leader 'riding the breakers, triumphantly poised at the crest of a surging wave' only to come to grief since 'breakers cannot be ridden for ever; the pace slackens, the board dips and the balance and mastery are gone' in *Modern Revolutions*, C.U.P., 1972.

7. Export prices for mineral and timber production were also higher in 1972—logs, plywood, gold, diamonds, manganese, bauxite. (Figures taken from the *Quarterly Economic Review*, E.I.U. No. 2, 1973.) By 1974, however, the quadrupling of the price of oil imports had more than offset these gains.

CHAPTER I

MILITARY AND POLICE RULE

Robert Dowse*

In 1966 the Ghana army consisted of some 600 officers and 14,000 other ranks. It was then the largest in West Africa and the cost of maintaining it the fifth highest in the continent. It had been expanded rapidly since 1960 when it had 7,000 men and (at officer level) it was entirely Africanised. Similarly, the police force, which at independence had numbered about 6,000 men, had grown to 14,000 some ten years later.[1] The army was officered primarily by men from the coastal areas; the other ranks, despite efforts to broaden the pattern of recruitment, were still predominantly from the north. Such was the composition of the armed forces which brought down the party regime on 24 February 1966. It was shortly before dawn that day when Col. Kotoka, Commander of the Second Infantry Brigade Group, declared in a radio broadcast:

> Fellow Citizens of Ghana, I have come to inform you that the Military, in cooperation with the Ghana police, have taken over the government of Ghana today. The myth surrounding Nkrumah has been broken. Parliament is dissolved and Kwame Nkrumah is dismissed from office. All ministers are also dismissed. The Convention People's Party is disbanded with effect from now.

Compared with the forces of other African countries, neither the army nor the police had been badly paid or poorly equipped, and although there were complaints (after the coup) that the army had been starved of resources, it is difficult to believe that this was the main motive for intervention. The conspirators seemed primarily to have been moved by a combination of fear and resentment. They feared that the President's Own Guard Regiment, built up by Nkrumah with Russian help, might displace regular units of the army in presidential favour; they resented Nkrumah's sporadic interference with the army's internal affairs, including not only promotions and retirements but the party's meddling (as the army officers saw it) in the very difficult Congo operation. And both emotions were strengthened by the belief that Nkrumah was dragging the country towards economic collapse under a single party dictatorship. The coup almost failed through poor coordination, nor was it wholly bloodless—those killed included Maj. Gen. Charles

* The writer would like to thank B. Amamoo, E. Feit, H. Frimpong and R. Parkes for their comments on early drafts of the chapter.

16

Barwah, Chief of the General Staff, in addition to those of the President's Own Guard Regiment who remained loyal to Nkrumah—but it was quickly brought to a conclusion, and a distinct pattern of military-police rule began almost immediately to take shape.

At 1 p.m. on 24 February, a spokesman on Accra radio justified the coup by the misdeeds of Nkrumah who had 'been running the country as his own personal property', the result being 'gross economic mismanagement' from which 'all of us have suffered in one way or another'. Inflation and unemployment were rampant—'the country is on the verge of national bankruptcy'—and there was need for 'a radical rethinking of economic and financial policies'. Nkrumah was accused of ruling capriciously and dangerously, but the case against him was not spelled out in detail. The underlying professional grievances could be seen in the announcement that Maj. Gen. Ankrah, who had been forcibly retired by Nkrumah, had now been reinstated and promoted to Lt. General. (It was one of several promotions self-bestowed.) The President's Own Guard Regiment was absorbed into the main body of the army after its Commander, Col. David Zanlerigu, had been placed in protective custody. And the broadcast, which announced that a National Liberation Council had been brought together to govern the country, ended with an appeal to the civil service: 'All principal secretaries, heads of department and other members of the public service are asked to stay at their posts.' Since, in the earlier announcement, the soldiers had dissolved the C.P.P. and the 1960 constitution, and were shortly to declare all political activity illegal, the rudiments of an administrative state emerged immediately. In a further broadcast later that evening, the N.L.C. announced that some five hundred political prisoners, held under the Preventive Detention Act passed by the former regime, were to be released, and that all the party posts throughout the country were to be controlled by the administrative secretaries to the now dismissed C.P.P. Commissioners.

The N.L.C. had acted quickly to erect the new administrative structure. And it acted equally quickly to destroy the old C.P.P. The leading cadres of the party were immediately arrested and placed in 'protective detention' by the police which, since it had branches throughout the country, was in a very strong position to know who might be a danger to the new regime. It was this aspect of the 'coalition coup' that made it so successful: the army had the force to overthrow at the centre; the police had the intimate local knowledge to enable it to prevent potential opposition before it could take shape. But although many of their grievances were of a quite specifically professional nature, that is not to say that the military and police were acting contrary to the wishes or even to the interests of the majority of Ghanaians. It is, indeed, difficult to think of any interest in Ghana that immediately stood to lose from the coup, apart from those employed by the government on state projects of one kind or another, and the various officials and agents of the now disbanded C.P.P. which by 1966 was quite incapable of offering resistance to the combined police and army.

Initially the N.L.C. consisted of seven men: Lieutenant-General Ankrah, three other soldiers—E. K. Kotoka, A. K. Ocran and A. A. Afrifa—and three policemen: J. W. K. Harlley the Inspector General, B. A. Yakubu his deputy, and J. E. O. Nunoo. Neither the air force nor the navy was involved. Thus the army had a majority until early March when another policeman, A. K. Deku, was added, bringing about an even balance within the army-police coalition. Ethnically, the admission of Deku upset the previous balance since it gave the Ewe-speaking community three—Kotoka, Harlley and Deku—of the eight places; moreover, Harlley and Kotoka were the chief architects of the coup, and both Ankrah and Nunoo were from the Ga community in Accra. Thus, the N.L.C. was numerically dominated by the minority communities, a fact which did not escape local notice. To offset this imbalance, however, there were other considerations. Afrifa, the third principal instigator of the coup, was an Ashanti, Ocran, a Fanti, and Yakubu, a northerner. Equally important was the fact that on the very important eight-member Economic Committee, only R. S. Amegashie was an Ewe; its leading member, E. N. Omaboe, was a Ga but the rest were Akan. Hence, at first sight, the ethnic element seemed less significant than the anti-political and pro-administrative bias of the N.L.C. The initial success of the N.L.C. also owed much to the commonsense of the original leaders who were very quick to include their senior colleagues—including Ankrah who had played no part in the coup—in their joint council of command. In addition, there was that widespread sense of grievance against Nkrumah among the military—a professional sense of danger—which cut across lines of possible tribal difference. And acting as a united group, the military and police had a strong base from which to seek allies.

From the first day of its rule the N.L.C. did everything it could to win over the civil service. There was not only the replacement of politicians by civil servants in the District and Regions. The N.L.C. also turned to the administration for help at a national level through an Economic Committee of senior civil servants, plus two directors from the Ghana Commercial Bank and the Bank of Ghana. It was on the advice of this Committee that General Ankrah (in a broadcast on 28 February) announced that Ghana would be seeking I.M.F. advice.[3] Not until July was a Political Committee appointed (consisting eventually of twenty-three members) and it was then regarded as much less important than the Economic Committee whose chairman had almost daily meetings with the N.L.C.[4] The N.L.C. also brought order into what had bordered on administrative chaos, reducing the number of Ministries to seven-teen, dismantling the alternative civil service which had grown up around the President's Office, and reducing the number of districts con-siderably.[5] On 14 March, the soldiers actually delegated the policy functions of the ex-Ministers 'to Principal secretaries or other heads of Ministries for which the Ministers were responsible'.[6] Similarly, the N.L.C. displayed a high regard for professional competence in the foreign service, relying for advice on the career diplomats who were said to have 'enjoyed far greater influence in decision-making under the N.L.C. than in the preceeding period'.[7] In addition, it closed a large number of expensive and distant embassies, and concluded limited economic and defence agreements with Togo and the Ivory Coast. It took altogether a much more modest administrative assessment of Ghana's role in Africa and the world.[8]

The N.L.C.'s economic policy was similarly cautious in the sense of being calculative and rational rather than political and demonstrative. It might, for example, have refused to recognise at least that section of the foreign debt which had been incurred by ex-Ministers, and in many cases incurred simply for the 10 per cent commission which foreign contractors had paid. Such a move would certainly have been popular; it would have been largely justified; but it might also have proved ad-ministratively embarrassing, and almost certainly it would have been frowned on by the I.M.F. from whom help was expected. Instead, the N.L.C. accepted the I.M.F. arguments for deflation, the rescheduling of loans, the encouragement of private enterprise, the shuffling off of ad-ministrative responsibilities, such as the state farms, and the attempted sale of state enterprises.[9]

Further evidence of the administrative bias of the N.L.C. came with its curious decree of October 1966 which made the spreading of rumours illegal, and the appointment of an enormous number of com-missions and enquiries into all aspects of Ghanaian life. And its en-dorsement of the commission's reports, often without change, was itself indicative of the common frame of reference between the soldiers and the administrative-cum-technical élite. So, too, was the ban on politics for the election of representatives to the Constituent Assembly—a ban which prevented the formation of parties until the very eve of the 1969 election. Politics, for the N.L.C. and its administrative allies, were evidently an extravagance which sensible people could well do without. No wonder that potential politicians complained; and, although they did not press their disagreement too far, it is clear that Busia and those who began to gather round him did not approve of the time-table of reform, and wanted an earlier lifting of the ban.

The alliance with the civil service sprang from a number of related factors. After all, the alternatives available to the N.L.C. were very restricted. Under Nkrumah, Ghana had become, *per capita,* one of the most debt-ridden countries in the world. A policy of deflation and economic caution was held to be vital, and civil servants were natural instruments for such a task. The training and background of the Ghanaian military and civil service were also broadly similar. Both were relatively rigid hierarchies, both had a strong predilection for caution and order, both had traditions pre-dating the political arrival of the 'verandah boys' of the C.P.P.,[10] and both were under severe attack during the latter years of the Nkrumah regime. The civil service had a further reason for its continued co-operation with the N.L.C. since it was under strong and sustained criticism from a section of the population—notably the 'new intelligentsia'—during the period of the N.L.C.'s rule. Two assertions, drawn from many, illustrate the point. In July 1966, B. D. G. Folson of the University of Ghana wrote that 'it is clear that those who have benefited most [from the coup] are the civil servants' and that in relation to N.L.C. policy 'they have, with the expert hands of bureaucrats, doubtless been slanting their recommendations in the usual way'.[11] In April 1967 Professor Adu Boahen (also of the University of Ghana) asked why, alone among Ghanaians, civil servants had not been investigated by the various N.L.C. Commissions when 'most people complain that it is the same Civil Servants who helped Nkrumah on his golden road to dictatorial and tyrannical rule [and] who are still at the helm of affairs'.[12]

The civil servants' immunity was not difficult to explain. Lacking the resources of a political party, the N.L.C. was necessarily more reliant on the public service than any party-based successor was likely to be. The N.L.C. had every wish, too, to expose the misdeeds of the former regime without jeopardising its own rule. The role of the civil service was greatly expanded therefore under the N.L.C., in sharp contrast with its earlier position under Nkrumah. Senior administrators were brought into policy making; they dealt directly with foreign and local business interests, and were 'relied upon as a major communication link between the new military leadership and the general public'.[13] And although the N.L.C. may have had no option but to rely upon, and therefore to protect, the civil service, it did so with evident enthusiasm. During his speech on the first hundred days of the N.L.C., General Ankrah commented that at independence in 1957 the civil service had been excellent and free from politics, a state of affairs eminently desirable, but that Nkrumah had abolished the Civil Service Commission and demoralised the service. The N.L.C. had replaced the Commission, 'thus ensuring fair play and security for all civil servants'.[14] The civil service responded with similar courtesies, the Auditor General being reported as saying 'that when the Armed Forces and the Police succeeded in restoring freedom to this country, the N.L.C. demonstrated their appreciation of the proper role which top civil servants should play in a democratic country'.[15]

The civil service was the most important corporate ally of the N.L.C. but it was by no means the only one. The military also courted the judiciary, the legal profession, the universities, the chiefs, and the leaders of the former United Party opposition to Nkrumah. In September 1966, the N.L.C. reconstituted the judicial system. It appointed a new Chief Justice, E. Akufo-Addo, and terminated the appointment of 17 judges. It also replaced the old local courts with new district courts which were increased in number, included in the regular judicial hierarchy, and opened to members of the legal profession. Thus the age-old Ghanaian lawyers' complaints about local courts were satisfied, and the number of professional openings for lawyers increased. Confidence in the profession was also shown in the appointment of judges to diplomatic missions, investigating commissions, the Electoral Commission, the Constitutional Commission, and the Press Council, until it began to look almost as though Ghana contained only lawyers, judges and ex-judges. Indeed, with the publication of the *Report of the Constitutional Commission* in January 1968, it appeared that Ghana was to become a Platonic Republic ruled by the guardians of the law.[16]

Another group whose support the N.L.C. sought assiduously was the chiefs, and that was easy to understand since in both the (Ashanti) National Liberation Movement and the Northern People's Party the chiefly element had been important and had opposed Nkrumah. Moreover, the former political opposition to Nkrumah—and the N.L.C. should be regarded to some extent as a continuation of this opposition—had sought to argue that chiefs should play a political role in modern Ghana, while the C.P.P. had not. In practice, of course, the institution of chieftaincy still received widespread support and affection both in the urban and rural areas of Ghana; and when the N.L.C. sought approval from chiefs it was perhaps trying to secure a degree of legitimacy which it otherwise lacked. And in gaining such authority, the soldiers could not only play down the coercive basis of the regime, but win practical support from an alliance which 'clearly [resembled] the relationship between chiefs and the colonial administration under indirect rule'.[17] Certainly both Harlley and Ankrah worked hard to bring the chiefs to their aid. On 4 March 1966 Ankrah declared: 'We shall respect the institution of chieftaincy and recognise the role that chiefs will play in the development of the new Ghana'. At the opening of the first meeting of the Chiefs' Standing Conference since 1957, Harlley assured the assembled chiefs that he regarded 'chieftaincy as an essential element in Ghana's national life'. The N.L.C. also made sure that the right kind of chiefs were given official recognition when in December

1966 nearly 200 chiefs, recognised as paramounts by Nkrumah, were demoted; a further 134 had their chiefly status withdrawn, and the previous incumbents were told that they were reinstated. These changes were reinforced in February by the withdrawal of recognition from a further 92 chiefs, and their replacement by former office-holders.

The renewed influence acquired by the chiefly estate during the post-coup period was reflected in the composition and recommendations of the Siriboe Commission on Electoral and Local Government Reform, the Constitutional Commission, and the Constituent Assembly. The two latter bodies are the subject of later chapters but it is worth noting here that the spokesmen of the chiefs in the Constituent Assembly took good care to ensure that traditional constitutional matters were left in their own hands, and not in those of the government. On the other hand, the reform of local government was left to the new civilian government to implement, and the N.L.C. went no further than asking the traditional authorities to nominate members of the management com-mittees which were created to assist the administrative officers of the districts.

What appears to have happened is that, since the N.L.C. felt that it could not rely upon the social groups supporting Nkrumah, it had per-force to rely upon those least associated with the former regime. Hence, the political participants in many instances, though not in all, had a pre-coup Opposition look to them. For example, on the Political Committee which, in the words of the decree establishing it, enabled the N.L.C. 'to serve more closely the public's interest and meet legitimate public objec-tions', a majority were ex-United Party members, including Busia, the Committee's Chairman from December 1966. Similarly, on the Elec-toral Commission, the Board of the Centre for Civic Education, the Constitutional Commission, and the National Advisory Council (which replaced the earlier Political Committees) there was a strong sprinkling of the older opposition. Not only was there continuity in membership between these new bodies and the former opposition; one could also detect similarities in policy, although the regional particularism which had been such a distinct feature of the N.L.M., the N.P.P. and other par-ties brought together by the former United Party was notably absent.

Even more striking was the similarity between the former colonial and the new military government. Support for policies at the centre in favour of administration and administrators, and rule at local level by a combination of chiefs and centrally appointed advisers, was character-istic of the British, and it re-emerged under the N.L.C. Similarly, the various committees of notables composed of those trusted by the a-political administration had more than a superficial similarity to the former Legislative and Executive councils.[18] These parallels were in-teresting, and they derived essentially from a basic similarity between the N.L.C. and the colonial government. Neither was a 'mobilising regime' in the sense of being concerned to involve the 'masses' in politics. On the contrary, a major concern of both was to govern through consultation with various selected groups. Under the N.L.C., the élite was wider and more complex. It involved, for example, a much larger university population and a more experienced trade-union leadership: but the basic principle remained the same—'trust only the established'.

Economically, too, the N.L.C. went as far as the dangerously exposed Ghanaian position would allow them to go in reversing the direction taken by Nkrumah. Like the former president, the soldiers and their advisers stressed the desirability of a private sector to the economy; but, unlike him, they went some way to making such a sector viable. In the Budget speech of 20 July 1966, Afrifa argued that 'the slow-down in Government activities should also release a greater proportion of the available foreign exchange for the use of the private sector'. In August 1966, commercial radio was introduced, in February 1967 commercial television; later in the year, Omaboe—the most influential of all the N.L.C.'s advisers—speculated on the possibility of establishing a stock exchange, a proposal that was later to be implemented by the N.L.C.'s civilian successors. The sale of the state farms also went forward. From the beginning of the N.L.C. period, the cry of Ghana for Ghanaians, and for more import licences for Ghanaian businessmen, was loud in the land, and it did not leave the government unmoved.[19] One attempt to meet the demand was the scheme outlined by the Ministry of Trade in September 1967 by which small Ghanaian traders were advised to form associations which would then be granted bloc import licences. The intention was made clear that: 'when the time comes for the eventual elimination of the foreigners from the retail trade, there will not be any vacuum'.[20] At the end of the year it was announced that the government would impose a stricter control of immigration, although it was Busia's Progress Government which was to take the draconic step of expelling all aliens without residence permits. On 31 December 1968 the Ghanaian Enterprises Decree was issued. It stipulated that, within five years, all retail trading establishments with an annual sales volume of under N.C. 500,000, all wholesale establishments with sales of under N.C. 1 million a year, and all extracting, processing, manufacturing and transport enterprises with a capital of less than N.C. 100,000 or employing less than 30 people, would be reserved solely for Ghanaians. A time limit of two years was also set, within which all taxi owners, and all local representatives of overseas manufacturers, should be Ghanaian. And one of the first measure of the civilian government which succeeded the N.L.C. was to shorten the time limits.

In these different ways the N.L.C. sought to bind itself to those groups who, between 1947 and 1957, had thought it their due to inherit the political power which would have complemented their economic and professional importance. Although by no means drawn from the older Ghanaian élite families,[21] the soldiers had a common interest with them in excluding the possibility of a new Nkrumah-type party arising once more to win political power. This possibility was certainly in the minds of the older élite, as an interview with Nene Azu Mate Kole by members of the editorial board of the *Legon Observer* illustrates:

> Q. Under that Committee (Coussey) it was generally believed that the well-educated, and the chiefs of substance, could operate a system of government and rule this country like gentlemen, but in the course of events, the lower strata captured political power. Is this still a possibility today, in the sense that although the present period has been under fairly middle-class administrators, etc.?
>
> A. The likelihood of that happening is very real.[22]

In order to achieve a peaceful transition to the kind of regime which the soldiers were prepared to accept, the N.L.C. had to remain united not only to prevent a counter-coup but to create the conditions needed for the transfer of power. The essential presupposition for such action was that the N.L.C. would not remain permanently in power, and here the writer simply asserts that the military and police leaders intended from the beginning to relinquish control: they went willingly, and were not driven out. But it was also essential that the N.L.C. itself should hold together, and that neither the police nor the army would fall into competing factions. The problem in relation to the police was relatively simple. It was dispersed, and only lightly armed, and consequently none of its members could challenge for control. There was of course an advantage in its dispersion, in that it could keep in close contact with public opinion, although since it was in touch it could also be bribed—and it was widely alleged to be corrupt at rank and file level. With regard to the army, the position was a little different. Being concentrated in barracks, disaffection could spread more rapidly than among the police, and that there was some degree of discontent could be seen from the attempted counter-coup of April 1967. In general, however, there was no clear evidence of *organised* factionalism within either the army or police forces. The main problem of unity was actually between the two, not in the sense of the army *versus* the police as organisations, but because the leaders of each became divided on personal and ethnic grounds. More general problems were settled quite easily. Such demands as arose for freedom from political interference, quicker promotion, better salaries, better barracks, the re-arming of the police, the restoration of the Border Guards to police control, the disbanding of the P.O.G.R., better uniforms, and the like, were gradually met for both forces.

It was apparent from the beginning that, although political activity was banned, the N.L.C. was anxious to ensure that it would be succeeded by a regime of which it could approve. It looked kindly on particular individuals and groups, and frowned on others. What mattered was membership of the various commissions and committees, access to the press, radio and television coverage, and who could gain admission to the Constitutional Commission, the Constituent Assembly[23] and to the lecture platforms of the N.L.C. supported Centre for Civic Education. Broadly speaking, those who succeeded were the individuals and groups which came within the electoral regulation which stated that candidates for the proposed assembly must have at least a Middle School Leaving Certificate and an income of N.C. 450 a year, but the N.L.C. also placed difficulties in the way of its potential opponents by a series of sometimes contradictory disqualification decrees which made it illegal for specified categories of the ex-C.P.P. functionaries to hold any public office. And it made sure, through a series of widely-publicised investigations into the general chicanery of the Nkrumah regime, that no-one would be left in doubt that the prominent C.P.P. adherents had been corrupt. Most of the former party leaders, therefore, had no part in drawing up the constitution, and were banned not only from membership of the Constituent Assembly but from the proposed National Assembly.

Yet although the N.L.C. was in broad agreement on the constitutional delineation of a successor regime, there was no accord about who should control the new government. After 1966 the division of opinion within the N.L.C. was sharpened by ethnic differences, despite the early optimism within the military and the police about 'tribal conflict'; and the division sprang not only from the fact that Harlley and Kotoka—two of the three principal leaders—were Ewe, but from the belief which grew among many of those who had welcomed the coup that the Ewe were 'politically on the offensive'. Despite the ban on rumour, it was widely whispered that the Ewe were disproportionately represented among the constellation of advisory bodies established by the N.L.C.—even though the actual facts did not lend much support to the allegations. And (as was noted in the introduction) this underlying ethnic division was confirmed by the emergence of the two rival civilian leaders—K. A. Gbedemah, an Ewe, and K. A. Busia, an Akan.

The interaction of ethnic with other forces operating on the N.L.C. could be seen in the three principal and critical events of these years: the abortive counter coup of April 1967, the Abbott Laboratories controversy during the last three months of 1967, and the question of Gbedemah's exclusion from politics during 1968.

During the early morning of 17 April 1967, Lieutenant Arthur, acting commander of a Ghana Army Reconnaissance Squadron, attempted to seize power. He had the help of two other officers, Lt. Yeboah and 2nd Lt. Osei Poku, 120 men, and a few armoured scout cars. They drove the 99 miles from Ho in the Volta Region to Accra, without challenge from military intelligence, attacked and almost captured Osu Castle, and took the radio station, from which they broadcast at 6 a.m. the names of three men—Lt. Col. Assasie, Major Asante and Major Achaab—who were to be the leaders of a new military junta. Arthur and his two accomplices were captured, but not before they had killed Captain Avevor, who was in charge of the armoury, and Kotoka, together with his ADC and his batman. During the short period of total confusion when the N.L.C. lacked any direction, when Ankrah had disappeared, and Afrifa was away from Accra in command of the Fifth Battalion in Tamale, the capital was rife with rumours, including a belief that the attempt heralded the return of Nkrumah. Although none of those initially involved, nor those mentioned in the broadcast were Ewe, a major story was that the counter coup had been aimed against the Ewe who controlled Ghana.[24] Ankrah denied that this was so at a press conference: 'It has come to the notice of the Armed Forces H.Q. that there are rumours going round to the effect that the insurrection was planned by Ashanti and Fanti against Ga and Ewe. This is a wicked rumour which is absolutely untrue.'[25] None of those brought before a court martial mentioned this aspect: they stressed the N.L.C.'s incompetence, and the difficulties junior officers had in passing examinations for promotion—Arthur had been told on 4 April 1967 that he had failed a promotional examination—but that was not the interpretation popularly held. Lt. Arthur and Lt. Yeboah were then shot in public on 26 May before a large and approving crowd, and the danger was quickly ended. None the less, this abortive attempt at a second coup marked a turning point in the N.L.C.'s rule, and it brought to the surface latent tensions on the Council. It was Harlley, for example, who broadcast the news that the coup had failed, while Ankrah was still in hiding, and who publicly criticised the army, saying that: 'There is a strong feeling that the failure of the army to take prompt action against the mutineers damaged its prestige,' and he went on to say: 'Some have gone so far as to question the loyalty and efficiency of the army.'

The attempt reflected a weakness characteristic of such regimes—that if one group of soldiers effects a coup, its action may encourage others to follow its example. Only 120 men were involved in the attempt which, *au fond,* seems to have been motivated primarily by specific grievances about promotion and a general discontent with the N.L.C.'s rule. Popular reaction was sharp. The people of Accra demonstrated against the rebellious soldiers, and students at Legon prepared to march in protest. But the attempt also gave those who were agitating for further civilian representation under the military, an opportunity to argue that 'the soldier-members of the N.L.C. should be released and made to devote more time to military matters; . . . the more routine matters of administration should be left to experienced, trusted civilians'. In June 1967 the N.L.C. did agree to institute a new Executive Council which included not only Ankrah, Harlley and Afrifa but a number of well-known civilians—it was charged with 'the general direction and control of the Government of Ghana' under the N.L.C. Each member was given the title of Commissioner and put in charge of a government department. The new Commissioners were civil servants or academics: the politicians still waited on the side lines. But a new National Advisory Committee was also formed to advise the military 'during the preparatory period to civilian rule', and Busia was chairman until he resigned at the end of 1968.

A second major controversy arose over the N.L.C.'s decision to participate jointly with Abbott Laboratories, an American pharmaceutical firm, in operating a drug-producing company in Ghana. The terms offered, or demanded, were extremely generous to the Americans although, given the perilous state of the Ghanaian economy, it would probably have been difficult to get better ones. When they were made public, they were attacked in the press, most notably in the fortnightly *Legon Observer* published at the University. A leading protagonist was Jones Ofori Atta, a university lecturer in Economics and later a junior Minister under Busia. And two lines of criticism were developed.

One was directed against the Commissioner of Trade, R. S. Amegashire, an Ewe. At a public debate on the agreement, a strong undertone was the dominant position in Ghana 'held by one ethnic group', despite the fact that Amegashie was the only civilian Ewe on the Executive Committee, and the only Ewe on the Economic Committee of the N.L.C. Harlley publicly suggested that the attacks in the press were ethnically motivated, and that they were aimed also at K. A. Gbedemah.[27] Late in December, Abbott withdrew from the negotiations, but the N.L.C. had its revenge for in January 1969 four senior editors on the government-owned press, the *Graphic*, the *Ghanaian Times*, and the *Evening News*, all of whom had attacked the agreement, were dismissed.[28]

The other strand of criticism was resentment over the onerous terms of the agreement, and a general feeling that the economic policy of the N.L.C. was working badly, most notably because of the high level of unemployment following the closure of uneconomic projects and a general reduction in government expenditure.[29] The N.L.C. had tried to expand the rural sector of the economy—cocoa prices were increased and taxes on agricultural implements were reduced—but the fact remained that agricultural production remained at a low level despite attempts to tackle the problem.[30] The devaluation of the cedi also affected the relatively badly off, since they had little with which to cushion themselves against a rise in the price of basic commodities. And it was against this background that opposition to the Abbott agreement and similar contracts had to be seen. Criticism was harsh, and the significance of the quarrel lay not only in the strength of the language, but in the fact that its overtly nationalist and veiled ethnic criticisms were voiced by the younger intelligentsia, many of whom were later to belong to Busia's Progress Party.

The same *motif* was to be heard in the debate on exclusion. The prime concern of the N.L.C. was to make it impossible for the ex-C.P.P. leaders to form the basis of the sort of populist coalition which had swept Nkrumah to power in 1951. The soldiers could not, of course, destroy the social base for such a coalition; but they did ensure that, if it arose, it would not do so with ex-C.P.P. politicians at its head. Given the course of events after February 1966, their fears were not difficult to understand. In January 1967 there was a strike of 5,000 workers in the goldfields of Obuasi, in September 1968 a strike of railwaymen; in November that year 2,000 men stopped work in the ports. A more serious outbreak occurred in Obuasi in March 1969 when some of the mineworkers were shot dead, and B. A. Bentum, whom the N.L.C. had appointed Secretary General of the Ghana T.U.C., was reported in 1968 as saying that 'the workers of the country were gradually losing confidence in the N.L.C.'.[31] The N.L.C. became increasingly alarmed; Kotoka threatened firm action and blamed 'subversive elements among the workers', Harlley saw the strikes as 'part of a plot hatched outside Ghana since November 1966'.[32] The groups which had supported Nkrumah were still present, and presumably still capable of being harnessed, and it was feared that some of the former C.P.P. leaders might make the attempt.

The regime's civilian advisers were as much concerned to prevent the resurrection of the C.P.P. as was the N.L.C. itself. It was on the advice of the Constitutional Commission that the N.L.C. decreed the exclusion from politics of all the major figures of the previous regime—the argument being that it was better such an exclusion should be part of the short-term arrangements for the transfer of power, than that it should form part of a long-term political settlement embodied in the Constitution. In January 1968 all those who had held public office, or party posts in the C.P.P., since independence were excluded by Decree No. 223 from further office for a period of ten years.[33] A series of later Decrees altered the criteria for exclusion, adding or subtracting various categories of persons—such as those belonging to the various 'integral wings' of the C.P.P., like the T.U.C. or the Young Pioneers. The overall effect was to preclude a good proportion of those with direct political experience from taking part in the work of the Constituent Assembly which was established later in the year. The January 1968 Decree, however, provided an escape clause. For it set up an Exemptions Commission which could free from the ban those who could prove to its satisfaction that they either had been forced into the C.P.P. by circumstances beyond their control or had opposed the party from within.

It was around this escape clause that political controversy arose. The most important of its potential beneficiaries was Gbedemah who, having left the C.P.P. and Ghana in 1961, was one of the leading aspirants for power in any future civilian regime. There were those who feared, or pretended to fear, that he might be able to fit together a coalition of the kind that had brought the previous regime to power in 1951—although one may doubt whether he himself had any such intentions since the party he was to form to fight the 1969 general election (the National Alliance of Liberals) was hardly different from Busia's Progress Party. It was dominated by much the same group of professionals and businessmen, though with a little more emphasis perhaps on business than the Progress Party. He had, moreover, allies within the N.L.C. in Harlley and Deku—all three being Ewe. Yet he was still brushed with the mark of Nkrumah, and his connections with the N.L.C. were open to the hardly less damaging charge of being motivated by Ewe political ambitions.

In November 1968 Gbedemah was declared to have been successful in his application to the Exemptions Commission—whose chairman was Mr. Justice Apaloo, an Ewe, the other two members being a Ga and an Ashanti—after witnesses as diverse as A. L. Adu, the former Secretary to the Cabinet, Nana Ofori Atta II, William Ofori Atta a former UP leader, and P. K. K. Quaidoo, a former C.P.P. rebel, had given evidence in his behalf. At this point, Afrifa called a press conference and condemned the whole process of exemption: it had become so complex that it was futile, and should be abandoned as it 'does not any more advance the objectives of the events of 24 February 1966'.[34] Three days later the Exemption Commission adjourned its hearing indefinitely. The matter was held in abeyance until February 1969 when the N.L.C. issued Decree No. 332, which repealed all the earlier edicts and stipulated that the disqualifications would cease to apply except to 152 specially listed persons. Gbedemah was not among those listed; but his tribulations were not at an end. In April 1969 two Political Parties Decrees, passed within two days of each other, reinstated many of the categories of disqualification, and brought within their provenance membership of the political parties which were then about to be established. The first of the decrees had the effect of rebanning Gbedemah, and the second of exempting him once more.[35] Then in May 1969, the government published and accepted the recommendations of the Jiagge Commission which, having found that Gbedemah (like other ex-C.P.P. politicians) was not able to account completely for his total assets, ordered the confiscation of the relatively small sum of N.C. 30,000. Shortly afterwards, the Constituent Assembly, in the course of a long and acrimonious discussion (set out in Chapter 4) decided to include the controversial Article in the Constitution which disqualified from public office anyone against whom a Commission of Enquiry had made adverse findings. Because there was still room for disagreement as to the interpretation of the clause, Gbedemah was able to contest the 1969 election, though under a cloud of uncertainty about the future—only to be finally disqualified after the election when the Supreme Court found against him in the constitutional case of *Awoonor-Williams* v. *Gbedemah*.

A major event which showed how deep were the divisions which had grown within the N.L.C. was the Otu affair. Air Vice-Marshal Michael Otu, Chief of Defence Staff of the Ghana Armed Forces, and his Aide de Camp, Lt. Kwapong (of the Ghana navy), were arrested on 20 November 1968 for alleged complicity in subversive activities. At the Commission of Enquiry, Harlley claimed that there was evidence to show that Otu and Kwapong had met members of the C.P.P. in London and that they had agreed to the return of Nkrumah in December 1968 following a further coup. Harlley also announced that Otu had been questioned, and that he had denied his complicity.[36] (It was later claimed in evidence before the Commission that the plot was actually to assassinate Ankrah, Harlley and Deku of the N.L.C., and Gbedemah.) Otu and his aide refused early in January 1969 to plead before the Amissah Commission, and demanded trial before a court of law; they also submitted to the N.L.C. a petition which included the suggestion that Otu was a 'victim of a carefully planned conspiracy with tribal undertones'.[37] When the High Court upheld their refusal to plead, the matter was left in abeyance, and the Commission eventually exonerated Otu and Kwapong. The matter was never satisfactorily explained, Harlley lost considerable prestige, and rumours sped thick and fast in an attempt to find hidden political and ethnic rivalries among those involved.[38]

These events suggested that there were serious differences within the N.L.C., of which the rift between Afrifa on the one hand, and Harlley and Deku on the other, was perhaps the most important. But it must be emphasised that the situation was not at all hard and fast. Parallel differences also developed among the various groups of politicians who began to contest for power after May 1969. And these too were similarly fluid. As late as the spring of 1968, it was said that Busia was still not averse to forming a party jointly with Gbedemah (with whom, after all, he had co-operated in exile) until he was apparently persuaded by Afrifa and a number of young university teachers at Legon that he could win a future election on his own.

The links between these various civilian and military factions were for the most part covert and indirect. Nevertheless, there was one incident which gave special weight to the dangers which the N.L.C. faced and from which it could perhaps be argued that by 1969 the N.L.C. was beginning to fall apart to such an extent that it might not have been able to continue to rule the country even if it had so wanted. The incident was the enforced resignation of Ankrah in April 1969 and his replacement as chairman by Afrifa shortly before the ban on party politics was lifted. Some months earlier, in August 1968, Ankrah had denied rumours that he was encouraging the formation of a political party—rumours that became linked to a public opinion poll conducted by a Nigerian, Mr. Nzeribe, which purported to find that a majority of Ghanaians would have liked to see Ankrah as the first civilian President. The rumour was dismissed by Ankrah as a 'wicked and malicious fabrication', saying that 'soldiers don't have the temperament for political acrobatics'.[39] Acrobatics there were, however, and Ankrah was told by his colleagues to resign on 2 April 1969, after he had been accused of collecting money through Nzeribe from business firms on behalf of certain politicians. Three of the four politicians named were (like Ankrah) Ga, the fourth being an Ewe.[40] All of them were shortly to become members of the United Nationalist Party, led by Joe Appiah in the 1969 election.[41] Soon afterwards, Nunoo (also a Ga) was removed from the N.L.C., having stated at a press conference on 3 May that the government's statement on Ankrah's resignation was inaccurate, and that Victor Owusu (then Attorney General) had used the episode to discredit his opponents.[42]

Ankrah was not the only member of the N.L.C. to have political friends, though perhaps none went quite so far into the political labyrinth as he. Nor were relations between the N.L.C. and the future party leaders always cordial. Most of the politicians had been organising covertly for some time, and although attempts were made from time to time to associate N.L.C. members with their cause, many were also actively exhorting the military to hand power back to civilian hands. As early as March 1967 Busia was using the occasion of a public lecture to urge the N.L.C. to establish a timetable for an early return to civilian rule, suggesting February 1968 as a suitable date, and claiming that people were 'generally sceptical about the professions of military regimes either to stability or democracy'.[43] At the same time, he was using his (N.L.C. appointed) position as chairman of many committees—the Political Committee, the National Advisory Committee which succeeded it, and the Centre for Civic Education after it was established in June 1967—to extend and reinforce his political connections. Each step towards civilian rule increased the tempo of political activity and stimulated party rivalries—the appointment of the Constitutional Commission and the presentation of its Report, the announcement by Ankrah in May 1968 of a timetable for the transfer of power by 30 September 1969, the establishment of a Constituent, Assembly in November 1968, the dissolution of the National Advisory Committee in order to leave its members free to prepare for politics, the Political Parties Decree of April 1969 permitting the formation of parties from 1 May 1969, and (at the last) the announcement of a date for the general election in August.

That such rivalries should have penetrated the N.L.C., and given rise to conflicts among its members, was hardly a matter for surprise. What is more worthy of note is that the N.L.C. actually held together despite these crises. What kept it intact? It is difficult to give a simple answer. It was partly due to the considerable popularity which the regime enjoyed, the strength and importance of which were clearly demonstrated in the lack of public support for the attempted coup of April 1967. Part of the explanation, too, was that although the members of the N.L.C. differed among themselves on personalities and transient political alignments, they were in accord on fundamentals—to keep Nkrumah and those who had supported him out, to clean the political stable, and to hand power back to an acceptable civilian regime. Another factor was that the military itself was not as divided as the N.L.C., since the bulk of the army was not exposed directly to political pressures. The number of policemen or soldiers who were given any governmental responsibility was small, being limited to members of the N.L.C. and the eight Military Administrators of the Regions. Military and political responsibilities were kept fairly well separated, therefore, and the N.L.C. may be regarded in many respects as a junta of police and military men who happened to be ruling, rather than as the command of a political army. In this respect, the presence of the police alongside the soldiers may have added an element of flexibility since neither one could dominate the other; and the police were able to relieve the military of some of the regime's political functions, since their mode of operation was more closely interwoven with society in general than was that of the soldiers. The troubles which did afflict the N.L.C. were instructive in this sense, in that they illustrated the strains endemic in trying to maintain a separation between political and military matters as well as showing the degree of success with which the distinction was maintained.

This, then, was the military side to the withdrawal from politics. The army was always near enough to the political whirlpool to be uncomfortable, and to want to pull away; but it never reached the point (as in Nigeria and Sierra Leone) when it was unable either to withdraw or to govern without breaking up. To a much greater extent than the rest of the army, the N.L.C. was divided and uncertain of itself: yet it, too, held together. Its uneasiness over the possible consequences of withdrawal grew as the self-appointed date for the ending of its rule drew near. As is explained in later chapters, the N.L.C. faltered, and held back on the very eve of the 1969 election. It asked the Constituent Assembly, which was still sitting, to reconsider the proposal that a Presidential Commission, to be composed of the N.L.C. Chairman (Afrifa) and Deputy Chairman (Harlley), and the Chief of Defence Staff (Ocran), should assume the functions of President under the constitution for a five year period in order to watch over the birth of the new republic. The request was acceded to; but the Presidential Commission did not last long, and the soldiers soon disappeared from the scene.

In looking back over the three or four years when the military governed the country, one can hardly say that its rule was an unqualified success. Its economic policies are examined in the following chapter, but one may reach the tentative conclusion here, that the major economic hardships during these years were endured by the very large group of unemployed which all the N.L.C.'s whistling in the wind about private enterprise did little to reduce. Politically—and one can certainly use the word about the period of N.L.C. rule—this first bout of military government saw a brief return to the pre-Nkrumah alliance of administrators, chiefs and intellectuals (old and new style, from the professions and the universities). But the alliance was never an easy one, for the civil service looked with some apprehension at the ending of military control, while the would-be politicians pressed constantly for a rapid transfer of power. The end to military-police rule was, at first reckoning, a brave and decisive return to parliamentary government; yet within three years the military had returned, and by 1972 it was clear that the process begun in 1966 could not be undone: that the army had become an integral element in politics, not merely in the sense of competing with other organised interests for scarce financial resources, but as a mechanism of political change. And as long as politics in Ghana remains balanced between competing sections of the élite, on the one hand, and the very diffused interests of the general populace on the other, so the military (or a segment of it) will be able to seize and retain control by appealing to the interests temporarily out of favour.

Notes

1. Details taken from J. M. Lee, *African Armies and Civil Order,* Methuen, London 1963.
2. There are three well documented accounts of the February Coup: A. A. Afrifa, *The Ghana Coup,* Frank Cass London 1966, A. K. Ocran, *A Myth is Broken,* Longmans, London 1968, and P. Barker, *Operation Cold Chop,* Accra 1969. See, too, the useful account by Robert Pinkney, *Ghana under Military Rule,* Methuen, London 1972.

3. *Africa Research Bulletin*, February 1966, col. 467A.
4. B. D. G. Folson, *Legon Observer*, 8 December 1967.
5. H. L. Bretton, *The Rise and Fall of Kwame Nkrumah*, Praeger, 1967 is useful on Nkrumah's policies of setting up competing administrative structures.
6. *Africa Research Bulletin*, March 1968, col. 489B.
7. W. Scott Thompson, 'Ghana's Foreign Policy Under Military Rule', *Africa Report*, May–June 1969.
8. Other examples of this approach were the closing of the guerrilla training establishments in Ghana, the publication in October 1966 of a booklet dealing with *Nkrumah's Subversion in Africa*, and the dismissal of Chinese and Russian 'experts'. Ankrah, in his broadcast to the nation on 28 February, warned that 'subversive elements from Independent African States should leave Ghana forthwith'.
9. See the following chapter.
10. The writer has developed the theme of the civil-military coalition in some detail in 'The Military and Political Development' in Leys (ed), *Political Change in Developing Countries*, (Cambridge, C.U.P., 1969). See also the interesting note by N. Kasfir 'Prismatic Theory and African Administration', *World Politics*, Vol. 21, No. 2, 1969, pp. 295–314 and V. C. Ferkiss, 'The Role of the Public Services in Nigeria and Ghana' in F. Heady & S. Stokes, *Papers in Comparative Public Administration*, (Michigan, University of Michigan Press, 1962), pp. 173–206.
11. *Legon Observer*, 8 July 1966.
12. *Ibid.*, 14 April, 1969. The always perceptive journal *West Africa* noted in its issue of 27 April 1968 that 'some top civil servants don't want a return to civilian rule because they are afraid that the politicians might turn the enquiries on them'. During February and March 1970, 568 civil servants were dismissed by the new Progress Government. See below, page 88.
13. R. L. Harris, 'The Effects of Political Change on the Role Set of Senior Bureaucrats in Ghana and Nigeria,' *Administrative Science Quarterly*, Vol. 13, 1968; see also E. Card, 'Ghana Prepared for Civilian Rule,' *Africa Report*, April 1968; 'Leaning heavily on the experience of top civil servants, most of them retained from Nkrumah's staff, the N.L.C. has become accustomed to decision-making by administrative fiat,' and J. S. Annan, 'Ghana's Brain Drain Under Nkrumah,' *Venture*, June 1966.
14. *Africa Report*, June 1966, pp. 21–5. Ankrah was referring to the powers vested in the President under the 1960 Constitution (article 51) of 'appointment, transfer, termination of appointment, dismissal and disciplinary control' of civil servants. See below, ch. 4.
15. Ahenkora Osei, *Ashanti Pioneer*, 22 January 1969.
16. See below, Chapter 3.
17. N. M. Miller, 'The Political Survival of Traditional Leadership', *Journal of Modern African Studies*, 1968, vol. VI, No. 2. It is interesting that Ankrah, in his justification of the coup, invoked the 'oldest and most treasured tradition of the people of Ghana', the custom of destoolment.
18. See D. Kimble, *A Political History of Ghana*, Oxford Clarendon Press, 1963, esp. pp. 301–500, and M. Wight, *The Gold Coast Legislative Council*, London, Faber & Faber, 1947.
19. Two typical examples: *Daily Graphic*, 29 May 1967, 'The time has now come for indigeneous private enterprise to be shielded from the competition of Lebanese, Syrians and Indians in retail trade'; *Ghanaian Times*, 22 April 1967 insisted that N.L.C. policy must be 'to transfer the control of . . . trade from the hands of resident foreign nationals into those of Ghanaians'. For a full account of the N.L.C.'s economic policies, see Chapter 2.
20. *Africa Research Bulletin*, 9 September 1967. Statement by the Ministry of Trade.

21. Thomas Hodgkin's account 'Counter-Revolution in Ghana', *Labour Monthly*, April 1966 overestimates the influence of 'bourgeois Sandhurst-trained officers'. Geoffrey Bing, 'The Coup for Martial Freedom', *Venture*, June 1966 is much nearer the mark: 'The officers of the armed forces do not come from any easily identifiable social class and represent . . . a cross section of the population.'

22. *Legon Observer*, 30 August 1968.

23. For a detailed examination of the kind of people who sat on the Constitutional Commission and in the Constituent Assembly, see Chapters 3 and 4.

24. At the rank of major and above in 1967 there were 6 Ewe officers out of 52 in the Ghana Army (11.5 per cent); of colonels and above 5 were Ewe (24 per cent). The Ewe could be said to be strong therefore at Army *command* level. Data taken from J. M. Lee, *African Armies and Civil Order*, (London, Chatto & Windus, 1969), p 113.

25. *Legon Observer*, 28 April 1967.

26. *Legon Observer*, 28 April 1967. The academics on the *Observer* let few such opportunities slip to remind the N.L.C. that it *was* temporary.

27. *Legon Observer*, 21 December 1967 and *West Africa*, 13 January 1968. Immediately prior to publication of the agreement, Afrifa declared that the country was becoming 'too tribalistic' and that tribalism 'holds great danger for the future', *Ghanaian Times*, 24 October 1967. The warning was echoed in the *Legon Observer*, 27 October 1967; but the *Ashanti Pioneer* continued: 'It seems to me that he (Gbedemah) has some tribal backing, most of them in very important official positions,' 19 January 1968.

28. A typical comment had been that in the *Ghanaian Times*, 2 November 1967, 'Our power-centre and most of our public services . . . are known to be dominated by one or two tribes.'

29. See below, Chapter 2.

30. *Africa Research Bulletin*, May 1969. Food prices also increased from 1963 = 100. 1965 = 153, 1967 = 157, 1969 = 176, *Monthly Bulletin of Statistics*, U.N. November 1969.

31. *Daily Graphic*, 16 December 1968.

32. *Ghanaian Times*, 20 December 1968. There were 71 strikes during the N.L.C. period and 51 in the last five years of Nkrumah's rule, C. E. Welch, 'Return to Civilian Rule in Ghana', *Current History*, May 1969, pp. 286–91.

33. There were reports that Ankrah was against excluding anybody, but that Afrifa insisted on a formal banning, *Legon Observer*, 27 October 1967. The advice of the Constitutional Commission was almost certainly decisive in resolving this disagreement in favour of exclusion, and indeed the Decree was originally drafted by the Commission.

34. *West Africa*, 23 November 1968.

35. The main purpose of the Decrees (Nos. 345 and 347) was to provide for the re-establishment of political parties and to lay down a framework of regulations within which they should work. N.L.C.D. 345 banned various categories of people holding specified public or C.P.P. offices on or since 1 July 1960, the date of the establishment of the first Republic; but N.L.C.D. 347 limited the ban to those who held such office on 24 February 1966.

36. *Africa Research Bulletin*, December 1968.

37. *West Africa*, 4 January 1969.

38. An interesting feature which emerged later was that da Rocha, who had been Otu's counsel before the Commission, became the Progress Party's General Secretary when open party politics were resumed in May 1969 and Otu was reappointed Chief of Defence Staff by Busia shortly after winning the 1969 election—until the disagreement over defence expenditure in 1971. See below page 304.

39. *West Africa*, 17 August 1968.

40. M. K. Apaloo was the Ewe, the three others being Peter Adjetey, Alex Hutton-Mills and Attoh Quarshie, who had been in detention for many years under Nkrumah as a member of the Ga Shifimo Kpee (see Austin, *op. cit.,* p. 374).
41. See below, Chapter 6.
42. Accusations were used on all sides. Owusu had by this time resigned from the Executive Council, and he too held a press conference at which the charges made by Nunoo were countered with charges by Owusu against Nunoo.
43. *West Africa,* 8 April 1967.

CHAPTER 2

ECONOMIC POLICIES

J. D. Esseks

At the beginning of 1966, on the eve of the February coup, the country was insolvent. Its funds were insufficient not only to cover current imports but the air and shipping fares owed to foreign carriers, and the debt repayments due to its many external creditors. Sizeable arrears on import bills had already accumulated,[1] and overseas suppliers were beginning to balk at shipping to Ghana. Western governments had been approached by the C.P.P. administration for help, despite several years of anti-Western rhetoric in the party-controlled press, but none was prepared to underwrite the substantial aid that was needed. Aid had also been solicited from the International Monetary Fund, but a number of the Fund's conditions for a stand-by credit were politically unacceptable to Nkrumah and his party advisors.[2] With the Communist countries, Ghana traded on the basis of bilateral agreements which allowed import surpluses within specified money limits; but, by the end of 1965, the government had exceeded the permissible limits with a majority of the country's ten Communist partners,[3] and there was no evidence that the Soviet Union or the other major Eastern suppliers were ready to extend special credits on the scale needed to replenish Ghana's depleted stocks or to compensate for supplies lost from Western sources.[4] Such limited new credits as might have been negotiated from any source would very likely have been offset by the heavy capital and interest payments on the external debt which in February 1966 stood at £120 million.[5] Because of the predominance of medium-term suppliers' credit, the capital and interest payments for 1966 were scheduled to be £28 million, or about 29 per cent of the year's total export receipts.[6]

At stake in this acute crisis was not merely the curtailment of luxury imports and foreign travel, but the viability of the country's major export industries, its infant manufacturing sector, almost all public services, and the daily habits of thousands of Ghanaian families long accustomed to a variety of foreign goods. High export earnings from cocoa in the 1950s had engendered fairly rapid economic growth (about five per cent per annum from 1955 to 1962);[7] and as purchasing power increased among cocoa farmers, civil servants, teachers, and many other groups, the demand for imported consumer goods soared. Between 1954 and 1961 (the last year of largely unrestricted imports) imports of dairy products rose by 145 per cent, sugar by 174 per cent, wheat flour by 99 per cent, and motor cars by 100 per cent.[8] Domestic production of these items, and of most other processed or manufactured goods was either non-existent or in limited quantity.[9] Moreover, the small industrial sector depended on imported raw and semi-finished materials, machinery and spare parts. Ghana's three principal export sectors were also not viable without large, regular supplies of imported goods—including insecticides and hand tools for farming, bulldozers and other heavy equipment for timber extraction; and chemicals, explosives and drilling machinery for mining. The country's rapidly expanding public services comprised another sector dependent on foreign supplies: hospitals imported antibiotics and vaccines, schools needed books and paper, piped water systems required pumps and lubricants.

From 1959 until the fall of the regime in 1966, the value of Ghana's annual exports stagnated at about £110 million, principally because as Table I (page 56) indicates world market prices for cocoa declined sharply in response to increased supply. (Despite an increase in output, the Ghanaian share of the world market declined.) In 1960 there was a substantial balance of payments deficit on current account, followed by serious shortfalls in all of the remaining years of Nkrumah's rule. In 1960 the deficit was financed primarily by running down Ghana's sterling reserves which at the end of 1960 stood at £149 million, the equivalent of almost fourteen months of imports.[10] Then in 1961 heavy taxes were imposed on major consumer imports and exchange controls were tightened; yet such measures failed to end the drain on Ghana's sterling reserves and by the end of the year they were down by 50 per cent to £74 million.[11] The apparent inadequacy of the steps taken then led to the fateful decision early in December 1961 to ration imports through the licensing of individual shipments. It was fateful because the licensing practices of the following four years failed in their major economic purposes of improving the country's balance of payments, and because the shortages which they caused contributed more than any other category of government actions, to popular disaffection. As Table II (page 57) indicates, in no year after the introduction of specific import licensing was a trade surplus attained; and by January 1966, after six consecutive years of payments deficits, the country's reserves had sunk to £3.5 million, the equivalent of about two weeks of imports.[12]

The shortage of consumer goods, and of materials required in both manufacturing and export industries, had reached serious proportions by 1964. Scarcities of sugar, drugs, tyres, and vehicle spare parts were reported, and by the following year, milk, flour, and fabrics began to disappear from the shops for prolonged periods. Municipal water systems ran out of water-purifying chemicals; hospitals reported shortages of X-ray fluid, vaccines, and other vital supplies. Whereas in 1964 a government survey had found that 'some' factories were forced to curtail production because of inadequate raw materials imports, in 1965 'most' manufacturers were affected.[13] There was an explicit policy in favour of state enterprises in the allocation of licenses, but at least eight of the thirty-eight state-owned factories and four of the five state gold mines suffered losses in production because of failures in the licensing system.[14] Production also fell in most of the country's saw mills because of a shortage of spare parts for the logging enterprises which supplied the mills.[15]

The puzzling inconsistency between the high 1965 import figures given in Table II, and the clear evidence of serious shortages that year, is explained by three factors. The aggregate figures for large categories masked contrary trends for significant individual items. Delays and bad phasing in the issue of licenses resulted in the bunching of imports towards the end of the year, with little relief from scarcities until then.[16] And because of the psychological climate of scarcity which had existed since early 1964, retailers tended to hoard supplies—new shipments were quickly bought up, or merchants kept them off their shelves until maximum profits were likely. The economic consequences produced a serious price inflation and the cancellation or postponement of new investment in the private sector. In the first half of 1965 the writer interviewed representatives of eight major timber companies, one of the country's biggest mines, and four large-scale manufacturing enterprises, each of which reported that uncertainty over obtaining import requirements was blocking investments for expansion or diversification. The government's Capital Investments Board encountered similar fears among foreign investors in its efforts to attract new capital into the country.[17] Between January 1964 and December 1965 the national consumer price index for imported food rose sixteen points, and for durable goods (most of which were imported) by fifty points.[18] A rapid expansion in the money supply greatly compounded these inflationary pressures—the average volume of cash and bank deposits available to the public and the government increased by 46 per cent between 1963 and 1965.[19] The principal cause was the government's heavy borrowing from the banking system in order to finance its budgetary deficits. The state sector pumped into the economy more money than ever before, but it was chasing too few goods. The economy was estimated to have grown by only 2.8 per cent in 1964 and 0.2 per cent in 1965.[20]

The political consequence of these shortages, and of the attendant inflation of 1964–65, meant that many Ghanaians turned away from the party and its leader. Sceptical about the government's indictments of local merchants, and of 'foreign perpetrators' of the crisis, they blamed the regime whose own socialist rhetoric had emphasised the central role of government in the economy. In retrospect, the popular view of who was to blame for the 1964–65 shortages was largely correct. It is true that the government's responsibility for what took place was not simply due to inefficiency and malfeasance, since any system of detailed import licensing is notoriously difficult, particularly in the first years of its operation. Nonetheless, two official inquiries—one commissioned by Nkrumah, the other by his successors—uncovered an extraordinary degree of poor planning, administrative blundering, and corruption.[21] In addition, there was the government's hungry appetite for foreign exchange. It successfully restricted private access to foreign goods and transport services: but it vastly increased its own claims on Ghana's export-earning and credit-negotiating capabilities. In comparison to the fiscal year 1960–61, the central government's expenditure on new machinery and equipment in 1965, virtually all of which was foreign-made, was 34 per cent higher; its investment in new buildings and construction, most of which had major imported components, was up by 66 per cent.[22] And in 1965 the public sector's share of gross fixed capital formation reached 66 per cent, compared with the 20 per cent of 1958.[23]

Part of this growth in capital investments—about a fifth—resulted from the expansion, according to political imperatives, of educational, health, and other social services.[24] Most of the rest resulted from Nkrumah's insistence that 'the public and cooperative sector of the productive economy should expand at the maximum possible rate. . . .'[25] Beginning in 1961, there was a rapid expansion of the state's role in trade, insurance, banking, agriculture, transport and manufacturing. Foreign exchange costs were especially high in the last two sectors. Between 1961 and 1965 the government's Black Star Shipping Line purchased fourteen new cargo vessels, six of them being acquired during 1964–65, when the payments crisis was particularly acute. In 1965, the state-owned Ghana Airways took delivery of two VC10s, at a combined contract price of £5.6 million. Both planes, and apparently all of the ships, were bought through suppliers' credits. Ideally, they should have paid for themselves through the convertible currency earned from foreign customers or saved because Ghanaian passengers and shippers would use them rather than foreign carriers; in practice, their annual foreign exchange costs (loan repayments and fuel bills) exceeded their hard currency earnings plus savings.[26]

The expansion of the public sector in manufacturing contributed to the eve-of-coup crisis in much the same fashion. From 1961 to the end of 1965 the number of state-owned factories increased from twenty-three to thirty-eight, and work was begun on twenty-six others. The new enterprises tended to be far larger and more expensive than those built previously. The combined cost of the three government factories commissioned in 1965—£13.5 million—was more than three times the investment in all the state factories as they existed in June 1961.[27] Six of the new enterprises, and all except one of those under construction, were financed partly by suppliers' credits; but the downpayments, loan instalments, and other foreign-exchange costs (including management fees and imported raw materials) exceeded the foreign exchange savings from substituting locally made products for imports. In 1965, the gross output of government factories was £10.4 million of which at least £3.3 million was taken up by the cost of their imported materials;[28] and the aggregate capital and interest payments due that year on both the existing factories and those being constructed amounted to £10.4 million.[29]

The problem was not only one of an excessive number of industrial investments crowded into a narrow span of years, but of the kind and size of the enterprises being established. Through the inexperience and venality of Ghanaian officials, as well as the greed, bribery and political machinations of project salesmen from both East and West, the Government contracted for many overpriced, poorly designed enterprises.[30] Among the contracts which Nkrumah and his ministers signed without adequate feasibility studies, or in contradiction of advisers' recommendations, were those for a steel mill designed to turn out construction rods of the wrong size for local building needs, a meat processing plant not assured of an adequate supply of meat, and a gold refinery with a capacity many times larger than the output of the country's mines required. A similar tale could be related of the government's schemes for mechanised farming. By 1965 the State Farms Corporation had expanded to 105 farms and was liberally equipped with tractors and other imported machinery; but the results were disappointing. Throughout 1965 (except for rice and maize) food crop harvests were negligible, and since production in the private sector also lagged behind demand, consumers had to face rising prices for local foodstuffs. In effect, the State Farms Corporation succeeded only with oil palms. In some instances, low production was due to the newness of the project, but in general the farms suffered from incompetent management, excessive interference from headquarters in Accra, and an insufficient number of trained personnel to operate the mechanised equipment.[31]

Ghana's private sector dwindled, a process hastened by the state's entry into the distributive as well as the productive sectors of the economy. In 1961 a quasi-state agency pushed all private buyers and four large cooperatives out of the internal marketing of cocoa. The following year, the government took over the large Cypriot trading firm, A. G. Leventis, at the latter's initiative and at an inflated price. The firm was merged with the Ghana National Trading Corporation which extended its distributive network to over 200 retail outlets and virtually monopolised the importing of five basic consumer items: milk, rice, flour, sugar and tinned fish. In addition, the rapidly growing Ghana

National Construction Corporation preempted almost all the small-scale public undertakings which had been the mainstay of most Ghanaian private contractors.

Cocoa farming (it is true) remained in private hands, but the government continued to control the price received by farmers. As Table I indicates, cocoa production almost trebled between 1957 and 1965, but after the record 1964–65 crop year of 557,000 tons, output declined the following year to 410,000 and to 376,000 in 1966–67. The drop in production resulted partly from adverse weather conditions, but it was also the consequence of neglect. Among other economies, the service of distributing insecticides directly to farmers was curtailed, and the subsidy on spraying machines discontinued. By the 1965–66 crop year, insect damage to cocoa trees had developed to crisis proportions, and farmers complained that they could not obtain adequate supplies of insecticides nor afford the unsubsidised spraying machines.[32] In addition, since the government depended on the cocoa duty for a substantial share of total revenues (an average of 20 per cent in this period),[33] when the world market price declined, it lowered the producer price. When the average f.o.b. price fell from £303 per ton in the crop year 1957–58 to only £125 in 1965–66, the producer price was dropped from £134 to £75.[34] Faced with a diminishing cash return on the one hand, and with higher labour and materials costs on the other, many farmers reduced the amount of time and money devoted to their farms—except those fortunate enough to farm along the borders who frequently smuggled cocoa into Togo and the Ivory Coast where a higher producers' price prevailed.

By the beginning of 1966, therefore, the government's handling of the economy had generated grievances in most sectors of local society: cocoa farmers, businessmen, workers (whose real wages fell as the result of rapid inflation), young persons unable to find employment in a stagnant economy, and consumers of varying income levels unable to obtain sugar, milk, sardines, and other common items. From such grievances the group which staged the February 1966 coup could be sure of ample support. And it was to the problems of the economy that the military leaders turned immediately after their seizure of power.

The same broadcast which gave to the public the names of the National Liberation Council also announced the formation of a seven-man National Economic Committee, consisting of five senior civil servants and two financial specialists. The Committee's Chairman, E. N. Omaboe, having been for the past five years in charge of the government's Central Bureau of Statistics, brought to this key position a sober realism. Omaboe himself described the first four months after the coup as 'an emergency period', when the N.L.C. government applied 'ad hoc measures' to ease the supply crisis.[35] Foreign help was indispensable, but because Nkrumah had developed close economic, cultural, and military ties with the Communist powers, and because it was feared that he might look to them for assistance to restore his rule, Ankrah turned to the West. It was for this reason that the N.L.C. tried to make it clear that it had not carried through simply a palace coup which promised little or no change of a kind likely to interest prospective donor government. In its first week of rule the government expelled Soviet and Chinese technical assistance personnel, some of their diplomatic staff, and the whole of the official East German community. The expulsions resulted partly from the tensions of the immediate post-coup period, but it was presumably hoped that Western governments would look favourably on Nkrumah's successors.

The N.L.C.'s appeals for emergency aid, backed by this shift in external policy, did win early agreement from the West to provide food, pharmaceuticals and other essential supplies on the basis of soft loans or grants. Although promising some relief, these early commitments could supply only a fraction of Ghana's needs. What was urgently required was to restore the confidence of Ghana's traditional commercial suppliers. And what they wanted was assurance of payment for the goods shipped. To this end the International Monetary Fund was approached both for a stand-by credit, and for assistance in rescheduling the country's external debt payments, so that a greater supply of foreign exchange would be available to finance current imports. In May, after securing commitments from the N.L.C. to reduce government spending, the I.M.F. opened a £13 million credit.[36] In June the principal Western creditors were persuaded to accept a temporary moratorium on debt payments, pending an I.M.F.—sponsored meeting in December. In July, imports began a gradual rise in value after dropping steadily and steeply from January to June, when the lowest monthly total in more than seven years was recorded.[37] Nonetheless, although the nightmare of a massive withholding of imports by commercial suppliers had receded, the basic problem persisted. Ghana's consumers, the public services, established industries and business interests all demanded imported goods and services to a greater extent than current export earnings could fund.

As the new government surveyed the 220 separate contracts for foreign credits signed by the former regime, they must surely have been tempted to repudiate the many agreements which provided for unviable projects, including the supply of goods and services at excessive prices: they might well have justified their policy—as Colonel Acheampong was to do six years later—on the grounds that many of the commercial suppliers had adopted fradulent practices. Only eight projects, however, representing £27 million were cancelled or suspended.[38] The great bulk of the inherited debt burden—about 90 per cent—continued to be carried, as the N.L.C. had pledged to do on the day of the coup. Since Ghana's major creditors (Britain and West Germany) were the same sources from which urgent emergency assistance was sought, the pledge may have been indispensable in the first months of the new regime. But why some repudiation of the debts was not declared later is less clear. During 1967, officials in Omaboe's Ministry of Economic Affairs advised him to cancel the most grossly overvalued and otherwise unjust credit agreements.[39] He rejected such recommendations on the grounds that, if acted upon, they would have diminished the chances of new, long-term loans, and because he believed that current debt relief of the same or greater magnitude could be achieved through a rescheduling of payments. The N.L.C. government's principal means, therefore, for coping with the debt burden was to negotiate the deferment and prolongation of payments. At the I.M.F.—sponsored meeting in December 1966, the twelve creditor countries agreed to the principles of postponing 80 per cent of the debt originally due in the period July 1966 to December 1968, and to stretching out those deferred payments over an eight-year period ending in June, 1979.[40] Bilateral agreements based on these principles were then concluded with separate creditors. The relief covered only two and a half years, but it was a period with heavy concentration of payments. Without the rescheduling, £58 million would have been demanded—the equivalent of five months of imports: with the relief, only £11.6 million was required.[41] Another meeting with Western creditors in 1968 extended the '80 per cent deferment formula' to payments which were due between January 1969 and the middle of 1972. And two sets of rescheduling agreements were negotiated with eight Communist governments.

When, after the election in 1969, J. H. Mensah, Finance Minister in the New Progress Government, calculated the total annual payments due in the 1970s on these re-scheduled debts, and on the new credits of £115 million obtained by the N.L.C., he concluded that the servicing burden was more than the country could be expected to bear:

> With the best will in the world, with the most determined management by Government and whatever sacrifices the people of Ghana will agree to make, it is going to take much more than seven and a half or eight years for this economy to generate a surplus of resources [on a scale needed to service the external debt].[42]

There was massive substance to his complaint. It is true that, apart from £42 million in I.M.F. credits and one small twelve-year loan, the new agreements provided for repayment periods of twenty to forty years: and their interest rates averaged 2.7 per cent.[43] But these new credits, on top of the policy of rescheduling rather than cancelling most of the old, meant that the N.L.C. actually handed its successors a heavier external debt in 1969 than had existed in February 1966. The net increase was 20 per cent, amounting to a total figure of £394 million.[44]

In order to pay off external debts without sacrificing essential imports, the N.L.C.—and each successor regime—clearly needed to expand the country's export earnings. One approach was to try and stimulate a greater output in the traditional export industries. After 1966 cocoa farming benefited not only from higher import license allocations for insecticides and cutlasses, but improved producer prices. Between the coup and July 1968, the Cocoa Marketing Board increased the price for a standard sixty pound load of cocoa almost 100 per cent, and (as Table I shows) the downward trend in production which began in the 1965–66 crop was reversed. Good crops were harvested in 1967–68, there was a very bad weather season in 1968–69, but bumper crops came in for the following three years.

The N.L.C.'s efforts to expand timber and mining exports included a devaluation of the cedi. On 8 July 1967 the sterling value of the New Cedi was reduced 30 per cent. Timber production had declined by 13 per cent from its 1965 level largely because of a cost-price squeeze.[45] Devaluation was helpful in this respect, and it does seem to have stimulated log exports. Between 1966 and 1969 they rose 46 per cent in volume, and the greater output—plus higher market prices—provided a 54 per cent increase in foreign exchange earnings, even with devaluation.[46] The N.L.C.'s success in promoting new export industries was much more limited, being confined to allowing a number of international oil companies to take out prospecting licenses for Ghana's offshore areas, and to arranging for the sale of electricity from the Volta dam to Togo and Dahomey *via* transmission lines which were scheduled to be completed late in 1972. The American-owned aluminium smelter also started production in 1967, using imported alumina, and locally-generated electricity to convert the alumina powder into metal. In this way, export earnings finally broke from the stagnation which prevailed between 1959 and 1966. As Table III (page 58) shows, export receipts rose markedly each year from 1966 to 1970, with only a small trade deficit in 1967 and then surpluses in the following three years. These improved trade balances were also the consequence of a much more effective control over import licensing and of a number of deflationary measures. Capital expenditure was cut by 54 per cent between 1965 and 1966,[47] and then kept at that general level for the next three years, and it brought about a greatly reduced demand for imported goods both in the state sector and by private business.

The N.L.C. significantly retrenched the state sector of the economy. The Black Star Line, Ghana Airways and the State Fishing Corporation reduced their fleets, the Ghana National Construction Corporation lost its near monopoly of public works contracts and was forced to lay off about 10,000 workers, and the State Farms Corporation closed down more than a quarter of its 105 farms. All thirteen of the government's 'rural industries' (including bamboo and rattan factories), and eighteen (mostly small-scale) state industries, were offered for sale. And by the end of 1969 eight of the state factories had been sold to Ghanaian buyers. For the larger enterprises, the N.L.C. sought foreign equity partners who would contribute investment capital as well as managerial and technical skills, and they were successful for the tyre and match factories and two cement plants. No new, wholly state-owned enterprise was launched in any sector: instead, the government's National Investment Bank was permitted to form partnerships (with itself as a minority shareholder) with foreign investors.[48] From a peak in 1965 of about 66 per cent, the central government's share of fixed capital formation dropped in 1968 to about 20 per cent—the level experienced in 1958.[49] Such policies were well in keeping with I.M.F. advice—except there was no increase of taxation. As a member of the original N.L.C. Economic Committee commented: 'We could not tax the people more. We might well have invited another coup.'[50] Instead, in both the 1966–67 and 1967–68 budgets, the N.L.C. reduced import duties on basic consumer items and raised the exemption limit for taxable personal income.

To the policy-makers of this period, retrenchment gave promise of a better use of resources in the state sector and of a higher output from private enterprise. Economic good sense also appeared to dictate a scaling down in the operations of the large state corporations. But arguments based on economic rationality were unlikely to appeal to the 20,000 for whom retrenchment in the public sector between 1965 and 1967 meant losing their jobs.[51] Another critical group were local businessmen, journalists and university teachers who disliked the foreign 'partnership policy'. As noted in the previous chapter, their main target was the agreement with the American firm, Abbott Laboratories. Following sharp public criticism, Abbott asked to be allowed to cancel the contract, and the civilian Commissioner for Industries, who had negotiated the agreement, was transferred to another ministry. Had a party government functioned in the place of the N.L.C. it is probable that other partnerships agreements (with Firestone to revive rubber plantations and operate a tyre factory, with French and Swiss interests to reorganise the Kade match factory, and with a Norwegian company to run two cement plants) would have been blocked. The enterprises would then have continued to limp along or remained idle (as did the pharmaceutical factory) for lack of new capital and skilled personnel. Similarly, a democratically elected government might also have found it a great deal more difficult to ignore the problem of unemployment which followed these reductions in the public sector.

An important by-product, however, of the policy of retrenchment was the greater availability to private enterprise of foreign exchange, bank credit, and skilled manpower. Between December 1965 and the end of 1968, commercial bank credit to state institutions dropped by 33 per cent but increased for the private sector by 31 per cent.[52] And whereas the Nkrumah government had planned to allocate to the state sector about 70 per cent of all 1966 imports, the N.L.C. worked on the basis of 61 per cent in favour of private enterprise.[54] Omaboe argued that this reallocation of resources to the private sector would yield a higher output and greater efficiency, and the available production figures for manufacturing seem to vindicate him. In three years, from 1965 to 1968, the total output from privately owned factories (with thirty or more workers) increased by 54 per cent.[55]

The N.L.C. deliberately promoted the expansion of local Ghanaian enterprise. Towards the end of 1967, for example, it began a feeder road programme which by August 1970 had built almost 1,000 miles of roads at a cost of £4.5 million.[56] The Public Works Department was instructed to favour Ghanaian contractors, and up to August 1970 they had obtained over 97 per cent of total contracts.[57] A parallel policy was followed in respect of imports. A firm's allocation of licenses depended largely on its financial classification in the government's Register of Importers. An importer classified in Group 'A' could receive £1 million or more in licenses; Group 'B' to allocations of from £500,000 to £1 million; Group 'C' under £500,000. When the Ministry of Trade revised the Register of Importers in 1966, it was directed by the N.L.C. to waive the criterion of past performance in order to raise twelve Ghanaian firms to Grade 'B' and a number of others to 'C'.[58] The only Ghanaian enterprise in Group 'A' was the state-owned Ghana National Trading Corporation. The upgrading of private Ghanaian importers continued, until by January 1970 there were fourteen of them in Grade 'A' and nine in 'B'.[59] They thus obtained licenses which would have otherwise gone to foreign importers or the G.N.T.C., and the latter's share of commercial imports declined from about 30 per cent in 1965 to 21 per cent in 1967.[60] It was a very significant shift from the state enterprises of the Nkrumah era.

Since the early days of the 1948 boycott, Ghanaian merchants had looked to the government for help to free them from expatriate competition. The Nkrumah government's policy after independence had been to edge out both Ghanaian and foreign traders by expanding the role of the G.N.T.C. The N.L.C., in contrast, curbed the state corporation, and published a decree at the end of 1968 which required that all retail trade establishments with an annual sales volume of N¢500,000 or less (N¢2.45 then equalled £1), and wholesale business with turnovers not exceeding N¢1 million, should be Ghanaian-owned by July 1973.

In addition, the Ghanaian Enterprises Decree of 1968, called for the 'Ghanaianisation' by 1971 of all taxi enterprises, and of businesses representing overseas manufacturers. A further provision specified that by mid-1973 the government must force the closure, or the sale to Ghanaians, of any enterprise 'employing thirty persons or less which in the opinion of the Committee [established by government to implement the decree] requires simple production or operational techniques, or any enterprise with a capital of one hundred thousand new cedis or less. . . .'[61]

These determined efforts to promote local private enterprise resulted from a combination of three related factors: a general resentment of the economic power enjoyed by foreigners in Ghana, a similar disenchantment with state enterprises, and the persuasive pressure applied by Ghanaian business interests. During the last four years of Nkrumah's rule, several sectors of the economy had been 'localised' through the growth of state enterprises; but in many fields, and particularly in wholesale and retail trade, foreign-owned enterprises continued to be conspicuous and were resented. In explaining the background for the Ghanaian Enterprises Decree, a member of the N.L.C.'s Executive Council commented:

> It is no secret that this legislation was directed against the Lebanese and Indians . . . They were here doing things which Ghanaians can easily do, like buying and selling goods. They came with little capital. They do not train Ghanaians to succeed them . . . They are a serious drain on our balance of payments with their personal remittance quotas, and they have been deeply involved in illegal transfers and currency smuggling.[62]

For Omaboe, a major purpose of the decree was to protect Ghanaians from the competition of well-established, financially stronger, expatriate firms in fields where Ghanaians had the ability to succeed—small-to-medium-scale trading enterprises, taxi businesses, and the like.[63] Another member of the Economic Committee pointed to the anomaly of foreign businessmen and their families—many of them employed in the same business—flourishing while Ghanaians with the same skills either struggled along in tiny businesses or were unemployed.[64]

Reliance on state enterprises was rejected because of their poor performance in recent years, and because it was believed by those who now advised the N.L.C. that a large part of the public equated socialism with shortages. R. S. Amegashie argued that the average Ghanaian wanted economic independence but not 'something abstract like more economic power to the state. He wanted new opportunities for himself, his relatives, and friends to earn a living in trade or other fields."[65] Similarly, it was believed that in operating small-scale enterprises which were protected from expatriate competition, many Ghanaians would serve fruitful apprenticeships from which they could move on to managing larger enterprises, whether state or private.[66]

In addition to the economic arguments for encouraging private enterprise, there was undoubtedly a good deal of lobbying on the part of local businessmen. Omaboe, Amegashie and their principal secretaries were visted frequently by representatives of various interest groups and individuals who wanted to be heard on how government should assist them. Both the N.L.C., and the senior civil servants responsible for economic policy, were susceptible to such pressures. The N.L.C. members cultivated political support in many quarters, but particularly from those whose interests Nkrumah had neglected or victimised, and Ghanaian businessmen were one such group. Among other sources of support were members of the former opposition United Party and ex-C.P.P. adherents who had broken with Nkrumah, many of whom had been businessmen or, when forced out of politics, had turned to private enterprise for their livelihood. For example, P.K.K. Quaidoo, a former minister from 1958–61 went into textile manufacturing, and in 1966 was appointed by the N.L.C. Chairman of the Black Star Line. In the same year E. K. Dadson, who had served as a parliamentary secretary from 1957 to 1961, and had various business investments, was named Chairman of the State Gold Mining Corporation. And there were many others.

The N.L.C.'s policies actually fostered political action among Ghanaian businessmen, as well as being partly a response to such action. New interest groups were formed (the Association of Ghanaian Businessmen, the Indigenous Ghanaian Manufacturers' Association and the Crusade for the Protection of Ghanaian Enterprises), and old ones (for example, the Ghana National Contractors' Association) were revived. The President of the Indigenous Ghanaian Manufacturers' Association, Mrs. Esther Ocloo, explained that her organisation was transformed from a 'dinner club' into a formal interest group largely in response to the Ghanaian Enterprises Decree and its promise of decisive protection for 'indigenous entrepreneurs'.[67] In 1969 she stood for parliament, as did E. Acquah-Harrison, President of the rival Ghana Manufacturers' Association, K. Amuah-Seki, Treasurer of the Association of Ghanaian Businessmen, and J. C. Yeboah, Secretary of the Ghana National Contractors' Association. All four were candidates either of the National Alliance of Liberals or of the Progress Party, both of which promised substantial aid to businessmen and endorsed the principles of the Ghanaian Enterprises Decreee.

The policy of the Progress Government after October 1969 differed from that of the N.L.C. in the sense that it both broadened the scope, and accelerated the pace, of this 'Ghanaianisation' of the economy. In their second month of office, Busia's cabinet ordered all aliens lacking residence and work permits to obtain them within the very short period of only two weeks, or leave the country. Almost all those affected were West Africans engaged as traders, artisans and labourers along with their families: enforcement of the order began in December, and between then and April 1970 an estimated 155,000 left Ghana for lack of permits.[68] Exceptions were made for mine workers, cocoa farm labourers, and categories where Ghanian replacements seemed unlikely to come forward, and many filtered back into Ghana after the initial expulsions. Nevertheless, there was a large-scale exodus with the result that, on balance, new employment and local trading opportunities were opened for many Ghanaians.

The same policy was followed with the Ghanaian Business (Promotion) Act of June 1970 which superceded the N.L.C.'s Ghanaian Enterprises Decree by flatly excluding aliens from small-scale trading in markets and at kiosks; it also moved the effective date for terminating foreign participation in small- and medium-scale trading operations from mid-1973 to August 1970. The N.L.C.'s deadline for localising taxi services was also brought forward, from 1971 to 1970. And in place of the former intention of forcing aliens out of unspecified 'small-scale industries' by mid-1973, the Progress Party legislation listed seven categories of business which were to be reserved to Ghanaians by July 1971: road transportation, baking, printing (other than textiles), beauty culture, produce brokerage, advertising and publicity, and the manufacture of cement blocks for sale. As with the Compliance Order, the government took enforcement seriously and both the 1970 and 1971 deadlines were largely observed.

Theory could not always, however, be matched with practice. Although non-Ghanaians were forced to surrender their businesses, it was not always clear that local people could take their place, if only for lack of capital to buy the stocks and other assets. For example, when no Ghanaian buyer came forward in July and August 1970 to take over a 100-cab taxi company, the state-owned Ghana National Trading Corporation was ordered to operate its services. Later in the year, the G.N.T.C. successfully petitioned Parliament for a N₵5 million loan to increase its imports so as 'to fill the vacuum left by the aliens till Ghanaians are able to be on their own'.[69] The problem was plain enough. To 'be on their own', in the sense of effectively replacing expatriate entrepreneurship, Ghanaian businessmen required managerial assistance as well as financial aid, and the government was prepared to help. It funded special loan programmes for small and medium-scale businesses, launched a scheme to guarantee commercial bank credits to local borrowers, and expanded business training opportunities. But the government was not always ready to give way. Some of the state-owned enterprises, after being reorganised under the N.L.C., were now strong enough for renewed growth, and they were encouraged to step in, not only where local enterprise was lacking, but where indigenous business could not operate so efficiently, as in construction.

Despite its 'private business bias, therefore, in practice the Progress Government followed a largely pragmatic approach. In areas where Ghanaian business showed some competence—as in constructing feeder roads and providing certain agricultural services—public enterprise was restrained. Where indigenous private enterprise was lacking, and state corporations appeared to have the necessary skill—as in importing, large-scale agriculture, and marine fishing—they were allowed to expand again. For example, the net sales of the G.N.T.C. fell from a peak of N₡147.5 million in 1965 to 54.5 million in 1967, but climbed to N₡78.2 million in the fiscal year ending 30 September 1970.[70] And where neither the state nor local private enterprise could shoulder full responsibilities, new direct foreign private investment was welcomed and offered various incentives, including government loans.[71] Unlike the Nkrumah regime, the government did not regard the expansion of the state sector as a social and political good in itself but simply as a necessary expedient.

Whatever the mix of state, indigenous-private, and foreign-private enterprise, the C.P.P., N.L.C., Progress and (after 1972) the N.R.C., were faced with much the same overall problem—how to increase employment opportunities and the output of goods and services in order to generate political resources which could be used to underpin their rule. Yet the shift in policy from an emphasis on the state sector prior to 1966, to that of promoting Ghanaian private business, was very marked. In the 1969 elections, both the major parties stressed the need to advance local, private enterprise and, in the two years of civilian rule, the Progress Government was conspicuously pro-business while the main Opposition—though criticising the implementation of particular programmes—did not dissociate itself from the general aim. And the short-term effect was clearly beneficial. Manufacturing, fishing, and the output of locally produced foodstuffs did expand significantly. Between 1966 and 1970 the value of manufactured goods grew in constant prices by an annual average of about 25 per cent compared with an average yearly increase between 1962 and 1966 of 13 per cent.[72] At the same time, efficiency in the state factories greatly improved until by mid-1971 all except one of the twenty divisions of the government's Ghana Industrial Holding Corporation were making profits.[73] Even the output of fish increased an estimated 45 per cent —mainly from the Volta Lake![74] Maize output increased from about 206,000 tons in 1965 to an estimated 900,000 at the end of 1970. And the Progress government continued the N.L.C.'s encouragement of local foodstuffs. It offered credits from the state's Agricultural Development Bank, constructed feeder roads to aid in marketing, guaranteed prices for certain commodities, and entered directly into food production via the state corporations.

Nonetheless, despite the expansion, employment did not keep pace with the growth in the labour force. The government's tally of employed persons showed an increase of only 5.8 per cent between the 1961–65 average of 365,000 and the 1966–70 figure of 386,000,[75] while the total unemployed at the end of 1970 was estimated at 200,000, or about half as much as the number of recorded employed.[76] The failure of the economy to generate more jobs was related to the low overall growth rates (an average of only 1.6 per cent for 1966–68 and 3.4 to 4 per cent for 1968–70) and caused by two persisting structural weaknesses: the inability to generate sufficient savings, particularly in the form of the foreign exchange which was needed to finance the imported components of investment, and the lack of entrepreneurial skills. With very little domestic production of capital goods, and only a modest development in the manufacturing of intermediate goods, most investment in Ghana required imported materials. But (as Table III shows) the sterling value of capital imports dropped below the 1965 level for the years 1966–69. More effective entrepreneurship might have engineered greater growth from the same or even lower levels of imports, but it could scarcely have made good the short fall in the imports which were needed.

Table III points to the two prime causes of the shortage of foreign exchange—the relative stagnation in export receipts prior to 1968 and the failure to restrain the import of consumer goods. For example, between 1968 and 1970 imports of machinery and transport equipment increased by £9.2 million but food imports rose by £11.7 million. Similarly, imports of passenger cars averaged 2,912 in 1964–65 but rose to 5,562 in 1969–70.[77] The main problem of course was the continued and excessive dependence on the one commodity —cocoa—which was unstable both in domestic production and in world market prices. From 1965 to 1970 cocoa receipts averaged 65 per cent of Ghana's total export receipts.[78] In the crop years 1964–65 to 1970–71, output fluctuated by an annual average of nearly 16 per cent,[79] while market prices first fell, then soared, and once again collapsed (see Table I). As discussed above, the N.L.C. and Progress sought to encourage greater output, but the problem of stabilising world market prices was quite beyond the control of any one country, despite the fact that Ghana produced about 30 per cent of total world output.

Yet very little could be done to diversify the economy. The same five commodities (cocoa, logs and timber, gold, maganese, and diamonds) which represented 98 per cent of total export receipts in 1957, still accounted for 92 per cent in 1967 and 80 per cent in 1972. The only major new export (earning more than 5 per cent of total revenues) was aluminium, but since the industry depended entirely on imported alumina, and ran up considerable other foreign exchange costs, the net benefit to the balance of payments was limited. Exports of aluminium in 1970 were valued at N₵31.9 m, the cost of aluminium oxide and hydroxide imports was N C 18 m. Both the N.L.C. and Progress Party governments might perhaps have done more to encourage agricultural exports, such as rubber or palm oil, but the gestation period tends to be several years and no sizeable contribution to foreign exchange earnings could have been expected in the short term. There was the possibility also of a new petroleum or bauxite-extraction industry, but that would have meant a loss of control over the country's own resources. Unable on its own to mobilise the capital and skilled-manpower resources required by such industries, the government—each and all Ghanaian governments—depended on foreign entrepreneurship. Some oil companies did respond to invitations to take out prospecting licenses; one promising strike was made in 1970, but subsequent drilling failed to identify sufficient quantities for commercial exploitation. The bauxite deposits were known to be extensive, but it was not at all clear that future market demand would justify investing in new mines, and again it was a question whether foreign investors would agree to risk their capital. The Progress Government was criticised for dragging its heels over negotiating a bauxite prospecting licence with the Kaiser and Reynolds aluminium companies,[80] which were also the owners of the $100-million-plus aluminium smelter in Ghana; but there was a genuine and perplexing problem which had to be faced—whether to seek the investment of a further $150–200 million, which might mean excessive economic power being concentrated in the hands of two foreign companies, or to block the injecting of capital into a stagnant economy which was critically in need of a new export industry.

Whether the Progress government was right to follow the N.L.C.'s policy of honoring its debt obligations is a matter for debate. It succeeded in obtaining agreement for a further stretching out of the payments, with the result that in 1971 only about 10 per cent of the amount originally due was actually being paid out.[81] The key consideration of course was whether the actual inflow of foreign aid would exceed the outflow in debt payments. In fact, the net balance was positive for the period February 1966 to April–May 1969,[82] negative (by about £1.3 million) in the fiscal year 1969–70, and then positive again in 1970–71. The critical mistake in policy, however, was the departure from the N.L.C.'s control of imports. The dilemma was clearly there. To continue physical controls through detailed licensing might prevent severe trade imbalances, and make possible some trade surpluses (as in

1968–70); but such a policy also led to bureaucratic delays, corruption, the discouragement of new investors through problems of supply, and the danger of a gross shortage of consumer goods with all the attendant evils of inflation, hoarding, black market selling and massive discontent at popular level. The decision was taken in 1970 when the Busia government extended open licensing to several categories of raw materials and capital items, and to basic consumer goods, until about 60 per cent of the total value of the country's import trade was free from controls.[83] In August 1970, appreciating that there was 'a very large backlog of demand for imported goods of all sorts',[84] the government conceded the need for some restraint on imports; and it chose fiscal measures. It was thought that regular import duties, and 'temporary import surcharges', would curb effective demand for goods, and that despite the freedom to import, merchants would not order what they could not sell. The backlog of demands, however, was not only large; it was also resistant to price increases, and overall imports grew by 18.3 per cent between 1969 and 1970, then expanded by 7.6 per cent from 1970 to 1971, particularly large increases occurring in the unwelcome area of food imports (see Table III). Part of the problem derived from the government's own spending, including payments to Ghana-based companies which in turn used the money to buy imports. The revised figures for total government expenditure in the fiscal year 1970–71 were 25 per cent above the 1969–70 level, and the 1971–72 budget called for a further expansion of 28 per cent.[85] Mensah recognised the risk of increasing government spending while the balance of payments situation remained weak,[86] but he (and presumably the cabinet) chose expansion, gambling on reasonably high cocoa prices and the success of fiscal measures to prevent excessive imports.

The gamble failed in both senses. In 1971 cocoa prices plummeted, and import costs outran export receipts by 16 per cent, with the result that the country's short-term debt (due within a year or less) mounted to the equivalent of the import bill for about half a year.[87] To stop the slide towards bankruptcy, an austerity budget of N₵459 m was presented to parliament in July 1971 which had an all too familiar ring to it. It introduced a National Development Levy of between one and five per cent on all incomes above N₵1,000 p.a.; it withdrew housing and car subsides for civil servants and army officers, imposed a 10–25 per cent tax on foreign exchange transfers, raised the price of petrol, increased the bank rate, introduced hospital charges and banned the import of a number of consumer goods, including all motor cars. There were, said Mensah, three major problem areas within the overall difficulty of the economy—food shortages, unemployment and the adverse balance of payments. A United Kingdom loan of N₵8.6 m helped a little to ease the debt repayments; and a tighter check was imposed on import controls and frontier trade while trying to increase local production of both cocoa and food. But the price continued to fall for the main autumn crop, and on 27 December 1971 the government devalued the cedi by an extraordinary 48 per cent. It was cushioned by a number of counter measures, including the abolition of the import surcharges and an increase in both the minimum wage and the producer price for cocoa. But that was little consolation for the immediate future, or for the middle-income 'salariat'. The effect of the budget and the massive devaluation was particularly bad since the economic hardships they imposed coincided with growing political dissatisfaction across a broad range of former party supporters—trade unionists, university students, civil servants and, most ominously, the policy and the army. And it was from a particular section of those most affected, the officer corps of the army, that the January 1972 coup came.[88]

The new military government—the National Redemption Council under Colonel Acheampong—reimposed a detailed licensing system and began to work towards an almost 50 per cent reduction in imports. The cedi was revalued, scaling down the 48 per cent devaluation to 20 per cent, and a sizeable proportion of the overseas debts dating from the Nkrumah period was repudiated, particularly those owed to overseas firms which had acted on a contractor financed basis. The N.R.C. showed a commendable energy in its policies, and gave particular emphasis (in military terms) to an 'Operation Feed Yourself' in an attempt to cut back on food imports. Fortunately for the soldiers, there was a large rise in cocoa and gold prices, and the beginning of a reversal of the adverse trade balance of previous years. New efforts were made to discipline imports and restrict smuggling, and Colonel Acheampong talked of trying to persuade, and (through import licensing) to oblige Ghanaians to live without the comforts of a high import economy. It was, and remains, an awesome task which will certainly require at least as much political skill as military fortitude on the part of the 1972 regime.

TABLE I
Cocoa Statistics
Crop Years 1957–58 to 1971–72

	1957–8	1958–9	1959–60	1960–1	1961–2	1962–3	1963–4	1964–5	1965–6	1966–7	1967–8	1968–9	1969–70	1970–1	1971–2
Average Price (£) per long ton	352	285	226	180	170	208	191	141	185	205	220*	365*	327*	260*	—
World Production ('000 long tons)	771	908	1,039	1,175	1,123	1,158	1,220	1,485	1,209	1,338	1,340	1,230	1,422*	1,353*	
Ghana's Production ('000 long tons)	207	255	317	433	410	422	436	557	410	376	415	334	415*	385*	460
Ghana's Share of World Production (percentage)	26.8	28.1	30.5	36.8	36.5	36.4	35.7	37.5	33.9	28.1	31.0	28.1	29.2	28.4	

Sources: Ghana, *Economic Survey(s)*, 1965, 1967, 1969, and Food and Agricultural Organization, *Production Yearbook, 1970*, and F.A.O. *Monthly Bulletin of Agricultural Economics and Statistics*, 1968–72.

* Data for metric tons.

TABLE II

Ghana's Foreign Trade Deficits and Total Balance of Payments Deficits on Current Account: 1960–65

£ Million	1960	1961	1962	1963	1964	1965
Imports						
Consumer goods	64.7	70.6	55.9	51.3	40.8	54.9
Raw and semi-finished materials	30.9	39.5	33.0	39.5	41.4	50.3
Capital equipment	28.0	26.7	21.3	32.3	32.4	48.3
Fuel and lubricants	5.9	6.0	6.5	7.2	7.0	6.5
Total Imports	129.5	142.8	116.7	130.3	121.6	160.0
Total Exports	116.0	115.1	115.0	108.9	114.6	113.4
Trade Deficit	13.5	27.7	1.7	21.4	7.0	47.6
Estimates of Total Deficit on Current Account	33.5	52.7	28.3	45.8	33.6	74.5

Source: Ghana, *Economic Survey(s),* 1961, 1966.

TABLE III

Ghana's Imports and Exports 1965–71

£ Million

	1965	1966	1967	1968*	1969*	1970*	1971*
Imports							
Consumer Goods	54.9	38.8	42.9	37.0	43.7		
(food)	—	—	—	(20.8)	(22.5)	(32.5)	—
Raw and Semi-finished Goods	50.3	43.0	50.0	50.6	57.9	—	—
Capital Equipment	48.3	38.3	29.9	31.9	33.8	—	—
(Machinery and transport equipment)	—	—	—	(35.0)	(38.6)	(44.2)	—
Fuel & Lubricants	6.5	5.2	7.7	8.7	9.4	—	—
Total Imports	160.0	125.3	130.5	128.2	144.8	171.0	184.0
Total Exports	113.4	95.7	123.4	139.5	162.0	199.5	158.5
Trade Deficit or Surplus	−46.6	−29.6	−7.1	11.3	17.2	28.5	−25.5

Sources: Ghana, *Economic Survey*, 1968, p. 44; *ibid.,* 1969, pp. 35, 37; and Standard Bank, *Annual Economic Review, Ghana*, October 1971, p. 2 and *Standard Bank Review*, April, 1972, p. 15.

Notes

1. On 23 February 1966, current payments arrears in respect of matured import bills and other obligations totalled £35 million. *Developments in the Ghanaian Economy between 1960 and 1968* (Accra; Ghana Publishing Corporation, 1969), p. 17.
2. Kwame Nkrumah, *Dark Days in Ghana*, (New York: International Publishers, 1969), p. 61. The I.M.F.'s conditions included a reduction in overall government expenditure, a 'temporary halt ... on the launching of new projects financed by supplier's credits', a more 'liberal attitude toward foreign investment', and a review of the existing trade pacts with Eastern countries. Ghana, *Economic Survey 1965* (Accra: Central Bureau of Statistics, 1966), p. 50.
3. *Economic Survey*, 1965, p. 48.
4. See the chapter, 'The Big Lie', in *Dark Days in Ghana.*
5. *Developments in Ghanaian Economy*, p. 17.
6. *Ghana, Economic Survey*, 1966, (Accra, Central Bureau of Statistics, 1967) pp. 27–28.
7. Walter Birmingham, I. Neustadt, and E. N. Omaboe, eds., *A Study of Contemporary Ghana*, Vol. I, *The Economy of Ghana* (London: Allen and Unwin, 1966), p. 55.
8. Cf, *Annual Report on External Trade and Shipping and Aircraft Movements, 1954*, Vol. I. (Accra: Office of the Government Statistician, 1955) with Ghana, *External Trade Statistics of Ghana, December, 1961*. (Accra: Central Burea of Statistics, 1962.)
9. *1962 Industrial Census Report*, Vol. I, *Industry* (Accra: Central Bureau of Statistics, 1965), pp. 120–124.
10. *Economic Survey, 1961* (Accra: Central Bureau of Statistics, 1962), pp. 122, 126, 127.
11. *Ibid.*, pp. 125, 127.
12. *Developments in the Ghanaian Economy*, p. 14.
13. *Economic Survey, 1964*, (Accra: Central Bureau of Statistics, 1965), p. 84 and *Economic Survey, 1965*, p. 75.
14. *Report of the Commission of Enquiry into Trade Malpractices in Ghana* (Accra: Office of the President, 1966), p. 14 and *Economic Survey, 1965*, p. 73.
15. *Economic Survey, 1965*, p. 65.
16. *Ibid.*, p. 35.
17. Interview with an officer of the Board, Accra, May 1965.
18. *Economic Survey, 1964*, p. 151 and *Economic Survey, 1965*, p. 148.
19. *Economic Survey, 1965*, p. 43.
20. *Ibid.*, p. 14.
21. *Ibid.*, and *Enquiry into Trade Malpractices*, and *Enquiry into Irregularities in Licences* (Accra, 1967).
22. *Economic Survey, 1965*, pp. 110, 112.
23. E. N. Omaboe, *The State of Ghana's Economy Today* (Accra: State Publishing Corporation, 1967), p. 6.
24. Cf, *Economic Survey, 1961*, p. 109, and *ibid.* 1965, p. 114–5.
25. *Our Goal: Osagyefo launches Seven-Year Plan* (Accra: Ministry of Information and Broadcasting, 1964), p. 3.
26. *Economic Survey, 1965*, p. 92.
27. Cf, *Ibid.*, p. 75 and The Ghana Industrial Development Corporation, *Twelfth Annual Report and Accounts* (Accra: Guinea Press, n.d.), Statements 1 and 2; and Ghana, *Report and Financial Statements by the Accountant-General and Report Thereon by the Auditor-General for the Year Ended 30 September 1961*, (Accra: Ministry of Information and Broadcasting, 1963), pp. 78, 79, 82.

28. This estimate is 50 per cent of the value of the state sector's consumption of raw materials, fuel, and electricity. Ghana, *Industrial Statistics: 1965–66* (Accra: Central Bureau of Statistics. 1967), pp. 34–35.
29. *The Budget, 1966–67*, Table IX.
30. *Report of the Auditor-General on the Accounts of Ghana for the Period 1 January, 1965 to 30 June, 1966* (Accra: State Publishing Corporation, 1968), pp. 23–46.
31. See: Marvin P. Miracle and Ann Seidman, *State Farms in Ghana* (Madison. Wisconsin: The Land Tenure Centre, University of Wisconsin, 1968).
32. *Report of the Committee of Enquiry on the Local Purchasing of Cocoa.* Accra. Ministry of Information, 1967, pp. 50–51.
33. *Economic Survey, 1963* (Accra: Central Bureau of Statistics, 1964), p. 127 and *Economic Survey, 1965*, p. 108.
34. *Local Purchasing of Cocoa*, p. 39.
35. *The State of Ghana's Economy Today*, p. 8.
36. *Economic Survey*, 1966, p. 45.
37. £6.4 million, *Economic Survey, 1966*, p. 32.
38. *Developments in Ghanaian Economy*, p. 18.
39. Interview with one of those officials. June 1970. In July 1967 Omaboe and a number of other civilians became the executive heads of ministries and bore the title Commissioner.
40. Albert Adomakoh, Governor, Bank of Ghana, 'Ghana's Foreign Debts', *Legon Observer*, (Legon, Ghana), 15 September 1967, p. 24.
41. *Ibid.*
42. *The State of the Economy and the External Debt Problem* (Ghana Publishing Corporation: Accra 1970) p. 10.
43. For the particulars of these loans, see: *Developments in the Ghanaian Economy*, pp. 23, 25, 27. For the I.M.F. debt, see *Ibid.*, p. 18.
44. *Ibid.*, pp. 16–17.
45. *Economic Survey, 1966*, p. 56.
46. Ghana, *External Trade Statistics*, December 1966 and December 1969, p. 222 in both issues. In the same period, however, the growth in sawn timber exports was slight and the net gain in foreign earnings was only 4 per cent.
47. *Economic Survey, 1969*, p. 114.
48. National Investment Bank, Ghana, *Directors' Report for the Year Ended 31 December, 1969*, (Accra, n.d.) pp. 22–29.
49. *Economic Survey, 1968*, p. 120–123.
50. Interview, Accra, July 1970.
51. *Economic Survey, 1968*, p. 102.
52. *Economic Survey, 1968*, p. 138.
53. *1966 Budget Statement* (Accra: State Publishing Corporation, 1966), p. 12.
54. *Ghana's Economy and Aid Requirements in 1967*, p. 29.
55. *Economic Survey, 1968*, p. 148.
56. Interview with a senior officer of the Public Works Department, Accra, August 1970.
57. *Ibid.*
58. Interviews with two senior officers of the Trade Division of the Ministry of Trade and Industries, Accra: July 1970.
59. *Commercial and Industrial Bulletin* (Accra), 24 January 1970.
60. The 1968 allocation was 23 per cent and that for 1969 totalled 25 per cent. Interview with a former senior officer of the Ministry of Trade and Industries for the 1966–69 period, Accra, August 1970. The 1965 estimate is from a letter to the author in June 1967 from Sir Patrick Fitzgerald, then Managing Director of the Ghana National Trading Corporation.
61. *Ghanaian Enterprises Decree, N.L.C.D. No. 323*, p. 5.

62. Interview in Accra, July 1970.
63. Interview with Omaboe, Accra, 16 July 1970.
64. Interview in Accra, June 1970.
65. Interview with Amegashie, 13 July 1970.
66. Interview with Omaboe, 16 July 1970.
67. Interview with Mrs. Esther Ocloo, Madina, Ghana, 10 July 1970.
68. *Ghanaian Times,* 5 August 1970.
69. *Parliamentary Debate, 4 December 1970.*
70. Interview G.N.T.C. Accra, July 1970.
71. *Parliamentary Debate, 6 September 1971.*
72. *Economic Survey 1969* and *Parliamentary Debate, 27 July 1971.* Figures based on manufacturing enterprises of thirty or more employees.
73. *Parliamentary Debate, 3 September 1971.*
74. *Economic Survey 1969*, p. 67.
75. *Parliamentary Debate, 27 July 1971.*
76. *Ibid.*
77. *Quarterly Dig. of Stats. December 1970*, pp. 29–30.
78. *Economic Survey 1969*, p. 41 and *Ghana, External Trade Stats. December 1970,* p. 199.
79. *Ibid.*
80. *West Africa,* 31 December 1971.
81. *Ibid.,* 27 August 1971.
82. *Development in the Ghanaian Economy.*
83. *Standard Bank, Annual Economic Review October,* 1971, p. 6.
84. *Parliamentary Debate,* 25 August 1970.
85. *Annual Economic Review November 1970* and *October 1971.*
86. *Parliamentary Debate 27 September 1970, 27 July 1971.*
87. *Af. Res. Bulletin, Vol. 9 No. 2*, p. 2272.
88. See below.

CHAPTER 3

THE CONSTITUTIONAL COMMISSION 1966–69

Robin Luckham

We turn now to more particular matters—to a discussion of the Constitutional Commission which the N.L.C. established in September 1966 as part of its attempt to turn the military power it had unlawfully acquired into some more permanent structure of civilian authority. The constitution which resulted from the Commission did not stand the test of time, being swept away by the second coup. But although no more than a paper tiger, it exemplified in a very interesting way the tensions which necessarily exist (particularly in post-colonial states) between political intentions and actual achievement. There were also specific problems encountered by Dr. Busia's government which flowed directly from the document itself, and from the intentions of those who made it—not least the assumption that every possible danger to a future civilian regime could actually be provided against. Hence the very detailed clauses of the 1969 constitution which were as unrealistic as they were undemocratic in the battery of prohibitions they placed in the way of a future elected government. The temptation to bend or disregard such rules was likely to beset any government having to act within them, and Dr. Busia's administration was to show itself unable to resist such temptations. There was, in addition, a more general problem of trust since the division of functions among a number of constitutionally protected 'guardians', and the pluralist image of a society composed of autonomous social estates such as the military, the chiefs and the professions, caused many to believe that the Constitution had been fashioned in defence of privilege rather than 'in defence of democracy', as the third Article of the Commissioners' Draft attempted to proclaim.[1]

A further reason why the 1969 Constitution is of interest is that there have been relatively few occasions in the life of an independent state when its citizens have engaged in so self-conscious an exercise in constitution-making, in which the basic principles of state power and political life were discussed thoroughly and publicly, as in Ghana under military rule. Yet one must also admit that the Constitution was as much a blueprint for the past as it was for the future. As Yaw Twumasi has said, the spectre of Nkrumaism still walked abroad.[2] Provision for change in the future was all too often sacrificed to provide strict constitutional guarantees against the alleged abuses of the past. There were,

62

it is true, a number of innovative and useful features of the Constitution such as the independent Electoral Commission, the Ombudsman set up to investigate complaints against the administration and the guaranteed recourse of citizens to the courts to enforce their rights. Yet the Constitution was heavily burdened, both by the opprobrium attached to provisions like Article 71—specifically meant to exclude from power the men who had ruled under Nkrumah—and by the rigidity and complexity of the sections which were designed to prevent the recurrence of the past by setting limits to the power of a future executive and legislature.

Constitution-making also provided a chance for both established and newly emerging social groups to define and promote their interests. Any legal order will generate contradiction between its universality in a Kantian sense—its ability to create legal rules independently of current configurations of group interest—and the recalcitrant fact that it will usually and systematically promote the interests of some groups over others. Equality before the law is at the same time reality and myth, for some are always more equal than others. The classic problem in the sociology of knowledge is how to show the connections between the general principles of a system of thought—whether it be an ideology or a configuration of scientific and cultural ideas, or a Constitution—and the interests, status and concerns of the men who manipulate it. Because constitution-making in Ghana in 1967–68 took the form of a public debate it is possible to trace the links between principle and interest, theory and practice, with unusual precision.

What were the interests served by the Constitution and how did they emerge in the debate? A number of changes had taken place in Ghanaian society since the time Nkrumah came to power. The fabled victory which took place of the verandah boys over the old intelligentsia can easily be understood when we reflect how small and poorly organized a body of men the latter were. The logistics of power, as described in Nkrumah's *Autobiography* were all too simple—a few devoted men, a modicum of party organisation at grass roots, moderately attended mass meetings and, of course, widespread discontent with the colonial government. Since those times, however, striking changes have taken place. In the first place there has been that huge expansion in the size of the educated élite of which the best indicator was the large numerical (and percentage) increase of Ghanaians with university degrees and of those passing through secondary school. Even the lawyers, who were the single most important occupational group among the old intelligentsia, increased in number from about 60 in 1948 to 230 in 1960 and over 600 in 1969. Secondly, Ghanaians took the control of the major instruments of state power—the government bureaucracies, especially the civil service, the police and the military. In

1951 there were only a handful of Ghanaians in the senior civil service and still fewer in the senior ranks of the police force and the officer corps of the army; by independence, in 1957, Ghanaians were numerically superior at the lower but not yet at the higher levels; but by 1961 they filled the entire military and police command structures and almost all that of the civil service. The division between these groups, whose authority rested on their control of Bureaucratic hierarchies or of force, and that of the politicians, which rested on the more diffuse popular support gathered together by the ramshackle C.P.P. party machine, developed apace. The C.P.P. not only cut back the power of the older status groups—the intelligentsia, the lawyers and the chiefs—but invaded the corporate privacy of the government bureaucracies and the armed forces. The result was the 1966 coup. Thereafter, the alliances forged by the military brought together all the major segments of the educated class, and it was broadly speaking these same groups to which the N.L.C. entrusted the making of a Constitution. Their interests, we shall argue, converged on two basic constitutional issues: limitations on the power of a popularly elected legislature, and a pluralist vision of government in which authority was distributed between autonomous centres of power, the major status groups being free to pursue their own interests undisturbed. That is not to say that there were no differences among them—between the old intelligentsia, the chiefs and the younger educated public servants and university teachers, or between the supporters of Busia and those of Gbedemah, which intertwined in a complex skein of conflict during the making of the constitution. The final document can be seen in many respects as a compromise between the political ideas of the older intelligentsia and the younger intellectuals, the former tending perhaps to prevail more often in the Constitutional Commission and the latter in the Constituent Assembly. Nevertheless, on the fundamental objective of preventing populism in politics, they were all agreed.

The making of a constitution for the return to civilian rule was a good indicator of the N.L.C.'s self conscious desire to take the army out of politics. The establishment of a Constitutional Commission was announced on 1 September 1966, barely seven months after the coup. The Commission began its hearings on 1 December 1966, and held its last meeting on 15 December 1967. The Draft Constitution and the elaborate Memorandum which sought to explain and justify it were published in January 1968. But it was not until December 1968 that the Draft was entrusted to a larger and more representative Constituent Assembly for debate, and not until August 1969 that the Assembly finally ratified the Constitution, a matter of days before the election which brought Dr. Busia's party to office. By that time, it had become clear that the N.L.C. had no intention of transferring power until it could be sure of an acceptable successor regime, or at the very least of a set of constitutional rules which would provide a framework within which such a regime could establish itself. Yet one of the most remarkable features of the deliberations of both the Commission and the Assembly was the way in which the N.L.C.—except on one occasion only[3]—kept out of the proceedings and left the civilians to get on with the job of providing a Constitution.

The probability that the military would accept the Constitution lay of course in the N.L.C.'s choice of the people who were to draft it. The Constitutional Commission was made up of respectable public figures. Eleven of its seventeen members were members of the Political Committee which the N.L.C. had established in June 1966.[4] Most had been leading figures in the nationalist movement in the late 1940s and early 1950s. The majority had either opposed the C.P.P. from the start or became disillusioned with it later on. The Chairman, the Hon. Mr. Justice Edward Akufo-Addo, like his brother-in-law W. E. A. Ofori-Atta, and R. S. Blay who became the Speaker of the Constituent Assembly, had been a founding member of the United Gold Coast Convention in 1947. He had also been a member of the Coussey Committee on constitutional reform in 1948–49, together with Nene Azu Mate Kole, J. A. Braimah and K. A. Bossman, three other members of the Commission. B. A. Bentum was the only Commissioner whose aversion to the C.P.P. dated from 24 February 1966 when, instead of being held in Protective Custody, he was appointed General Secretary of the Trades Union Congress.[5]

A number of the Commissioners were also among the beneficiaries of the return to civilian rule. The Chairman was elected President of Ghana in August 1970 after the Progress government had put out an unofficial whip in his behalf through Saki Scheck, who had by then become Chief Whip for the Progress Party in the National Assembly; W. E. A. Ofori-Atta and Victor Owusu became Ministers, Adam Amandi and Kweku Baah (a joint-Secretary to the Commission) were appointed Ministerial Secretaries. J. A. Braimah became Regional Chief Executive of the Northern Region. Nene Azu Mate Kole and D. J. Buahin were made members (in December 1970) of the Council of State. Abayifa Karbo remained Chairman of the Public Services Commission, to which he had been appointed by the N.L.C.; B. D. G. Folson was made acting Chairman of the Centre for Civil Education, and Mr. Justice V. C. R. A. C. Crabbe became a Supreme Court Judge, following a period of office as Interim Electoral Commissioner when he supervised the elections which brought the return to civilian rule. That the Commissioners were men of independent mind and character is attested by the open opposition of nearly all of them to the C.P.P. and by the arguments which took place within the Commission over a number of issues during its hearings. B. A. Bentum was later to withstand an attempt by progress to dislodge him from the General Secretaryship of the T.U.C.; Miss Akua Asaabea Ayisi, M. K. Apaloo and Dr. E. V. C. de Graft Johnson stood against Progress in the 1969 elections—as an independent, for the U.N.P., and for the A.P.R.P. Nevertheless, they shared common political assumptions arising out of their experience under the previous regime —assumptions that were broadly accepted by the members of the military government.

On the face of it, the procedure by which the Commission set about its task was democratic. At its first meeting it divided into three working groups which held public meetings throughout the country and listened to anybody who cared to talk. A questionnaire was sent out to selected organisations, and memoranda were invited from all groups and members of the general public who wished to submit them. In all, 567 individuals and organisations 'gave oral evidence' at the hearings and 721 sent in memoranda. They were as varied as the Aborigines Rights Protection Society (still in existence from the earliest days of protest under British rule) and the Assin Drivers Union; the First Century Gospel at Sekondi, the Yendi Catholic Teachers, and the Ahmadiyya Movement of Saltpond; the Ghana Bar Association, Employers' Associations, the Trades Union Congress, the Ghana National Farmers Union, the Juaben Ratepayers Association, the Paternoster Square Stores of Obuasi and the Ghana Law Students Association (U.K. and Ireland). Among individuals who sent memoranda, the variety was as great, including the leader of the emergent (and soon to subside) 'Third Force' (Dr. J. S. Bilson), and veterans of the struggle against Nkrumah like Nana Bafuor Osei Akoto and Kwesi Lamptey. There were prominent lawyers—A. Akiwumi, Cobbina Kessie, Joe Reindorf, Reginald Bannerman, David Effah and Mr. Justice Sowah—as well as ordinary members of the public, several chiefs and a junior army officer.

The fare provided to the Commission by this procedure was indigestible. Consultation gave legitimacy to the exercise rather than shaping the Constitution itself in a definable way. In two instances at least when the Commission's views differed from substantial numbers of the public—when, for instance, it expressly deviated from the majority of the memoranda which were in favour of a purely ceremonial Head of State, or when it decided against a review of Regional boundaries—it followed its own, rather than the public's predilections. As one might have expected, it was debate in the closed hearings of the Commission and its Standing Committee which was decisive. And within the Commission itself there were narrowing circles of influence. The Standing Committee, composed of Akufo Addo, Andoh, Apaloo, Bentum, Folson, Karbo and Ofori-Atta,[6] together with the joint secretaries, Crabbe, Baah and Minta, debated all the draft provisions before sending them to the full Commission for the final decision, and disposed of the Commission's administrative arrangements. The Secretariat of the Commission prepared several background papers—including one on Fundamental Human Rights which formed the basis of the corresponding clauses in the Constitution—and exercised great influence simply by the fact that the draft articles which were submitted to the Commission emanated from the pens of its draftsmen, especially the inexhaustible V. C. R. A. C. Crabbe, the Special Commissioner.

The lengthy *Memorandum on the Proposals for a Constitution for Ghana* was prepared by Crabbe, Baah, Minta, Folson and the Chairman. If the part played by the first four was a good example of the influence that can accrue to expertise in such a setting, that of Akufo Addo demonstrated the importance in post-Nkrumah Ghana of the social connections and prestige of the old intelligentsia. Akufo-Addo —impressive despite his diminutive stature, having a red rose in his button-hole, a cigar at his fingertips, dressed in a black coat and pinstripe trousers, with Edwardian sideburns and a liking for champagne—was a visible incarnation of the ethos of that intelligentsia. His skill in chairmanship and behind-the-scenes negotiation was consumate, and he seems to have taken it as his personal responsibility to ensure that the document (as expressed in a characteristic passage in the *Memorandum on the Proposals*) would 'span generations, even centuries' and gather around it 'a respect, an aura of sanctity and inner strength that, by itself, [would go] a long way to daunt even bold spirits who may harbour designs against it'.[7] The Minutes of the Commission are full of phrases like 'the Chairman emphasised the need for', 'the Chairman explained that', 'the Chairman suggested and the members agreed' or 'on this point the Chairman reminded members that. . . .' There were times, indeed, when ordinary members of the Commission became restive, so much so at one point that the Standing Committee was accused of imposing its own recommendations, in particular those having to do with the nature of the executive, and the Chairman felt it necessary to make a statement in reply.[8] There was to be more than one occasion later when sceptics described the document as 'Akufo-Addo's Constitution', and there were at least some ways in which they were right.

The Chairman's influence could also be seen in the Constitution's extreme length and cumbersome complexity: 172 articles and 2 schedules take up 160 pages in the draft document. [177 articles, 2 schedules and 186 pages in the final constitution passed by the Constituent Assembly]. There were to be no loopholes, even if this meant a constitution that was half an inch thick and virtually incomprehensible to the layman. And the procedure the Chairman followed almost guaranteed this result. For instead of deciding general principles first, and then drafting the rules which best expressed them, the different chapters and sections were drafted by the Secretariat (and on occasion by the Chairman himself), and then submitted to the Standing Committee and the full Commission successively. Both first principles, and the minutiae of drafting, were discussed simultaneously, and the results were far from elegant. There were, it is true, occasions when vigorous internal debate from the floor of the Commission secured important alterations in detail—causing, for example, the abandonment of a property, income or employment qualifications for M.P.s, and the abandonment of a proposal to give the President powers to make subsidiary legislation on his own responsibility. Subtlety of argument sometimes secured modifications—as when Folson brought the *Proposals* closer to the conventional model of cabinet government by stating an effective case against secret voting in Parliament, which the Commission had earlier decided to introduce. But disagreements on fundamentals—like Dr. de Graft Johnson's proposals for a non-parliamentary executive or Miss Akua Asaabea Ayisi's memorandum sharply criticising the proposal that Ministers could be appointed from outside Parliament—got short shrift.[9]

As one might have expected, the interests of the military and the civil service were more than adequately safeguarded. On many points—such as the desirability of an independent Public Service Commission—the views of the Commissioners did not differ significantly from those of the N.L.C. or of the civil servants and there was little need for specific consultation with them. But the Chairman took care to sound out the feelings of the Commander of the Army on the arrangements for the Armed Forces in the Constitution, raising in particular the question whether or not there should be a single Chief of Defence Staff with powers of command over all three branches of the armed forces. An official of the Ministry of Foreign Affairs attended a meeting to make suggestions on the proposed National Security Council; and an official of the security service was actually asked for information about the control of expenditure in the American C.I.A. Such tender concern was easy to understand, since the civil servants, policemen and soldiers were a constituency that the Commission could not afford to neglect. It is significant that the Draft Constitution gave the armed forces in certain respects the kind of functional autonomy that it conferred upon other key institutions, such as the judiciary and the Electoral Commission. Though the General Officer Commanding (renamed 'Chief of Defence Staff' in the Constitution itself) took his operational orders from the Cabinet, he was appointed by the President acting in consultation with ('on the advice of' in the final Constitution) the Council of State; he was also responsible to an Armed Forces Council, in which were vested powers of commissioning, appointments, conditions of service and discipline. The provision for his appointment was explicitly intended by the Commission to be 'on the same lines as the provisions made for the appointment of the Chief Justice'.[10] On the other hand it recognised that the Armed Forces-unlike the Judiciary —had ultimately to be subordinate to the Executive, and this was achieved by empowering the Prime Minister to appoint the majority of the members of the Armed Forces Council (in the Constitution itself all except the Chief of Defence Staff) so that the Council would not be unduly 'weighted in favour of officer representation'.[11] Nor was the General Officer Commanding to enjoy the same protection from arbitrary dismissal as a Judge, the Electoral Commissioner or the Ombudsman.

The starting point of the Constitution was Westminster; but there were important variations drawn from other common law traditions, the Secretariat being specifically enjoined at the outset to produce working papers on the 'interesting features' of the American, the Irish and the Indian Constitutions.[12] Explicit references may be found in the Commission's *Minutes* to India in relation to the position of the President, the enforcement of Fundamental Rights and the role of the Attorney-General, to the U.S.A. concerning the separation of powers, and to Pakistan concerning the disqualification of the President. The Commissioners also ventured outside the common law tradition to Scandinavia for the Ombudsman and to the Fifth Republic in France in relation to the separation of powers and the Presidency, though such excursions were relatively less frequent.

The Commission's heritage comes out even more strikingly in the *Memorandum on the Proposals for a Constitution for Ghana* prepared at the conclusion of its hearings to give the Draft Constitution an intellectual backcloth. It begins with a quotation from Plato—'the punishment which the wise suffer who refuse to take part in government is to live under the government of worse men'. Appendix 2 to this chapter enumerates all the sources of the quotations with which the *Memorandum* is studded. Particularly conspicuous are the philosphers of western liberalism—J. S. Mill, Montesquieu and Locke; late 19th or early 20th century British constitutional historians—Lord Bryce, Erskine May, Morley, Bagehot and Dicey; and luminaries of the common law tradition on both sides of the Atlantic—Chief Justice Marshall and Blackstone. It is surprising that the Commissioners did not quote from Sarbah, Caseley Hayford, Danquah or the other leaders of the intelligentsia in the nationalist past (though one could well imagine these figures quoting from the same sources as the Commissioner, had they too been given the task of drawing up a Constitution). There are only two references to socialism in the entire document; and both are pejorative.[13]

If the British liberal tradition was the shared language of the Commissioners, discussion of the actual distribution of power under the
Constitution was overshadowed by fears of a revival of the immediate
past. One way of dealing with such fears was to exclude those who had
supported Nkrumah from politics. But should this exclusion form a part
of the constitutional document? And if so, should it be confined to those
against whom specific allegations of misconduct could be proved, or to
all who had supported the former regime? After some argument, it was
decided that a specific ban on the C.P.P. and its adherents in the
Constitution would not be appropriate. It should exclude from Parliament, and public office, only those found unfit to exercise power by
Commissions of Enquiry on specific allegations of misappropriation of
public funds and other misdemeanours.[14] It was argued that a blanket
exclusion would be unfair on those who had joined the C.P.P. but then
left the party, or who had co-operated under duress. Nobody's hands
were completely clean, and two members of the Commission, Bentum
and Braimah, had actually held office at the time of the coup. A total
ban would also have made the Constitution too political a document,
for:

> Open disqualification on the national scale might also presuppose that the
> country was not politically sure of itself. Moreover, there was the greatest
> need to avoid creating the impression that the new Constitution was being
> carved out for another political party.[15]

The matter was left, therefore, for the N.L.C. which was able to
legislate temporary exclusions by decree. As the *Minutes* put it:

> One of the advantages of promulgating the law on exclusions by decree
> would be to put any possible blame arising out of it squarely on the N.L.C.
> Members also shared the view that if the exclusion provisions were
> promulgated by decree of the N.L.C. the political excitement likely to arise
> over it would have died down before the enactment of the Constitution.
> Tactically, this will be an added advantage.[16]

The Secretariat was asked to prepare a draft Decree, including a
procedure whereby those disqualified might appeal for exemption; and
this, in essentials, was the Decree No. 223 enacted by the N.L.C. in
January 1968, of which a fuller account is given elsewhere.[17]

Another possibility—and one that was favoured by certain N.L.C.
members—was to dispense with party politics altogether. At one of its
earlier meetings the Commission debated the merits of an article by K.
B. Asante on 'A No Party State for Ghana' which had been published in
the journal *West Africa,* but it was found to be too radical. It was
argued that it would not only be unworkable to ban parties, but that it
would infringe the right to freedom of association which was to be
guaranteed in the Human Rights sections of the Constitution. Parties as

such were not undesirable, only party organisations like the C.P.P. under Nkrumah, which sought to arrogate all power unto themselves.

In the discussions which followed, the Commission settled for three broad strategies to prevent the recurrence of the past. The first one may describe as the 'Plato game', since it is called to mind by the quotation from Plato which heads the *Memorandum*. The sections of the Constitution which corresponded to this model were those establishing a division of powers within the executive, entrenching the independence of the President, the Council of State, the Electoral Commissioner, the Ombudsman and the Attorney General, and those securing the independence of the judiciary and making it the ultimate arbiter of all conflicts. A select number of wise men were to be guardians of the political order—statesmen 'above' partisan politics, protected by the Constitution, active in settling conflicts, and making sure that they did not harm the institutions set up by the Constitution.

The second might be called the 'John Stuart Mill' game—essentially one of parliamentary government with additional safeguards to make sure that the rules of the game were observed. The people were the ultimate check against arbitrary government; vigorous debate among their freely chosen representatives in parliament the best foundation for democracy. The Commissioners were less enthusiastic about this strategy than their nineteenth century liberal rhetoric would have led one to expect, for was it not by using so ruthlessly his parliamentary majority that Nkrumah had overridden all safeguards against arbitrary power? To be sure, the electoral process was to be heavily protected under the Constitution, but the Commissioners were also on record in their *Memorandum* as saying that parliamentary sovereignty was a 'superstition' to be 'exorcised'[18] by very real constraints on the law-making powers of parliament, as well as on the executive discretion of the government.

Thirdly, there was the strategy to which we may lend the name of Chief Justice Marshall, the 'government of laws not men'.[19] Arbitrary power was to be curbed by the law, by the ground-rules laid down by the Constitution itself. The comprehensive protection given to human rights, the extremely complex division of powers between the different branches of government, the cumbersome and difficult amendment procedure, and the central importance of the Supreme Court, all followed from this kind of thinking. There is a sense in which Chief Justice Marshall was logically prior to the other two games because it defined which of the two, whether Plato or John Stuart Mill, the government of the few or of the many, was to be played in any given situation. But in spite of the massive proliferation of articles, clauses and rules—of a constitutionalism that was at once the joy and the despair of the lawyers—the total situation was never defined satisfactorily.

It is the writer's belief that 'the Plato model' is the key tò some of the most distinctive features of the Constitution. The guardians of the political order were to be a small and select group. The two most powerful personages were to be the President and the Chief Justice. The former was to be considerably more than a formal Head of State. He had powers to delay legislation of which he did not approve and to refer legislation which he believed to be unconstitutional to the Supreme Court.[20] He was also given several, by themselves quite minor, powers which cumulatively bestowed on him considerably more initiative *vis à vis* the legislature and the government than a head of state under a Westminster form of parliamentary government usually has. Above all, he was to be the central figure in a unique separation of powers within the executive branch through

> the placing under the Umbrella of the President's office of certain institutions or agencies of the government which in our view need to be kept away from the Government so as to ensure that political considerations do not interfere in matters like appointments and the running generally of such institutions.[21]

By this means the Commissioners sought to guarantee the independence of a great battery of auxiliary guardians. On his own initiative, the President was to appoint about half the members of the Council of State[22] and (in consultation with this body) he appointed the Chief Justice, the Attorney General, the Public Services Commission, the Auditor General, the Audit Service Board, the Governor and the governing body of the Bank of Ghana, the Electoral Commission and the Ombudsman; he also had powers to determine the salaries and emoluments of members of certain of these institutions and to make subsidiary legislation regarding them.[23] These provisions clearly presupposed that it was possible to insulate the judicial process, the bureaucracy, the electoral process and to some extent even the economy from 'politics', and that the best way of achieving this end was to protect by means of the Constitution the independence of a small number of wise men.

Behind these proposals were interesting assumptions also about the control of conflict. When, for instance, some members of the Commission felt that the powers given to the President to delay legislation might lead him to clash with the Prime Minister and Cabinet, they were offered the reply, recorded in the *Minutes* as the opinion of the majority, that conflict:

> is inherent in the nature of democratic behaviour and can only be resolved whenever it arises by the *moral behaviour* (our italics) of those operating the Constitution, for which the Constitution cannot provide an answer.[24]

Such an assumption involved 'behind the scenes . . . counselling, warning, encouraging and arbitration which do so much to smooth the rough edges of political conflicts and encourage compromise and moderation'.[25] The institution on which the Constitution specifically relied was the Council of State, an 'august body' which brought together representatives of different centres of state power such as the President, Prime Minister, Speaker, Chief Justice, Attorney-General, the General Officer Commanding the Armed Forces and the leader of the Opposition, with other notables who were co-opted by the President.[26] It was assumed that informal consultations within the Council of State, and between the Council and the government, would make the formulation of more explicit rules unnecessary. The Commission argued, for example, that there was no need to check the Prime Minister's patronage by setting a limit to the number of Ministerial Secretaries

> because of the provisions elsewhere making it obligatory for the P.M. to consult the President before tendering his advice on public appointments. In the general view of the Committee this provision would serve as a check on the tendency to make appointments through political patronage.[27]

The Commissioners embodied their philosophy in clause (4) of Article 3 of their Draft Constitution, saying:

> (4) So far as possible Ghana shall be developed to be a society in which all conflicts, disputes, disagreements and grievances, in whatever form or from whatever source, shall be resolved and settled by discussion, negotiation, arbitration and judicial adjudication, and accordingly any enactment or contract or any form of political, economic or social relationship which expressly or by implication prescribes or encourages any other form of resolving or settling conflict, disputes, disagreements and grievances shall be unlawful void and of no effect.[28]

The provisions regarding the Chief Justice and the Supreme Court—perhaps even more than those dealing with the Presidency —were the touchstone of the Constitution, for:

> should a clash or confusion nevertheless occur, the Supreme Court is the only legal body to resolve the conflict by interpretation in such a way as to leave no confusion or conflict unresolved ... Any attempt by any office-holder, no matter how august his office may be, to put his notions of right or wrong, justice or injustice or his notion of the interest of the country above the Constitution interpreted by the Supreme Court is a reprehensible act worthy of the sternest reproach, if necessary, the severest punishment.[29]

Under Article 2 of the Constitution, any person alleging that legislation or an action of the executive was in contravention of the Constitution could bring an action in the Supreme Court for a declaration to that effect. Members of the judiciary could be dismissed only by an elaborate judicial procedure involving a tribunal of three of their peers; their salaries could not be varied to their disadvantage; and they were retired

on full salaries, in order to reduce the temptation to feather their retirement nests. The Chief Justice had very wide areas of paternal discretion
within the judicial domain, including the power to make binding
recommendations to the President for judicial appointments,[30] to em-
panel courts and the tribunals which investigated judicial misconduct,
and to settle the administrative arrangements of the judiciary.[31]

The whole edifice depended very much on a set of assumptions about
the character, behaviour and legitimacy of the holders of 'conflict-
regulating' positions in the Constitution. And a great many questions
were raised by them. Would the judiciary really be capable of objectivity
and, still more important, would there be the belief that it was free of
bias? Would the President be sufficiently respected by all sides in order
to be able to mediate between them or to guarantee the independence of
the institutions under his umbrella? Would the Electoral Commissioner
escape the charge of political bias in the conduct of the elections? These
were questions that were actually raised during the short period the
Constitution was in force. Yet it seems to have been the Commissioner's
assumptions that they would all be answered quite simply in the affir-
mative. It was epitomised in their discussion of the proposal that the
President be empowered to refer legislation to the Supreme Court for
determination as to its constitutionality before it passed into law. For
they were apparently persuaded by the Chairman's argument that

> it cannot be argued that the Supreme Court will be dragged into politics,
> because the lawyers on both sides will merely come to support one view or
> another in a general desire to assist the Supreme Court in coming to the cor-
> rect view.[32]

Conflict was seen as a groping after Platonic forms, the 'correct
view'—an assumption which was to be wholly out of line with what actually happened after the Constitution came into force.

A notable feature of certain of the institutions placed under the
President's protective umbrella—the Electoral Commissioner, the
Attorney-General, the Ombudsman and the Auditor-General—was
that their authority was largely personal. As will be seen, the Commission explicitly rejected proposals for a multi-member Electoral Commission and the argument that both the government and opposition parties should be given a say in the election of its members. The authority of
the President—in so far as it was exercised independently of the Prime
Minister—was also largely individual, since in most instances he was
able to act merely 'in consultation with' the Council of State rather than
being compelled to act on its advice. And we have already remarked on
the wide area in which the Chief Justice exercised his own discretion.

There was a presumption, too, as to the sterling qualities of the men
selected for these offices. It was regarded as unnecessary, for example,

that the President be required to declare any acquisition of property by him in addition to that admitted in the declaration of assets and liabilities on his assumption of office. For:

> the point was made in discussion ... that a reasonable minded President would always take the Cabinet into confidence when he acquired any additional property during his term of office. Members therefore agreed that there was no need for the Constitution to stipulate a declaration by the President of any subsequent acquisition of property by him.[33]

The guardians of the constitution were presumably expected to behave in a dignified and responsible manner because of their innate character rather than because the Constitution compelled them to do so, and it was for this reason no doubt that there were fewer ascriptive qualifications for office than one might have expected in so conservative a document. It was assumed that, in the new political order, the right people would rise as a matter of course to positions of power. There was, however, an age qualification for the Presidency, which was raised 'from 45 to 50 years to ensure that only seasoned, mature and elderly statesmen commanding an aura of respect would be appointed'.[34] In addition, the Ombudsman, the Chairman of the Audit Services Board, the Chairmen of Commissions of Enquiry and the Attorney-General—all had to be either Judges of the Superior Court of Judicature or persons qualified to be appointed as such, that is to say, lawyers of several years standing. And the Council of State included both a proportion of *ex-officio* members and a minimum number of Chiefs as well as members selected by the President in his discretion.

The Commissioners debated the respective merits of income, property or employment qualifications for Members of Parliament,[35] but rejected them, more because they seemed impractical than because they were undesirable. In the end, they agreed on not paying salaries to the M.P.s, endorsing John Stuart Mill's argument that, if paid,

> the business of a member would ... become an occupation in itself, carried on like other professions, with a view chiefly to its pecuniary returns, and under the demoralising influences of an occupation essentially precarious,

rather than those of the Leveller Cpt. Rainboro', also quoted in the Memorandum.[36] The archetypical M.P. was to be the independent professional, or entrepreneur; and he was not interdicted from making a livelihood out of government contracts.[37]

If authority—at least in those parts of the constitution that were meant to be 'above' politics—tended to be seen in personal terms, it was an entirely different kind of personal authority from that which prevailed under Nkrumah. At one of the first meetings, 'it was agreed that the President should be a father figure, who would represent the conscience of the nation'.[38] Authority, instead of being charismatic and capricious, was to be traditional, in the sense at least that it was not clearly differentiated from generally superior status. The relevant tradition, of course, was not so much that of the chieftaincies of the pre-colonial order, but that of the founding fathers of Ghanaian nationalism, of Mensah Sarbah, Aggrey, Casely Hayford and Danquah.

One may say that *all* Constitutions rely on tradition. All depend to some extent on personal authority, and all perforce assume the good faith of the men who hold political office since it is impossible to lay down rules for every situation. The argument, however, is that these assumptions were exercised by the Commissioners in a very selective manner. For good faith was not so freely presumed in other parts of the Constitution where (as we shall see) there was an unusual degree of emphasis on the government of laws not men, and on formal rules which lift little room for discretion—in marked contrast with the élitism of the sections of the draft constitution which set out the appointment and functions of the political guardians. The security bestowed on the Supreme Court, the Electoral Commissioner, the Ombudsman and like institutions, was very considerable: but constraints against *their* abuse of power were less in evidence. Who was to guard the guardians? Nor was the procedure for their selection immune from manipulation. Although it was intended that the President should not be chosen on a partisan basis, the procedures adopted did not make it likely that his election would be free of party politics.[39] And, once chosen, the president was, as we have seen, the key to several other nominations. Similarly the Chief Justice—whom the President appointed and who, as events under Dr. Busia's regime were to show, could by no means be *assumed* to be above the political struggle—held the key to the composition of the Judiciary.

Apart from the sheer length of the document and the elaborately spelt out division of powers, the 'Chief Justice Marshall' strategem of emphasising the government of laws, not men, was most in evidence in the very lengthy amendment procedure and the sections on Human Rights. The exact details of amendment are too complex to describe in detail. They laid down four categories of Articles in the Constitution: firstly those, such as the Articles making the Constitution itself supreme or forbidding the levying of taxes and the raising of armed forces without authority of Parliament, which could not be amended under any circumstances; a second category which could be amended in detail only to the extent that the changes did not derogate from the principles contained in the Constitution,[40] a third category which could only be changed after a delay of twelve months, a two thirds vote of the National Assembly, a dissolution and a two thirds vote of the new Assembly elected after the dissolution; and a fourth category of less vital provisions which could be altered by a simple two thirds vote of the

Assembly. Nothing illustrates the paradox of the whole constitution-making exercise so well as these cumbersome provisions. Since a government with a dominant control, such as the Progress Party secured after the 1969 election, could force through many of the changes it wanted. And no amendment procedure, however ironclad, was proof against a further coup.

At first glance, the most striking aspect also of the Human Rights provisions was their specificity, for 'the consensus of opinion reached was that where the fundamental freedoms are concerned certainty should not be sacrificed at the altar of brevity'.[41] Equally notable was the ease with which, in theory, they could be enforced. Under Article 2, any person could bring a constitutional case before the Supreme Court, even if he did not have a material interest in the ruling; and under Article 106 it was no longer necessary to obtain the Attorney-General's fiat (or consent) to bring civil proceedings against the government. But the edge to these provisions was blunted by the lengthy lists of exceptions.[42] To what purpose was freedom of movement and assembly protected if it could be infringed by actions that were 'reasonably required in the interests of defence, public safety, public order, public morality, public health or the running of essential services'? The effect of the provisions, therefore, would have depended almost entirely on what the judiciary made of them. It is arguable that rights would have been just as well protected had they been spelled out less exactly and had the Commission felt less need, as a consequence, to proliferate exceptions to them. The position was rendered still more ambiguous by Article 3 of the Constitution which was aimed at legislating against the recurrence of the past by declaring unlawful 'the existence, organisation, activity or propaganda by speech, writing or any other means, of any organisation which seeks to establish in Ghana a system opposed to democracy'. Had this not been altered by the Constituent Assembly, it might well have destroyed the effect of the clauses protecting freedom of association.

From the point of view of the ordinary citizen, the most promising innovation was probably the Ombudsman, with his wide-ranging powers to investigate the abuse of power by administrative agencies, developing a tradition of public enquiry into administrative action which the Expediting Committee had already begun under the N.L.C. The provisions for the Electoral Commissioner were also highly elaborate. The Commissioners were in no doubt that they wanted an end to rigged elections, and that they should make protection against political interference as explicit as possible. Not only was the Commissioner to have sole power to make the Rules governing the elections to the exclusion of Parliament; he was also to be appointed independently of the government and entrenched in the Constitution on the same terms as a

Justice of Appeal. The exact procedure to be used in voting was also entrenched (only to be cut out by the Constituent Assembly which found it
to be unduly cumbersome).

These two institutions were probably the Commission's most
positive contribution to the cause of parliamentary democracy in the
tradition of John Stuart Mill, the one in making the administration
responsive to citizen complaints—at least potentially,[43] the other in ensuring genuinely free votes in fair elections. Another innovation was the
writing into the Constitution of an officially recognised leader of the
opposition who was to be paid a salary and who was to be *ex-officio* a
member of the Council of State. Thus the Commission made explicit
what other constitutions usually leave implicit.

The Draft undoubtedly assumed a closely structured form of
democracy which was basically that of a parliamentary system on
British (plus some American) lines. Other forms were held to be
'charismatic' in the pejorative sense, since they verged on the irrational
and unpredictable. In deciding against the use of a referendum in the
amendment process, for example, it was argued that such a device
'would almost smack of a yearning for Athenian democracy, for the
basis of modern democracy is the principle that the people's elected
representatives can do their thinking for them'.[44] In addition, it was
argued that the power of the legislature had to be protected not only
from the people but from the political parties. The Commissioners set
out to find ways of reducing party control over members of parliament
in order to enable the latter to play a more positive and critical role.
Initially they decided that M.P.s should have the right to cast their votes
in secret and that the roll-call be abolished, only to change their minds
later[45] after Folson and Andoh had argued that this would reduce the
accountability of parliamentarians to the electorate. They also sought
ways of diluting the doctrine of collective cabinet responsibility so that
it would not:

> be possible for the P.M. to dominate his colleagues unduly in a manner which
> would only be reminiscent of the way the former Cabinet was so severely
> dominated by the ex-President.[46]

The appointment of each Minister had to be submitted to Parliament for
its approval; he was to be individually responsible to Parliament for the
policy of his Ministry as well as collectively in his capacity as a member
of the cabinet, and Parliament was specifically empowered to pass a
vote of no confidence 'in the Prime Minister or any other Minister'. But
the cabinet was also accorded protection from too close a control by the
Assembly, in that a mere defeat of the Government did not amount to a
vote of no-confidence compelling it to resign: a motion of no-confidence
could only be moved under stringent procedural restrictions and not
before the expiration of twenty-four months after the assumption of

office by the Prime Minister.[47] The intention—though seemingly at variance with the above provisions which were meant to limit the power of the prime minister—was to reduce the political nature of the executive. It was underlined by the fact that the Prime Minister was to be allowed to appoint up to eight Ministers from outside the Assembly. In theory at least, such a provision would have allowed him to appoint the entire Cabinet—except himself—from outside.[48] For it was argued that

> It is desirable to make use of the best available avenues for people who may not wish to submit themselves to the rough and tumble of party politics to serve in the Government. It is necessary to look beyond Parliament for the selection and appointment of a certain proportion of the executive because the success of democracy depends not only on the political process, but also on the efficiency of the government.[49]

This took the Commissioners all the way back to Plato. And it was a thoroughly managerial view of the constitution which could be expected to recommend itself in a period of military government. Nevertheless, the proposal was attacked by Miss Akua Asaabea Ayisi who argued in a memorandum that it was undemocratic, and 'harked back to a colonial period when the Governor-General was able to nominate *ex-officio* Ministers from outside the legislature',[50] a criticism renewed in the Constituent Assembly, which finally decided that all Ministers should be selected from Parliament.

In conclusion, we may repeat that the Constitution which emerged from the Commissioners' debates contained three different strategies for preventing the occurrence of the kind of politics which had occurred under Nkrumah. Firstly, an élitist strategy, that is to say, the insulation of parts of the Constitution from partisan politics and the creation of a category of guardians of the Constitutional order whose authority was to be personal and 'legitimised' in the tradition of the old intelligentsia. Secondly, a constitutionalist strategy—the erection of a wall of precisely-formulated prohibitions of a rational—legal kind, such as the constitutional division of powers, the amendment procedure, and the provisions on Human Rights. Thirdly, a democratic strategy, in the belief that a truly democratic order would prevent the excessive concentration of power in a single set of hands, although this was the strategy about which the Commissioners expressed most doubts.

At the root of the Constitution's incoherence was the fact that the rules of each game—the government of the few, of the law or of the many—differed from those of the others, and there were few criteria by which to make a satisfactory choice between them. In relation to the underlying models of the Constitution suggested earlier, we may perhaps conclude that the Chairman of the Commission, and those who supported him, were playing Plato most of the time, whereas the Secretariat of the Commission—being responsible for the complicated draftsmanship as well as the lengthy Human Rights provisions—were veritable Chief Justice Marshalls; and a minority of the members of the Commission, like Folson, espoused John Stuart Mill, though of course there was a good deal of shifting among them from one game to the other. The Constituent Assembly, as we shall see, shifted the whole document towards John Stuart Mill, although it did not take it the whole way. Still more did Dr. Busia and his cabinet insist that they had a mandate to play John Stuart Mill after the Progress Party won its sweeping victory in the 1969 election, with the result that they were very discomforted when the Judges of Appeal who sat as the Supreme Court in the Sallah case decided to play Chief Justice Marshall.[51] The Supreme Court was the institution in which the élitist and constitutionalist strategies converged, to set the limits within which democratic politics could operate. And it was both the strongest and weakest point in the Constitution. The Court was to enforce the ground rules of politics from above, but it was not very realistic to expect it to stay immune from the political pressures generated from below, given its strategic position in the hierarchy of political values. And when, after Busia's election victory, the courts and the legal profession came into conflict with the Government many people came to the conclusion that, whatever the Constitution might say, Ghana had already begun to revert once again to arbitrary rule. The Constitution which was hammered out of the Constitutional Commission Draft did not, therefore, match the Commissioners' own standards, that it should:

> have the advantage of being flexible whilst maintaining its defined limits. It should develop a capacity for coping with new and unsuspected problems without forcing its operators to resort too readily to formal amendment or to invite its violent overthrow.[52]

APPENDIX I

BACKGROUND OF MEMBERS OF CONSTITUTIONAL COMMISSION

Members

E. Akufo Addo (*Chairman*)

> Prominant in private legal practice in 1940s and 50s. Member of Coussey Committee, 1949. Founding member of U.G.C.C., 1947, of Ghana Congress Party, 1952. Secretary, Bar Association in late 1950s. Made Supreme Court Judge by Nkrumah 1962 and dismissed by him from Supreme Court in 1964. Member, Political Committee of N.L.C. 1966. Made Chief Justice by N.L.C., 1966. President of Ghana August 1970–72.

K. Adumua-Bossman, (died 1967 during hearings of Commission)

> Prominent in private legal practice in 1940s and 50s and secretary Bar Association for many years. Member of Coussey Committee 1949. Stood election against C.P.P. 1951 on National Democratic Party ticket. Later a Judge of Supreme Court and dismissed with Akufo Addo in 1964. Member of Political Committee of N.L.C. 1966–67.

Adam Amandi

> Teacher. Northern People's Party M.P. 1954–56. Joined United Party, detained 1960, released and left Ghana until coup. Ministerial secretary in P.P. government 1969–72.

A. S. Y. Andoh

> Former Secretary to Asanteman Council, Lecturer, Department of Extra-Mural Studies and Secretary, Institute of African Studies, University of Ghana. Organiser for National Liberation Movement against C.P.P. in Ashanti in 1950s. Became Registrar, University of Science and Technology, Kumasi, during membership of Commission. Secretary of Ashanti Youth Association, but resigned 1969 after vainly attempting to keep it independent of politics.

M. K. Apaloo

> Journalist. Became M.P. 1954 and 1956 on ticket of Anlo Youth Organisation, later joining G.C.P. and U.P. Accused before Granville Sharp Enquiry 1959 of collusion with Major Awhaitey in plot against Government. In Preventive Detention 1958–66. Political Committee of N.L.C. 1966–67 and National Advisory Committee 1967–68. Broke with Busia 1969, stood election on U.N.P. ticket and lost.

Miss Akua Asaabea Ayisi

> Early member of C.P.P., a 'Prison Graduate' in 1950. Disillusioned with C.P.P., went to Cambridge to read History, read for the Bar and returned to Ghana as a private legal practitioner 1963. National Advisory Committee of N.L.C. 1967–68. Independent candidate in 1969 elections and lost.

B. A. Bentum

> Trades Unionist with power base in Agricultural Workers' Union in Nkrumah period. General Secretary of Executive Board of T.U.C. until made Minister of Forestry by Nkrumah. Appointed General Secretary of T.U.C. by the N.L.C. after 1966 coup, a post later held (by election). Political Committee of N.L.C. 1966–67 and National Advisory Committee 1967–68.

J. A. Braimah

Northern Chief. Member of Coussey Committee 1949. Became extraordinary member of Legislative Council 1950, Elected to Assembly 1951, appointed by Nkrumah to Executive Council, resigning after confession to Korsah Commission that had accepted a bribe. Joined N.P.P. 1954, re-elected M.P. 1954, deputy-chairman U.P. 1957, but withdrew from active politics shortly thereafter. Later a C.P.P.-nominated M.P. in 1965 General Election. Political Committee of N.L.C. 1966–67. Northern Region Administrator in civilian government 1969–72.

D. J. Buahin

School teacher and timber merchant. Stood against C.P.P. in 1951 election. Member of Constituent Assembly 1968–69. Stood down in contest for Progress Party nomination in Sunyani in 1969 in favour of J. H. Mensah. Member of Council of State December, 1970–72.

Dr. E. V. C. de Graft-Johnson

Lawyer in private practice. Political Committee of N.L.C. 1966–67 and National Advisory Committee 1967–68. Member of Constituent Assembly 1968–69. Leader of A.P.R.P. in 1969 General Election, but failed to win a seat in Assembly.

Rev. Dr. F. K. Fiawoo (died 1970)

Teacher, school-proprietor and reverend Minister. Elected to Assembly 1951 and joined C.P.P. Became Deputy Speaker before leaving active politics.

B. D. G. Folson

Senior Lecturer in Political Science, University of Ghana. Political Committee of N.L.C. 1966–67. Chairman of Centre for Civic Education 1970–71. Associate Professor, University of Ghana 1971–72.

Abayifa Karbo

Upper Region Chief (Lawra-Na) and lawyer (his father had also been Lawra-Na and was a member of Coussey Committee). N.P.P. and U.P. M.P. 1954–64. Studied at Ghana School of Law and became lawyer 1965. Detained under Nkrumah. Political Committee of N.L.C. 1966–67. Member of Constituent Assembly 1968–69. Chairman of Public Services Commission.

Dr. Hilla Limann

A Northerner. Stood for election on N.P.P. ticket in 1956. Studied in France, later joined diplomatic service and still a serving diplomat.

Nene Azu Mate Kole

Paramount Chief of Manya Krobo. On Coussey Committee 1949. Political Committee of N.L.C. 1966–67 and National Advisory Committee 1967–68. Member and Deputy Speaker of Constituent Assembly 1968–69. Member of Council of State and member of Judicial Council 1969–72.

W. E. A. Ofori-Atta

Graduate teacher (economics) and lawyer. Son of Nana Ofori Atta 1 of Akim Abuakwa, nephew of J. B. Danquah, brother-in-law of Akufo-Addo. Founding member of U.G.C.C. and G.C.P. M.P. 1951–54. Deputy Opposition Leader and Chairman Public Accounts Committee. Lost seat in 1954 and went to U.K. to read law. Returned 1959 to private practice. Member of U.P. and detained twice 1963 and 1964. President of Bar Association 1966–67. Chairman Cocoa Marketing Board 1966–68. Political Committee of N.L.C. 1966–67. Member of Constituent Assembly 1968–69. Minister of Education 1969–71, External Affairs 1971–72.

Victor Owusu (resigned from Commission owing to pressure of work as Attorney-General, March 1969)

Lawyer in private practice 1962 onwards. Member of Central Committee of C.P.P., resigning 1955 to join N.L.M. and later the United Party. M.P. 1956–61. Accused of indirect involvement in plot against government before Granville Sharp Committee 1958. Detained 1961–62. Acting President Ghana Bar Association after J. B. Danquah's incarceration 1964. Made Attorney-General by N.L.C. October, 1966, remaining in the post until April 1969. Member of Constituent Assembly 1968–69. Minister for External Affairs 1969–71, Attorney-General 1971–72.

Saki Scheck

Lawyer. Early associate of Nkrumah in Committee on Youth Organisation; founding member of C.P.P.; 'prison graduate'. Resigned and joined Ghana Congress Party 1951. Went to U.K. to study law, returning 1959. Political Committee of N.L.C. 1966–67. Constituent Assembly 1968–69. Government Chief Whip 1969–72.

Secretariat

V. C. R. A. C. Crabbe

Lawyer in government legal service until appointment as Judge 1967. Legal draftsman and first Ghanaian Parliamentary Counsel. Seconded to East African Common Services Organisation as a legal adviser 1963, and while there helped draft Uganda Constitution. Returned to Ghana to work with Constitutional Commission 1966, being promoted Judge and made Special Commissioner 1967. Subsequently made Interim Electoral Commissioner and Special Parliamentary Draftsman to Constituent Assembly. Promoted to Supreme Court 1970, lost position when Court abolished 1972.

Kweku Baah

Lawyer. Studied at Ghana School of Law early 1960s. U.P. backroom boy. Went to U.S.A. and Canada for post-graduate work in law and international relations and organiser there for Dr. Busia. Became legal consultant I.C.F.T.U. Returned to become Joint Secretary Constitutional Commission 1966. Joint Clerk, Constituent Assembly 1968–69. Ministerial Secretary for Interior 1969–71 and Defence 1971–2.

E. K. Minta

Career civil servant.

APPENDIX II

SOURCES OF QUOTATIONS IN CONSTITUTIONAL COMMISSION'S MEMORANDUM

1. J. S. Mill—five times.
2. Lord Bryce—four times.
3. The Bible—three times:
    (i) Leviticus,
    (ii) Deuteronomy, and
    (iii) the Sixth Commandment.
4. Case of *Baffuor Osei Akoto and Others* v. *the Minister of the Interior and Another*
   æ. See below pp. 115–16.
5. Hobbes—twice.
6. Erskine May—twice.
7. Montesquieu—twice.
8. Lord Hewart (Chief Justice of England)—twice.
9. John Morley—twice.
10. *In Re Yusufu Interiba Aminu* (Ghanaian constitutional Case, 1967)—twice.
11. Chief Justice Marshall (the early 19th century American Chief Justice) in the case of *Marbury* v. *Madison*—twice.
12. Plato.
13. Sir Alladi Krishnaswani Ayyar (a Pakistani Judge).
14. Sir Sidney Phillipson (report on Regional Administration in Gold Coast).
15. Bishop Butler.
16. Cicero.
17. Lord Kilmuir (English Judge).
18. United Nations Universal Declaration of Human Rights.
19. Blackstone (the Commentaries).
20. Harold Laski.
21. The African Times, 1875.
22. King Tackie (19th century Fanti ruler).
23. Voltaire.
24. Rousseau.
25. American Declaration of Independence.
26. John Wilkes.
27. Edmund Burke.
28. John Locke.
29. Captain Rainboro (the Leveller).
30. Albert Johnson Machulloch (?).
31. *Report of the Constitutional Adviser Ghana, 1955* (Sir Frederick Bourne).
32. *Report of the Achimota Conference to consider the Report of the Constitutional Adviser, 1956.*
33. *Liversidge* v. *Anderson and Another, 1941* and *R. V. Home Secretary, ex Parte Budd, 1942* (British constitutional cases).
34. Judgement of Lord Camden in *Entick* v. *Carrington, 1765* (British Constitutional case).
35. dissenting judgement of Lord Denning in Conway v. Rimmer (British Constitutional case).

36. Magna Carta.
37. Act of Settlement.
38. Mme. Nicola Questiaux (member of French Council of State).
39. Mr. Kurt Holmgren (Justice of the Administrative Court, Sweden).
40. Dicey.
41. Leckey (the constitutional historian).
42. Wade and Phillips (British textbook on constitutional law).
43. Woodrow Wilson.
44. Bagehot.
45. Lord Samuel.
46. Lord Acton.
47. Sir William Harcourt (late 19th century British politician and authority on the constitution).
48. *Report to H. E. the Governor by the Committee on Constitutional Reform* (the Coussey Committee), 1949.

Notes

1. Changed in the final Constitution to 'Defence of the Constitution'.
2. See the debate in *Transition*, 1968 and 1970, between Yaw Twumasi and B. D. G. Folson.
3. See below pp. 115–16.
4. Messrs. Akufo-Addo, Adumua-Bossman, Apaloo, Bentum, Braimah, de Graft Johnson, Folson, Karbo, Mate Kole, Ofori-Atta and Scheck.
5. A decision less surprising than might seem at first when it is remembered that he had already been 'elevated' by Nkrumah from the post of General Secretary of the Executive Committee of the T.U.C. to that of Minister of Forestry; he was also close to Harlley and other members of the N.L.C. before they staged the coup.
6. Victor Owusu was a member of the Standing Committee until his resignation in March 1967.
7. *Memorandum on the Proposals for a Constitution of Ghana* (Accra: State Publishing Corporation, 1968), p. 16.
8. *Minutes of the Plenary Meetings* p. 85, minutes of meeting of 30 May 1966: 'the Chairman made a brief statement in which he outlined the nature and purpose of the work of the Standing Committee', which 'was not a Committee meant to take decisions for the Commission. It only served as a central body for exercising, in the first instance, all issues affecting the basic aspects of the Constitution, carefully sifting out various proposals, and submitting recommendations for discussion, acceptance or rejection by the Commission . . . any feeling that the Standing Committee was trying to impose its views on the Commission would therefore be unjustified . . . There was no valid case for asking the Commission to go back on decisions already taken on the nature of the executive and the Commission would not go back on such decisions.' As a result of this incident, however, it was decided that the Minutes of the Standing Committee would, for the first time, be circulated among the other members of the Commission.
9. One subject on which initiative was more widely entertained was that of Chieftancy and Local Government, which was consigned initially to a Sub-committee under Nene Azu Mate Kole, a Paramount Chief in his own right. The other members of the Committee were Andoh, Amandi, Buahin, Fiawoo, Limann, Miss Ayisi. Of these Andoh was the only member of the Standing Committee, as was Kweku Baah who acted as Secretary. Nevertheless the Committee was required in the first instance to report back to the Standing Committee rather than to the Plenary Commission.
10. *Minutes of the Plenary Meetings*, p. 174, meeting of 10 October 1967. The details of the military's constitutional position given here are the broad outlines of the provisions of the Draft Constitution, ch. 16. The Constitution itself, Ch. 15, differs only in detail from the Draft. Most of the changes that were made by the Constituent Assembly tended to increase Executive control over the Armed Forces, e.g. by doing away with the *ex officio* representation of members of the military in the Armed Forces Council and by providing that all members of the latter except the Chief of Defence Staff should be either members of the Cabinet (the Minister of Defence or Minister for Interior) or appointed by the President on the Prime Minister's advice.
11. *Ibid.*
12. *Minutes of the Standing Committee Meetings of the Constitutional Commission* (Accra: State Publishing Corporation, 1968) p. 2, minutes of the first meeting, 5 December 1966.
13. As in the discussion of protection from deprivation of property in the section of Fundamental Human Rights: 'it had been the practice under the guise of socialism

for the former Government of Ghana to arbitrarily deprive Ghanaians of their property' *Memorandum on the Proposals for a Constitution for Ghana*, p. 57.

14. Article 71(2)(b)(ii).
15. *Minutes of the Plenary Meetings*, p. 54, 31 March 1967.
16. *Minutes of Standing Committee*, p. 45, meeting of 3 April 1967.
17. p. 109 seq.
18. *Memorandum*, p. 18.
19. In the eyes of an American constitutional lawyer we might seem to be maligning Chief Justice Marshall who, in his own time and context, was an advocate of a flexible interpretation of the U.S. Constitution. We keep the name, however, as the Constitutional Commissioners use his celebrated judgement in *Marbury* v. *Madison* principally to justify their constitutionalism as the 'government of laws not men'.
20. Under Article 84 of the Draft, the President could withhold his assent to Bills unless passed by the National Assembly by a two-thirds majority of all its members or by a simple majority after six-months. The Constituent Assembly (see below) rendered this virtually a nullity by providing that the National Assembly could consider and repass legislation from which the President held assent by an ordinary majority without delay. It also did away completely with the President's power to refer legislation to the Supreme Court.
21. *Memorandum on the Proposals for a Constitution for Ghana*, p. 88.
22. The *ex-officio* members were the Prime Minister, the Speaker, the Leader of the Opposition, the Chief Justice, the Attorney-General and the General Officer Commanding Armed Forces. The three latter were excluded in the final Constitution, whereas the President of the House of Chiefs was added.
23. The Constituent Assembly deprived the President of the power to make subsidiary legislation on behalf of institutions under his 'umbrella'; removed the Attorney General from under that umbrella altogether; made the President act on the Prime Minister's advice in appointing the Governor and governing body of the Bank of Ghana, made him act on the advice of the Council of State in appointing the Electoral Commissioner rather than in consultation with it; and in sundry other ways reduced the protection he could provide. Nevertheless a substantial degree of pluralism in the sources of executive power remained a feature of the Constitution.
24. *Minutes of the Plenary Meetings*, p. 86, meeting of 30 May 1967.
25. *Memorandum*, p. 99.
26. Note that the Constituent Assembly altered the Composition of the Council of State; see p. 107.
27. *Minutes of Standing Committee*, p. 79, meeting of 30 May 1967.
28. This clause was, however, deleted from the Constitution by the Constituent Assembly.
29. *Memorandum*, p. 92.
30. The President was specifically enjoined by Draft Article 115 to accept the Chief Justice's recommendations. The Chief Justice himself had to consult the Judicial Council, though he was not (until this section was altered by the Constituent Assembly) obliged to accept the Council's advice.
31. A large part of this discretion, however, was removed by the Constituent Assembly in favour of the more collegial but still independent Judicial Council. See the discussion below, ch. iv.
32. *Minutes of Plenary Meetings*, p. 92, 2 June 1967.
33. *Minutes of the Standing Committee*, pp. 58–59, meeting of 10 May 1967.
34. *Minutes of Plenary Meetings*, p. 196 meeting of 12 December 1967. The limit was reduced again by the Constituent Assembly to 40.
35. *Minutes of the Plenary Meeting*, pp. 59, 62, and 114.
36. *Memorandum*, pp. 117–18.

37. See *Minutes of Plenary Meetings*, p. 115, meeting of 27 June 1967: 'Members of Parliament should not be barred completely from undertaking Government contracts, provided the necessary checks against fraudulent practices ... can be devised, the point being that in a developing country such as Ghana where the majority of contracts obtain in the public sector ... it would be unfair to debar Members of Parliament from tendering ... A Member ... who acquires an interest in a Government contract should however be made to disclose it.'

38. *Minutes of Plenary Meetings*, p. 14, meeting of 6 January 1967.

39. The Commissioners argued: 'to give the power to elect him to the National Assembly will give the impression that the President is dependent on the National Assembly. There is also the danger of the President becoming a purely partisan choice. We think this would be highly undesirable' *Memorandum*, p. 94. The election of the President was by secret ballot without debate in an Electoral College which included members of the Assembly, Chiefs and representatives of District Councils, the former, however, being in a clear numerical majority over the two latter categories.

40. These had to be passed by two-thirds votes of the National Assembly, separated by six months, be sent to the Supreme Court for a determination whether the changes did not detract from the principles of the Constitution and then be repassed by another two thirds vote of the Assembly. The Constituent Assembly deleted the reference to the Supreme Court, arguing that the Court would still be able to strike such an amendment down if referred to it after it had passed.

41. *Minutes of the Standing Committee*, p. 13, 11 January 1967.

42. See *Minutes of the Plenary Meetings*, p. 31, meeting of 17 February 1967 which record a disagreement whether the words 'public interest' should be retained as a qualification to the rights provisions: 'it was argued, on the one hand, that the provision could be used by an unscrupulous Government in suppressing the people on the pretext that the public interest demanded it, and on the other, that it was an indispensable prerequisite of executive power to be used in good faith when the interest of the state so required'. The latter view won the day.

43. Potentially, because Dr. Busia's government was very tardy in drafting the required legislation for the establishment of the Ombudsman's office, and the President had no appointed the first holder of this position before the regime was overthrown.

44. *Minutes of Plenary Sessions*, p. 185, meeting of 14 November, 1967.

45. Except as regards constitutional bills, voting on which remained secret.

46. *Minutes of the Standing Committee*, p. 75, 29 May 1967.

47. Article 66 clause (5) of Draft, which was deleted by the Constituent Assembly.

48. According to Article 61(1) and (2) of the Draft, the cabinet was the Prime Minister and not less than eight or more than seventeen other Ministers of State; the P.M. could appoint not more than eight Minister of State from outside the Assembly, so that if he was willing to have a Cabinet of only eight members, all could be appointed from outside Parliament.

49. *Minutes of Plenary Meetings*, pp. 102–103, meeting of 13 June 1967.

50. *Minutes of Plenary Meetings*, pp. 105–106, 16 June 1967.

51. In the Sallah case, the government's right, under Section 9 of the first Schedule of the Transitional Provisions of the Constitution, to terminate the employment of public servants appointed prior to the N.L.C.'s assumption of power, was challenged in the Courts. Not only did the Supreme Court refuse to uphold a preliminary objection by the Attorney-General as to the composition of the judicial panel hearing the case, but it ruled against the government on the substantive case, precipitating a series of bitter public statements about the judiciary by Dr. Busia and other members of the government. See D. Austin, 'Progress in Ghana', *International Journal*, Vol XXV 1970.

52. *Memorandum*, p. 18.

CHAPTER 4

THE CONSTITUENT ASSEMBLY—A SOCIAL AND POLITICAL PORTRAIT

Robin Luckham and *Stephen Nkrumah*

The Constituent Assembly was formally inaugurated by Lt. General Ankrah on 6 January 1969 at Parliament House. The N.L.C. had originally intended to follow the Constitutional Commission's advice that the Constituent Assembly be chosen at a general election on a non-party basis:

> the result of the Constituent Assembly elections . . . would indicate where the wind was blowing and whether the objectives of the Coup had been achieved. Moreover, a Constituent Assembly nominated by the N.L.C., or appointed by indirect elections or though the collegiate system, would not be acceptable to a large body of opinion in the country.[1]

In the event, the N.L.C. decided against a directly elected body. The ostensible reason was that the initial response of the public to the registration of electors had been poor, and that the return to civilian rule would be unduly delayed by the holding of two elections, one for the Constituent Assembly and the other for the new civilian parliament. A more plausible explanation was that the N.L.C. was still not sure of itself.[2] The politicians were beginning to use the prospect of elections as an argument for lifting the ban on party politics, but far from welcoming the fact that an election would enable them to see where the winds were blowing, the N.L.C. was apprehensive that, if it did not exercise greater control over the process, the wind might blow in the wrong direction. Moreover, if politicians were allowed to contest a public election—even if prevented from forming parties—they might challenge the military regime, including its right to preside over the return to civilian rule. These apprehensions also help to explain why the N.L.C. never gave a clear reply to repeated enquiries by the Constituent Assembly as to whether it was to be allowed to enact or promulgate the Constitution; the Council preferred to hold the issue open as a bargaining point until the very last days of the Assembly in August 1969.

In order to establish the Assembly, the N.L.C. decided to proceed by way of indirect election from statutory bodies and voluntary associations, adding a small number of members directly nominated by itself. The procedure left much less to chance than a direct election would have done, and reflected a tendency among its military and police leaders to see society in corporate terms. The total membership of the Assembly was 150. Among them were forty-nine chosen by electoral colleges made up of the local councils within the administrative districts of each region, and six by city and municipal management committees in Accra, Kumasi, Sekondi-Takoradi, Cape Coast, Koforidua and Tamale. The electorates were hardly representative. They were made up of local notables appointed to the councils after the coup, the councils varying in size from sixty-eight members in Winneba to eight in Accra which elected the Chairman of its Management Committee, R. E. Bannerman, unopposed.[3] Nor was it very difficult to forecast the outcome of many of these limited contests—as in Wenchi between Dr. Busia and Bediako Poku (a former C.P.P. Ambassador), although the expected did not always happen: the veteran opposition leaders, Kow Richardson and W.E.A. Ofori-Atta, lost in Winneba and Asamankese, the former to a newcomer, Haruna Esseku, the latter to the 'local son', A. A. Aboagye de Costa.[4] With very few exceptions, however, the electoral colleges chose local 'men of prominence'—K. A. Busia, B. K. Adama, R. R. Amponsah, S. G. Antor, O. Y. Asamoah, Abayifa Karbo, Imoru Salifu—whose local standing as educated men was reinforced by their professional qualifications or by a record of opposition to the former regime.

The eighteen representatives of farmers and market women were selected in each of the nine regions by 'electorates' varying in size from six to fifty-six persons, who in turn had been chosen by electoral colleges throughout the Region. They, too, turned to local men and women of prominence. The farmers of the Eastern Region selected Kankam Buadu, the Managing Director of the State Cocoa Marketing Board; those of Ashanti chose B. D. Addai, a timber merchant, and another prominent member of the former opposition; those of Greater Accra turned to Alex Hutton-Mills, a businessman and scion of one of Accra's old élite families. The farmers of the Central and Western Region, and the market women of the Central Region, Brong/Ahafo and Ashanti all chose lawyers, including Mrs. Bertha Amonoo-Neizer, representing the Ashanti market women.

The traditional order was also represented, the Chiefs sending nine representatives to the Assembly, one selected by each regional House of Chiefs. Some were extremely articulate and well educated spokesmen for the chiefly estate—like Nene Azu Mate Kole, the Deputy Speaker and former member of the Constitutional Commission, Nana Agyeman Badu II Dormaahene, Nana Obiri Yeboah II (Isaac Amissah-Aidoo) a lawyer who was to become Deputy Speaker of the National Assembly, and the Adansihehe Nana Kwaantwi Barima II. In addition, fifty-five members were elected by 'recognised institutions and organisations'. They included professional bodies like the Ghana Bar

Association, the Ghana Registered Midwives and the Ghana National Association of Teachers; economic groups like the Greater Accra Cooperative Fishing Union, the Ghana National Building Contractors Association, the Ghana Manufacturers Association and the Trades Union Congress; voluntary associations, like the Women's Society for Public Affairs, the Ex-Servicemen, and the Ghana National Youth Council; religious organisations like the Christian Council of Ghana; and such statutory bodies as the Universities and the Judiciary. The remaining fourteen members were nominated by the N.L.C., although it is not clear what special interests its nominees were expected to promote. They included R. S. Blay, a retired judge and founding member of the U.G.C.C. in 1947, who was elected Speaker of the Assembly; Richard Quarshie, former Resident Director of a mining company (Consolidated African Selection Trust) and Commissioner for Trade and Industries under the N.L.C.; Victor Owusu, the Attorney-General; and four men who had been unsuccessful in other contests, W. E. A. Ofori-Atta, a lawyer and opposition politician, G. K. Agama an economist teaching at the University of Ghana, who was later to become leader of the opposition under the civilian regime, James Mercer, a Sekondi Barrister, and J. G. Amanoo—a lawyer and editor of the *Ghanaian Times* and a former C.P.P. Ambassador—who had failed to get the nomination of the Ghana Journalists' Association.

A distinguishing feature of the Assembly was the 'élitist background' of the majority of its members. The commoners or 'verandah boys' of the formative years of the C.P.P. were conspicuously absent. There was a discernable difference in the social composition of the Constituent Assembly from that of the Constitutional Commission, but it was mainly one of generation and position within the élite. For alongside the old intelligentsia and politicians of the former opposition, there were now numerous younger men with no political past, 'new men' from the professions, the civil service, the universities and business—E. H. Boohene, R. E. Bannerman, B. J. da Rocha, J. A. Kufuor, T. D. Brodie-Mends, Jones Ofori-Atta, Richard Quarshie, P. A. Adjetey, Issifu Ali, G. K. Agama, and S. A. Okudzeto, some of whom (e.g. Boohene, Bannerman, Kufuor, Quarshie, Issifu Ali) had already been given important posts in the N.L.C. administration. Both the Assembly and the Commission were thus recruited from the upper strata of Ghanaian society. And it was in this sense that both differed from the legislature under Nkrumah, as can be seen clearly in the Appendix to this chapter. The large number of M.P.s in the Nkrumah Parliament, who by 1966 could only be classified as 'politicians', or as functionaries of the party and its wings, is indicative of the vast political patronage network under the C.P.P. which absorbed many who would formerly have been classified as clerks, schoolteachers, traders and workers as well as the proverbial 'verandah boys'. Exact comparison is difficult. Nevertheless, it is possible to contrast the relatively small number of 'professionals' in the 1965 Parliament with comparable groups of the Constituent Assembly and the 1969 Parliament.

Occupation	1969 Constituent Assembly	1969 Progress Parliament	1965 C.P.P. Parliament
Lawyers	36*	33	10
Doctors	8	3	0
University Teachers	11	9	3
Other professions	14	10	8

* including three judges.

Of these occupational groups, the lawyers were not only the largest, but had an influence over the proceedings which was quite out of proportion to their numerical representation. To begin with, they did most of the talking. Of the twenty-five most loquacious members, ten were lawyers. Peter Ala Adjetey the Accra barrister who was to become Secretary of the Bar Association in 1969–71, was particularly articulate, taking up approximately eight and a half of the ninety eight days the Assembly sat; Joe Appiah, the Kumasi barrister and President of the Bar Association from 1967 onwards, came second. No less than 47 per cent of the Assembly's entire debating time was taken up by lawyers' arguments and perorations.

Lawyers were often their own—and the Constitution's—severest critics, and Peter Adjetey was on record as saying the 'the Constitution was too complex to be readily understood by a layman and that it should not be comprehensible to lawyers only'.[5] Nevertheless, they were sometimes strongly resented. After criticising the entrenchment of the provisions relating to the Judiciary, in which he spoke of the 'whims and caprices' of Judges (for which he was challenged by Mr. Justice Azu Crabbe 'on a point of order') Kwesi Lamptey exclaimed: 'It seems to me —some people do not like us to talk about Judges—that this Constitution is a Constitution by Lawyers for Judges'.

Similarly, Nene Azu Mate Kole defended Article 2 of the constitution against a lawyer's suggestion that constitutional issues, like any other cases, should be heard in the first instance by the High Court rather than going straight to the Supreme Court.

Mr. Chairman, I was a little astonished that any member should have anything to say against Chapter One of the Constitution. I think those persons who raised objections against Clause 2 should have realised that the Supreme Court in the context of the Constitution, was set up as a Court to interpret the Constitution—(Some Members: no, no) Members can say 'no', but that is the purpose—interpretation of the Constitution should not lend itself to the opinion of many; it should only be decided by one constituted body . . . Therefore if there are any lawyers who want to earn legal fees, will—(Uproar)

Mr. Joe Appiah (Bar Association): Mr. Speaker, on a point of order, I am very sorry, Sir, that this statement should come from the Deputy Speaker. If I may say so in all humility, it is a sad reflection on the legal practitioners of this country.

Nene Azu Mate Kole: I should like to withdraw without reservation.

Mr. Joe Appiah: Thank you very much.[6]

Loquaciousness, to be sure, is not the same as influence, and many words were spilt on contentious issues, like Article 71(2)(b)(ii), to little effect. That particular article was a good example of an issue on which the lawyers, like good advocates everywhere, were among the foremost protagonists on *both* sides—Joe Appiah, T. D. Brodie-Mends, W. E. A. Ofori-Atta (and his brother, the economist, Jones Ofori-Atta) tried to secure the disqualification from public office of persons against whom commissions of enquiry had made adverse findings: S. A. Okudzeto, P. A. Adjetey, O. Y. Asamoah, R. E. Bannerman attempted to reduce its scope or do away with it altogether. Mr. Justice S. Azu Crabbe, Victor Owusu and James Mercer tried to steer a middle course by insisting that there should be a right of appeal from commissions of enquiry. In the end, the result was probably not very different from what it would have been had none of them spoken at such length.

When, however, the majority of the members of the legal profession believed they had interests in common, they could not be restrained. And such interests did emerge in the constitutional debate. For, during the N.L.C. period of rule, lawyers had been undergoing an important crisis. Under Nkrumah they had been cowed: special courts had been created, judges had been dismissed, and leaders of the Bar like J. B. Danquah imprisoned; the Bar Association atrophied and ceased to meet in order to ensure that it was not 'packed' by the Nkrumah-ist lawyers. At the same time there had been a rapid increase in the number of lawyers in practice, particularly after the University of Ghana began to produce its own graduates in law, the effect of which had been not only to weaken the hitherto strong sense of community at the Bar but to lead to a serious increase in professional misconduct. When Akufo-Addo was appinted Chief Justice by the N.L.C. late in 1966, he had set about such problems by developing more regular means of communication with the Bar and by proposing to give the judiciary and the gover-

ning body of the profession—the General Legal Council—greater disciplinary powers. Meanwhile the Bar Association revived under the
vigorous Presidency of Joe Appiah and it insisted that its conduct
should be regulated by the profession itself rather than by authority.
The specific issue over which conflict came out into the open was a cir-
cular issued by the Chief Justice in the name of the General Legal Council instructing Judges to deny audience in the courts to lawyers who did
not hold a current solicitor's licence, which could only be obtained if
they had paid their taxes. Three leading members of the Bar, acting on
behalf of the Bar Association, actually obtained a High Court injunction against the Chief Justice.[7]

Conflict between the Bar and the Chief Justice had a profound influence on the Assembly's debates, because Akufo-Addo was closely
identified in many people's minds with the Draft produced by the
Constitutional Commission of which he had been Chairman. And this
was so despite the Socratic ignorance professed in one of the early
debates by Mr. Joe Appiah in the following exchange:

> Mr. Justice C. A. Owusu (Oda Administrative District). . . . Now the
> Judiciary. I shall suggest for the serious consideration of Members that they
> should not allow the conflict between the Ghana Bar Association and the
> present Chief Justice to bias their minds against the noble work of the
> Constitutional Commission.
> Mr. Joe Appiah: On a point of order, Mr. Speaker . . . I do not think that so
> far anybody who has spoken has said that there is any conflict between the
> Bar Association of Ghana and the Chief Justice . . . Nor indeed can it be
> said that any member of the Bar Association has instructed anybody to say
> that. We can speak for ourselves and if it is necessary to avoid conflicts
> between the Bar and the Chief Justice we shall do so openly and fearlessly.
> Until then, I would, Mr. Speaker, strongly suggest that this digression be
> withdrawn.[8]

There were, as we shall see, six subjects in respect of which the
Assembly introduced really substantial changes in the Draft: the
Chapter on the Judiciary; the provision for Presidential recognition of
professional bodies under the new Article 51; the powers of the
President; the emasculation of Article 3 'Defence of Democracy'; the
restoration of the doctrine of collective cabinet responsibility; and the
provisions on Chieftaincy and Local Government. The changes in the
first two directly reflected both the conflict between the Bar and Bench,
and the Bar Association's efforts to increase its own powers. Article 51
was a good rallying point around which the lawyers struck up alliances
with members of other professions—the doctors, pharmacists, surveyors, accountants and engineers—who were equally anxious to improve their professional recognition, autonomy and status. The discussion of the Presidency was also indirectly affected by the conflict since

the office was cast in the same Platonic-guardian mould as the position of Chief Justice.

In spite of the omnipresence of the lawyers, procedure was one of the Assembly's weakest points. (This was certainly one of the reasons why it did not introduce a larger number of changes in the Draft proposals.) The N.L.C. Decree under which the Assembly was established had provided that its procedure be governed by the standing Orders in force in Nkrumah's first National Assembly after independence in 1957, together with such modifications as the N.L.C. might approve. In practice, it meant the use of British parliamentary procedure in the time-honoured tradition. At the beginning of its proceedings the Assembly elected a Speaker, R. S. Blay, and a deputy, Nene Azu Mate Kole. It also appointed parliamentary-type committees—including a Privileges Committee; later in the proceedings it found it necessary to establish a Drafting Committee to give attention to the problems of putting a constitutional document together in manageable shape. The various stages in the debates were also more or less equivalent to the First, Second, Consideration Committee and Third Reading stages of parliamentary procedure in handling public bills. Observers were quick to note that Westminster was not perhaps lost to Africa after all;[9] and if only for this reason alone, experienced politicians like Joe Appiah and William Ofori Atta were very much at home. Some members, however, had their misgivings. B. J. da Rocha for instance:

> I will turn now to Standing Order No. 101 which states: 101(1). In cases of doubt these Orders should be interpreted in the light of the relevant practice of the Commons House of Parliament of Great Britain and Northern Ireland (laughter) Why? Why?
> Mr. Speaker: Are you asking me a question?
> Mr. da Rocha: It is a rhetorical question. I think it is time for these anachronisms of a colonial era to be done away with.[10]

Yet all did not go smoothly. The original intention had been that the Assembly should end its deliberations within three to four months, but it was still holding emergency sittings in its eighth month, meeting for the last time on 22 August, a week before the general election. It had been hoped that the debates would be over, or almost over by the time the prohibition of politics was lifted, but the ban was lifted on 1 May and thenceforth leading members of the Assembly tended to be absent, nursing their parties or constituencies; political alignments hardened, enthusiasm flagged, and it became increasingly difficult to obtain a quorum. Throughout the debates there was a good deal of bickering over points of detail, and the Speaker did not have a good grasp of procedure. Some of the amendments which found their way into the Constitution were extremely ambiguous,[11] often as a consequence of several amendments being put forward in a heated and confused debate. This happened despite the fact that Members sometimes drew attention to the ambiguities, as in the final debates on the sections of the Transitional Provisions under which 568 public servants were later to be dismissed by the Progress Government early in 1970.[12] Some important amendments disappeared altogether in the quagmire of procedure, never again to see the light of day. Such was the fate, as we shall see later, of the proposals put forward at consideration stage, to cut down the number of qualifications with which the Human Rights provisions are hedged, and of Mrs. Susana de Graft Johnson's motion that a statement of Directive Principles be included at the beginning of the constitution. If, therefore, the Assembly did not change the Constitutional Commission's Draft radically, the explanation was as much the inertia of a large and unwieldy assemblage as it was that most of its members had political assumptions in common with the Commissioners. And this was despite the fact that the lawyers had more than their share of the membership of the six committees which steered the Assembly through its deliberations, filling 19 out of 43 committee positions, taking the Chair in all six Standing Committees and being much in evidence in the key Business, Standing Orders, and Drafting Committees. In addition, when the House resolved itself into Select Committees for consideration of individual sections of the Draft, three of the five Chairmen were lawyers. And members of the legal profession were very much more active in committee than the laymen. Lawyers were responsible, for example, for no less than 92 out of a total 105 amendments moved in the Select Committee on the Judiciary, even though there were only nine of them among the Committee's twenty-eight members.

A further reason for the Assembly's incoherence was the absence of organised party politics, including party discipline and the whole paraphanalia of whips and caucuses, not only to ensure majorities as and when required, but to reduce the possibility of measures being diverted or delayed by procedural manoeuvres. True, political alignments were beginning to form from the Assembly's early sessions, well before the lifting of the official ban on party politics. Dr. Busia instituted weekly meetings at his house around a core of his close associates at which the proceedings of the Assembly was discussed, and within a short time he could probably have commanded a majority on most issues. He was Chairman of one of the Select Committees; he was also a member of the Business Committee, and two of the other four members, Kwesi Lamptey and B. K. Adama, were in his close circle. Yet there were remarkably few issues on which he tried to use his concealed majority. He himself kept studiously clear of controversial issues like Article 71(2)(b)(ii), the position of the Chief Justice or the voting age. Indeed, almost the only issue when he brought out his support in full force, was in the vote on the establishment of a Presidential Commission under the Transitional Provisions at the very end of the Assembly's debates. He was harbouring his resources for other battles, gathering together the threads of political support in the struggle for political power which he was to win at the August 1969 elections. He spoke relatively infrequently compared with some other members, and when the ban on politics was lifted he was very rarely to be seen in the Assembly at all, giving a watching brief to lieutenants like Kwesi Lamptey, W. E. A. Ofori-Atta or–in the later stages–Victor Owusu.

Busia could afford not to show his hand since the basic structure of the Constitution was one which he approved, and such amendments as he desired could for the most part be expected to emerge from the debates without any need for his intervention. In his contribution to the initial debate on the Principles of the Constitution in February 1969 he went on record as saying that, although he thought an independent judiciary was necessary,

> we see, for example, that this idea of sovereignty of the law in practical terms tends to mean the ultimate power tends to be wielded by judges, and the view we have expressed about this is that we do not want judges to wield ultimate power because they are not sensitively and directly responsible to the people. The people cannot remove them as they can those who are elected.[13]

Similarly, said Busia, the Presidency could be a means of providing a check on the executive, but such checks ought not to prevail 'to the extent at present provided in the Constitution'.[14] He argued, in particular, that the Prime Minister should have an unencumbered right to choose his own colleagues, and that he should also select the Attorney-General who would thus be a political rather than a constitutional (or presidential) appointment as provided in the Draft.[15]

In terms of the intellectual games or models of the Constitution put forward in the preceding Chapter, Dr. Busia was 'playing John Stuart Mill' rather than Chief Justice Marshall or Plato—naturally enough, since he was the most likely successor to executive power. And he found ready support from the majority of the other members of the Assembly, who also saw themselves as future M.P.s, and for whom such arguments were already part of the politics-of-going-back-into-politics.

As has been pointed out, the N.L.C. had tried to take steps (including the continued ban on parties until May 1969) to ensure that the Assembly would not be influenced directly by politics. But such precautions did not exclude from the Assembly men who intended to contest for political office, except those banned under the Disqualification Decrees. Several of the members of the Assembly had been active opponents of the C.P.P., and of these some, including Joe Appiah,

William Ofori-Atta, R. R. Amponsah, Victor Owusu, and S. G. Antor, had been detained for political reasons. There was also a scattering of former C.P.P. members—for example J. G. Amamoo—who had been accepted by the new order following their renunciation of their past, though there were none of the major figures of the former regime. To most of the former politicians, as to some of the newcomers like T. D. Brodie-Mends, H. Esseku, G. K. Agama, O. Y. Asamoah or C. O. Nyanor, membership of the Constituent Assembly was part of the journey back to politics or into politics for the first time: 54 of the Assembly members stood at the general election in August 1969, of whom 36 were elected; 36 stood for Dr. Busia's Progress Party; 18 stood for other parties or as independents.[16]

Nevertheless, there was surprisingly little division on party lines even after the lifting of the ban on 1 May 1969. The politics-of-going-back-into-politics cut across future party alignments. G. K. Agama, S. A. Okudzeto and O. Y. Asamoah of the NAL-to-be were in complete agreement with Dr. Busia and his lieutenants on the desirability of giving more emphasis in the Constitution to parliamentary government and cabinet responsibility. These men were initially aligned (as were others among the young politicians and intellectuals like Jones Ofori-Atta or J. G. Amamoo, who later joined the Progress Party) with the 'Third Force', (the radical ginger-group which formed around Dr. Bilson, but which failed to materialise as a political party when the ban on politics was lifted). This group was responsible for some of the more scathing attacks on the Draft in the early debates, usually in favour of a much more thoroughgoing return to parliamentary and popular sovereignty than Busia had cautiously advocated.

Party politics in the usual sense had hardly any influence on the debates except in the closing stages. The turning point came with the debate on Article 71(2)(b)(ii) which it was believed would exclude Gbedemah from office in the 1969 election. Yet although Gbedemah's own supporters were to vote solidly against the clause, the members of other parties were by no means united on the issue. The U.N.P. was split, Joe Appiah being one of the main advocates of disqualification and Peter Adjetey one of its main opponents. Although many Progress members, particularly Jones Ofori-Atta, W. E. A. Ofori-Atta, Kwesi Lamptey and R. R. Amponsah, were fervent supporters of disqualification, Busia kept away from the debates, either because of a lingering doubt as to the political wisdom of excluding his main adversary, or because he did not wish openly to appear to be doing so. Victor Owusu, as we shall see, actively argued against disqualification, though he did not vote in the final divisions on the subject. The Constituent Assembly, in sum, was never a political body in the conventional sense, and therein lay both its strength and its weaknesses.

We now turn to the debates. For the first few days, members of the Assembly concerned themselves with their own powers—what would happen to the Constitution as approved by them? The N.L.C. had merely authorised them to consider the Draft and to return it to the Council, without giving them full powers to enact and promulgate, and the uncertainty expressed by the Assembly was over what would happen to the document once it was in the hands of the Military Government. The suggestion that the N.L.C. be relied on to promulgate the consitution was resented; Kwesi Lamptey declaring that 'the N.L.C. has no right to give a constitution to this country'.[17] Here was an indication at least that, although the Assembly was a creation of the N.L.C., its members were unwilling to be dictated to by the military. The fact that they were elected, albeit indirectly, encouraged the feeling that they were at least more representative than the N.L.C., and that they should not play a role subordinate to that of the army and police. At first it was resolved to ask the N.L.C. to empower the Assembly to enact the Constitution, then that the N.L.C. should be allowed to promulgate the constitution by signifying the date on which it was to come into effect after enactment by the Assembly. In the event, the N.L.C. did not decide on who was to enact and promulgate the Constitution until the dying days of the Assembly.[18] But having made its claim public, the Assembly began to consider the Constitutional Commission's proposals.

There was a general acceptance of their provenance, despite the note of dissent voiced by Agboloh, representing the Association of Junior Civil Servants (which was soon to be suspended by the N.L.C. for threatening to strike in support of wage claims):

> The Constitutional proposals now before us seemed only to have been designed to guarantee firmly the social economic and financial position of certain declared privileged persons in our society. I disagree with certain persons who claimed to be convinced that the text before us represent the true aspirations and wishes of the people of this country.[19]

Other members were selective in their criticism, although there was a wide measure of agreement that the Akufo-Addo Commission had been influenced unduly by the past.[20] It was also feared that the Constitution might become unworkable among the several centres of power envisaged, and that a constitution of 172 detailed Articles might be 'so unwieldy that the average person in the country is not going to understand it'.[21]

Specifically, opposition was expressed to the Prime Minister's having to share executive responsibility with the President, to the ubiquitous role of the Chief Justice in the proposed Constitution, and to turning the Attorney-General (as one member put it) into a constitutional 'astronaut',[22] independent of the government of which he was the chief legal adviser. It was also felt that the judiciary's powers exceeded its proper limits and, in particular, that it should not be able to strike down legislation before it is passed. Arguing as a lawyer and not as a chief, Nana Obiri Yeboah II said that it was enough that the Attorney-General's power to give or withhold assent to actions against the government had been abolished—it ought to be accepted that, when judgement is given against the government in favour of a citizen, 'the government of the day will have the decency to satisfy that judgement'.[23] Some members also complained that the Constitution would prevent the government from managing the economy effectively. The economist and future Leader of the Opposition, G. K. Agama, found much support for the argument that the government's control over the economy should be increased by transferring the power of appointment of the Governor and Members of the Bank of Ghana from the President to the Prime Minister. Obed Asamoah, on the other hand, elicited much less enthusiasm for his complaint that the protection of property under the Human Rights Chapter would make it very difficult for a government to nationalise parts of the economy if circumstances made this necessary.

There were attacks by a vocal minority of Members, many of them devotees of the 'Third Force', on the position of the Supreme Court as an additional layer on top of the existing hierarchy of courts; criticism, too, of the special procedure under Article 2 for the reference of constitutional cases to the Supreme Court, and of the extreme rigidity of the amendment procedure, though none of these criticisms found general favour with other Members of the Assembly. As a possible substitute for the guardian powers of the President and Judiciary some of the Members advocated a Second Chamber of the legislature, but without the Assembly's approval. As one Member commented later when opposing the suggestion: 'the multiplicity of controls and checking bodies is getting out of control'.[24]

Few members were prepared to go as far as the lawyer Obed Asamoah who argued that Judges should not be selected by the Chief Justice but by 'the representatives of the people',[25] by which it seems he meant the Prime Minister. J. A. Kufuour suggested that an electoral college of legislators, judges and the Attorney-General (representing the executive) should choose judges after candidates had been investigated by the Special Branch; but this too was rejected, despite the cogency of the argument that the Constitutional Commission's assumption of a Supreme Court which was 'above' politics was unrealistic:

> by the very nature of its exercise of judicial review, the Supreme Court is already in the thick of politics and rightly so ... the Court, to work successfully, must have Judges not only versed in legal interpretation; they

must also be responsive to the political and social aspirations of the country. It has been said that such Judges must not only be good lawyers; they must also be statesmen.[26]

Perhaps the most disliked proposal was Article 3, entitled 'Defence of Democracy'. Sub-clause (1) provided that 'the existence, organisation, activity or propaganda by speech, writing or any means of any organisation which seeks to establish in Ghana a system opposed to democracy or which commits any act prejudicial to the National Sovereignty is hereby declared unlawful'. The Commission presumably had in mind the need to proscribe any organisation like the former Convention People's Party, but the Constituent Assembly was also aware that such a provision could be used to suppress harmless organisations. Kwesi Lamptey thought that it was 'diabolical and dangerous'; B. J. da Rocha could not see how it could possibly defend democracy. Only a lone voice from one of the women members pleaded for its acceptance because it sought to prevent 'the growth of communism in Ghana'.

Members of the Constituent Assembly were divided on a number of issues. Various speakers attacked provisions which were thought to discriminate against the youth in favour of Chiefs, judges, and older people generally, such as the age qualification for the office of President. The representative of the Youth Council, Sam Okudzeto, complained 'that most Ghanaians still laboured under the impression that knowledge, wisdom and experience are synonymous with age';[27] Mr. Edjah, for the Students of Ghana, talked of a conspiracy of the rich and the old and asked 'How shall it profit a man if he shall be guaranteed all his civil liberties and be without economic status?'[28] To which the reply came:

Nana Obiri Yeboah II: Mr. Speaker, I have noted with a lot of concern that the previous speaker (Mr. Edjah) has accused Members of this House and Members of the Constitutional Commission of being fraudulent, of being wicked and devoid of shame. I think this House should dissociate itself from this point.
Mr. Speaker: I asked the Member to withdraw those words and he did.
Nana Obiri Yeboah II: It is not a case that Students should be excluded from this House?
Mr. Speaker: You are quite right. This House is not a Students' debating class. (A member: It is a mature House.)

These early sessions also showed that Members were anxious to defend group and local interests. Nana Agyeman Badu II, the Omanhene of Dormaa-Ahenkro, welcomed the role given to chiefs in their proposals, but asked that constitutional protection be given to the traditional Councils. B. D. Addai proposed that Ghana should be a monarchy under a Chief; and some of the Chiefs argued that the President should be chosen by the Chiefs from among themselves. Nana

Agyeman Badu II and Nana Obiri Yeboah II wanted Regional and National Houses of Chiefs included in the Constitution, a demand in which the Chiefs were ultimately successful. The engineer, M. N. B. Ayiku, suggested that the Constitution provide some recognition of the status and autonomy of professional bodies, a point taken up later by the pharmacist, B. E. D. Ofori-Atta, and by Joe Appiah in their opening addresses, and which they were to press to a successful conclusion in Article 51 of the Constitution. The Christian Council wanted the inclusion of a clause guaranteeing 'non-interference by a government party or the government or Head of State with the administrative process and functions of a religious body'. The Ga-Adangbe wanted a separate region for themselves. Northerners demanded a new Ministry of Northern Affairs. The representative of the Association of Junior Civil Servants pointed out that their members wanted 'more pay, better housing facilities, more promotions in the junior grade, revision of the General Orders and above all, reduction in prices of commodities to suit every pocket'. Such demands followed a time-honoured pattern whereby Ghanaian M.P.s sought to secure maximum benefits for his constituents and his home area.

Many speakers were also anxious about future relations between the military and civilian authorities. Obed Asamoah felt that the Constitutional provisions for the Armed Forces might make them tend to feel they were too independent of the civilian power. T. A. Bediako wanted control over the armed forces to be written into the Constitution, and suggested that it be made illegal for a civilian administration to surrender power to the army, even during an emergency. Moreover, when the present N.L.C. handed over power they must withdraw completely from politics. To facilitate this, R. A. Quarshie suggested that the members of the N.L.C. ought to be rewarded with generous pensions, and retired from the Army and the Police Service on the coming into force of the Constitution. A very different view was expressed by Air Commodore Hayfron, the representative of the Ghana Ex-Servicemen: 'After the experience of February, 1966, it will be difficult to expect the military to turn their back completely on government affairs. The best thing to do is not to isolate the Armed Forces, but to devise a means to regulate satisfactorily the relation between the army and the civilians'—an argument which went through many changes before the final withdrawal of both army and police on 1 October 1969.

After several days of initial debate on the principles underlying the Constitution, the House formally adopted for consideration the proposals of the Constitutional Commission and started a clause by clause discussion in a Committee of Whole House. It was soon discovered that this approach was time consuming in the extreme, since almost every member wanted his voice heard if only to attract public notice. Accordingly, it was decided to divide the House into five Select Committees each of which would consider some aspects of the proposals in detail before placing their conclusions before the whole House for approval. It was in these Committees that nearly all the important changes were made.

It was at this stage too that the professions mustered their forces. In the Committee on the Executive, the engineer M. N. B. Ayiku, with the assistance of the lawyers, produced a draft Article providing for the recognition by the President of professional bodies whereby they would be empowered to issue their own regulations governing such matters as the training for, entry to, control of, and discipline in, each profession. The proposal had revolutionary implications for the power structure of many of the professions, giving them in theory greater status and autonomy than they had ever enjoyed before—and this eventually passed into law.[29] In the same Committee, members began to chip away at the Presidency and the other independent centres of executive power, to restore something more like normal cabinet government. At the same time, the Committee on the Judiciary began to whittle down the powers of the Chief Justice in favour of the other Judges, the Bar Association and the Executive. There was a good deal of interchange between the Committees, since Members were allowed to appear in Committees other than their own to move amendments and take part in the discussions on them: a leading figure, like Joe Appiah, though belonging to the Committee on the Legislature, appeared in the Committees on the Judiciary and the Executive to propose amendments, take part in discussions and marshall support.

The Select Committee on the Legislature was preoccupied much of the time with the issue of disqualification, excising Article 71(2)(b)(ii), only for it to be restored and reworded when put back to the plenary Assembly. However it, too, managed to limit the President's power to refuse assent to a Bill; and it put an end altogether to his power to refer impending legislation, which seemed to him to contravene the Constitution, for pronouncement on its constitutionality by the Supreme Court. The Committee which was labelled Miscellaneous 1, with Busia in the chair, introduced important changes in chieftaincy and local government, although it left the Human Rights Chapter, also entrusted to it, virtually intact.

Since the proceedings of the Select Committees were unfortunately only partially documented, we had to rely to a large extent on the debates which arose from their recommendations. For this reason we now look at the debates at Consideration stage, when the Committees brought their proposals to the plenary Assembly, for the final detailed discussion and decision.[30]

Chapter 1 on 'The Constitution' contained the controversial Article 3

embodying provisions for the 'defence of democracy'. Opposition to it
was so strong that it was amended out of recognition. The T.U.C.
representatives managed to secure the abolition of sub-clause (4) and (5)
which threatened the right to strike.[31] Many members wanted subclauses
(1) to (3)—declaring unlawful organisations seeking to establish a
system opposed to democracy—deleted from the Constitution
altogether, and they probably would have been but for an acceptable
compromise whereby, after a lengthy debate spreading over several days,
Article 3 was amended to 'defend the Constitution' instead of
'democracy', and Parliament was denied the power to pass any law establishing a One-Party State.

The debate on 'The Territories of Ghana' (Chapter 2) revealed the
changed position of those who had formerly been opposed to the cen-
tralisation of power in the hands of the C.P.P., and who were now in control of the central machinery of government. The unitary form of government proposed by the Constitutional Commission was accepted without
question. Indeed, members were eager to check any moves that would
have a disruptive effect. The request by the Member for Kpandu Administrative District, S. G. Antor, that the Volta Region should be re-
named the Volta-Togoland Region was rejected, on the grounds that it
might revive the moment among the Ewe for unification with Togo.
Similarly, the motion by the Ga/Adangbe Members for a separate
Region was defeated, Ironically, the opposition was led by the Adansihene, Nana Kwaantwi Barima II from the Ashanti House of Chiefs, a
group that had backed the N.L.M.'s demand—supported by Busia—for
a federal constitution for Ghana in the days before independence.[32]

The debate on citizenship (Chapter 3) testified to the claim that much of
the Constitution approved by the Constituent Assembly was hardly dis-
tinguishable from the Constitutional Commission's Draft, since the
proposals on citizenship were accepted without substantial amendment.
They were designed to restrict citizenship to indigenous Ghanaians, and
two attempts by Joe Appiah (himself married to an English lady) to extend citizenship as of right to foreigners who married Ghanaians were
defeated. E. Acquah-Harrison, a businessman, spoke against any easy
way of acquiring Ghanaian nationality lest 'all the trade in the country
is taken away from us'. He was echoing a popular resentment against
the preponderant role of foreigners, particularly Lebanese, Syrians and
Indians, in commerce—a resentment which both the N.L.C. and the
Progress government were willing to assuage.[33] In similar fashion, the
debates on Chapter 4, dealing with the freedom of the individual, indicated a general acceptance of the work of the Akufo-Addo Commission. The Select Committee which studied the clauses in detail, included
Victor Owusu and William Ofori-Atta who had first hand experience of
the way in which the Preventive Detention Act had operated under the

C.P.P. To the Draft's provision that 'any person who is unlawfully arrested or detained by any other person shall be entitled to compensation therefore from that other person', the Assembly added a rider that, when convicted persons who had served the whole or part of their sentences were acquitted on appeal, they might be awarded compensation by the Courts. They also tightened up constitutional restrictions on the declaration of a Public Emergency by the government by compelling the authorities to publish monthly in the Gazette the names of people detained under emergency regulations, together with details of cases reviewed by the tribunals appointed under the provisions.

Several members complained that the Human Rights provisions were excessively complicated and encrusted with qualifications and exceptions. The limitations were said to be necessary to ensure that an individual's enjoyment of his rights should 'not prejudice the right and freedoms of others or the public interest',[34] but phrases such as the 'public interest', 'public order', 'public safety' abounded so much as to make it seem that what was given with one hand was taken away with the other. So at least it seemed to several Members. The lawyer R. E. Bannerman complained that:

> What we have to consider is whether this is a Constitutional Document or a Legislative Document and this sub-Clause (2) with all its sub-sections (a), (b), (c) and (d) is an attempt to legislate in a constitutional document. Now a Constitutional Document must state broad principles and the broad principles we are concerned with is the right to life. That must be stated in positive terms. If anybody thinks that protection is being interfered with it is up to him . . . to go to Court for redress . . . But you cannot give a person the right with one hand under 16(1) and take it away with the other hand under 16(2).[35]

At the time, such objections seemed decisive to Members and they voted to remove all the qualifications. The vote seemed to indicate that the same fate might befall the qualifications appended to all the other Rights in the Constitution until there were cries of alarm from Busia and other members of the Select Committee which he had chaired. It was therefore agreed to appoint a small committee under Mr. Justice S. Azu Crabbe to look into the question, and it was by this procedural manoeuvre that the proposed amendments were by-passed.[36]

During the debate on Chapter 5, on the Representation of the People, the Assembly approved with little controversy the setting up of an independent Electoral Commission to conduct both general and local elections. It decided, however, that the Commissioner need not necessarily be a Judge, and that the detailed procedure for elections could be left in his discretion instead of being prescribed by the constitution itself as in the Draft. Members then added a recommendation of their own to those of the Commission by banning (Article 35) the formation of tribal, religious or communal parties. This amounted to little more than the entrenching in the Constitution of a Section of the *Avoidance of Discrimination Act*, passed by Nkrumah's legislature in 1957. Nevertheless, it is surprising that there was so little dissent from among the members of the Assembly, since they included several former supporters of the N.L.M. in Ashanti, the N.P.P. in the North, the Togoland Congress in the Volta Region, and similar organisations against which the legislation had originally been directed. A cynic might say that things looked different, now that so many of them saw themselves as the prospective inheritors and beneficiaries of power.

In contrast, discussion of the Executive, Legislature and Judiciary was contentious. Three reasons can be put forward to explain why this was so. Firstly, the proposals were unconventional in certain respects and needed scrutiny. Secondly, there was the residue of the conflict between the Bar Association and the Chief Justice. Thirdly, and perhaps of greatest importance, the Chapters were concerned with the allocation of powers among the various branches of government, and it is a reasonable assumption that those who hoped to succeed the military were determined to prevent too many restrictions being placed on the offices they coveted. The general effect of the changes introduced was to redistribute executive powers away from the President (and the institutions under his protection) towards the Cabinet, to reduce the President's powers *vis à vis* the Legislature, and to reduce (but certainly not to do away with) the judiciary's powers to set constitutional limits to the powers of both the executive and the legislature. *Within* each branch the primary emphasis was on cutting-back the non-responsible power of the individual 'guardians' of the constitution, remarked on in the preceding Chapter, in favour of conciliar authority. The Chief Justice and the President, in particular, were compelled to heed the advice of advisory bodies like the Judicial Council, the Rules of Court Committee, and the Council of State in a much wider variety of situations.

The President was to be chosen (as in the Draft with some minor modifications) by an electoral College consisting of the National Assembly and representatives of Chiefs and District Councils. The Constituent Assembly preferred a four-year term rather than the eight years suggested by the Commission, but agreed that the President should be eligible for re-election for a second term. The age limit for the Presidency was reduced from fifty to forty, thanks to the cries of 'conspiracy against the youth'. The office was, however, deprived of many of the functions bestowed on it by the Constitutional Commission. No longer could the President select on his own responsibility the Attorney-General, the Governor and members of the governing body of the Bank of Ghana, and the chairman and members of the Council for Higher Education: he had now to appoint them on the advice of the

Prime Minister. The government's chief legal officer and its key instrument of financial policy were thus brought back under the control of the cabinet. The change in relation to the Attorney-General was particularly far reaching since he was deprived of all of the protection against variation in his terms of service, or his removal from public office previously afforded him under Draft Article 68. Nor was the President any longer empowered to make statutory instruments relating to the various institutions under his protection or to 'deal with any matter relating to the election, installation and destoolment of Chiefs', a power which now passed to the Houses of Chiefs. He also lost to the Prime Minister and Cabinet the responsibility for administering the affairs of the country on the dissolution of the National Assembly.

Even so, he was still more than a purely ceremonial Head of State, retaining several of the constitutional functions the commission had given him, in respect of which he was not obliged to act on the advice of the Prime Minister. But the Assembly decided that he should usually act on the advice of the Council of State when performing them, as in the appointment of the Chief of Defence Staff of the Armed Forces, the Auditor-General, the Ombudsman, the chairmen and members of Commissions of Enquiry and certain public corporations; and in the appraisal of Regulations by the Electoral Commissioner for the conduct of elections. The Assembly did however retain the President's right to nominate the Chief Justice and certain members of the Council of State on his own responsibility.

The Assembly approved the establishment of the Council of State to advise the President in the discharge of his constitutional duties, and increased its responsibilities. In his contribution to the debate, Busia saw the Council as a welcome return to tradition by 'adopting the practice of our Chiefs being advised by their elders',[37] and perhaps the most interesting aspect is the fact that it included both the Prime Minister and the Leader of the Opposition, a feature enthusiastically endorsed by the Assembly. Presumably it was hoped, as Jones Ofori Atta remarked, that this would have a moderating influence on party politics. But the Assembly went on to reject the Commission's proposal that the Chief Justice, the Attorney-General and the head of the Armed Forces should also serve on the Council. The decision was in keeping with its desire to reduce the 'ubiquity' of the Chief Justice in the Constitution, and make the Attorney-General an agent of the executive, and an affirmation of its view that the transfer of power to civilians should be complete and permanent. There was, however, an important qualification to be made to the argument that the President's authority was now shared with the Council of State, namely, that since he appointed a majority of its members, his influence over it was likely to be considerable.[38] An unfriendly President might still, therefore, have put considerable

difficulties in the way of the Prime Minister, though he was not as for-
midably armed with powers to do so as in the Commission's proposals.

In its debate on the Prime Minister and Cabinet, the Assembly placed
greater emphasis than the Commission on the desirability of a
Westminster-style of cabinet-government. It restored the doctrine of
collective responsibility, the Constitutional Commission having
preferred the less precise wording that 'each Minister (should be)
responsible for the business of the government relating to his portfolio
within the general policy of the government as determined by the
Cabinet'. Parliamentary approval was no longer required for the appointment of individual Ministers; nor could it pass votes of no confidence in individual Ministers. The Prime Minister's hand was
strengthened by being empowered to appoint the Attorney-General to
the Cabinet, but he was no longer able to choose Ministers from outside
the National Assembly. The Constituent Assembly thus did away with
one of the Constitutional Commission's more distinctive efforts to
establish a degree of separation of powers between executive and
legislature. It is clear that the politicians in the Assembly were determined that there should be no 'back-door' way of entering the Cabinet:
all must pass through the twists and turns of party politics.

Further concessions to cabinet responsibility were made by obliging
the President to act on its advice in delivering messages to the National
Assembly on the state of Ghana, and he was no longer empowered to
'recommend for the consideration of the National Assembly such
matters as he shall judge to be necessary or expedient'.[39] Similar restrictions were imposed on the President in the selection of a new Prime
Minister since he had now to appoint the leader of the majority party in
the National Assembly, and only when no party enjoyed an absolute
majority was he, himself, able to propose a name for the first ballot in a
vote by the National Assembly.[40] There was a comparable reduction in
the role of the President in the chapter on the Legislature. Although he
retained the right to veto, or recommend amendments to, Bills of the
National Assembly, the right was so hedged with qualifications as to be
almost meaningless. For the Constituent Assembly rejected the
proposal that the President might refuse his assent for six months to
Bills which he had returned to the National Assembly unless they were
passed again within that time by a two-thirds majority. He could still
return a Bill for further reconsideration, but was now bound to give his
assent if the Bill were again passed by a *simple* majority.[41] Moreover,
even this procedure could be by-passed under an additional sub-clause,
Article 84(12), whereby a Committee of the National Assembly could
decide a Bill that was 'of an urgent nature'. Nor was the President any
longer permitted, as he was under the Draft, to refer a Bill, or provision
thereof, to the Supreme Court for determination as to its con-

stitutionality: the Assembly now insisted that the Supreme Court should only pronounce on the constitutionality of legislation (on a petition brought before it) *after* the legislation had been enacted.

The Assembly upheld the Constitutional Commission on most other matters relating to the legislature, especially where its powers had actually been extended—as in Article 81, which authorised the National Assembly to set up committees to review the activities and administration of government departments. The principle of 'government by committee' did not lack opposition. But J. A. Kufuor expressed the general view when he argued that:

> . . . One of the greatest set-backs in governments of the developing countries is corruption in the administration—in Ministries and Departments; distortion of legislative intent of Acts when they were being executed; delays and inefficiences in the execution of important measures; all these can easily be exposed where you have specialised Committees of the House dealing publicly with individual ministries.[42]

The Assembly also confirmed the proposal that M.P.s should not be paid salaries, which was not as drastic as it sounded since they were still to receive tax free allowances and gratuities on retirement or death. These, like the salaries of Ministers and Ministerial Secretaries, were to be determined by the President in consultation with the Council of State.

By far the most passionate debate of the whole Assembly took place over Article 71(2)(b)(ii) under which a person was disqualified from membership of the National Assembly if judged incompetent to hold public office by the report of a Commission of Enquiry. Had the proposal been discussed immediately after the coup in 1966 it would almost certainly have been accepted without challenge since public resentment against corrupt politicians was the universal. But much had happened since those early days. The Siriboe Commission of Enquiry into Electoral and Local Government Reform had recommended disqualification for life of all persons against whom adverse findings involving dishonesty had been made by a Commission of Enquiry[43]—an extreme penalty, reduced by the Constitutional Commission to disqualification for five years. The N.L.C. (as described in earlier Chapters) had passed Decrees, on the Constitutional Commission's advice, disqualifying several categories of former office holders in the C.P.P. hierarchy unless exonerated by the Exemptions Commission. And by the time the Constituent Assembly considered the matter, embryo political groups had been formed: the leader of one of them, Gbedemah, actually obtained exemption from the Exemptions Commission, an event which brought about the suspension of the Commission's hearings. Meanwhile, Gbedemah's assets had been looked at by the Jiagge Commission of Enquiry, which reported to the N.L.C. in June 1968. It was widely believed that the Report contained adverse findings against him, and this was confirmed halfway through the Assembly's sessions in May, 1969, when the Jiagge Commission's Report was published with its accompanying White Paper. As a result, Article 71(2)(b)(ii) threatened to have the effect of disqualifying one of the main contenders for the office of Prime Minister from membership of the Assembly. What might earlier have been seen as a matter of debarring dishonest people from the National Assembly was now bound up with a struggle for power.

The passage of the disqualification provisions through the Assembly was stormy, beset with numerous procedural wrangles. In the Select Committee on the Legislature, Gbedemah's supporters, together with those who opposed this kind of disqualification in principle, managed to secure the necessary majority to cut 71(2)(b)(ii) out of the Constitution. But, as soon as the Chapter on the Legislature came before the whole House again, a motion was passed approving disqualification in principle and asking the Select Committee to reconsider the matter. The Committee was unable to agree even upon what actually transpired at its meetings,[44] and the sub-clause was brought back to the House. A motion in the name of the Rev. C. G. Baeta, that disqualification be included subject to appeal to a Review Committee set up by the Chief Justice, failed to pass. Finally, an amendment sponsored by Jones Ofori-Atta not only restored disqualification by reason of adverse findings of a Commission of Enquiry, but also left out any provision for appeal. It was passed and incorporated in the final Constitution, but not before there had been further acrimony over a complicated procedural wrangle.[45] It led to a number of Gbedemah's supporters' walking out of the Assembly and threatening not to sign the final constitutional document: in the end, they signed; but twenty-four members expressed reservations in a public statement and sent a minority report to the N.L.C. The latter acted upon the report by referring 71(2)(b)(ii) back to the Assembly once more for reconsideration at its last but one sitting—only to be told by the members, by now with some impatience, that they refused to discuss the matter further.

In this protracted and angry debate the opponents of disqualification produced several arguments against it. Firstly, that the provisions were undemocratic in seeking to prevent the people from deciding for themselves who should represent them. Secondly, that they were unjust since the Commissions of Enquiry did not follow strict judicial procedure in examing those that appeared before them, and there was no right of appeal to a superior adjudicatory body. Thirdly, disqualification on the basis of adverse findings of a Commission of Enquiry might be dangerous in that a future government might harrass Opposition

members by arraigning them before Commissions packed with government sympathisers. As the Sekondi barrister James Mercer put it: 'we
have an adage in Akan that if you are digging a hole for your enemy,
please do not dig it too deep—so that if you fall into it yourself you may
come out'.[46] Finally, some Members argued that it was a move
calculated to remove Gbedemah from the political scene by his rivals
for office. There was some truth in the argument that politics had eaten
into the debate since of the 11 members and 2 tellers who opposed its inclusion in the Constitution, 7 subsequently contested the election as
members of Gbedemah's party, and none stood for Busia's P.P.; while
18 of the 55 and two tellers who voted for disqualification stood for
Progress, none for N.A.L.[47] Yet politics was not everything. The
followers of the other parties were split, and there were men like James
Mercer, Peter Adjetey, Victor Owusu and the Rev. Baeta who either
argued against 71(2)(b)(ii) *per se*, or at least thought that an appeal from
decision of Commissions of Enquiry should be provided. Victor
Owusu's arguments, coming from a leading member of Dr. Busia's party
was of particular interest. From his experience as Attorney-General
under the N.L.C. (he said) Reports of Commissions of Enquiry were
very uneven in quality. Although they might form the basis for exclusion under the ordinary electoral law, such exclusion should certainly
not form part of the Constitution, and since Commissions of Enquiry
could be appointed by a government to discredit political opponents, it
was most dangerous to allow disqualification without any provision for
appeal.[48] The supporters of disqualification, on the other hand, claimed
that theirs was a moral rather than a political case—they were fighting
for the principle of debarring from office people of proven dishonesty in
public affairs. As Jones Ofori-Atta said:

> We have heard that perhaps we are attempting to make it impossible for
> Mr. Gbedemah to carry out his political activities successfully. This may be
> so, this may be consequential, but I stand for principle and I should like the
> Pressmen to know that this principle is far larger than myself, Mr.
> Gbedemah or anybody in this country.[49]

The sentiment was noble, the morality impeccable: yet one may still
conclude that it was peculiarly unfortunate for Ghana's new start in
democracy that one of the main contestants for power should be
caught in the tangled web of a disputed principle.

The debate on the Chapter on the Judiciary was less contentious,
although the changes that were made were important, following in most
instances the Select Committee's well prepared Report drafted by B. J.
da Rocha's subcommittee. Members of the Constituent Assembly were
as aware as the Constitutional Commission of the threat posed to the
judiciary by Nkrumah's dismissal of judges, and they endorsed, in

general terms, the provisions guaranteeing its independence: namely, that the judiciary was to be subject to the Constitution but to no other authority or person; that (Article 2) any citizen might bring an action in the Supreme Court for a declaration that an enactment, or anything done under the authority of an enactment, was unconstitutional and (Article 171) might obtain legal aid to do so; that (Article 170) any person might bring an action against the government without need for the Attorney-General's fiat (or consent); and that the procedure for the appointment of judges and their dismissal (which should only be for proven incapacity or misconduct) be protected from politics. Members agreed, too, that the more important of the provisions relating to the judiciary should be protected behind the special amendment procedure under Article 169 of the Constitution (Article 5 of the Commission's Draft) which permitted amendments only to the extent that they did not derogate from the provisions or the principles embodied therein. The Constituent Assembly approved all these proposals and embodied them in the Constitution, despite the doubts expressed about the superimposition of the Supreme Court as an additional layer on top of the existing Court of Appeal. It also approved (with supporting speeches from da Rocha, Busia and Agama) the proposal that judges should retire on full salary—although it limited the privilege to judges with at least ten years service behind them. Ghana, it was said, needed judges of unimpeachable integrity, and it was assumed that the way of attracting such men to the bench was through favourable conditions of service—though there were some Members who bitterly opposed the proposal up to the Assembly's final sittings.

Nevertheless, the Constituent Assembly set tighter limits on the powers of the Judiciary. No longer was it the supreme corporation, the guardian of guardians, as in the Commission's proposals. The Assembly marked this change in symbolic terms in its debate on the Preamble by replacing: 'Determined to secure for all of us a Constitution which shall establish the SOVEREIGNTY OF THE LAW as the foundation of our society' by '. . . THE SOVEREIGNTY OF THE PEOPLE and the RULE OF LAW as the foundation. . . .' In practical terms, too, the judiciary lost several of its powers and privileges. The Chief Justice in particular lost a number of his extra-judicial functions. He was removed from the Council of State and from the Presidential Commission. The Assembly also struck out Draft Article 124 which sought to make the actual work of the judiciary independent of financial control by the government: the salaries of judges were protected, but the administration of the courts still depended on government money. The judiciary was also made subject to investigation under Article 100 by the Ombudsman. And the office of Judicial Secretary—the chief administrator of the courts—was excised from the Constitution, another casualty of the conflict between the Bar Association and the Chief Justice.[50]

The balance of power *within* the judiciary was also altered. In general terms the Chief Justice now had to act on the advice of, rather than in consultation with, the Judicial Council of which he was Chairman. In addition, the members of the Bar Association in the Assembly took good care to put three of their own representatives on the Judicial Council and two on the Rules of Court Committee[51] (as well as succeeding, during the debate on Chapter Thirteen on the Police Service, in putting their own representatives on the Police Council and Regional Police Committees)—a good example of a pressure group at work. On the other hand, those who were to be appointed Ombudsman, or Chairman of a Commission of Enquiry, or Chairman of the Audit Service Board, no longer had to be Judges or persons qualified for appointment as such.

Much of the remaining discussion centred on further proposals designed by the Commission to diffuse power and prevent its abuse—the setting up of the Public Services Commission, the Police Service Council, the Armed Forces Council, the Prison Services Board, an Audit Service and the Ombudsman. These proposals were accepted, subject to a few changes in detail. It is interesting that the *ex-officio* representatives of the Armed Forces and Police on the Armed Forces Council and the Police Council were reduced to the Chief of Defence Staff and Head of the Police Service: the Assembly clearly wished to make civilian control over these bodies effective by minimising the number of serving officers on each of the councils. The Chief of Defence Staff and the Head of the Police Service also lost their *ex-officio* position on the National Security Council, and the former ceased to be a member of the Council of State and the Presidential Commission. The Assembly also followed the Commission in adopting the provision from earlier constitutions that 'no person shall raise any armed force save by or under the authority of an Act of Parliament': it had not forgotten the danger posed by President Nkrumah when his bodyguard, the President's Own Guard Regiment, was used to act as a check on the regular forces.

So far very little had been said in the Assembly about the role assigned in the Constitution to traditional rulers. Although the C.P.P. government had several allies among the Chiefs and gave high public office to a number of them, the fact was that chiefs had begun to lose most of their former powers. In effect, the declaration in the 1960 Republican Constitution that chieftaincy would be preserved was meaningless; and it was understandable that many of the chiefs saw Nkrumah's overthrow as a return to the days when they had a great deal of influence. The Constituent Assembly was on the whole a sympathetic forum. There was little opposition to the Constitutional Commission's proposal that chieftaincy be guaranteed and entrenched in the Constitution (Article 153). The chiefs even succeeded in getting their name written into the Preamble—'We the Chiefs and People of Ghana ...', in spite of the fact that not all the Members wished to increase their power. As S. K. Opong commented: 'We are talking about democracy, but we must know that in the traditional system the democracy we are talking about does not exist.'[52] More important, they were able to write into the Constitution a National and Regional Houses of Chiefs. This met one of their most long-standing wishes—that the government's power through the process of recognition to influence the enstoolment and destoolment of the Chiefs be withdrawn, since the Regional Houses of Chiefs were given original jurisdiction and the National House of Chiefs appelate jurisdiction in all chieftaincy matters, subject to further appeal to the Supreme Court.

To obtain such concessions, the Chiefs had to concede some reduction in their role in local government, compared with the Commission's proposals. While the traditional authorities (as in the Draft) made up one-third of the membership of the District Councils, they were now restricted to no more than half of the members of Local Councils.[53] The chiefs were quite willing to make such concessions in order to increase their corporate autonomy, for many saw themselves as constitutional monarchs exercising their authority through informal channels and they were not particularly enthusiastic about involving themselves in the formal machinery of local government, with its attendant political dangers.

As part of an effort at administrative decentralisation, the Assembly also accepted the Commission's proposal to create Regional Councils and a Regional Administration to be presided over by a Chairman who, like his predecessor under the N.L.C., was to be the central government's nominee. It was certainly the intention of the constitution-makers to introduce a greater degree of autonomy in local government. Yet the Constitution provided only a bare framework for local, district and regional government which was left very largely for later legislation to fill out. The Local Administration Bill introduced by the Progress government in 1971 in no way indicated, however, that the party in power was anxious to relinquish its day to day control of local government, whatever its leaders might have said before they took office.[54]

Towards the last days of the Constituent Assembly, the Members debated the 'Transitional Provisions'—that is, those parts of the Constitution which had only temporary significance since they concerned the actual period of the transfer of power from the N.L.C. to a civilian government. The Assembly accepted, with a few minor amendments, the proposals on the election of the first President and the National Assembly, and those protecting the members of the

N.L.C. from legal proceedings against them in connection with and since the coup. It also made financial provision for the N.L.C. by approving the proposals that its members could retire from the Army and the Police on full salary at any time before or after the coming into force of the new Constitution. In addition, they were to be paid 'as a token mark of the nation's gratitude such gratuity by way of a terminal award as shall be determined by the Government under the Constitution which immediately succeeds the N.L.C.'.

On the eve of the promulgation of the new Constitution on 22 August 1969, the N.L.C. began to waver in its decision to withdraw fully its control. On 12 August, the Council informed the Constituent Assembly that the Constitution should be enacted by the Assembly and promulgated by the N.L.C. There followed a complicated series of manoeuvres. When the Assembly rejected a motion by Nana Agyeman Badu II that a three-man army-cum-police Presidential Commission be set up to exercise the functions of the President for the first five years, the N.L.C. passed a Decree (N.L.C.D. 380) which, reversing its previous decision, empowered the Assembly to bring into force as well as enact the Constitution. In the same Decree however it directed that, before enacting the Constitution, the Assembly should reconsider the rejected motion. The decision to allow the Assembly both to enact and promulgate the Constitution was naturally interpreted as an inducement to persuade its members to approve of the troika Presidency, especially as the members had already (15 August) put their signatures to the Constitution. A critical debate ensued. Many recalled the promise by the N.L.C. not to cling to power one day more than was necessary, and argued that a Presidential Commission would have serious repercussions for the working of the Constitution. Peter Adjetey, in a long and well-argued attack, said that, however good their intentions, members of the N.L.C. night find it difficult to shake off the habit of ruling, and asked what would happen if the future members of the Commission kept their military and police jobs: how could the Inpsector-General of Police and the Chief of Defence Staff be expected to act as the ceremonial (and not-so-ceremonial) Head of the executive while at the same time being responsible to Ministers in the Government? On the other hand, there were those who saw practical advantages in making such a concession to the N.L.C. since a return to civilian government under the guardianship of military figures was preferable to continued army rule. Certain members of the Assembly spoke darkly of threats to security, a warning presumably connected with rumours of a plot in the army and a reshuffle in the military which was then taking place. Others replied that if there really was a threat to security, serious enough to justify a last minute change in the Constitution, then surely they had a right to be taken into confidence.

116   POLITICIANS AND SOLDIERS IN GHANA

The crisis ended as rapidly and mysteriously as it had begun. Victor
Owusu moved an amendment to Nana Agyeman Badu's original motion which differed from it in certain important details. Word was
passed among Dr. Busia's supporters that it should be passed, and it
was.[55] It established a triumvirate Presidential Commission—consisting
of the Chairman of the N.L.C., Brigadier Afrifa, the Deputy Chairman,
John Harlley, and the then Acting Chief of Defence Staff, Major-
General Ocran—to exercise the functions of the President for not more
than three years. Unlike the original motion, it reserved the right to the
new Parliament to dissolve the Presidential Commission before the
three-year period had elapsed: and that was precisely what happened in
1970. In this way a very difficult question was settled. And having
turned aside the N.L.C.'s other requests—to reconsider Section 9 of the
First Schedule of the Transitional Provisions, and the controversial sub-
clause 71(2)(b)(ii)—the Members of the Constituent Assembly enacted
and promulgated the Constitution on 22 August 1969.

To conclude this account of the debates of the Assembly we need to
look finally at the procedures adopted for amending the Constitution.
Once again the past was the main determinant of the Assembly's
decisions for the future. As the Rev. Baeta argued: 'It is precisely
because of the ease of making amendments under the old regime that
our Constitution became what it did become, the travesty of the
original.'[56] In consequence, there was wide-spread agreement that
amendments must be difficult to achieve. Nevertheless, a few members
expressed doubts about the rigidity of the procedures proposed by the
Constitutional Commission, especially the protection of certain articles
of the Constitution from any amendment whatsoever.[57] As M. N. B.
Ayiku put it:

> We have been told in this House that there are certain things which are
> called a parallelogram of forces—social, political and economic forces.
> These three variable forces are given expression through representatives of
> the people in Parliament. It is these people who represent these forces and
> they represent the interest of the people directly and we are saying here in
> 1969 that 150 of us nominated by certain identifiable groups are writing a
> constitution which the representatives of the people cannot amend at any
> time in the life of this nation. It is totally illogical.[58]

Nevertheless, the provisions adopted in Chapter Nineteen of the
Constitution were those proposed by the Akufo-Addo Commission outlined earlier. The main differences were that the Assembly slightly
reduced the number of articles that were entrenched behind the complicated special amendment procedures, and increased those that could
be amended by a simple two-thirds majority vote of the Assembly. If
one judges the Constitution approved by the Constituent Assembly on

the basis of its amendment procedures, it is a rigid one.[59] One wonders, however, how many of the members of the Assembly agreed with Harry Sawyerrs' prophetic statement that if there were a need for change in the future that could not be achieved within the rules for amendment laid down under the constitution, then:

> ... the whole Constitution can be thrown overboard. If there comes a time when the people for whom we are now drawing the Constitution think that the Constitution has outlived its usefulness, the whole Constitution can be changed.[60]

What can be said by way of conclusion and general comment? Firstly, that the influence of the N.L.C. on the work of the Assembly was indirect and occasional rather than constant and pervasive, not because of any divergence of interest but because both bodies were in broad agreement on what was needed. Nevertheless, the shadow of the military fell across the Assembly debates: the soldiers were there in the castle and their readiness to surrender power had to be seen against the fact of their intervention in 1966. The N.L.C. followed the debates closely, and their refusal, until the closing stages, to authorise the Assembly to enact and promulgate the constitution, gave rise to speculation that they might withhold their approval if it were not to their liking. The Assembly was willing to indemnify the soldiers who had staged the coup from all future legal proceedings against them, and to bestow on them a very generous financial settlement on their retirement from politics; but it insisted on complete control over the army and police in the new constitution. And there is no evidence that the N.L.C. even tried to modify the decisions which reduced the autonomy of the military, including the removal of the General Officer Commanding the Armed Forces from the Council of State. The one area of the constitution where the influence of the N.L.C. appeared decisive was, of course, in the provision for a presidential commission. Simply by asking the Assembly to reconsider its decision not to discuss Nana Agyeman Badu's proposal for a 'troika presidency', the N.L.C. was able to have its way. Yet within a year the Presidential Commission had been replaced by a civilian elected President—Akufo-Addo, one of the main architects of the Constitution.

Secondly, the constitution of the second republic, as approved by the Assembly, was substantially that of the Constitutional Commission. The Assembly scrutinised its proposals, modified some, altered others, and added clauses of its own. But the form and structure of the constitution, approved after ninety-eight sittings, were essentially those of the draft proposals. The Constitutional Commission tried to devise a constitution which would break not only from the Nkrumah model of a centralised, single-party dictatorship but from the familiar pattern of a centralised cabinet government and a parliament tightly controlled by the government-of-the-day. In so far, therefore, as the Assembly changed anything, it brought the constitution closer to an archetypical Westminster pattern of cabinet government, and only to a relatively limited extent did the Assembly heed the plea by Nana Kwaantwi Barima II:

> No doubt we have produced sons and daughters who went overseas and graduated in other fields and disciplines and who have come back with ideas so alien to us. They quote people like Ivor Jennings and they quote constitutional cases here and there. I am of the opinion that we as a Ghanaian society should produce something of a Ghanaian nature so that people elsewhere will also come to us to copy from us.[61]

Thirdly, the Constituent Assembly, like the soldiers and policemen of the N.L.C. and the Constitutional Commissioners, thought of society in a pluralist image—in marked contrast to Kwame Nkrumah's unitary vision of a mobilising society in which the political kingdom had supremacy. The élite in this pluralist image was made up of self-regulating, though interdependent, status groups. The Chiefs were one such autonomous estate, although the majority of the status groups which espoused such a view belonged to the modern sector of society with some claim to professional status, like the military, lawyers, doctors, engineers, or civil servants. If it is partly true that the military had intervened in February 1966 in order to preserve its 'martial freedom', then it is equally true that other groups took constitution-making as their opportunity to develop and entrench their own autonomy. And in some respects the Assembly carried this tendency even further than had the Commission, as in making provision for the status and self-regulation of professional bodies under Article 51.

The political analogue of this occupational pluralism was the concept of the division of powers: the entrenchment of autonomous centres of power, each with its distinctive contribution to the political order—the Judiciary, the Legislature and the Executive—and, within the Executive branch, further divisions of functions and power between the Prime Minister, President, Ombudsman, Electoral Commissioner, Chief of Defence Staff and so on. At a cursory glance, it might be said that the Assembly was less enthusiastic than the Commission about the political as opposed to the occupational aspect of pluralism since it pulled back under executive control a number of the independent power centres, such as the Attorney-General or the Governor of the Bank of Ghana. But if one looks more closely, the Assembly often brought such institutions back behind their previously-recognised, pre-Nkrumah boundaries rather than actually reducing their freedom of action. It gave a different emphasis to these many centres of power, but it did not in any fundamental sense abandon the pluralist vision of society that the

Commissioners had put forward. Thus the judiciary was deprived of its right to strike down legislation before it was passed: but it was still heavily protected against outside interference in matters like the appointment and dismissal of judges. Indeed the reduction of the Chief Justice's powers in favour of the collegial view of the Judicial Council may have helped the judiciary to resist governmental control to a greater extent than was provided for under the Commission's Draft, although it could not prevent the judiciary from being subjected to other forms of political pressure.[62]

In much the same way the role of the Chiefs in the formal machinery of local government was cut back by the Assembly; but they were given more power through the Regional and National House of Chiefs to regulate their own affairs. This was fully in accord with the Chiefs' own realisation that they had to recognise the appropriate limits to their power in order best to preserve it. As Nana Agyeman Badu II put it:

> I want to make it clear to Members that the Chiefs in this country will not be involved in party politics (hear, hear). We want to make it clear that we are not going to be used as tools in the hands of future politicians in this country . . . Chiefs should not finance political parties, chiefs should not speak on party platforms, chiefs should not chair party functions . . .[63]

Fourthly, we should note the early emergence of party politics in the Assembly, despite the fact that by far the greater number of clauses of the new Constitution were agreed to without serious division on party lines. The N.L.C. had originally intended not to lift the ban on politics until the work of the Assembly was complete, but the latter continued to sit much longer than the N.L.C. had anticipated; and when Afrifa took over as Chairman of the N.L.C. in April 1969, following the resignation of Ankrah, he lifted the ban on 1 May without waiting for the Assembly to finish its work. This hastened the tendency, already begun, for the Assembly to become a political workshop in which the 'threads of electoral' support (as described later by Yaw Twumasi) were being woven. These politics-of-going-into-politics were, however, quite different from normal party conflict. The emphasis was on picking up support from as wide a spectrum of political opinion as possible in order to build up a majority, rather than on *using* such a majority for political purposes declared in advance. The lines of cleavage were played down and voting was only 'political' when the very existency of one or other of the newly emergent political groupings was called in question, as in the debates on disqualification.

Finally, there is the question of the 'representative nature' of the Assembly. Did the members 'represent' the various bodies which chose them? Our examination of the manner in which groups like the farmers or market women chose men or women 'of substance' rather than their own kind would suggest not. The Assembly was not very sympathetic when groups sought to use the House as a forum for their own grievances—when for example, the Junior Civil Servants complained about the ban imposed on their Association by the N.L.C. Even the Chiefs were given scant attention when they asked for the restoration of their lands or that their salaries be increased. On the other hand, powerful groups like lawyers and the chiefs were often able to get what they wanted, *provided their interests could be articulated in terms of wider constitutional issues.* Even so, the 'interests' that were pressed were often not those of the original 'constituencies' which sent Members to the Assembly but those of their professional or political friends. Was the Assembly in any broader sense, therefore, representative of the demands and aspirations of the Ghanaian people as a whole? The educational, social and economic gap between its members and those they were chosen to represent was of course very wide, and its members concern with the liberty of the individual is easier to understand when seen from the perspective of men who had already achieved a degree of economic and social security for themselves. Many of the electors who were later to vote in the 1969 election would no doubt have liked a constitution which not only ensured the freedom of the individual but guaranteed employment and prosperity. But that is simply another way perhaps of saying that the legitimacy or acceptability of the Constitution of the second republic depended at least as much on the actions of political leaders working with its terms of reference as on the framework of rules and regulations approved by the Constituent Assembly. And that was something no number of articles and clauses in a constitution could provide.

Composition of Constituent Assembly Compared with Nkrumah (1965) and Busia (1969) Parliaments

Occupation	National Assembly (1965)	Constituent Assembly	National Assembly (1969)
'Politicians'	78 (4)	—	1
Functionaries of party and wings [a]	41 (2)	—	1 (1)
Private Business	7 (1)	16 (2)	20
Corporate business [b]	0	9 (3)	5 (2)
Chiefs	1 (1)	13 (3)	2 (1)
Doctors	0	8 (1)	3
Lawyers	10 (3)	36 (8)	33 (5)
Other professions [c]	8 (2)	14 (1)	10 (2)
University lecturers	3	11 (2)	9
Teachers	13 (2)	16 (2)	23
Journalists	8 (2)	2 (1)	3 (1)
Senior civil servants [d]	0	6 (2)	4 (2)
Executive and clerical workers [e]	14 +	14 (1)	13
Trades unionists, manual workers	5 (2)	9	1
Farmers [f]	16	1	15
Unclassified and others [g]	4	8	4
Total	198	150	140

Notes: Occupational details of Nkrumah Parliament are from Ghana:,*Official Gazette*, Nos. 28, 31 and 33 of 1965; of Busia Parliament from lists of candidates at 1969 elections prepared by Electoral Commission; of the Constituent Assembly from the latter and the list of members prepared by Clerks of Constituent Assembly; these are supplemented by other sources of information at the writers' disposal, e.g. the Annual List of lawyers.

The numbers in brackets indicate those in each occupational category who are also included in another category. For this reason the figures when added up come to more than the totals shown.

[a] Includes functionaries of parties, Kwame Nkrumah Ideological Institute (Winneba), Young Pioneers, Young Farmers League, National Council of Ghana Women, political appointees to state corporations or state bodies like the State Cocoa Marketing Board (e.g. 'loans supervisors').

[b] Directors/managers in large concerns like CAST, PTC, etc., plus public relations and advertising practitioners.

[c] 'Other professions' includes engineers, surveyors, architects, accountants, economists and statisticians, research workers, social workers, pastors, pharmacists and nurses.

[d] Senior civil servants—in administrative class or equivalent in other public bodies or in specialist grades.

[e] Executive and clerical grades in civil service and equivalent in corporations and private firms. A figure of 14 (+) is given for the Nkrumah Parliament, because an indefinite number of functionaries in party and wings might also fit in this category.

[f] An elusive quantity. There can have been few (or almost no) politicians engaged in full-time farming without other sources of livelihood. Equally there are many in other occupations who own land or farms as a sideline. Because it is an emotive thing politically there are many of these who would *claim* to be farmers at election time, and this may explain the difference in the number of 'farmers' elected to the Nkrumah and Busia Parliaments and those selected on a non-political basis to the Constituent Assembly.

[g] The Constituent Assembly included 2 students and 5 women whom it is not possible to assign except under the doubtful category of 'housewife', which would not exclude other economic activities like trade (there were 11 women in the Assembly altogether).

Notes

1. *Minutes of the Plenary Meetings of the Constitutional Commission* (Accra: State Publishing Corporation, 1968), p. 45, meeting of March 17 1967. In view of the controversy (see below) about who should enact the Constitution it is interesting that the Commission went on to state unequivocally that 'It would also not be desirable for the N.L.C. to be either the enacting body or tinker with the Constitution to the extent of issuing a White Paper on it on the advice or otherwise of its legal advisers'.

2. The Interim Electoral Commissioner's view was that it was administratively feasible to organise an early election for the Constituent Assembly. See the following chapter.

3. In the Interim Electoral Commissioner's view it was administratively feasible to organise an early election for the Constituent Assembly. See Chapter 6. The Cape Coast and Koforidua municipalities also elected their Chairmen, T. D. Brodie-Mends and M. K. Osei, without contests.

4. Ofori-Atta was standing outside his own district of Kibi, but he reached the Assembly on an N.LC. ticket.

5. *Proceedings of the Constituent Assembly*—No. 6, Col. 171–172.

6. *Proceedings* No. 15, Col. 723.

7. The barristers who agreed to institute proceedings against the Chief Justice were Messrs. J. B. Quashie-Idun, B. J. da Rocha and Joe Reindorf. There is a discussion of some of the legal implications of the case in *Review of Ghana Law* Vol. II, No. 1 (April, 1970), pp. 64–73. Although the injunction was later quashed by the Court of Appeal, Akufo Addo gave up his efforts to make the lawyers pay taxes and allowed his other disciplinary proposals to lapse with them. The Bar Association boycotted the opening of the Legal Year in September 1968 en bloc, and the periodical informal meetings between their Executive and the Chief Justice (which had been instituted by the latter) ceased.

8. *Proceedings*, No. 10, Col. 433.

9. See Dennis Austin 'A Month in the Country' *West Africa* (London) 23 August 1969.

10. *Proceedings*, No. 6, Col. 162
11. E.g. Art. 51 on professional associations, and Art. 61 on freehold interest in land.
12. The provisions—under Section 9 of the First Schedule of the Transitional Provisions—were referred back to the Assembly for reconsideration under Decree 380 (see p. 116) by the N.L.C. precisely because of the ambiguity as to whether they gave the government the right to refuse to continue the appointment of *any* public servant after the Constitution had been in force for six months, or whether this applied only to public servants appointed by the N.L.C. itself. The Assembly failed completely to resolve the ambiguity, and retained the original wording, mainly, it seems, because the protagonists of both positions believed it favoured their own interpretation.
13. *Proceedings* No. 12, Col. 518.
14. *Ibid*, Col. 519.
15. *Ibid*, Col. 520.
16. Nine for N.A.L., 4 for U.N.P., 1 for A.P.R.P. and 4 independents.
17. *The Proceedings of the Constituent Assembly*, No. 4, Col. 91.
18. See below, p. 115.
19. *Proceedings*, No. 11, Col. 489.
20. See too *Legon Observer* (Accra) 6–19 June 1969, p. 7.
21. Obed Y. Asamoah, *Proceedings*, No. 2, Col. 46.
22. M. N. B. Ayiku, *Proceedings*, No. 3, Col. 26.
23. *Proceedings*, No. 8, Col. 282. A somewhat optimistic statement in the light of some of the actions of Dr. Busia's government in its first year of office.
24. *Proceedings*, No. 23, Col. 1019.
25. *Proceedings*, No. 3, Col. 51. He did not specifically mention the Prime Minister in his contribution to this debate, although he was later to move an amendment to this effect in the Select Committee.
26. *Proceedings*, No. 6, Col. 199.
27. *Proceedings*, No. 11, Col. 476.
28. *Proceedings*, No. 8, Col. 294.
29. Article 51 of the Constitution. While the professional bodies of the engineers, the architects and the accountants were already incorporated under legislation or in process of being so, the doctors were still beholden to a government appointed Board and the lawyers to the General Legal Council (a body which included representatives of the Judiciary, the Executive, the Faculty of Law at the University of Ghana and the Bar) rather than to their respective professional associations, the Ghana Medical Association and the Ghana Bar Association.
30. Chapters 1 and 2 were dealt with by a Committee of the whole House before the Select Committees brought their reports on the other Chapters to the Assembly for debate.
31. Even if these did not directly make strikes illegal, they might well have made it possible for the government to legislate against strikes, claiming exemption by virtue of Article 3(4) and (5) from the guarantees of freedom of association provided elsewhere in the Constitution.
32. For details, see Austin, *Politics in Ghana*, 1948–60, p. 263 seq.
33. See Chapter 2.
34. Article 15.
35. *Proceedings*, No. 45, Col. 1405.
36. By the time the Chapter came before the Assembly again on 5 June, the report of the Committee had somehow been mislaid and was not available to Members. Crabbe complained bitterly to the Speaker at the treatment his Committee had received, alleging not only that the report had been delayed at the printer but also 'by a further conflict here and there'. But time was now running short, the political season was on, Dr. Busia's supporters were gathering closer around him, and the Human Rights provisions were passed with relatively few changes.

37. *Proceedings*, No. 21, Col. 929.
38. He was able (Article 53) to appoint up to 12 members out of up to 16, and could terminate these appointments in his discretion in consultation with the Council of State. On the other hand, the likelihood of his being able to control the opinions of ex-Presidents, Prime-Ministers and the like who sat in the Council as of right was clearly limited.
39. Article 46 of Draft.
40. If his nominee in this ballot was not elected Prime Minister, the Assembly was given a week to choose a Prime Minister itself, failing which the President dissolved Parliament. (Article 60 of the Constitution.) In the Draft, the President was to nominate candidates for election by the Assembly as Prime Minister; and only if three successive candidates failed to obtain a majority was the Assembly left to its own devices to elect one of its members without any further proposal from the President.
41. In the Constitution, as in the Draft, the President was unable to withhold his assent from Bills of a financial nature.
42. *Proceedings*, No. 59, Col. 1924.
43. Parts 1 and 2 of the Report of the *Commission of Inquiry into Electoral and Local Government Reform* (Accra, 1967), p. 22.
44. *Proceedings*, No. 76, Cols. 2627–2638.
45. It arose because the wording of 71(2)(b)(ii) which was agreed between Jones Ofori-Atta and the Special Parliamentary Draftsman, V. C. R. A. C. Crabbe, had still fewer loopholes than that contained in Ofori-Atta's own motion introduced earlier from the floor of the House. The new wording also differed from that agreed to by the Drafting Committee. The matter was raised in the House by representatives of the latter committee, and settled by a vote in favour of Jones Ofori-Atta. It was raised again by the Speaker, on his own initiative, but was dropped when he ruled against himself after a bitter dispute over the propriety of his bringing it back to the house. Ofori-Atta's original wording made the unlawful acquisition of assets the *grounds* on which a Commission of Enquiry could find a person 'incompetent to hold public office' unlike the final wording which read: 'No person shall be qualified to be a member of the Assembly who ... has been adjudged or otherwise declared by the report of a Commission of Enquiry to be incompetent to hold public office or that, while being a public officer, he acquired assets unlawfully, or defrauded the state of ...'
46. *Proceedings*, No. 77, Col. 2668.
47. *Proceedings*, No. 78, Col. 2723. A vote taken the previous day on the motion that 72(2)(b)(ii) be excluded from the Constitution had produced less clearcut alignments.
48. *Proceedings*, No. 77, Cols. 2660–2662.
49. *Proceedings*, No. 78, Col. 2701.
50. The Judicial Secretary was named alongside the Chief Justice and the General Legal Council in the action brought by Quarshie-Idun and others relating to the refusal of rights of audience in the Courts in 1968.
51. Previously the Bar Association was not represented at all in the Judicial Council, while the two Counsel represented previously on the Rules of Court Committee would not necessarily have been Bar Association nominees, being under Draft 122(1)(c) nominated 'by the professional organisation recognised by the Chief Justice as representing the interests of the legal profession in Ghana'.
52. *Proceedings*, No. 10, Col. 433.
53. The provisions of the Draft had been more complicated, stipulating that traditional members be no *less* than half and up to sixteen out of twenty-one members.
54. See the criticisms of the Bill by a former member of the Constituent Assembly, Peter Adjetey, in the *Spokesman* (Accra) 9 March 1971. The features of the Bill

which seemed inimical to local government autonomy were the powers given to the Prime Minister to appoint executive Chairmen to head the District Councils, and to the Minister of Local Administration to take functions away from the Regional Councils as he saw fit or to dissolve or suspend Local and District Councils if he were satisfied that they were not performing their functions satisfactorily.

55 The party vote was as clearcut as that on 71(2)(b)(ii)—indeed more so, there being no P.P. abstentions. See the *Proceedings,* No. 97, Cols. 3368–3369.

56. *Proceedings,* No. 89, Col. 3093.

57 The provisions relating to the supremacy of the Constitution (Chapter One), forbidding the levying of taxes and the raising of armed forces without the authority of Parliament (Article 127 and 149) and the institution of Chieftaincy (Article 153).

58 *Proceedings,* No. 89, Col. 3036–7.

59. John Griffiths—to whom we are indebted for a number of useful comments on this and the preceding chapter—disagrees with us at this point, pointing out, for instance, that amendment of the U.S. Constitution is as rigid. On the other hand the U.S.A. is a Federation, and the difficulty of formal amendment is more than compensated for by judicial review of a very generally worded constitutional document. In contrast the Constitutional Commissioners in Ghana deliberately drafted an extremely complex, detailed and legalistic document with, as we say in the preceding Chapter, the explicit intention of reducing the scope for 'judicial amendment' of the Constitution.

60 *Proceedings*, No. 89, Col. 3084–5.

61 *Proceedings*, No. 97, Col. 3390.

62. As in the Sallah case.

63 *Proceedings*, No. 10 Col. 396.

CHAPTER 5

THE WORK OF THE ELECTORAL COMMISSION

V. C. R. A. C. Crabbe

One immediate result of the Constitutional Commission and the Electoral Commission of Enquiry was the publication on 29 January 1968 of the Interim Electoral Commission Decree (no. 221) under which an 'Interim Electoral Commissioner' was appointed on 3 April. He was given responsibility for:

(a) the registration of electors, (b) the annual revision of the registers of such electors; (c) the conduct of all elections, including referenda and plebiscites; (d) the periodic delimitation of the boundaries of the constituencies; (e) the appointment and dismissal of registration, revising, and returning officers and their supporting staff. (He could delegate his functions in regard to these matters to such other officers as he thought fit); (f) the issue of such procedural rules and regulations for the facilitation of the registration of electors and the fair conduct of elections; (g) the proper storage and use of all election materials; (h) the registration of political parties and their symbols; (i) the division of electoral districts into wards and sub-wards; (j) the rejection of the nomination paper of candidates; (k) declaring whether or not a candidate has been duly elected to the proper chamber; and (l) such other functions as may be prescribed by regulations under this Decree.

The first task was to set up the Commission, and this was done on 1 June 1968.

REGISTRATION

The Constitution approved by the Constituent Assembly conferred the right to vote on every citizen not under 21 years of age who was of sound mind, and established an Electoral Commission for the demarcation of constituency boundaries not only for elections to the National Assembly but for local and district councils. It provided that the Electoral Commissioner should be subject only to the Constitution, and not to any other person or authority. It also provided that the appointment of officers and other employees of the staff of the Electoral Commission should be made by the Commissioner in consultation with the Public Services Commission.

The country was divided into as many constituencies as there were to be members in the National Assembly, in such a manner as the Electoral Commission prescribed, the number varying from 140 to 150.

Part II of the First Schedule to the Constitution provided that elections must be held within thirty days of the coming into force of the Constitution: sub-section (3) declared that elections should be held in 140 constituencies in accordance with the regulations made by the Commissioner with the approval of the N.L.C.

The Commissioner then had to consider objections raised by the public to the boundaries of the parliamentary constituencies. More than 100 memoranda were received. The Commissioner heard evidence from petitioners, not as an innovation but as part of a long-established electoral procedure. Under the Independence Constitution of 1957 and the Electoral Provisions Act of 1965, the report of a Delimitation Commission had to be published, and the views of the public invited thereon within three months of publication: the Commission was then allowed a further statutory period of six months within which to determine the representations received. Now, in 1968, the whole process of receiving and determining objections to constituency boundaries was completed within four instead of six months. By 30 July the Commissioner had heard all the objections to the boundaries of certain constituencies in the Greater Accra area and in the Central, Western, the Volta, and Eastern regions. Early in August, representations for the reconstitution of some constituencies in the Northern, Upper, Ashanti, and Brong Ahafo Regions were considered and dealt with, and the instrument finally determining the boundaries of all the 140 constituencies in the country was published on 31 August 1968.[1]

The problems involved in the registration of voters were made worse by a general suspicion of the machinery of elections arising from the malpractices of the Nkrumah period. The changes in procedure suggested by the Electoral Commission also presented difficulties. In the past, one could send a list of names of friends and relations to a registration officer for them to be enrolled: now, however, prospective voters were required not only to appear before a registration officer in person but to complete an application form in his presence. (Where an applicant, for one reason or another, could not actually complete the form himself, the registration officer had to do so on his instructions.) After the entries had been completed, the applicant signed or made his mark and affixed his thumb print to the form. To explain this procedure to the public, and to arouse interest in it, an intensive publicity campaign was mounted throughout the country. A mock registration was organised in August—a dummy register of voters having been prepared—and on 1 September 1968 registration began in the administrative areas of Accra-Tema City Council, Cape Coast, Kumasi, Tarkwa-Aboso, and Sekondi-Takoradi.

The first results were not at all discouraging, rising very steeply after a slow early start. In the Tarkwa-Aboso constituency, for example,

2,300 persons had been registered by 13 September 1968: within two days the number had increased to 3,886. In the Takoradi constituency, 1,495 persons had registered by the same date and 4,253 by the 15th, an increase of nearly 200 per cent. Like an avalanche, registration gathered its own momentum. In Sekondi about 1,500 had registered by 13 September; by the 18th the total was 2,983. In the Accra-Tema area and in Kumasi the number actually doubled within a few days. The final count showed that out of the country's estimated potential electorate of 3.2 m. about 2.4 m. had registered. The overall picture was as follows:

Registration of Voters

1 September 1968—6 January 1969

	Potential	Actual	%
Ashanti	479,830	401,590	83.7
Brong Ahafo	252,280	221,451	87.78
Central Region	376,044	270,927	72.05
Eastern Region	516,290	343,600	66.55
Western Region	283,940	224,542	79.01
Northern Region	281,530	198,586	70.17
Upper Region	395,960	302,807	76.47
Volta Region	355,320	226,304	63.60
Greater Accra	219,000	172,858	79.92
	3,160,194	2,362,665	75.76

These figures showed that those who talk about illiterates in Ghana should be careful not to imply that they do not know what is happening. They may be unlettered, but they are not devoid of wisdom. If anything, more sense abounds in the rural than in the urban areas: certainly, the difficulties encountered were mainly with the urban educated, not with the village illiterates. The latter easily understood the need to register, and made the task of the registration officer that much simpler.

The procedure was usually as follows. After the Odikro or headman of a village had been told about registration, he announced a day on which villagers should not work on their farms, beat the gong-gong, and the villagers came and were registered. Few under 21 attempted to enroll; among the small number who did, it was usually because some of them did not know their ages. There were no stories of registration forms being sold in the rural areas, in marked contrast with the urban areas where attempts were made to buy and sell the forms,[2] and where a number under 21 tried to register by all kinds of devices, using lipstick, wigs and make-up to look older. Some potential electors were disenchanted with politics and did not bother to register: but only in the Volta Region was there a general indifference to, and scepticism about, party politics: many looked upon the registration half-heartedly, and the final figures showed that out of 355,320 potential voters, only 226,304 registered. Even so, the highest percentage in the region was recorded by West Dayi, a rural area where, out of 26,190 potential votes, 21,836—83.38 per cent—registered. Keta—the 'metropolis' of the Volta Region, although Ho is the regional capital—registered only 53.62 per cent: 12,419 out of 23,160 potential voters. These figures alone show that the rural areas were more alive politically than the towns.

THE CONSTITUENT ASSEMBLY

Under sub-rule (2) of the Constituent Assembly Elections and Nomination Rules, the Interim Electoral Commissioner appointed Thursday 28 November 1968 for the election of representatives of the six Committees of Management of the Accra-Tema City Council, Kumasi City, Sekondi-Takoradi City, Cape Coast Municipal, Tamale Municipal, and Koforidua Municipal Council. In addition, rule 1 provided that each of the Committees of Management of the 43 existing local and urban Councils should constitute an electoral college for the election of a representative to the Assembly not later than 16 December 1968. Each member of the college was entitled to nominate a candidate of his choice who need not necessarily be a member of the Committee; the nominee had of course to consent to his nomination, and two other members of the Committee of Management had to support it. For such elections, one ballot box was used, placed in the full view of the members of the electoral college who voted by putting a cross against the name of the candidates of his choice. The counting of the votes was conducted in the presence of the members of the college and could be verified. Where two candidates obtained an equal number of votes, there was a recount; if the tie was confirmed, another ballot was held there and then for the two candidates. The chairman of the Regional and District Committee of Administration was given a casting vote if, and only if, the second ballot also resulted in a tie.

The Decree also made provision for various identifiable groups, such as the Houses of Chiefs, farmers' organisations, the lawyers, doctors, fishermen, market women, Christian and Muslim groups, students' organisations, and the civil service to elect 91 members to represent them in the Constituent Assembly. (To these 140 elected members—6 plus 43 plus 91—were added 10 persons appointed by the N.L.C. itself).[3] The first day of the meeting of market women at the Legion Hall in Accra was rowdy, and the Regional Administrative Officer was compelled to call in the help of the Commissioner who immediately cancelled the elections for that day. At the next meeting, the police ensured that all who were not market women were kept out of the premises: the elections were then very orderly, as indeed they were throughout the Regions.

THE LIFTING OF THE BAN ON PARTIES

On 28 April 1969 the Political Parties Decree was published, to come into effect on 1 May. It provided that the Electoral Commissioner should be the Registrar of political parties with the duty of registering and supervising (as a 'remote control') their activities. The decree prohibited the formation of any party on a discriminatory basis, in the sense that at least three of the founding members had ordinarily to be either resident, or registered, as voters in each of the Regions; and not more than six of the founding members could belong to any one particular community. Parties were forbidden to use identifying symbols or names which resembled those of a previously registered party, power being given to the Registrar to refuse registration if the law was not complied with or if the purposes of the party were unlawful. Appeal lay to the High Court. Political parties were also required to keep records for purposes of audit, so that all might know how they got their funds and how they used them, the Registrar being empowered to ask a particular party to furnish him with any information, with attendant penalties for refusal. Aliens were not only ineligible to be members of a party but were forbidden to contribute to its funds. Parties were also not allowed to use 'flags, standards, banners or ensigns', the use of such devices in the past having been a fertile source of tumult.

The day after the publication of the Decree, representatives of over twenty organisations came to the offices of the Commission. They included the All People's Party, the Black Power Party, the People's Popular Party, the All People's Congress, the Progress Party, the National Alliance of Liberals, the National Reconstruction Party, the Ghana Democratic Party, the Labour Party, the Ghana Workers' Party, the Ghana Youth Party, the People's Action Party, the Nationalist Party, the Radical Alliance Party, the Liberty Party, and the Jehova Party. Of those which collected the necessary forms, only nine applied for registration—the Popular Party, the All People's Congress, the Progress Party, N.A.L., P.A.P., the Nationalist Party, the Republican Party, the All People's Party and the G.D.P. On 6 June 1969 the N.L.C., acting under the Prohibited Organisations Decree 1969, banned the People's Popular Party. The Republican Party informed the Registrar in July that it had formed a merger with the All People's Party under a new name—All People's Republican Party; later the Nationalist Party and the G.D.P. also came together to form the United Nationalist Party.

On 25 June 1969 the Commissioner met each of the party leaders individually, telling them the date he had decided upon for the general election. The reactions of the leaders varied. Gbedemah was not sure whether the country was ready for elections on the date suggested; Busia was prepared for elections, since he thought his party had covered much of the ground, but he too complained that the authorities had not given them much time. Modesto Apaloo (U.N.P.) argued that there were still potential voters who should be registered and that the elections ought to be postponed until the Commissioner had secured the use of photomatic machines for the issue of identity cards. Similar arguments were used by the other parties. Before meeting the leaders, however, the Commissioner had arranged an interview with the Chairman of the N.L.C., Brigadier Afrifa, to see whether the government had changed its plans for the return to civilian rule by 30 September 1969. It was clear that there was no intention of changing the date, and the only problem therefore was that of choosing a particular day within the time available.

Regulation 1 of the Public Elections Regulations 1968 required the Interim Electoral Commissioner to issue a writ, whenever there was occasion to hold a public election, addressed to the Returning Officers of the constituencies in which it was to be held. The Commissioner had to specify the date and place for the nomination of candidates, and the day on which the poll should be taken—not less than 14, and not more than 30 days, after the nomination of candidates. Apart from these statutory requirements, the actual circumstances of 1969 made it necessary that the Commissioner should take into consideration the date on which the Constituent Assembly was likely to conclude its deliberations on a new Constitution, the Chairman of the Business Committee having announced that the Assembly would end its deliberations within the first week of July 1969.[4] The other consideration was the time required for the election of a President of the Republic,[5] the appointment of a Prime Minister, and the formation of a Council of State and Cabinet. None of these could be conceivably concluded earlier than three weeks after a general election. After careful consideration, therefore, the Commissioner came to the conclusion that the most suitable date for the election was 29 August 1969; the writs for the election were issued to all Returning Officers on 9 July. Candidates were required to deliver their nomination papers in quadruplicate to the Returning Officers for their constituencies between 8 a.m. and 12 p.m. on 1 August 1969. And it was announced that voting would take place between 7.00 a.m. and 5.00 p.m. on 29 August.[6]

The Commissioner now warned political parties that, with the announcement of the date for the general election, Part 2 of the Representation of the People Decree 1968, relating to election offences, had come into force. It was an offence to forge or fraudulently destroy a ballot paper, or to supply a ballot paper to any person without due authority. The sale of ballot papers was prohibited, and it was an offence for a person to vote when he was not entitled to or to vote more than once. There were also severe penalties for impersonation, bribery, treating, and undue influence. Similarly the use of force, violence or restraint to induce or compel any person to vote, or refrain from voting, constituted an offence. Finally, since the Political Parties Decree conferred authority on the Registrar to arrange for party accounts to be audited, the Commissioner asked the parties to declare (by 15 July 1969) all properties and funds held by them and the source of such funds. The request was made so that the Auditor-General might institute (on behalf of the Commissioner) whatever enquiries were thought necessary into the financial transactions of a political party, particularly for the purpose of enforcing the provisions of the Decree which forbade parties to receive financial contributions from foreign companies or from aliens. Such at least was the law.

THE ELECTION

The prime purpose of the 1969 election was to achieve a democratically-elected civilian government to which the N.L.C. could hand over the administration of the country. The method of voting differed from earlier contests in the sense that there was now a legal requirement that ballot papers should contain the name, and the symbol or colour, of a particular candidate and a serial number. In order to facilitate the nomination procedure, the Commissioner authorised returning officers to allot the symbols to the candidate officially sponsored by the party executives. (There were also a number of symbols for use by independent candidates.) But before this stage was reached there was the practical problem of getting the papers printed. Strict security measures were taken, the actual printing being done in two phases. The special ballot papers (together with the special tendered papers) were printed first, for the 'little election' on 25 August when the army, police, and the officials, who would be on duty on election day, cast their votes. The general ballot papers, and the tendered papers, for the main election on 29 August were then printed. The whole process took ten days, each fully occupied with the printing and binding of the books of papers.

In all, 10,125,800 general ballot papers, and 35,400 tendered papers were printed, a total of 10,161,200, each in the colours of the symbol used by the candidate and bearing his name. As the papers came off the press they were billed, labelled, boxed, and despatched under special transport arrangements. The object was to deliver the ballot papers as they became available, but it was also deliberate policy to send them to their particular areas at the last moment. At every stage the ballot papers were under armed guard, and representatives of the political parties were given an opportunity to sign their names on the seals of the strong rooms where the papers were kept, and to keep vigil if they wished—a precaution which some of the party agents observed. It was significant that no complaints were made that ballot papers had got into wrong hands before the actual day of the election.

The Constitutional Commission considered various methods of voting procedure and, taking into consideration the experience of previous elections in Ghana and in neighbouring states, tried to devise a means whereby the abuses of the past could be reduced to a minimum. The method adopted was as follows.

The name of every elector wishing to vote was checked against the register of voters. The polling assistant checked the voter's name, his house number, and other particulars, and asked as many questions (in English or a Ghanaian language) as was necessary to satisfy himself that the voter was the person whose name appeared in the register. The voter's number was then recorded on the counterfoil[7] of the ballot papers, and the papers bearing the symbol or colour of each of the candidates in the constituency were given to the voter after they had been stamped with the official mark. If there were, say, five candidates, the voter was issued with five different ballot papers, each bearing the symbol and name of one of the candidates. He was then given one of the special envelopes, went into another room or screened area where he selected the paper which carried the symbol of the candidate of his choice, folded the ballot paper, and put it into the envelope in such a way that it could not be seen by any other person. He then discarded the ballot papers he had rejected into a receptacle provided for them. As he came out from the screened area, the envelope was touched by an official to ensure that it did not contain more than one ballot paper, and the voter dropped the envelope into the single box in the full view of the public. One should add that, before the voter was issued with a ballot paper, the base of his left thumb nail was marked with indelible ink —guaranteed to last at least two weeks—and a cross was placed on the lower part of the left palm. In addition, before he left the polling station his right thumb-print was taken. Over and above these precautions, every candidate had a polling agent whose duty it was to detect impersonation. He was expected to watch and see that the polling staff performed their duties properly, and to be able to confirm that no one interfered with the ballot boxes.

On 29 August, all the efforts of the Interim Electoral Commissioner, and everything he had said, were put to the test. A very early tour of polling stations in Accra and Tema gave hopes that all would be well, although by as early as 5 a.m. voters began to queue, and the numbers soon began to reach alarming proportions. The 'vote early campaign' had been too successful. The polling stations were not due to open till 7 a.m. yet by 6.30 a very great number of voters had turned up. A few presiding officers were late in opening their polling stations; some did not arrive until very late, although they were expected to be at their posts at 6.45 a.m. to open the voting at 7 promptly. And in one constituency a returning officer could not be traced, although supporting staff were ready.

People became impatient, but fortunately did not lose their tempers. The Commissioner personally opened the voting at two polling stations in the Osu Klotey constituency of Accra; when he returned to his office, crowds had gathered to know why some presiding officers had not been punctual, and cries of sabotage were heard. By about 8 a.m. the situation in some polling stations was still serious. Although the Commissioner organised teams from the staff of the Electoral Commission, some stations did not open until 10 a.m. and they were ordered to extend their voting period by the number of hours by which they were late. Then other difficulties arose. Those who thought they had registered, but had not checked the provisional or final registers when they were exhibited, flocked to the office to ask why they could not vote. Fortunately some of these problems had been anticipated, and officers of the Commission were on hand to try and trace on a master register those who could not find their names in the registers at the polling stations. Thus order was eventually rescued from near disorder.

The reports from outside Accra were very encouraging. Voting was proceeding in a calm manner, there had been no incidents. By 1 p.m. even the queues in Accra were becoming shorter as people continued to vote. At some polling stations voting was complete by as early as 3.30 p.m., but by law such polling stations remained open and the counting of votes started after 5 p.m. At 2 p.m. it was reported that certain stations in Accra were short of ballot papers. The Commissioner travelled to Tema for more—only to find that when the papers were ready, and an army major had gone round to distribute them, the returning officers of the various polling stations told him that there were sufficient ballot papers for all their candidates. There were other incidents of a somewhat bizarre character. One story was that in a polling station in Accra a supporter of a particular party, having collected her ballot papers and envelope, went into the screened compartment singing the slogan of her party, dropped all the ballots (including the envelope) into the receptacle containing the rejected papers, and then started stirring the mixture with her hands, proclaiming the victory of her candidate.

Throughout polling day the police and the military were very little in evidence. This was deliberate. By an agreed plan between the Commissioner, the army, and the police authorities, certain precise measures had been taken to deal with any situation that would call for the use of security forces. There were about 8,000 polling stations, and it would have required at least 32,000 policemen and soldiers to man them effectively. As this would have been too much for the police and the army, other steps were taken: regular patrols were carried out, the bulk of the security forces standing by ready to deal with any situation that might arise. In the event, no incident occurred.

At each polling station, the votes were counted under the personal supervision of the presiding officer who then announced the results. Before he did so, the candidates (or their representatives) and their polling agents had to sign a declaration showing the total number of registered voters allotted to the polling station and the number of votes cast in favour of each candidate. The presiding officer put all the used papers back into the ballot box, which was locked and sealed so as to prevent the introduction of additional papers. The boxes were then sent, under police or army escort, to the returning officer at the counting centre, accompanied by representatives of the candidates. At the centre a ballot box was opened only when the previous one had been dealt with and its contents ascertained. After the counting of a box had been completed the contents were checked against the statement of the poll, and then put in an envelope, the envelopes being marked with the name of the candidates, the polling division code, and the polling station number. Tendered ballot papers were not counted. Each candidate was permitted to appoint not more than three counting agents. Then, as soon as the votes had been counted and checked, the returning oqcer announced the results, informing the Electoral Commissioner by telegraph or telephone or police wireless message.

An operations room had been set up in Accra and in all the regional centres to collate the results of the poll, and to communicate them to the press, radio, television and the more than 300 foreign correspondents who were covering the elections. A giant floodlit score board was mounted on a scaffolding near the review arch in Black Star Square, Accra, visible to the thousands of people who crowded the stands of the square. It was connected to the operations room, and as the results trickled in they were given to attendants who indicated them in florescent chalk on the scoreboard to the cheering and applause of the crowds. The police and the Workers' Brigade bands provided music, the Bottling Department of the Ghana National Trading Corporation opened beer gardens for the sale of refreshments to the public: nothing was left undone to improve the occasion!

The returns started coming in from about 10.25 p.m. By the early hours of Saturday morning (30 August) the results were widely known. The staff of the Commission began to hope for a long rest, but it was to be a brief hope. On 4 September a statement on behalf of 'the minority parties in the elections'—N.A.L., U.N.P., and P.A.P.— was read at a press conference. The statement regretted that events had taken place such as to 'impugn the conduct of the elections in the most serious manner, and raise questions as to whether the results truly reflect the collective will of the people of Ghana'.

It was alleged that the voting was not secret, since 'by an officially ap- proved device it was possible for anyone in authority to find out, to know exactly how every citizen of this country voted'. The device was said to be a simple one. 'Each voter had his registration number written on all the ballot papers issued to him, so that by checking the ballot papers placed in the boxes against the voters' register it would be pos- sible to find out who voted for what party.' Supporters of what were now the minority parties (it was argued) believed that their votes could be detected, and were therefore frightened either into casting their votes in another direction or into not voting.

It was also claimed that there was evidence of the involvement of the Electoral Commission with the Progress Party to the extent that the Commission had been used to procure electioneering equipment for Busia's party, and that most of the returning officers, in many of the areas where the results were overwhelmingly in favour of Progress, had been officers of the Centre for Civic Education whose chairman, until the eve of the elections, had been the leader of Progress. It was alleged, too, that a very large number of envelopes were ordered and collected under no security measures, the result being that they came into 'the hands of a party determined to win the elections' and that a much larger number than was 'necessary of tendered ballot papers were printed which were used for other purposes than they were intended for'. Since, therefore, the situation negated the cardinal principle of secret ballot, it was not fair 'to allow such a situation to remain unchallenged or un- corrected for the five year term of parliament'.

The minority parties demanded that the majority party:

> at the earliest opportunity and as a matter of serious national importance should give the nation a chance to reaffirm its will in a general election based on a new voters' register to be prepared by a national commission on elec- tions and on fresh rules to be approved by parliament which shall ensure that there can be no managing of the procedures and events of registration, balloting and counting of votes. We demand, at whatever price it will be procured, the use of the photomatic equipment for identification of voters on the register, which the nation was promised for this election, but which

was dropped for the flimsy excuse given the country. Ghana's future is too much at stake for anyone to plead financial stringency for this purpose.

They also claimed that

if a new registration is honestly done, if preparations for a new election are made by an impartial body unlikely to be influenced in any form, if voting is free and secret, without threats or promises of perquisites or rewards, if counting is done strictly according to a code of discipline and a high sense of public behaviour, we have no doubt that a different pattern will emerge which will confirm our faith in our people.

The Commissioner had made it clear on his appointment that he would not engage in controversy, particularly with political parties and their leaders: but the allegations against him personally, and against the Electoral Commission, were such that it became necessary for him to enter the arena of political controversy, and to meet the authors of the statement on their cherished ground of a press conference, at which the following refutations were made.

The complaint that the principle of secrecy had not been observed was based on the assumption that the serial numbers of voters on the register were entered on the ballot papers which 'were placed in the ballot boxes'. It was pointed out that this was incorrect. The serial numbers were entered only on the counterfoils of the used ballot papers, a practice which had been part and parcel of the voting system of Ghana since the introduction of free and democratic elections under the Guggisberg Constitution of 1925. The purpose was quite simple—to enable the courts to determine which candidate had won, should a petition be filed challenging the validity of the election on the ground of impersonation and allied malpractices. Under regulation 34 of the Public Elections Regulations 1968, the counterfoils of the used ballot papers (and the marked copies of the registers used for the poll) had to be put into bags sealed by the returning officer. These bags were preserved for twelve months and then destroyed. Neither the Electoral Commissioner, nor any member of his staff, had the right to open the bag. The only authority which was competent to do so was the High Court of Justice on an election petition.

The charge that the Electoral Commission machinery was involved with the Progress Party was also rebutted. The Commission had followed normal government practice, buses and generators all being purchased for it by the Ghana Supply Commission. The complaint that the returning officers in many of the areas were once officers of the Centre for Civic Education was similarly rejected. Of the 140 returning officers, 4 were principals of training colleges, 34 were local authority employees, 101 were established civil servants of senior grade, and one was an employee of the state Cocoa Marketing Board. None was on the staff of the Centre for Civic Education.

The fourth allegation, that large numbers of envelopes for the elections were ordered and collected without proper security measures, was dismissed as untrue: 3,474,500 envelopes, not 9 m. were ordered. The envelopes used for the election were not themselves ballot papers, and it is difficult to see how the printing of such envelopes could have influenced the outcome of the elections. The truth of the matter is that only 2.7 m. were used of the under $3\frac{1}{2}$ m. actually manufactured, the rest being kept in reserve for any future bye-election.

The additional complaint that large numbers of tendered ballot papers were printed, and then used for illegal purposes, was dismissed on the ground that such papers were issued only to voters who had presented themselves at polling stations and had found that some other person had already voted under their name.[8] They were not counted, and could not therefore have had any effect on the results. (Tendered ballots were put into envelopes marked with the name of a candidate whom the voter wanted.) The importance of the tendered ballot was that it enabled the court, in the event of an election petition, to determine whether the extent of impersonation, or similar malpractice, had nullified the election. No one, in 1969, brought to the notice of the Electoral Commissioner any instance of a constituency where there was so large a number of tendered ballot papers as to render the election unfair.[9] It is true that the Commissioner was told that one political party had about 20 tendered ballot papers in its possession. The *Evening Standard* also published, on 5 September, a picture of a tendered ballot paper. But who was to blame? Under sub-paragraph 1(g) of paragraph 11 of the *Representation of the People Decree 1968*, any person who (without authority) is found in possession of a ballot paper outside a polling station commits an offence and is liable to imprisonment for a term up to five years.[10] It appeared to the Commission, therefore, that there was distinct prima facie evidence of a criminal offence having been committed, and the matter was referred to the Attorney-General and the police for appropriate action.

To allegations that the names of voters in the registers were duplicated, and that the registers contained the names of deceased persons, the Commissioner replied simply that the registers of voters had been publicly exhibited, and revising officers had been appointed to adjudicate upon such issues. In addition, the registers of voters had been given free of charge to all political parties over a month before the election. Death, and the remarkable propensity of many Ghanaians to move from one part of the country to another, as well as the similarity of names, are natural occurrences which should not have been misconstrued to imply deliberate errors in the registers. A particular complaint was that the number of registered voters in the Mion-Nanton constituency was 4,154 whilst the total number of votes recorded at the election was 4,564. The number of electors in Mion-Nanton was actually 7,898—a fact which could have been verified quite simply by inspection of the master copies of the register authenticated by the signature of the revising officer. And, indeed, the election in the constituency was won by a candidate sponsored by the N.A.L.—one of the parties which made the allegations.

ENVOI

The soldiers and police on the National Liberation Council never for one moment sought to control the Interim Electoral Commissioner; nor did any member of the Council even attempt to interfere with him in the discharge of his duties. The N.L.C. gave the Commissioner a free hand, placing an absolute faith in the impartiality and integrity of the Commission and according its officers great respect.

Notes

1. *The Representation of the People* (*Constituences*) *Instrument, 1968.*
2. The Commission learnt that there were various motives for buying the registration forms. As a means of identifying the voter, they could be used for impersonation (so it was thought). They were also bought to decrease the potential number of supporters of one's opponents. As much as N₵4–5 was offered for a form. Hence the elaborate precautions for taking the thumbprints of voters on polling day.
3. See Chapter 3.
4. The Assembly did not complete its work until 22 August 1969. The election took place a week later.
5. The First Schedule to the constitution provided for the election of the President after all members of the Presidential Commission had ceased to hold office.
6. There were 'special voters', especially members of the armed forces and the public service, who voted four days before the main election.
7. Gbedemah, at a press conference soon after the general election, condemned this practice.
8. One lesson the Commissioner was surprised to learn was that most of the leaders of the political parties and a very large number of the candidates who stood for election did not acquaint themselves with the provisions of the electoral law. They tried to observe what they *thought* was the law.
9. At the time of writing there were two election petitions still pending. In the case of one of them, the Court of Appeal sitting as the Supreme Court declared the seat of the victorious candidate vacant on the ground that he was disqualified. A bye-election was held and the person who had presented the petition stood again for election. He lost.
10. This was a serious offence which could disqualify a person under art. 71 of the Constitution.

CHAPTER 6

THE 1969 ELECTION

Yaw Twumasi

As soon as it became clear that the August elections had resulted in an overwhelming victory for the Progress Party, Busia was called upon to form a government, and his principal opponents, the National Alliance of Liberals, constituted the main Opposition in the new parliament. In human terms, the elections resulted in a dramatic reversal of political fortunes. Those detained under Nkrumah, such as R. R. Amponsah, W. E. Ofori Attah, Victor Owusu, Kwesi Lamptey and S. D. Dombo, became Ministers,[1] while former Ministers such as Gbedemah and C. T. Nylander became members of the Opposition. Such a reversal of the roles of the pre-coup *dramatis personnae* was remarkable in itself, but the elections also altered for a time the careers of many young middle-class intellectuals who, even in their most Utopian dreams, had not thought of a political career under the Nkrumah regime. Five political parties, out of a total of more than twenty which had emerged by 1 May 1969, participated in the elections after being registered by the Electoral Commissioner: the Progress Party, the National Alliance of Liberals, the United Nationalist Party, the People's Action Party, and the All People's Republican Party; of these, only P.P. and N.A.L. were of major significance.[2]

In statistical terms, 63.5 per cent of those registered actually voted. Of the total votes cast, the P.P. obtained 58.68 per cent, N.A.L. 30.44 per cent, U.N.P. 3.8 per cent, P.A.P. 3.43 per cent, A.P.R.P. 1.83 per cent and Independents 1.82 per cent. Two candidates, one N.A. L. and the other P.P., were elected unopposed, and each of the major parties contested 138 seats. As described by the Electoral Commissioner in the previous chapter, the election was organised on the basis of universal adult suffrage in 140 single-member constituencies throughout the nine regions into which the country was divided; and of the 140 seats, the P.P. won 105 or 75 per cent, N.A.L. 29 or 20.71 per cent, and the minor parties 6 or 4.29 per cent. The evidence may be tabulated as shown in Table I.

The elections were conducted in a fashion derived from the classic, conventional British model, familiar in Ghana since 1954, though the precise manner of voting (as explained) was changed. Prominently displayed at each polling station were the photographs and symbols of all the candidates seeking election in the constituency, so that those who could not read were not handicapped; indeed, an essential feature of the latter stages of party campaigning consisted of mimed explanations, in various vernaculars, of the voting procedure and party symbols. Party manifestoes hardly raised any passionate hopes about a radical change of the political and economic world of Ghanaians; but what the manifestoes failed to do, the party symbols sought to achieve by displaying a variety of millenarian images. P.P.'s symbol was a red sun rising from black clouds on a white ground; for N.A.L. it was the full morning sun with nine jagged rays in red over a gold background; U.N.P.'s symbol was the broom and corn on a white background with green borders; P.A.P.'s a hand holding a blazing torch in red, black and white, and A.P.R.P.'s a torch crossed by a hoe and oar, all three in gold against a black background. At political rallies, various leaders impressed upon their audiences that their party labels symbolised 'a profound and total rejection of the present evil world, and a passionate longing for another and better one'.[3] To the P.P. a better world was emerging from an age of darkness and oppression; N.A.L.'s morning sun pictured the birth of a new era; and the U.N.P. told its supporters that the broom was to sweep clean the Augean stables of the Nkrumah era, the corn symbolising a new age of plenty and prosperity; for the P.A.P., too, the blazing torch heralded a brave new world. The various party mottoes, on the other hand, put the emphasis more on each party's perception of the most important political virtue: for P.P. it was *Progress in Unity, Liberty and Justice*; for N.A.L. *With Humility and Loyalty We Serve Our Nation*; for U.N.P. *One Country, One People, One Destiny*; for P.A.P. *Action Now*; and for the A.P.R.P.: *Fair Play*.

The one fact common to all the political parties was the cautious way in which they sought to avoid in their manifestoes any vision of a future Ghanaian society which would, in any real sense, conflict with that of

TABLE I

Party	Votes	%	Seats	%
P.P.	876,378	58.68	105	75
N.A.L.	454,646	30.44	29	20.71
Others	162,347	10.88	6	4.29
	1,493,371	100.00	140	100.00

the National Liberation Council. There was nothing which could be used as evidence for distinguishing one party from another, nor did any of the programmes threaten in any serious way the established interests of a substantial class or social group in the country. Indeed, they were all remarkably similar: they emphasised the need for a rural ren-naisance, for promoting and encouraging Ghanaian business enter-prise, and the importance of such commonplace goals as building more roads and hospitals, overhauling food marketing systems, expanding educational opportunities, and creating a favourable climate for foreign investment.[4] This very general appeal was perhaps a necessary response to the limits—ideological as well as legal—imposed by the ruling N.L.C. which had already made its intentions clear: 'to establish in Ghana a strong and progressive welfare society' in which there would be four major divisions of the economy: a private sector, a joint private/government sector, a government sector, and a cooperative sec-tor, '. . . the private sector remaining the largest . . . in terms of number of persons engaged and gross output'.[5] This rejection of the state in-terventionism of the pre-coup period constituted one of the limiting con-ditions imposed by the N.L.C. under whose auspices the elections were held. The issue in the elections, therefore, was primarily about who was best qualified on past political experience to exercise power, and only secondarily was the question asked as to what particular interests those who joined together were seeking to promote.

Table II (below) describes the regional and ethnic basis of the parties.[6] The Table at the end of this chapter provides a detailed portrait.[7] From these results we can obtain a national picture of the outcome of the elec-tion which has remarkably clear lines. First, there is the predominantly Akan basis of the P.P.'s victory, and the heavy electoral support given by the Volta Region to N.A.L. The P.P. won all the seats in the Ashanti, Brong Ahafo and Central Regions. N.A.L. won fourteen out of sixteen seats in the Volta Region. The Akan-v-Ewe basis of the victory is thrown into higher relief if we take a closer look at the seats lost by N.A.L. in the (Ewe) Volta Region, and those lost by Progress in the Akan-dominated regions. In the Eastern Region, Progress won all the Akan seats and lost the four non-Akan—largely Krobo and Ga-Adangbe—seats of Ada, Krobo, Manya and Yilo-Osudoku. In the Volta Region, N.A.L. won all the seats except the Nkwanta and Krachi constituencies which are ethnically polyglot—although it also won the ethnically mixed Buem and Biakoye constituencies. In the Western Province, another Akan-based region, the P.P. lost the two Nzima seats to P.A.P. in the home area of Nkrumah, where an efficient electoral machinery organised by the former President's ex-security officers—who had suffered a good deal as a result of the coup—succeeded in opposing both the two dominant parties. The

Nzimas, it must be remarked, are Akans: but they actually preferred to vote for a party led by a northerner, Imoru Ayarna, who had been a former Ministerial Secretary of Agriculture in the 1951–54 Nkrumah administration.[8]

The Akan–Ewe basis of the P.P.–N.A.L. conflict may therefore be represented as follows:

TABLE II

	Ashanti	Brong-Ahafo	Central	Western	Eastern	Volta
	AKAN					EWE
P.P.	78%	85%	71%	53%	61%	18%
N.A.L.	17%	14%	19%	16%	34%	77%

The number of seats in each region, when correlated with ethnic and linguistic identities was as follows:

TABLE III

Region	Main Linguistic–Ethnic Group	P.P.	N.A.L.	Others	No. of Seats
Ashanti	Akan-Twi	22	0	0	22
Brong-Ahafo	Akan-Brong	13	0	0	13
Central Region	Akan-Fanti	15	0	0	15
Western Region	Nzima, Wassaw and Sefwi	10	0	3	13
Eastern Region	Akan & Adangbe	18	4	0	22
Volta Region	Ewe	2	14	0	16
Upper Region	Non Akan	13	3	0	16
Northern Region	Non Akan	9	5	0	14
Accra-Tema Region	Ga	3	3	3	9
Total		105	29	6	140

There was some basis, therefore, for the assumption that 'tribalism' was a factor in the outcome of the elections—an assumption which was already in danger of becoming a cliché even before there was any evidence to support it. We shall show later, however, that such a conclusion lacked a sufficient explanatory force.

The second clear picture from the results is that both the main parties did well in the Northern and Greater Accra Regions, inhabited mainly by non-Akans and non-Ewes, despite the challenge of the Ga-dominated U.N.P. in Accra, and despite the intensity of local conflict in the Northern Region. In the Upper Region, which is also a non-Akan,

TABLE IV

| Occupation | Party Candidates | | | |
	P.P.	N.A.L.	U.N.P.	Others
Accountant	1	1		1
Pharmacist/Druggist	2		1	
Clerk	5		2	7
Educated, rich and middle-level farmer	7	10	8	3
Businessman/Merchant	16	16	10	16
Barrister/Solicitor	22	21	12	8
Printer				1
Public Officer/Civil Servant	9	9	3	
Teacher/Tutor	16	17	13	10
Trader/Storekeeper	1	5	5	4
General & Timber Contractor		3		3
Cocoa Cooperative Secretary	3	1		
Politician	3	2	2	1
Medical Doctor	1	1	3	
Works Superintendent/Technician	2	2	2	1
University Lecturer/ Research Fellow	4	5		2
Trade Unionist	1	1	2	
Quantity & Chartered Surveyor	2			1
Chief	1			
Journalist	2	4		1
Sociologist	1	1		
Housewife				1
Letter Writer			1	1
Pastor				1
Dentist				1
Unemployed			1	2

Source: Ghana Gazettes 18th–25th August 1969, supplemented by personal interviews.

non-Ewe area, the vote for Progress was substantial but N.A.L. was able to win three seats. The P.P. also won over 80 per cent of the seats in the urbanised and cosmopolitan areas, although here too opposition to its appeal was by no means negligible.

Finally, the evidence is plain, from a number of representative constituencies, that the occupational background of the candidates of the two major parties was broadly similar. The evidence is set out in Table IV, in which the information was drawn from 99 of the 140 constituencies. Classification of parliamentary candidates into occupational categories occasionally presented a number of problems since there were several candidates who could be grouped under more than one category. R. A. Quarshie, for example, a senior civil servant for more than 18 years, retired from the Civil Service, and qualified later as a lawyer; he had hardly practised law before becoming the resident Director of the London-based Consolidated African Selection Trust, and when filing his nomination papers he described himself as an industrialist. The formula used in the Table was to classify such a person as a Civil Servant/Public Officer on the principle of his life-long career. In addition, at the time of the elections, local government was separate from the Civil Service, but Local Government Officers—Clerks of Council and Treasurers—were classified as Civil Servant/Public Officer in anticipation of the recommended integration of the two services. (For a similar classification of the 1969 Parliament, and its relation to the Constituent Assembly and the 1965 C.P.P. National Assembly, see Chapter 4, p. 121.) In the constituencies for which no specific data were available—they were mostly in the Northern and Upper Regions—the candidates were, in the main, primary school teachers, local government workers, and traders. The better educated, professional candidates for N.A.L. came mostly from the Volta and Central Regions, while the professional Progress Party candidates were distributed throughout the country, although concentrated in Ashanti, Brong-Ahafo, and the Western, Central and Eastern regions. This occupational distribution was in itself an index of the spread of educated talent, and it had serious implications for both parties in the nomination of the candidates, although that is not our concern at the moment.

What is clear from Table IV is that the most numerous professional and business groups of lawyers, teachers and businessmen were equally well represented in both major parties, an important point since it indicates the extent to which candidates rejected by one major party were ready to join another in order to gain election. Lawyers constituted the largest professional group: 21 per cent. Next came businessmen (16 per cent) and teachers (16 per cent). N.A.L., however, had a much higher percentage of middle-level traders and farmers. The predominance of lawyers and businessmen in both major parties shows clearly the advantage that persons of independent financial means have over others in a country where a majority of the educated élite works in the civil service and state corporations.

Judged solely by the quality of candidates, therefore, there was little to choose between the two main parties. Furthermore, both parties were led by politicians whose involvement in Ghanaian politics went back to 1951; and both appeared well-endowed with financial resources for the four-month campaign. Why then did the Progress Party win so handsomely?

The answer lies as much in the political past as in the immediate circumstances of the election, particularly in the way in which public opinion was generated between the post-coup period and the actual date of the election. That is, a historical perspective is needed, since it was, after all, a time when Ghanaians re-lived a large part of their immediate political past. In particular, we need to look at the 'electoral mobilisation'[9] of a number of groups which played a dominant part in the political history of the country.

We might start with a militant group of urban employees—the Railway and Harbour Workers Union whose history of political and industrial action went back to the early decades of this century. By 1950, at a time of demonstrative nationalism, the dominant role of the Railway Union in Ghanaian trade union history was well-established; it had taken part in the general strike of January that year, and through the action of leaders such as Turkson Ocran and Pobee Biney, it had hitched its wagon to the political fortunes of the C.P.P. By the end of the 1950s, however, the alliance with Nkrumah's party was under strain. Pobee Biney and Ocran had been expelled from the C.P.P. in 1953 for alleged Communist sympathies and affiliations. And in 1958 the C.P.P. Government passed the Industrial Relations Act, whereby the existing trade unions were reconstituted into sixteen national unions each of which, while enjoying 'complete autonomy in negotiations', was 'subject to an overall policy to be decided by the central T.U.C.'.[10] The Act was particularly resented by the unions not only because it bolstered the power and authority of the T.U.C. in relation to the constituent unions, but because it deprived them of their two main weapons—the right to strike and collective bargaining. Not unexpectedly, they resisted the application of the Act. And there came about the series of events culminating in the Sekondi-Takoradi strike of 1961, for which the immediate occasion was the Budget of that year when the C.P.P. Government not only levied a new purchase tax on a wide range of consumer goods but imposed a compulsory saving scheme under which all persons earning over £120 a year were forced to accept 5 per cent of their wages or salaries in the form of National Investment Bonds, drawing 4 per cent interest and redeemable after ten years. No corresponding attempt was, however, made to curb the acquisitive activities of the *nouveaux riches* of the party leadership.

The first organised protest came from the Sekondi-Takoradi branch of the 8,000 strong Railway and Harbours Workers' Union and was of considerable political significance, since it marked a division within the C.P.P., the left seeking to use the strike to increase their political ascendancy in the party hierarchy. The most important consequence for our purposes is that the United Party Opposition (as it then was) tried to use the occasion to widen its base. It failed in 1961 and a number of its leaders, together with several local trade unionists and market women who had supported the workers, were detained. In 1966, however, the workers in Sekondi-Takoradi, in a most uninhibited fashion, demonstrated in support of the N.L.C., blithely assuming that the overthrow of Nkrumah would usher in an economic millenium. Their hopes were not to be realised. In 1969, they were to go on strike again, and V. K. Quist, Chairman of the powerful Location Association in Sekondi, who had returned from exile after the coup, was again confined in custody by the N.L.C. which dealt with the dispute hardly less severely than the former party regime had done. But between 1966 and 1969, Lamptey, Scheck and Quist, using their former contacts and links with the workers, were busy mobilising them around old accumulated grievances. It is significant that the first rally of the Progress Party, after the ban on parties was lifted, was held at the Old Methodist School Park, Sekondi, on 18 May 1969. At this mass meeting, Busia reminded his audience that he was not only aware of the social and economic problems of Sekondi-Takoradi (he had been District Commissioner in charge of a Sociological Survey of the area in 1947–49) but had also sympathised with the workers, as evidenced by the support given by his colleagues during the 1961 strike. He promised to give the workers their proper rewards, and Lamptey and Scheck were cheered by the over 50,000 people who had defied a two-hour rainstorm to witness the launching of the party.

On 7 June, Gbedemah also launched an equally well-attended rally at the same port and railway town. He too promised to create 'right conditions for a happy understanding between workers and management through the improvement in the working conditions of all Ghanaians'.[11] But the electors of Sekondi-Takoradi must have listened to his speech with mixed feelings, for he had a history behind him which he was not allowed to forget. As a member of the three-man Presidential Commission which had handled the 1961 strike in its initial stages, he had ordered the imposition of a dusk to dawn curfew, declared a state of emergency in the town, and ordered the arrest of the market women and the workers' leaders. Admittedly, shortly afterwards, he had gone into exile; but the image of Gbedemah which the C.P.P. Government had tried to create was that of a 'bourgeois Minister', scared by the radical directions towards which government policies were turning and seeking, in desperation, to forge conspiratorial relations with the Opposition. Somewhat unjustifiably, therefore, he came out of the crisis, on his return to Ghana after the coup, with the worst of both worlds: out of favour with the N.L.C. Government and out-flanked by Lamptey, Quist, and others among Busia's associates who posed as the authentic spokesmen of the workers. His contacts in Sekondi-Takoradi were thin on the ground, and his party suffered in consequence. During the elections the poll in these two key towns was a little low: only 56 per cent of the registered voters in Sekondi, and about 60 per cent in Takoradi, voted; nevertheless, Kwesi Lamptey won easily, and the N.A.L. vote was less than half that for Progress in the two constituencies.

If the historical odds against Gbedemah and N.A.L. in places such as Sekondi-Takoradi were heavy, they were no less unfavourable in the rural, cocoa-farming communities. Displaced by the N.L.M. in the Ashanti cocoa constituencies between 1955 and 1957 the C.P.P. had re-established its grip after independence, and by the time of the first Republic in 1960 the United Ghana Farmers' Council was under party-appointed leaders whose lack of any firm base among the farming community was reflected in the frequency with which they commuted between world capitals. It was they who assured the government in 1959–60 that farmers would be willing to have 6/- withheld from the price paid by the C.M.B. for every 60 lbs. cocoa—that is, 16 per cent of the price; two seasons later, farmers too were asked to accept government bonds maturing in ten years in place of a further 10 per cent of the price. It was indeed the very heavy burden on the cocoa farmer[12] which had led to an attempt by the C.P.P. government to widen the base of taxation in the 1961 budget. Once again the former Opposition United Party had tried to build on the farmers' grievance. There were few open channels of expression through which discontent could be voiced during the final years of Nkrumah's rule, but the opposition did what it could to keep itself alive not only in Ashanti but in the south, especially in migrant farming areas. And these (illegal) attempts to provide an alternative appeal and party brought their reward after the coup. The U.G.F.C. was disbanded; in its place the Cooperative Marketing Council, and the Cooperative Alliance (both of which had been abolished under Nkrumah), were re-constituted; and early supporters of the co-operative movement, such as K. B. Ntim (Progress M.P. for Kade), George Oteng (Progress M.P. for Ahafo-Ano) and B. D. Addai came into their own again. Similarly, Gbedemah and N.A.L., by their links with the former party regime, were at a disadvantage. As in the case of Lamptey and Quist in relation to the railway workers, so for Ntim,

Oteng and others, in relation to the cocoa farmers, a new set of political circumstances provided new opportunities for political action. They appealed to the farmers for support through the co-operatives, and in doing so found not only a base for their own election success but a potent source of strength for Busia and Progress in the cocoa growing areas.

How did other sections of local society respond? There was an immense variety in the re-awakening of political life during the post-coup period, but perhaps the most notable response to the fall of the C.P.P. was a general reaction to the party's attempt to assert the superiority of the central government over local bodies, including the weakening of traditional authorities. The process had gone through many vicissitudes: but, by and large, the centre had gained power under Nkrumah at the expense of localities, and popular discontent had been ruthlessly and foolishly suppressed as evidence of disloyalty to the state. After the coup, the reaction expressed itself in the proliferation and revival of Town Improvement Societies, Regional Organisations, Youth Associations, Ex-detainee Associations, and urban groups of one kind and another. Cautiously avoiding any brush with the law (since the N.L.C. had banned political activities after the coup), these various groups publicly declared that their main objectives were social and economic. Each region complained of neglect; and they needed activist groups to call the attention of the N.L.C. to their needs—bodies like the Volta Region Economic Association, The Northern Youth Association in the Northern and Upper Region; the Brong Ahafo Youth Association, the Ga Youth Association, and the Asante Youth Association—each drawing on earlier organisations of a similar kind. This manner of justifying their existence gave them a great deal of plausibility in the eyes of the soldiers and policemen who, immediately on assuming power, had committed themselves to an anti-centralist and voluntarist platform. But, as will be seen, in addition to being needed to fill the vacuum left by the banning of the C.P.P. and its 'apparat groups', these local associations provided powerful support for the politicians as they began to emerge.

Chronologically, the earliest groups were the local Town Improvement Associations which were later absorbed or overshadowed by Regional Associations early in 1968 and 1969. The following were typical of the various pre-party associations in Ashanti of which the writer had particular knowledge—the Juaso Town Improvement Association at the local territorial level, the Adansi Youth Association at the level of an historic community, and the Asante Youth Association at the regional level: and each is a good example of the way in which local threads of support were woven into an electoral net.

The Juaso Town Improvement Association was a revival of the Scholars Union, formed in 1948. Situated about 40 miles south of

Kumasi, Juaso was once an important trading town (as evidenced by
the ruined buildings of cocoa-buying firms) as well as an educational
centre after a government school opened in 1918; its commercial,
educational and administrative importance could hardly be rivalled
within a radius of 40 miles. Kumawu, Juaben, Bompata, Agogo and
Asokore, historically more important townships, were administered
from Juaso, a preeminence which came to be challenged, however, after
the discovery of gold in the 1930s at Konongo some 7 miles away. The
superior wealth of Konongo then began to be seen in its schools (both
Catholic and Presbyterian), a busy lorry park, important expatriate
shops, an impressive police station and such appurtenances of a commercial centre as night-clubs. After independence, its growing importance became more marked: a secondary school and a training college
were built, and the District Magistrate's Court came to hold its usual
weekly sittings here instead of at Juaso. And it was the growth of
Konongo at the expense of Juaso which constituted the foundations of
Juaso-Konongo relations. The early Juaso Scholars Union had been
formed precisely to protest against the decline of the town, but it was
short-lived until immediately after the coup when a meeting of citizens
was held and the name, 'Juaso Town Improvement Association',
adopted.[13] Branches were then formed in Accra and Kumasi by citizens
resident in the municipalities; the Accra branch was active, concerned
mainly with discussing the most effective strategy to adopt in presenting
petitions to the appropriate authorities. Before the ban on political parties was lifted, an unusually politically conscious man, K. A. Karikari,
a storekeeper of Messrs. U.A.C. Limited, Konongo, established links
with the Association and other similar groups. He had lived in Ashanti-
Akim for a long time (though his home town is in the Sekyere constituency) and had developed a wide network of influence through a
system of credit whereby people were enabled to buy a range of goods,
from corrugated iron sheets to textiles, on a system of hire-purchase.
His influence with the Juaso Association lay in the fact that he had no
emotional attachment to Konongo; hence his good faith was in theory
unimpeachable. As Chairman of the post-coup Management Committee of the Konongo-Odumasi Urban Council, he helped in the election of J. K. Boafo, a Cooperative Accountant, to the constituent
Assembly in December, 1968. After the formation of the Progress party
(he had been Busia's friend since the 1950s) he was made the Party
Chairman in the Ashanti Akim district, comprising two constituencies;
and he, in turn, appointed the Secretary of the Juaso Town Improvement Association to the post of local Progress Secretary at
Juaso—similar appointments being made in other towns and villages in
the two constituencies.

These appointments did not smother local jealousies. As Maxwell

Owusu shows in a later chapter, there was a pervading feeling in the country that a close, functional relationship existed between the origin of a parliamentary candidate and local economic development. On the basis of this belief, every sizeable town sought to nominate a candidate for adoption, and in the Ashanti Akim South constituency each of the three main towns presented candidates: Boafo, the Constituent Assembly man, for Konongo; K. Frimpong-Boadu, an Accra barrister, for Obugu; and J. A. Danso, a cocoa cooperative auditor, sponsored by the Juaso Town Improvement Association. It was the intervention of a fourth candidate, who transcended the local limitations of his rivals, that prevented what might have been an unpleasant crisis. N. Y. B. Adade (later, Attorney General) was born in 1927 at Obugu, where his father, a friend of Karikari, was a storekeeper before becoming the local manager of John Holt Ltd. at Konongo; he was educated at Juaso Government School and then lived at Konongo before reading economics and law at Legon and London University. His mother's home town was in the Juaben-Edweso constituency, his father's town was in the Ashanti Akim North constituency. With such a wide background, a sufficient number of the competing groups felt that he would work in the interest of all, and in this way Karikari was able on behalf of Adade to bind together the various associational threads of support to ensure a substantial victory for Progress. N.A.L. entered the constituency only after all this preliminary bargaining had been done. Free from the complex problem of nominating a candidate, it was only in the latter stages that one was chosen at all—K. Amoo Adare, a former C.P.P. Chairman of the Agricultural Development Corporation, who flew back from Nairobi where he was working for the U.N. High Commission for Refugees. Yet, despite his late entry, he managed to collect almost a third of the vote from among those who were still dissatisfied with the choice of the Progress candidate.

We move now to a different level to look at the Adansi Youth Association, a revival of a similar Association which existed before 1949.[14] Adansi was one of the numerous independent Ashanti states, strategically situated between Amansie (the Ashanti state nearest Kumasi) and the southern conglomeration of Fanti states. In the past, acting on a shrewd calculation of their interests, the Adansi either acted as scouts of the Asantehene—reporting British troop movements—or fought as the allies of the British. It was the discovery of gold, and the formation in 1897 of the Ashanti Gold Fields Corporation (A.G.C.) which led Adansi to align itself decisively on the side of the British since it now had a secure source of wealth.[15] Providing wealth and employment, the mines authorities at Obuasi had nothing but friendly relations with the traditional rulers. The state, however, lacked post-primary educational facilities, and it was only after independence that three training colleges were built in those towns which (for local reasons) had supported the Nkrumah regime in the 1954–57 period of conflict—Akrokerri, Dompoasi and New Edubiasi. But it still lacked a secondary school and, except in Obuasi, good hospitals and electricity. Educated young Adansis blamed the mining company which they believed had got so much out of their lands and given so little in return, and moved by the twin passions of a desire for the benefits of 'modernity', and a strong anti-company sentiment, they revived the Adansi Youth Association which had once existed as a local cultural society. The revival was well-timed, for the London-based Lonhro Company was now engaged in negotiations with the N.L.C. Government for a take-over of the Ashanti Gold Fields Corporation, and the immediate aims of the Youth Association were to exert pressure first on the N.L.C. to bargain for such terms of agreement as would be beneficial to Adansi as a whole, and then on the Adansihene and the State Council to use whatever new royalties would be granted for the development of the state. Revived as the *Adansi Odo Ye Kuo* (Adansi Fraternal Association), it met at Obuasi during Easter 1969, and began to put forward demands for development projects. After the lifting of the ban on politics, and through the influence of two of its leaders—F. N. Mensah who was in the Constituent Assembly, and Boateng who had been seconded to the Assembly as a second Clerk—the Association decided to support the Progress Party. Boateng (a son-in-law of the treasurer who was the mother-in-law of the first M.P. from the area in 1951—J. B. Abu Bekr) was nominated as the Obuasi P.P. candidate; Mensah, a prosperous timber contractor, was chosen as a candidate for the other constituency—in preference to Abu Bekr whose earlier nomination was vehemently opposed by the Youth Association.

The Asante Youth Association (A.Y.A.) differed from both the Juaso and Adansi associations in that it had much more precise political objectives. The original aim of the revival was to reconcile former political opponents, an aim which the N.L.C. itself had sought to pursue after the release of ex-C.P.P. detainees. Immediately after the coup, there was a general belief in Ashanti that the region had suffered the greatest number of detainees under the Nkrumah regime, and had been deprived of amenities because it was the main centre of Opposition in the 1950s. If politics was not to bedevil development once again, (it was argued) it was imperative to foster a spirit of 'one-ness' in the region. Such was the general impulse behind the revival of A.Y.A. in 1968, and the first meeting was convened on the initiative of Kumasi residents. It included Owusu Sekyere, the son of Baffuor Osei Akoto (former Chairman of the N.L.M.), James Owusu, (former C.P.P. Chairman of the Kumasi City Council), J. K. Akyeampong, (a Kumasi businessman). A. W. D. Adutwum (ex-Adansihene), and A. S. Y. Andoh (Registrar, University of Science and Technology and a former Secretary of the Asanteman Council).

Andoh was appointed as Interim Secretary, and set out energetically to establish branches in Ashanti and elsewhere, especially Accra. Throughout his travels he emphasised one theme: reconciliation; and he endeavoured to make the A.Y.A. independent of any forces that might emerge in the future. The contradictions inherent in this approach became apparent, however, early in 1969 when it was announced that the ban on politics would be lifted in May; they were such that Andoh's motives in fashioning the Association as an independent force became suspect. Divisions along former C.P.P.—U.P. lines came to the surface. Atta Mensah, C. C. Addai, Yaw Asamoah—ex-C.P.P. and founders of the pre-1949 A.Y.A.—were on one side; Owusu Sekyere, B. A. Mensah, Sam Boateng and Dr. Kwame Safo-Adu—a somewhat mixed group—on the other. Both groups sought to fashion the Association in directions they perceived would not be prejudicial to their interests in any future alignment of political forces. An inevitable struggle ensued; meetings, both in Accra and Kumasi, became noisy; Andoh was virtually forced to resign, and when elections for new officers were held in April 1969, Dr. Safo-Adu become President and swore an oath of allegiance to the Asantehene.

Dr. Safo-Adu was typical of a whole new generation of middle-class intellectuals who emerged in post-coup Ghana, notionally unencumbered by past conflicts. He had an extensive medical practice in Kumasi, was an active member of the Current Affairs Club, and Chairman of the Ashanti Advisory Committee of the Centre for Civic Education. His victory was seemingly a victory for the non-committed: in reality, by background and upbringing, he was sympathetic to pro-Busia forces. As a Progress candidate in Manhyia, a Kumasi constituency where he had his practice, he polled the highest number of votes in the whole country: 18,563 to his N.A.L. opponent's 4,335. But, although a Busia man, his 'non-committed' background was a significant factor in rallying the support of such ex-C.P.P. activists as James Owusu behind his leadership. The main influence of A.Y.A. was in Kumasi, but by organising youth wings of the Progress Party, it sent out campaigners into other areas of the region. A.Y.A. had a complex, almost Byzantine, relationship with many of the chiefs, including individuals of traditional importance, like Baffuor Osei Akoto, and with the Ex-Detainees Association which was banned by the N.L.C. and then re-named the Committee for the Defence of the Coup. But whatever the precise nature of such links, they were of considerable importance to Progress both in the election and in the mobilising of party support.

It would be wrong to convey the impression, as these examples tend to do, that leadership in the voluntary associations which emerged fell wholly into P.P. hands. That was not so. The Northern Youth Association, for example, was more N.A.L. than Progress. Formed in 1967, its founders were strongly committed to the welfare of the two northern regions (the Northern and Upper Regions) which are the major areas of economic deprivation compared with the rest of the country. Many of the Association's leaders tended to be of a more radical disposition than the earlier generation of northern leaders; and the Northern Region in particular, the more southern of the two northern areas, had no cogent reason to be bitter about the Nkrumah regime. It had received a good share of educational benefits; scholarships had been awarded by the C.P.P. government to anyone able to have the most expensive type of education which only money (in acute short supply locally) could purchase, and few people from the region were detained or suffered great hardship under Nkrumah. Many of the N.Y.A. members indeed looked back on the decade 1956–66 as a time when new leaders were able to challenge the earlier monopoly of power held by the then existing alliance of chiefs and their educated advisers. For a variety of reasons, therefore, Gbedemah had a first claim on the leaders of the N.Y.A., and one of the most active, Sibidow, an 'ex-graduate' of the Kwame Nkrumah Ideological College at Wineba, was instrumental in moving the association in a pro-N.A.L. direction. The region was also beset by traditional rivalries of a finely balanced nature, as in the sway of local interests between the Muslim chiefs and sub-chiefs over the Dagomba Skin dispute in Yendi, in which N.A.L. and Progress were in conflict not in national party terms but as opposed groups of interest drawn from rival mosques, villages, clans and families. The overall result in the Northern Region was therefore very close—whichever party actually won a particular constituency. As App. II shows, Progress won 47.8 per cent and N.A.L. 42.4 per cent of the votes in the contested seats.

Further north, two contrasting elements brought a different result. It is true that the N.Y.A. in the Upper Region included a new generation of educated leaders, like the London-educated barrister A. A. Luguterah, who was to stand for N.A.L. in the Chiana-Paga constituency, and Issifu Ali who was Commissioner for Information after the coup until he resigned to become N.A.L. candidate in Wa. But the region had been administered under the C.P.P. by a party Commissioner, A. A. Asumda, whose policies—especially towards his political enemies—had made the impact of the Nkrumah regime somewhat harsh. And the area was rich in able politicians of national stature who had consistently opposed the C.P.P., including S. D. Dombo, Duori-Na (Opposition leader in parliament after Busia's voluntary exile), Jateo Kaleo, and B. K. Adama, all of whom later become Progress Ministers. Their loyalty to local interests, their 'northern-ness', their local standing among Muslim and Catholic followers alike, and their non-subversive resistance to Nkrumah, gave them a particular aura of respect well beyond their own constituencies, as well as a solid base of support among their immediate kin. It was difficult for any challenger to compete with them—or with local leaders of great influence like Abayifa Karbo, a former opposition M.P. and later a lawyer, who had succeeded his father as Lawra-Na, thus combining a traditional stronghold with a wide following among the growing number of Christian-eduated young men in the north-west. None the less, N.A.L. was able to find clusters of support and willing candidates from among the many rival lineages which formed the little chiefdoms of the region in which local competition for power and status made it impossible for any one party—P.A.P., Progress or N.A.L.—to exert an exclusive appeal.

In the Volta Region, a Development Association came together in the belief that the Ewe-speaking region had stagnated economically, not least because of its anti-C.P.P. stance. Under the presidency of Chapman-Nyaho (an ex-secretary to the cabinet), who was not particularly enamoured of Gbedemah's leadership, the Association debated ways and means of developing the region now that the C.P.P. had disappeared. But the majority of the members believed that Gbedemah's political experience as a former Finance Minister would serve the region well, and certainly Gbedemah's political stature was greater than that of his (fellow Ewe) opponents, such as M. K. Apaloo (U.N.P.) S.G. Antor (P.P.) and Kofi Dumoga (P.P.). The split in Busia's support in the region, when Apaloo decided to join the U.N.P. instead of P.P.— quite apart from Ewe-Akan divisions— also contributed to the very poor performance of the anti-Gbedemah forces in the region.

The pattern of voluntary association examined in these examples was by no means universal. No such well-structured and active groups emerged in the Central or the Western Regions. Instead, there were clandestine manoeuvres among a group of 'new' leaders—mostly accountants, lawyers and university lecturers—who tried to find an associational base which would be free from the political strifes of the past. The 'Third Force', as they came to be generally designated, can be described as the political expression of halting attempts to transcend past political differences represented by Busia and Gbedemah. Its origins went back to the immediate post-coup period—more precisely to July 1966—when an idealistic and energetic Kumasi medical practitioner, Dr. John Bilson, brought together a debating club called the 'Libertarians'. The society was formed ostensibly to uphold the tenets of a free and open society and, in practice, to put forward the claims of the 'uncommitted youth' to participate in public affairs in a reborn Ghana. *A priori,* there was much to recommend such a group. But the military seizure of power had not wiped the slate clean, suddenly making Ghana an historical palimpset; old political memories lingered and, like other groups, the 'Third Force' came to be bedevilled by divisions based on blandishments from forces arranged behind Busia and Gbedemah. But, for a time, it attracted among its ranks lawyers, e.g. Luguterah (later N.A.L.), O.Y. Asamoah (later N.A.L.), A. S. Kpodonu (later P.P.) and Kwame Aidoo (later N.A.L.); it also attracted university teachers, e.g. E. H. Boohene (later N.A.L. vice-chairman), K. A. Karikari (later P.P.) and G. K. Agama (N.A.L. Parliamentary Opposition Leader until September 1970); it counted businessmen and accountants among its members—E. K. Dadson (later N.A.L. candidate) and J. K. Rockson (later P.P. candidate).

The outstanding feature of this grouping was that it was urban-based and lacked roots in the rural areas; its *modus operandi* consisted in trying to win the allegiance of the leadership of the various voluntary associations. What it lacked in popular appeal it made up for in enthusiasm until, lacking a *tabula rasa* on which to write a whole new chapter of Ghanaian history, it split into warring factions. By the time the Constituent Assembly was inaugurated, the 'Third Force' had already begun to divide.

The split was not, however, along ethnic lines: on the contrary, as the names indicate, they were based on the various members' assessment of their chances of winning a nomination and, should they win, on the probability that they would be given ministerial positions. This is best exemplified by Aidoo who joined the Progress Party immediately after deserting the ranks of the 'Third Force' and, on failing to win the nomination on a Progress ticket, joined N.A.L. and was adopted as a candidate, losing however to his P.P. opponent. After the split, one of the most energetic rumps regrouped as the Republican Party under the leadership of P.K.K. Quaidoo, an ex-C.P.P. Minister. The Republican Party then divided, one part under Rockson's leadership—keeping the name; the other, under Quaidoo, allied itself with Dr. E. V. C. de Graft Johnson's All People's Congress to form a new party, the All People's Republican Party. Before the open split, the Republican Party had mobilised support in many parts of the central and western regions, until it reached a position of strength when it seemed capable of altering the balance of support between the major parties. Rockson, in particular, had extensive contacts with chiefs and the various Asafo groups (he was a captain of an Asafo Company) in his native Ekumfi district of the central region. Then, barely four weeks before the election, the Republican Party announced a merger with the Progress Party. The decision appears to have been based solely on a 'games theory' assessment of the relative chances of the various contending parties for, as the former secretary, K. A. Sarpong, said: '... it is better to be swallowed by an elephant than by an ant'.[17]

Individuals were also active in ways (camouflaged by a variety of forms) aimed at enhancing their chances for adoption as parliamentary candidates against the time when the ban on politics would be lifted. Kingsley Abeyie, for example, a Kumasi-based lawyer and a founder member of the Current Affairs club, formed with other Kumawi residents in Kumasi the 'Descendants of Tweneboa Kodua Society'—Kodua being a Kumawu chief who is said to have sacrificed his life to ensure Ashanti success in war—in an attempt to create a nucleus of support for his future campaign.[18] In the southern Abura constituency, J. K. Fynn, a history lecturer at Legon, emerged as a 'favourite son' after he had joined the local Asafo Company—the traditional warrior organisation which is still powerful in the Central Region. The decision to join the Company was taken after his return from London in 1965 when he began research into the history of his native Abura district; he was installed a captain after the coup, his visits to Abura became more frequent, and there was hardly an alternative to him at the time of the election. He stood for the Progress Party and won in all the polling stations except those of his opponents' home area.[19] O. Y. Asamoah (later N.A.L. M.P. for Biakoye in the Volta Region) also built a personal electoral machine, in a constituency where the electorate is of four different ethnic stocks, through his services as a lawyer and frequent week-end visits while lecturing at Legon: it is arguable that he too could have won for any one of the contending parties. It was through such personal and group activities that a large fund of good will was built on which politicians traded at the time of the election; and in Accra Harry Sawyerr, standing as an Independent, successfully withstood the party networks of his Progress and U.N.P. opponents. On the other hand, it was easy to *over-estimate* the strength of a personal following—as Joe Appiah discovered in Atwima where he lost heavily to both Progress and N.A.L. It was not difficult to attract enthusiastic support for even a very small campaign, provided it was backed with some funds: the candidate was ensured by his followers of a growing support—for which more money was needed—until polling day when friends, followers, funds and votes melted away.

These local associations were not the only institutions through which support was mediated after the coup. State-sponsored bodies also played a part, notably the Constituent Assembly which—as we have seen—held 96 sittings, passed 177 Articles, and enacted and promulgated the new Constitution seven days before the General Election.[20] Thus the period of campaign coincided with the sittings of the Assembly. And this fact alone, coupled with the procedure for electing members to the Assembly, made its establishment notable. As described by Robin Luckham, the Constitutional Commission had recommended that the Assembly be elected by the people on the principle of 'one man, one vote', a procedure considerably modified by the N.L.C. The immediate effect was that the Assembly not only mirrored but reinforced the pluralistic character of post-coup society, and it provided the means whereby localities, chiefdoms, villages and voluntary groups were linked to national politics. Farmers, co-operative leaders, businessmen, trade unionists, and lawyers, debated the constitutional proposals under one roof. And, this bringing together at the national level of leaders who had hitherto had little or no contact with each other set the scene for intense political bargaining. To the Assembly from the Wenchi administrative district came Busia; from Takoradi, Sekondi, Mampong, Wa, Kpandu, Biakoye and Accra came Lamptey, Scheck, Amponsah, Adama, Kpodonu, Asamoah and Adjetey. Gbedemah was absent, fighting a legal battle for his exemption from being banned from active politics. Of the members, only a handful were in any sense loyal to Busia. The majority consisted of a generation of educated men whose political commitments, if they had any beyond a desire to be elected into a future Ghana parliament, tended to be pro-'Third Force': winning the loyalty of this new local leadership was crucial, therefore, and the opportunity was certainly seized.

On the evidence of the official reports of the Assembly, Busia spoke on only a few occasions—least of all on occasions when controversial articles came to be discussed. He was, however, busy interviewing, establishing links with the new leadership in the Assembly, and sounding opinions. He sought to formalise these loose relations in his suburban house, on the Accra-Cape Coast road, by instituting bi-weekly meetings of such members as were willing to discuss the constitutional provisions in detail. In January 1969, the hard core of this group consisted of those of his old colleagues who were in the Assembly; from March onwards the group had considerably expanded, and by July he could count on the loyalty of at least two-thirds of the members of the Assembly. By the time of the lifting of the ban on parties, the weekly meetings had evolved from a constitutional debating forum into the nucleus of a political party. Among the new additions from the Assembly were T. D. Brodie-Mends (Cape Coast Administrative District), later Progress member for Cape Coast; Haruna Esseku (Winneba Administrative District), later Minister of Transport and Communications, who was an enthusiastic member of the 'Third Force' until about six weeks to election day; S. K. Oppong, former principal of St. Augustine Secondary School, a 'Third Force' supporter and later Junior Minister of Education; B. J. da Rocha, previously 'uncommitted' and fiercely independent, and later Progress Party General Secretary; J. B. Kaba, a lawyer and formerly a 'Third Force' sympathiser, later Progress M.P. for Bolgatanga; A. S. Kpodonu, a staunch 'Third Force'

supporter, who lost the Ho West constituency as a Progress candidate
to N.A.L.: and J. G. Amamoo, previously opposed to Busia's
leadership, a former Ambassador under Nkrumah, and later a Junior
Minister in the Progress government. J. A. Kufuor, Town Clerk of
Kumasi City Council; Mohammed Abdul Saaka, a Northern lawyer
(later a Junior Minister); B. M. Akita from Shai and A. K. Boaitey (both
lawyers); C. O. Nyanor, a banker (later a Junior Minister); and
Rockson were also among the new acquisitions. In the absence of
Gbedemah, Busia was easily the most towering political personality in
the Assembly. And it made the task of knitting together the scattered
threads of élite groups relatively easy.

None the less, anti-Busia forces did emerge in the Assembly. Joe Appiah, representing the Bar Association, led one such group which included Peter Adjetey (Accra administrative district), Alex Hutton Mills
(Ga Farmers Association) and Dr. R. H. S. Bannerman. It was in this
fashion that smaller parties took shape, like the U.N.P. which appealed
directly to a particular group interest—the Ga—yet was able to attract
other candidates (like Joe Appiah) who saw some hope of a 'third party'
which might hold the balance between larger groupings. Another section, led at various times by G. K. Agama of the University at Legon,
and Sam Okudzeto, a lawyer, looked to Gbedemah and a solid core of
Ewe members. A loosely joined 'Third Force' group was led by Dr.
Asamoah until he, too, decided to join N.A.L. Despite this opposition,
the balance of forces by July/August among the members of the
Assembly, and among their electoral support groups in the country at
large, had shifted decisively in Busia's favour. Busia's presence in the
Assembly, coupled with his chairmanship of the Centre for Civic
Education, enabled him to have an initial purchase on whatever support
structures emerged in the pre-election period. He began to look like a
leader who might win, and his popularity—and support—grew with his
success. Organisation, adequate financial resources and hard work no
doubt played their part: but both the major parties had these in almost
equal proportions. Gbedemah, however, was still appearing before the
Exemptions Commission and it was not until 17 March 1968 that he
gave a precise indication that he would form a political party; in the
meantime, some of his prospective supports were either disqualified or
demoralised. It is true that his home region, which had never previously
given him unanimous backing, rallied to his support, and this coming
together of a pro-Gbedemah, pro-N.A.L. movement in the Ewe-
dominated areas created a degree of backlash in other regions; but it
was not *that* strong to account for the outcome of the election.
Gbedemah himself, in his political career, had never been greatly attached emotionally to his Ewe homeland: a man of cosmopolitan interests and tastes, he had had strong links in other regions of the coun-

try, and N.A.L. was able to put up candidates in all but one of the 140 constituencies.

It should be noted, finally, that these events took place in a political setting which was dominated by two considerations. One was that the *initial* policies of the N.L.C. (later policies scrupulously sought to be fair and were occasionally antagonistic to Busia) pointed in directions which left no one in doubt that the originators of the coup would not welcome the return of any one associated, even remotely, with Nkrumah and the C.P.P. And, for many, Gbedemah undoubtedly carried too much of the C.P.P. past with him still. Secondly, popular justification for the coup ran along lines which Busia had adumbrated in his long political career, thus giving him the image of a prophet. A constant refrain, in conversation, was: 'Busia said so and so . . . let us give him a chance.' And the results were an eloquent testimony of such beliefs.

Notes

1. Amponsah became Minister of Lands & Mineral Resources; Ofori Atta, Minister of Education; Owusu, Minister for External Affairs; Lamptey, Defence Minister, and Chief Dombo, Minister of State.
2. Coming together in 1970 to form the Justice Party.
3. E. J. Hobsbawm's phraseology, *Primitive Rebels* (Manchester University Press, 1963), p. 57.
4. Moses Danquah, *The Birth of the Second Republic* (Accra n.d.) is a compendium of useful contemporary material on party manifestoes, election results, etc.
5. *Rebuilding the National Economy,* a broadcast talk by the Chairman of the N.L.C., 2 March 1966. See above, Chapter 2.
6. See p. 143.
7. Appendix II.
8. Imoru Ayarna was defeated in his home constituency of Tempane Garu in the Upper Region.
9. See J. P. Nettl *Political Mobilisation,* London 1967.
10. See D. Rimmer, 'The Industrial Relations Act, 1958' in *The Ghana Economic Bulletin,* Vol. 3 No. 4, April 1959, p. 8.
11. M. Danquah, *op. cit.,* p. 47.
12. That farmers were harshly taxed was noted by Miss Polly Hill in 1958. By her calculations, '. . . when world cocoa prices stand around their present level at £350 a ton, the cocoa farmer, however large or small he may be, is allowed to retain only about £1 out of every £3 of his income (net). Such an average rate of income tax has never been known in the world in peace or war'. P. Hill, 'The Case Against Double Taxation of Cocoa Farmers' in *The Ghana Economic Bulletin* Vol. 2, No. 9, 12 September, 1958, pp. 15–16.
13. This account is based on the letters and *Record of Meetings* of the Juaso Town Improvement Association.
14. The writer is indebted to S. Fosahene, a founder member and journalist, for an account on the Adansi Youth Association.
15. See G. W. Eaton Turner, a *Short History of the Ashanti Goldfields Corporation 1897–1947* (n.d.), p. 20.

16. I am indebted to Dr. J. Bilson and K. Karikari for this account of the Third Force.
17. M. Danquah, *op. cit.,* p. 26.
18. See Chapter 10 for a close examination of the election struggle in Kumawu.
19. Result: J. K. Fynn, (P.P.) 4,227; I. K. Nkrumah (N.A.L.) 1,796; de Graft Johnson (A.P.R.P.) 1,116; P. Begyina (U.N.P.) 62.
20. See Chapter 4.

APPENDIX I

Percentage of Votes obtained

	National		Ashanti		Western		Volta	
	Votes	% total Votes	Votes	% total Votes	Votes	% total Votes	Votes	% total Votes
P.P.	876,378	58.68	215,707	14.45	71,240	4.77	28,491	1.91
N.A.L.	454,646	30.44	47,835	3.20	21,646	1.45	121,606	8.14
A.P.R.P.	27,328	1.83	622	0.04	9,896	0.66	91	0.01
P.A.P.	51,123	3.43	2,688	0.18	27,979	1.88	1,555	0.11
Indep.	27,216	1.82	5,228	0.35	2,991	0.20	929	0.06
U.N.P.	56,680	3.80	5,049	0.34	1,381	0.09	4,992	0.33
Total Votes	1,493,371	100	277,129	18.56	135,133	9.05	157,664	10.56

Percentage of Registered Votes

Total Registered Voters	23,51,658	100	401,590	17.07	224,542	9.55	226,304	9.62

APPENDIX II

	National		Ashanti		Western		Volta	
	Seats	% total votes	Seats	% regional Votes	Seats	% regional Votes	Seats	% regional Votes
P.P.	105	58.68	22	77.84	10	52.72	2	18.07
N.A.L.	29	30.44	0	17.26	0	16.06	14	77.13
A.P.R.P.	1	1.83	0	0.22	1	7.32	0	0.06
P.A.P.	2	3.43	0	0.97	2	20.71	0	0.99
Indep.	1	1.82	0	1.89	0	2.21	0	0.58
U.N.P.	2	3.80	0	1.82	0	1.02	0	3.17
Total	140	100	22	100	13	100	16	100

APPENDIX I (continued)

Percentage of Votes obtained

	Upper		Greater Accra		Brong-Ahafo		Central		Eastern		Northern	
	Votes	% total Votes	Votes	% total Votes	Votes	% total Votes	Votes	% total Votes	Votes	% total Votes	Votes	% total Votes
	94,315	6.32	43,608	2.92	127,707	8.55	114,734	7.68	130,275	8.72	50,301	3.37
	54,743	3.66	39,145	2.62	21,745	1.46	29,962	2.01	73,321	4.91	44,643	2.99
	3,201	0.21	—	—	—	—	9,420	0.63	1,342	0.09	2,756	0.18
	7,293	0.49	4,328	0.29	—	—	3,227	0.22	1,429	0.10	2,624	0.17
	5,286	0.35	6,174	0.41	—	—	71	0.01	4,156	0.28	2,381	0.16
	4,874	0.33	28,456	1.91	1,387	0.09	4,165	0.27	3,888	0.26	2,488	0.17
	169,712	11.36	121,711	8.15	150,839	10.10	161,579	10.82	214,411	14.36	105,193	7.04

Percentage of Registered Votes

	302,807	12.88	172,858	7.35	221,451	9.42	265,920	11.31	337,600	14.36	198,586	8.44

APPENDIX II (continued)

	Upper		Greater Accra		Brong-Ahafo		Central		Eastern		Northern	
	Seats	% regional votes	Seats	% regional votes	Seats	% regional votes	Seats	% regional votes	Seats	% regional votes	Seats	% regional votes
	13	55.57	3	35.83	13	84.66	15	71.01	18	60.76	9	47.82
	3	32.36	3	32.16	0	14.42	0	18.54	4	34.20	5	42.44
	0	1.89	0	—	0	—	0	5.83	0	0.63	0	2.62
	0	4.30	0	3.56	0	—	0	2.00	0	0.66	0	2.49
	0	3.11	1	5.07	0	—	0	0.04	0	1.94	0	2.26
	0	2.87	2	23.38	0	0.92	0	2.58	0	1.81	0	2.37
	16	100	9	100	13	100	15	100	22	100	14	100

CHAPTER 7

POLITICS IN ASUNAFO*

John Dunn

In the days of the Septennial Act, the English (as Rousseau mordantly suggested) were free once every seven years.[1] On current showing the Ghanaians will be doing well if they are free more than once every fifteen. The election of 1969 was the first unequivocally free national political act on the part of the unorganised populace since the election of 1954, the first election, that is, in which the coffers of the state did not enter sharply into the political choices of voters. To understand what most voters were doing when they went to the polls on this occasion is to understand something as central to the politics of Ghana as the operation of the machinery of government—it is to understand what the people of Ghana attempt to do politically when they are free.[2] Whatever they may have brought about, the action which they performed in choosing in this way retains its moral status. No doubt the Ghanaian electorate was confused and ignorant, and no doubt its wills were as particular as the next nation's.[3] But abstract though it was and politically null as it soon turned out to have been, there is to be read in its choices, as there may perhaps be in the choices of all nations allowed the privilege of choosing, the shadowy outlines of a *Volonté Générale*. Elections in Africa by now may be closer to rituals of affliction than to concrete embodiments of freedom, but the sentiments to which they give transient and paradoxical shape are no less profound for their failure to exemplify the assurance of a mastered world. In order to recapture

* The research on which this article is based was assisted by a grant from the Smuts Memorial Fund of Cambridge University. The writer owes his introduction to Ahafo and much of his understanding of its life to Dr. A. F. Robertson. He could not have done most of the research required without the skilful assistance of Susan McKaskie and Jonas Omersu. Two points of method require a brief note. Firstly, he has taken pains not to identify any actors whose conduct was in breach of the law or of publicly specified standards of propriety. This lends the account a rather abstract air on occasion. To have been more concrete would have been to betray the trust of the very many participants on both sides who attempted generously to enable him to understand what was happening. Secondly, it will be apparent that this article is not offered as a contribution to a value-free social science. It is nevertheless intended to be a contribution towards understanding the truth about the events which it describes. There is some danger that it may be felt that having incisively seen through (with the advantages of hindsight) the fantasy of transplanting 'proletarian truth' to Ghana, the writer has fallen a helpless victim to the fantasy that 'bourgeois truth' has been so transported. He wishes accordingly to record as a matter of historical fact that it was not because his feelings were biased in favour of these values at the outset that he perceived events in this fashion. Rather, he felt as he did at the end because this was what he saw.

some vague outline of these sentiments, this chapter attempts to discuss two separate issues: the question of what happened in the election campaign in the Asunafo constituency, and the question of what was meant by what happened.

The Asunafo division of Ahafo is situated in the western rain-forest to the south of the main road linking Kumasi, the capital of the former Ashanti empire, to Sunyani, the capital of the present Brong-Ahafo region. Its most direct political and administrative ties have been shared between these two centres for more than sixty years, for the greater part indeed of the British occupation of Ashanti.[4] The balance of significance between the two towns has changed with changes in the political relationship between the central government of the country and the traditional political system of Ashanti. Ever since the British conquest of Ashanti in 1896, the central government has manipulated the political structures of Ahafo as pawns in its relationship with Ashanti. The delicate balance of conflict and co-operation between Accra and Kumasi has always been close to the centre of the politics of the country as a whole, and in the light of this national preoccupation, the politics of Ahafo inevitably appear provincial and instrumental. But whereas, from the perspective of Accra or Kumasi, Ahafo may well seem a mere instrument, a counter in a game of altogether grander scope, it is important to remember that from the viewpoint of Ahafo this grander game is apt to appear as instrumental to more local purposes, and Kwame Nkrumah or even the Asantehene have thereby seemed to be reduced to the status of weapons in local factional struggles. The confrontation of national élites, whether colonial or postcolonial, with local communities has tended to be described in terms of the recalcitrance of local values to national ends, but its meaning lies (as throughout the period of indirect rule which is substantively far from terminated today) at least as much in the subservience of national power to very active local purposes.

The administrative links of Asunafo with Sunyani and Kumasi are paralleled by the lines of physical communication along which the economic products of the area pass in order to reach the national markets.[5] The economic development of Ahafo and to no small degree the peopling of this densely-forested area followed upon the administrative penetration of the area by the British. As a district it represents the most recent (and currently the most spectacular) example of the Ghanaian economic expansion of this century, the process of rapid capital accumulation through the exploitation of the virgin forest for cocoa cultivation,[6] supplemented over the last twenty years by the timber industry. The great majority of the present Ahafo population has derived ethnically within the last two generations from other areas of Ghana or from abroad.[7] Except for the town of Mim with its sawmills and intermittent union troubles, the economic activities and the political

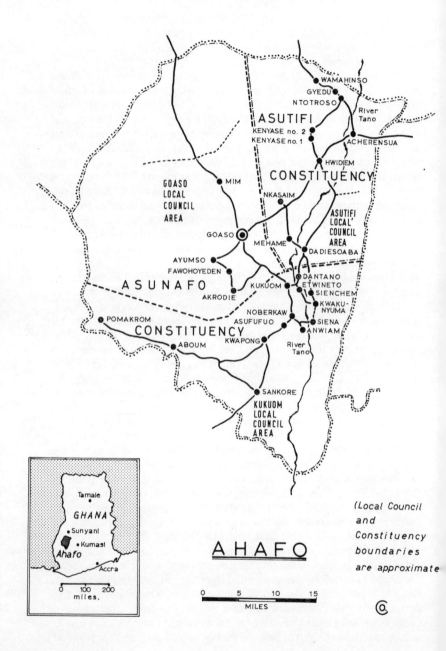

(Local Council
and
Constituency
boundaries
are approximate

structures of the area are entirely pre-industrial, though the equipment used in timber extraction is sufficiently massive in scale to remove any suggestion of undisturbed bucolic tranquillity. A great deal of wealth is produced in Ahafo and much money is made there. The rape of the forest is an enthusiastic and participatory response to the exigencies and enticements of the world economy.

The social relations characteristic of the area are extremely intricate. The continuing inflow, now somewhat slower than twenty years ago, of those with capital to take up new cocoa land and of those with nothing but their labour to contribute, produces a very complicated economic relationship with its environment. In some ways the area is in a neocolonial relationship, not just with the world economy but also with other parts of Ghana, in that a substantial proportion of its farmers, particularly of Ashanti origin, are 'stranger farmers'. Indeed they are resented as such since they are frequently absentees and tend to export the profits of their farms to their home areas instead of reinvesting them locally.[8] The major capitalisation of the timber industry in the shape of the Mim Timber Company and Messrs Glikstens is also foreign to the area (though at least two former M.P.s now work timber concessions within Ahafo) and its profits too are largely exported. The initial character of the district as thinly-populated, largely virgin, forest has meant that it has had to import most of its capital and thus to endure a continuing and exploitative outflow of resources to other areas. Indeed, because of the increased social responsibility exhibited (under some initial political pressure) by the expatriate timber concerns, and the intrinsically more inscrutable character of their economic operations, stranger farmers occasion more direct resentment among most Ahafos than do the European interests in the area. But although the productive resources are exploited by those outside the area—as was endlessly emphasised in the election campaign with respect to the depredations of the government—Ahafo also imports, besides the greater number of its capitalists, the greater part of what the American Marxists Fitch and Oppenheimer have conceived as its rural proletariat.[9] Much of the labour supply in the process of cocoa production—and virtually all the non-familial labour involved—consists of semi-migrant foreign nationals or northern Ghanaians. Luck, energy, and good judgement may enable some of these to take up farms on stool lands and to become in effect citizens of Ahafo too. But for the most part the money which they can accumulate over a year or two is sufficient only to make them substantially richer in status and power in their home countries and insufficient to give them preferential access to the more productive and now rather scarcer land supplies in Ahafo. There is a chronic labour shortage in the rich cocoa areas, since the earnings of cocoa labourers are not such as to make the employment enticing for most southern Ghanaians even in conditions of substantial unemployment. The economic viability of cocoa production has therefore come to depend increasingly upon the continued availability of extremely cheap labour from much poorer areas. There was some discussion during the course of the campaign of non-Ghanaian business enterprise and its effects in the constituency, both European and African, particularly that of Yorubas in the retail trade, but the dependence of large-scale cocoa farmers on cheap imported labour was little mentioned.

The system of social stratification on the national level (in so far as such a thing does *exist* on the national level) played no part in the issues of the election. The sharpest conflicts of economic interest within the area also did not appear since the most economically deprived group had for the most part no local status as citizens of Ahafo and in many cases no legal title to vote in a national election.[10] It is an important feature of class relations in the area that many cocoa labourers are in a semi-domestic relationship with their employers, while even those who are employed by wholly absentee owners enjoy some degree of economic protection. The forest food crops, especially plantains and cocoyams (a byproduct of the approved method of growing cocoa), provide a diet which is plentiful, whatever its nutritional deficiencies. Few go hungry in the forest, and its most economically deprived groups—the migrants from the often drought-stricken savannah regions—are thus distinctly less deprived than they might well be at home. The politics of Ahafo have always been in consequence a politics of faction at a lineage, a town, or divisional level, rather than a politics of class; a struggle between kinship groups and places rather than between geographically dispersed economic interests. Since the categories of class as such did not enter into either the vocabulary or the self-conscious political activities of the election, the intricacies of tenurial relations in cocoa production need not concern us here.[11] But two other self-identificatory roles which have come to Ahafo along with the purely economic aspects of modernity did play a part. Both the Christian religion and modern education had come slowly to Asunafo;[12] but both had appeared in a more vigorous form in the preceding ten years, and they undoubtedly had some weight in fixing the less traditional aspects of the election's meaning. The aspect of Busia's campaign which provoked most derision among some European observers and urban sophisticates, its vociferous god-fearingness, seems to have responded in this rural environment to some real needs.[13] At the same time the Progress Party's appearance as the party of respectability headed by a university professor made it the natural political vehicle in Asunafo, as in most parts of the country, for those who were admitted by the avenue of education to the participatory fruits of modernity, above all public office and the salaries which go with it.[14] The availability of post-Middle School education was a very crude symbol of the opening of modern opportunity to the people of Ahafo. The perfect candidate for the Progress Party symbolically (and the candidate whom they in fact ran) was a young man, not only Ahafo-born and graced with an Honours Degree from the University of Ghana but teaching in the local Secondary School at Acherensua in the neighbouring constituency, the provision of which had been the C.P.P. government's major local reward for political services rendered. Secondary education, in offering the possibility of dramatic social mobility through access to public office, is making an offer more resonant than that of *la carrière ouverte aux talents*. There is little bourgeois nonsense about meritocracy in the identification of the purposes of education. It is the fact that careers should in principle be open to *many*, not that they should be open to *talent*, which constitutes the progress. The symbolic offer made by education comes less as the wages of virtue than as the prize of a sort of social sweepstake. Its point is not that the rewards *will* accrue to virtue but that they *may* accrue to you. Education enshrines many of the most optimistic fantasies of Ahafo residents and in doing so it lends powerful support to the modern status hierarchy. The greatest achievement of the C.P.P. nationally, and its most concrete local service, paradoxically reinforced the political efficacy of its opponents.

In addition to the localist and ethnic categories discussed below, and the abstract categories of class, religion, and education derived from the recent social history of Ahafo, there remains one further categorical dichotomy—derived in this case from the political history of the area—which must play a part in the explanation of what happened in the election. In Asunafo, as in many other parts of the country, one way of seeing the election campaign for many of its participants was simply as a continuation of the political struggle between the former C.P.P. of Nkrumah (reincarnated uneasily in Gbedemah's N.A.L.) and the former United Party now led again by Dr. Busia. At the level of local personnel the continuity was often strong enough to represent a virtual identity. But both at what could be politely termed an ideological level, and at the level of local political accumulation, it was in the interest of both parties in the 1969 election to sophisticate this crude historical distinction. Gbedemah would have been unable to don the mantle of Nkrumah overtly, even had he wished to do so—political parties had been banned by government decree precisely for allegedly doing so—and both the circumstances of his breach with Nkrumah and his own personality presented him with little temptation to assume such an unequivocal identity.[15] At the same time it was an important feature of the rather pietistic pretensions of Dr. Busia's party that it was a party of reconciliation, not one of revenge.[16] In public testimony this pacific reconciliation of all values (which of course in practice might equally well be seen as the consolidation of all interests) was testified to by a number of former C.P.P. dignitaries (among them the former Regional Commissioner, Yeboa-Afari, who had had his own difficulties with Nkrumah before the coup) appearing in the constituency to speak for the Progress Party. It is, of course, a general characteristic of politics that all parties can do with the votes of those for whose opinions or beliefs they have no use whatsoever.

There can be no doubt that the legacy to this election from the history of party conflict in Ahafo[17] (despite such purposeful blurring of the historical boundaries by the two parties) extended much further than the political *équipes* of rival party activists. Indeed the former United Party M.P. for the area assured me with some plausibility, if not with total impartiality, that the election barely needed fighting. The P.P. (he said) had as good as won before it started, since he himself had consolidated the U.P. electoral allegiance of the area in the historic battles of 1954 and 1956 when the constituency had been almost three times its present size and when he had had to lavish thousands of pounds of his own money on the enterprise. The heroic age of political entrepreneurship, it was firmly suggested, was over, the market established; and those of less innovatory skill and personal energy, to say nothing of wealth and courage, could safely expect to reap the rewards of inheriting it.

In the early 1950s Ahafo was not a politically sophisticated area. In the first national election of 1951 it was part of the extensive Kumasi West Rural constituency. The C.P.P. candidate B. F. Kusi was a young Kumasi trader from Bisease, 12 miles from Kumasi but with family connections all over Ahafo. He won the seat easily. By the time of the next election Ahafo had split off as a separate constituency. Kusi had by this time quarrelled with the C.P.P. and he stood against the party without success in his home constituency. The C.P.P. candidate for Ahafo, B. K. Senkyire came from Kenyase. He was opposed, after a contested nomination, by two candidates, one of them A. W. Osei, a former state nurse from Goaso. Senkyire won by a comfortable margin after a vigorous campaign.[18] Over the next two years Ahafo was subjected to the full ravages of the N.L.M. struggle. At its height, in the election of 1956, Osei won the seat from the C.P.P., with the assistance of a number of local chiefs, most particularly the Chief of Mim.[19] Subsequent political conflict in the area was extremely savage by Ghanaian standards. The C.P.P. reimposed its control at the local level through extensive purges of traditional office-holders and the manipulation of local separatism, notably by the restoration of the paramountcy of the Kukuomhene in the course of the creation of a separate Brong-Ahafo region. Many people were beaten up and driven away from their lands into the forest—'to bush'. The life of the M.P., Osei, a man of striking courage and determination,[20] belied by his diminutive stature, was threatened on at least one occasion in a determined manner and numerous efforts were made to get him to transfer his allegiance to the C.P.P. He was one of the last M.P.s to remain in opposition and he continued to challenge the government intermittently (though without injudicious rudeness) in Parliament. Only the formal arrival of the one-party state and the elections of 1965, in which he was consequently unable to stand, produced his disappearance from the political scene and restored the public representation of Ahafo to C.P.P. hands. There can be little doubt that the area as a whole suffered for the obduracy of its resistance to C.P.P. control[21] and it is hardly surprising that there should have been substantial local enthusiasm at the prospect of a government of the reincarnated U.P., when the formal ban on party politics was at last lifted three years after the coup.

The official campaign for the 1969 election was naturally confined to the period after the lifting of this governmental ban on overt political activity. But in Ahafo, as elsewhere, politics never stops and there are some features of the campaign which can only be understood in the light of the entire period since the overthrow of the Nkrumah government. In one sense the most important feature of the election was that the machinery of government did not interfere in the election on behalf of either of the two major parties. Its neutrality as an organised interest may have derived more from internal dissensions along ethnic lines within the ruling N.L.C. than from the sheer force of its members' addiction to the proprieties of democratic election, but the motives for its organisational neutrality are of no significance in this instance. What matters is that it did not explicitly take sides and that any partisanship displayed by its agents at a local level was restricted in efficacy by a stringent need for discretion. The local administration, in Asunafo at least, ran the election to such high standards of propriety that despite the ebullient and far from polite atmosphere of the campaign, in which derogatory accusations were in profuse supply, for some two and a half months the writer never heard anyone allege that it had deviated from the strict demands of impartiality. Individual policemen or returning officers might have strayed from this path on occasion, but, in an exceedingly authoritarian environment, modern authority in the constituency attained impressive standards of purity in its performance of the rituals.

There is, however, a sense in which the ostentatious impartiality of the administration may have served in effect as the subtlest form of partiality. There can be no doubt that the most effective member of the local administration (the young Ga Administrative Officer) would have been happy, had not the intense rectitude of his public conduct precluded such a choice, to support the victorious party. A man of startling energy, allied with great charm and histrionic ability, he had had a very considerable impact upon the district in the two years of his administration.[22] Despite his maintenance of an elaborate mime of social distance,[23] he remained endlessly available to settle disputes, and he wrestled with *élan* against the lethargic reflexes of the central bureaucracy on behalf of the people of his district in an effort to dissipate their historical heritage of governmental neglect. The coming of piped water to the town of Goaso, the administrative capital of the district and the seat of his residence, while it was an achievement for which many claimed responsibility,[24] represented for him and indeed for the people of the town at large the consummation of his administration. As an incarnation of civic rectitude and sheer practical efficacy, he was himself for many the most reassuring political symbol—and one which plausibly united material benefit and moral purpose. If rectitude meant piped water at last, who did not want rectitude?[25]

One further sense, symbolically revealing although of small importance in this particular constituency, in which the propriety of the government's demeanour was less than impartial between the two major parties requires brief mention. Among the N.L.C.'s few specific political undertakings during the three years of its rule was the creation of the Centre for Civic Education, a government-sponsored and financed voluntary association for purveying instruction on the ethical character of the state. As one might expect with a post-colonial state, this ethical character was a pretty abstract affair, largely a question of being impartial between its subjects and of being owed duties by them. Civic education was clearly education in not voting, when the time came, for the former President (though even here the N.L.C. government showed its lack of confidence in the efficacy of the educational process by banning any party which attempted to provide this opportunity). But at least in its public dimensions it could not be asserted to have been education in voting *for* anybody in particular. The most that could be said was that earnest injunctions to exhibit virtue when voting might suggest to the innocent voter that to expend his ballot on a man whose public image was somewhat pietistic would be a more virtuous act than bestowing it on a man whose public image was distinctly more raffish. In any case it is hard to believe that the Centre for Civic Education can have exerted any very drastic electoral effect. Among the sixty or so men and women (not personally engaged in running the campaign of one of the parties) interviewed in Goaso in three months before the election, extended questioning revealed that at most four or five had *heard* of the Centre under any description, and of these none had any distinct idea of what it was for. What was more important from the point of view of N.A.L.—as Gbedemah complained on the occasion of his electoral visit to Goaso—was that the man placed at the head of this emblematically impartial body was to become, in due course, the leader of the party which eventually won the election. Gbedemah's complaint was not, of course, that there was anything inauthentic for Busia in the rôle of civic educator. (It was indeed the precision with which the rôle fitted him which served in the unsympathetic eye to blur its impartiality.) What had aroused Gbedemah's resentment was that the Centre had given the Progress Party's leader several years start in political organisation before the ban on politics had been lifted. Organisation had been the C.P.P.'s great talisman, a word of almost magical significance, pronounced reverentially even by the District Secretary of the Progress Party, and the practice of it had always been Gbedemah's forte. In his speech in Goaso he contrived to turn the start enjoyed by his opponents almost into an advantage for himself by the dramatic projection of the speed and the nationwide scope of his own organisational efforts. It was a fine performance. But the bravado rang a little hollow.

Organisation had always been an activity of slightly ambiguous meaning in Ghanaian political practice. It took in, under one of its aspects, the mastery of the modern technical aspects of political campaigning, a mastery which the C.P.P. had introduced to most of Ghana, the provision of propaganda vans, leaflets, newspapers, speakers and party paraphernalia in which N.A.L. often enjoyed something of an edge over its opponents in this particular campaign. The symbol of this modern aspect of organisation might simply be not missing the bus. In so far as it was in itself a sufficient condition for amassing votes, there is no reason to suppose that Busia's tenancy of the Civic Education platform gave him any significant organisational advantage. But, in another of its aspects, organisation always meant something distinctly less public or modernist in character: the attentive stitching together of national coalitions out of local élites, in which there remain necessarily almost as many seams along which to fray as there are strands in the local political cloth. There can be no doubt that Busia's travels around the country and his meetings with local notables had the effect of clothing the Progress Party, on its eventual emergence, in the mantle of local élite approval, making the respectable party into the party of national respectability in most areas of the country, and thus endowing with impressive political weight an ideology which had seemed to less sensitive foreign observers almost devoid of social purchase. The organisational talents of Gbedemah himself and the C.P.P. in general in this second activity had never been tested in an environment in which there existed real opposition, without the possibility of some more or less direct recourse to the coercive or economically rewarding powers of the state. The situation in 1969 demanded substantially greater political skill for their control, and Gbedemah certainly needed much more time to unpick the seams, though time alone would hardly have turned out to be sufficient. There was thus real political substance to the advantage enjoyed by Busia through his public institution, and he had in fact visited Goaso to inaugurate a branch of it. And yet the opportunity which it must have given him in Asunafo to consolidate local élite support was in practice quite supererogatory. The main seams of such a coalition had been stitched together, as A. W. Osei observed with pride, in the election of thirteen years before. The political memory of Asunafo was largely a memory of the costs of this choice, and the survivors of this élite coalition had no need of a visit from their former party leader to commit them energetically to the effort to secure the belated rewards of their past sufferings. As the bent old women who had been beaten from their villages under the C.P.P. danced in jubilation over their enemies at the Progress Party's election rallies, it was clear that the people of Asunafo had drawn their lessons from an education with roots in a soil deeper if more ambiguous than that of the civic.

The campaign which took place within the painstakingly neutral administrative framework was conducted by two different types of actors. One, a rather small group, comprised those who were overtly or covertly contenders for selection as electoral candidates for either of two major parties which alone in the end contested the constituency.[26] The other consisted of the political organisations of these two parties. The distinction between the two groups was in part one of status, a social matter, but also in part one of vanity, a personal matter. Becoming an M.P. in Ghana represents dramatic upward social mobility for all except the vastly rich. A seat in Parliament, with its combination of direct and indirect economic returns, is a prize of such a scale that only one eligible man in Asunafo—a large-scale timber contractor—was plainly too rich for it to be worth his while acquiring it. Selection as a majority party's candidate for Parliament is an economic opportunity for which the ambitious might well choose to contend for purely egoistic reasons. It is thus not surprising that some of those who did aspire to the parties' nominations without success should then have failed to take any part in the election campaign. The story of the Progress Party's triumph in the campaign is largely the story of the failure of a series of vanities, ruffled in political defeat, to give rise to the customary fissions.

The party's success in preserving its unity was facilitated in part by the timing of one of the most important contests over candidacy. The eventual Progress candidate, Alfred Badu Nkansah, first attained political prominence in a tripartite competition for the nomination as a member of the Constituent Assembly for the two Parliamentary constituencies of Asunafo and Asutifi (the Goaso Council area). The other two candidates were A. W. Osei, the former United Party M.P. for the area, a substantially older man, and a third rather shadowy figure, apparently an itinerant vendor of patent medicines who received little support and disappeared from political view immediately after the election. Nkansah had the advantage of a university education, important in the context of selection for constitution-making, without the disability which commonly accompanied this qualification of having chosen to live and work outside the area. He had recently played a prominent part in the successful struggle to destool the chief of his home town, Akrodie;[27] he was also an active member of the resuscitated Ahafo Youth Society, the modernist pressure group in the perennial conflict with the local state bureaucracy, a body of which Osei was probably the leading light. The electors for the representative of the locality to the Constituent Assembly were the government-appointed members of the Local Council for the area, of which, too, Mr. Osei was a highly effective member. The total number of electors was less than thirty and in no sense whatever could they have been said to be statistically representative of the area. But, whether because the prominence of officials in its composition gave it a more formalist sense of the qualifications required for constitution-making (and hence led it to put greater emphasis on youth and educational attainment), or whether for more direct reasons, the electors voted, somewhat to the surprise of a number of shrewd local observers, strongly in favour of Badu Nkansah.

In the subsequent months the latter's public performance in the Assembly was prominent enough to please the more attentive local political observers. Copies of Hansard containing speeches of his percolated through to Goaso and one or two members of the community, including the local representative of the Special Branch of the police, who observed him in action in the Assembly and professed themselves satisfied. In private, Badu Nkansah naturally aligned himself with the large group of members of the Assembly who favoured Dr. Busia and he began to attend some of the meetings of this group at Busia's private house on the outskirts of Accra. At the same time Osei was in extremely poor health for some months, and he became increasingly preoccupied with the problems of running his business and attending to his very extensive familial responsibilities. Whether or not the 1969 nomination would have been such a simple choice if he had been successful in his earlier candidature for membership of the Constituent Assembly, it was not a difficult matter in the circumstances which now prevailed to decide that he had had his fill of the travails of politics and could properly emulate Cincinnatus in abandoning public for private duties. The avoidance of any direct and embittered clash between the two men was of great significance, since the core political organisation of the party remained in essentials an inheritance from Osei's earlier campaigns.

Both the party's District Secretary (a nephew of Mr. Osei, who lived

in one of the rooms in his two-storey house in Goaso) and another
leading member (who was not only a close personal friend of Osei's for
many years but a former chief of Noberkaw, one of the premier chiefly
ranks in the Ahafo division) had worked closely with Osei in the Ahafo
Youth Society. There was a certain initial distrust towards these
men on the part of the most active supporters and advisors of Badu
Nkansah, a number of whom were not Ahafo-born, because they feared
a resuscitation of Osei's candidacy and there were intermittent minor
grumblings over matters like the control of campaigning funds as these
became available, and over the general unwillingness to undertake the
entertainment of visiting dignitaries due to speak at rallies. But, despite
the general scarcity of financial resources, the atmosphere remained
strikingly amiable and co-operative.

The maintenance of amity in this key relationship during the campaign did not mean that the party escaped the pains of a sharply contested candidacy. At the meeting held in the regional capital, Sunyani,
some 80 miles from Goaso, to inaugurate the party in the Brong Ahafo
region, another eligible figure from Ahafo appeared on the V.I.P. dais as
a potential rival to Badu Nkansah. He was a man of roughly the same
age as the latter, slightly more of an urban sophisticate in appearance,
and he possessed the additional advantage of a British M.Sc. degree in
engineering. He worked at the modern port of Tema and owned a rather
new-looking Mercedes, whereas Badu Nkansah, as became important
at some points of the campaign, did not possess a car and his salary as a
school teacher was totally insufficient for him to acquire one. (There
were, indeed, certain stages of the campaign in which the need to return
to Accra to draw his allowances as a Member of the Constituent
Assembly seemed to loom larger in his financial planning for the campaign than the need to participate in its deliberations did in his political
planning.) This rival candidate, Yaw Podiee, hailed from Mim, the
largest and wealthiest town in the constituency, and this fact, combined
with his greater personal wealth, appeared to threaten Badu Nkansah
with serious competition. The threat was not an entirely idle one. The
fairness of the first selection meeting of the party was successfully
challenged by Podiee through the regional organisation of the party;
and a second meeting, summoned for the town of Sankore deep in the
forest, led first to an attempt on the part of Podiee's supporters to persuade the police to close the meeting and then to an extended public
wrangle before the chief of Sankore about the circumstances in which
the meeting had been summoned. At the end of this dispute, the
representatives of Mim marched out of the meeting and Badu Nkansah
was confirmed as the candidate by an overwhelming (and clearly an absolute) majority of the delegates. Numerous subsequent efforts to settle
the dispute aborted, usually because of the difficulty of assembling all

the injured parties at one time and place, and it was not until a meeting (in Mim itself) shortly before the election—when the District Chairman of the party who came from Mim, and another even more determined Mim representative, grumpily condescended to take part in a rally—that the breach was publicly healed. Allegations of corruption and chicanery were passed energetically in both directions and it would be imprudent to attempt a conclusive causal analysis of the result. But it was clear, quite apart from the advantage which he enjoyed by having already appeared on the national political scene as the representative of Ahafo, that one reason for Badu Nkansah's success was that in the eyes of the electorate he was a much better candidate. Podiee, a slight figure with a quiet and rather delicate mien, who had studied in England for some years, had simply been away from home for too long. The air of urban sophistication which clung around him conveyed a powerful sense of social distance. Unlike his taller, charming, noisily articulate and slightly brash opponent he lacked the capacity to 'move with the people' and did not know how to dominate a beer bar. One could not imagine anyone saying of Podiee, as the District Secretary said over and over again with quiet and confident satisfaction of Badu Nkansah, 'The people like him.' Badu's stay away from Ahafo had left him still in possession of a reassuringly familiar local identity, and he had had the political good taste to return and find a job and make his home in Ahafo. Podiee had travelled too far and returned too belatedly to serve as a plausible vehicle for the assertive political demands of Ahafo. In the event, even the possession of the large car served, with his distant air, not to promise greater efficacy as an advocate of the interests of the area, but to accentuate the transiency of his relationship with it. What might have been seen as a testimony to its owner's effectiveness served in practice merely to emphasise the extent to which he had become exotic.

Even this account of the selection of the P.P.'s candidate represents, as will be apparent later, a distinctly tidied up outline of the shape of its campaign. For the selection of the N.A.L. candidate there is no way in which even this rather specious simplicity can be matched. It had at least always been clear that one of the parties which contested any election in Asunafo under N.L.C. auspices was certain to be some version of the former United Party. What was not clear up to the very day of nomination was what other parties, if any, might enter the lists. One reason for this was simply the much greater organisational fluidity of the other parties, a national rather than a local characteristic, though one which had distinct repercussions on the local pattern of political activity. Another was the distinctly more furtive character (it was referred to by participants quite explicitly as a largely 'secret campaign') of the N.A.L. approach in the constituency when it did in fact begin. This furtiveness was in a sense a rational response to the precariousness of the government's impartiality in the election. For while the government was indubitably impartial as a unit between the parties which were permitted to contest the election, it did actively maintain its right to determine the limits within which it *was* prepared to be impartial. Not only did it ban by decree at a national level parties for alleged complicity with Nkrumah; but, at a local level, C.I.D. or Special Branch officers attended a large number of election rallies and took conscientious notes on the proceedings, while full particulars of the secret selection meeting for the N.A.L. candidate, held in a private house in Goaso, immediately found their way into the hands of the local administration. Paradoxically, in Asunafo, the party which was assumed to enjoy most support in the senior ranks of the police force nationally was subjected locally to a certain amount of inconvenience as a result of this conscientious surveillance. On the national level the party enjoyed an irreproachable security rating. Gbedemah had not merely had the good fortune to be removed by Nkrumah from the Ministry of Finance for alleged corruption. He had also had the political prudence or personal pride to respond in due course to this treatment by leaving the country and engaging in bitter public recrimination against his former leader. But this political accreditation on the national level which, along with the economic resources at the disposal of his party, explained why in the end he was able to field the only candidate who did oppose the P.P. in Asunafo, could not suffice to provide an *a-priori* charter in the eyes of the local administration for the doings of his local agents.

   The N.A.L. campaign was organised by the licit residue of the former C.P.P. local hierarchy. The major organiser, and in fact the Parliamentary candidate in the neighbouring constituency of Asutifi, Kojo Bonsu, was a former chief of Kenyase and a brother of the leading C.P.P. dignitary from Ahafo, B. K. Senkyire, M.P. in 1954, and Minister in the final Nkrumah government. The latter was widely thought in Accra to have been one of the major figures behind the party organised by Imoru Egala, a party banned during the course of the campaign by the N.L.C. for its alleged intention to bring Nkrumah back from exile. Senkyire was in no position to escape from any of the versions of the government's Disqualification policies. But although he could thus, at no point, have taken an overt part in campaigning, there is no reason to believe that his brother (who used to appear in a Mercedes universally described as Senkyire's own) would not have been able, had governmental licence permitted, to swing his support behind a party which appeared to be a more authentic inheritor of the C.P.P. mantle. As it was, it was said, rancorously by his opponents, that he had dallied politically and economically with at least two further parties before settling his favours finally upon NA.L. Such inconstancy is not a trivial matter since, if it is ignored, the insistence of N.A.L. members on the degree to which their membership of the party had been a matter of course would be seriously misleading. There is no reason to doubt the claim made by one of the most impressive local C.P.P. organisers that he had always esteemed Gbedemah, even as against Nkrumah, as the epitome of the true, pre-tyrannical (and, one may suspect, pre-ideological) C.P.P., a man whose advice, if followed, would have averted the calamity of the coup and the loss of many good jobs. Having acquired Gbedemah as a leader, the N.A.L. supporters were in no danger of being short of attributes to ad-mire in him. But rationality should not be confused with causality: the quality of the determination of their allegiance seems to have been a largely *a-posteriori* characteristic of it. One could not say that necessity had made strange bedfellows in this instance. But governmental licence might certainly have made different ones. Gbedemah's economic resources, and the character of his party as the contender least unlike the C.P.P. to contrive to survive within the limits of governmental tolerance, made him the natural inheritor of a local political *équipe* which increasingly looked to be all dressed up with nowhere to go. But although this *équipe* was an excellent example of what could be acquired for cash on a decidedly oligopolistic political market, one characteristic of it points up a general dilemma in Gbedemah's national campaign strategy.

Whereas much local political support could be picked up on a purely market basis, there were few places in which a preponderance of sup-port could be picked up on this basis alone; while organisational sup-port of any political weight acquired on a purely market basis tended to carry intrinsic costs above and beyond those of its political purchase. A political *équipe* authentically N.A.L. in its ideological identity (whatever such an *équipe* would have been like outside the Ewe areas) would not have been unduly embarassed. by administrative scrutiny. But a local C.P.P. apparatus, in which former C.P.P. District Com-missioners were covertly promised their jobs back if the party won, might well appear to the local administration as intrinsically closer to its protracted historical identity than to the decorous political label which it had so recently adopted. In this guise it might well seem to require all the administrative surveillance which it could conveniently be given. Without the government's exclusion of a potential competitor Gbedemah, then, might well have failed to garner the political support which he did acquire in Asunafo.

It is a mark of the equivocal status of N.A.L. as a contestant in the constituency that, whereas the first public P.P. meeting of the campaign was held in Goaso on 1 May, in the immediate aftermath of the lifting of the ban on politics, no major N.A.L. activity was discernible in the con-stituency at all (though a N.A.L. van did drive through on 8 June) until the middle of June when a meeting was held in the smartest Goaso beer bar. The Special Branch representative in the district claimed that as late as 7 August the party had still not secured a permit for holding an official public rally some three weeks before the election was to take place. The two campaigns represented a dramatic contrast in styles. To a very substantial extent they went their separate ways, resolutely ignoring the existence of one another. The competition between them took on many different guises, but one form which it never assumed was that of a rational and explicit debate between the two parties about how the state could best be governed. The Schumpeter image of conflicting élites blandly offering their managerial talents to discriminating consumers in an assured environment was as inept a picture of the efforts of the vendors as it was of the expectations of the purchasers. The loyalties reached for were deeper and more pervasive, and the enterprise to which electors were summoned was altogether more urgent than the practice of marketing. The rewards for success and the penalties for failure were of quite a different scale both for élites and masses, and the prospects for failure were known by all not to terminate with the election results. The image of cementing unity in the struggle against a nebulous but menacing foe, captures the language in which the activity of electioneering was described much better than that of the compulsory but attentive choice between rival schemes of hire purchase. It will be more illuminating to discuss the recruiting campaigns of the two armies separately, as they happened, and it is convenient to begin with the first to appear on the scene.

The opening meeting of the Progress Party in Goaso on 1 May, summoned by the Chief of Goaso beating gong-gong, in a sense epitomised the problems of the party in the coming months. Although it claimed to be the official inauguration of the party in the constituency, it was in fact a meeting unauthorised by the central machinery of the party: it was organised by the faction in the longstanding Goaso chieftaincy dispute which opposed the faction to which Osei belonged. As far as was then publicly known, the latter was still a prospective candidate and it was assumed that the holding of the meeting at this time was an effort to preempt the political ground for another candidate. Organisationally the meeting also foreshadowed much of the rest of the campaign: it had to be closed and reconvened some hours later because of the paucity of the attendance. The subject matter of the speeches, appropriately enough, was the need to come together to represent the interests of Ahafo in view of the dreadful damage to these interests caused by past local disunity. Three weeks later, on 21 May, the national machinery of the party, in the masterful person of A. A. Munufie, a Sunyani lawyer and interim Regional Chairman of the party, appeared in the constituency to reimpose some order on the proceedings. The meeting was supposed to be a meeting of the party executives, rather than the public, but it took place very publicly at the courthouse. Munufie was somewhat late and the chief of Goaso attempted to have the meeting postponed to another occasion. Munufie's powerful voice quieted the hubbub briefly and he explained that all the offices in the party were merely interim until the formal regional inauguration in Sunyani, three days later. Then a representative of the alternative faction in the local chieftaincy dispute complained that the self-selected party executive did not represent the people of Goaso and the meeting broke up noisily.

The regional inauguration on 24 May duly saw many important Ahafo figures at Sunyani. The former Paramount of Ahafo, the Kukuomhene, was among the chiefs sitting in state beneath their umbrellas, while Mr. Osei and his nephew (the aspiring District Secretary) and both candidates for the party nomination were also conspicuously in attendance. Busia arrived to speak to a substantial crowd, flanked by numerous policemen and traditional state executioners. It was a gay and festive occasion, featuring sundry party dignitaries from Accra, a band or two, some dancing, men with megaphones, party motor-cyclists, a carload of girls dressed in white and red, and a good deal of genial disorganisation. If the party shrank from the distribution of bread (or its Ghanaian analogue, sardines), it clearly had no inhibitions about supplying the people with circuses. A main theme of Busia's speech was an assurance that he did not propose to dismantle the Brong Ahafo region (Sunyani's sole industry). It was in essence a denial (made rather anxiously by Munufie in Goaso three days before) of the charge of being a lackey of the Ashanti, which the former U.P. leader was clearly under strong pressure to make.

In three weeks after this inauguration the decisively national focus of the campaign's objective, and the external political resources which this made available within the constituency, began to impose order on the ebullient particularism of Ahafo to the extent of providing it, by mid-June, with an authorised District Executive, the election of which had been duly supervised by party officials from outside the constituency. Osei's nephew, Benson Anane, duly became the Secretary and his election was made more generally palatable by Osei's own public declaration that he was not prepared to stand as a candidate. The self-elected Goaso executive was largely supplanted outside the town itself, but it swallowed its pride and continued to co-operate in the campaign. Further public meetings, at both of which Munufie spoke, were held at Mim and (in the second week of June) at Kukuom, in the immediate aftermath of Kukuomhene's acquittal celebrations,[28] a piece of timing which secured an optimal audience but which clearly irritated the chief himself. On 29 June Badu Nkansah was chosen as the candidate, Yaw Podiee having, as the Executive judged, improperly submitted his application to the regional office and thus being ineligible. The consequences of this dispute dragged on for several more weeks, exhausting most of the energies available. Taken with the unavailability of a party van for the district, and with Badu Nkansah's modest personal means and his need to leave the constituency for substantial periods to participate in the Constituent Assembly, it resulted in there being a temporary respite in the public campaign—a respite which lasted until a meeting in Badu Nkansah's home town Akrodie in mid-July to which a leading U.P. former detainee, R. R. Amponsah, came to speak.

The remainder of the P.P. campaign was more continuous and less eventful. There were a substantial number of further public meetings, held at least once in all the major population centres in the constituency, several with visiting speakers. A promised visit by Busia himself never materialised, though on two occasions leading party supporters in the constituency made extended trips outside it in order to hear him speak. The content of speeches did not vary very much, though the tone of persuasion wavered in sophistication and delicacy from the purely pietistic to the sharply and personally minatory, and from the grandly universalistic to the meanly ethnic. Apart from the intermittent character of the candidate's presence, the most striking organisational problem throughout was one of transport. The modern party van from the regional organisation was shared with several other constituencies and was thus only occasionally available. Bedu Nkansah, out of the not very extensive campaigning funds raised at local rallies and made available to him by the party's central organisation, contrived to borrow or hire a motley array of decrepit vehicles ranging from a Land Rover with a wooden body to a pair of exhausted Volkswagens, none of which spent as much time available for use as they did being repaired. The constituency was of substantial size, and its population was scattered through the forest in clusters most of which, because of the rather uncharacteristically low rainfall in 1969, could be reached by road in a fairly robust vehicle. There can be no doubt that the party organisers were compelled to devote more energy and money to actually getting to as many places as possible in the constituency to campaign than they did to any other part of their enterprise. When they actually did get to most of the more rural villages, they confined their political activities, apart from consultations with the party's local representatives where such were to be found, to a brief introduction of the candidate, an identification of the party emblem (which illiterates had to remember if they were to be able to vote at all) and an extensively mimed representation of the activity of voting. The procedure for voting was in fact fairly elaborate and the mime consequently took up most of the time available at each halt. The entire procedure was described throughout by the party organisers as 'educating the people' in how to vote. It was certainly true, too, that what was transacted was more aptly described as educating them in how to vote for those for whom it was assumed they would already wish to vote, than as attempting to persuade them to vote for a particular party. The P.P. assumed throughout (quite correctly as the results demonstrated)[29] that their problem was simply one of getting electors to the polls with an understanding of the mechanism of casting a ballot, not one of persuading them to vote for the P.P. rather than for their opponents. On occasion they pressed this exercise in civic education rather hard—as when they visited a primary school and attempted to get the Headmaster to teach the children to identify the P.P. symbol in order to assist their parents in doing so when the opportunity in due course arose. The neutrality of this undertaking was greeted with some incredulity by the predominantly Ewe schoolteachers and in fact the N.A.L. vote in this village was one of the highest in the constituency.

The N.A.L. campaign began later and proceeded in an altogether more covert and less assured fashion. A bus load of supporters from one village deep in the forest was alleged to have gone to Gbedemah's inauguration rally but the P.P. resolutely denied that this had happened. A N.A.L. propaganda van, painted in the party's striking red and yellow colours, had appeared in the constituency on a number of occasions in the first half of June. The P.P. organisers claimed to know the identity of the N.A.L. candidate as early as the middle of June, and indeed gave the (true) fact that he came from Mim as an argument against the chances of Podiee's being selected as P.P. candidate. But it was not until shortly after this that N.A.L. held their first Goaso executive meeting, presided over by one of the party's regional officials, Mr. Essel, the Kukuomhene's clerk. T. N. Baidoo, a former C.P.P. District Commissioner, a relative and long-time rival of Osei's and a colleague on the first official agency for the development of the area seventeen years before,[30] spoke at length at this meeting. It was clear that the organisational talent of the party was a direct heritage from the C.P.P., though the preliminary District Chairman, a male nurse, S. K. Dontor, was a Fanti and a relative newcomer to the district. On 5 July after a series of postponements an official candidate selection meeting of the party began. There were three competitors for the nomination. One, J. K. Osei, a quiet schoolteacher from Mim at that point teaching outside the constituency at Bechem, was a member of the Ahafo Youth Society and agreed by all to be an excellent candidate. The other two contestants were an agricultural survey officer from Akrodie, said to lack force of personality and a large bull-like man, recently admitted to the University of Ghana as a mature student, who had studied meat technology in Germany and served as production manager of the government meatpacking factory in Bolgatanga. He had expressed a vehement and pungently cynical interest in politics at his University interview and was clearly a formidable figure. But, as one of the executive remarked quietly before the meeting began, he had little prospect of success since he came from Ashanti and his eligibility derived solely from his mother's ownership of a farm in the district at Ayumso: 'If we are not going to have a candidate who is Ahafo-born, then let's stop the party.' Most of the meeting was taken up with a dispute over the choice of the party District Chairman in which the geographical divisions, Kukuom side and Mim side, were reflected in a bitter conflict as to whose candidate should be selected as Chairman, a conflict in which the even balance of forces might well have foreshadowed (and was clearly expected by all participants to foreshadow) a conflict between the two localities over the Parliamentary candidature. Some of the structural problems of the party were revealed by the subject matter of the dispute—the significance of having a literate rather than an illiterate (sc. the Kukuom representative), the desirability of having a local man rather than a stranger (sc. the temporary chairman, S. K. Dontor), and the usual range of accusations of chicanery in the distribution of information. The valiant endeavour of the regional presiding officer, Kojo Bonsu, and his determined insistence on the need for unity and propriety, did not prevent the meeting from breaking up after some hours (and before the Parliamentary candidate had been selected) in what the District administration rather unsympathetically described as a riot. The one determinate result of the meeting, the election of a District Executive, by confirming Dontor as District Chairman, further emphasised the tension in the party's local identity. Since, as one of the Executive observed *sotto voce*, the party's leader was very much a stranger to Ahafo, it would have been a pointless exercise to attempt to portray itself as more indigenous than the indigenes. N.A.L. was forced therefore into the pursuit of the allegiance of the relatively large local stranger population, above all the Ewes and Krobos. But in doing so, it risked discrediting itself as an authentic representative of the locality. Even the eventual running of an Ahafo-born candidate could not quite dissipate the whiff of the alien which hung about it and any more purposeful attempt to elude this identity would have risked the sacrifice of a more or less guaranteed core of electoral support in exchange for a highly speculative (and in all probability non-existent) chance of a majority.

    The day after the fracas at the courthouse N.A.L. applied for a police permit to hold another candidate selection meeting but the request was refused because the District Administration thought it likely that a week of cooling off might be required to prevent further trouble. In the event a N.A.L. van returned to the constituency from Sunyani on the following day and a secret meeting was held at the house of T. N. Baidoo, rather mysteriously reported as a public rally in one of the national newspapers, at which the offer to the former C.P.P. District Commissioners that they should regain their jobs in the event of a N.A.L. victory was allegedly made by the party official from Sunyani. Thereafter the party contrived to conduct what was referred to, both by its own adherents and the P.P. with varying admiration or censure, as its 'secret campaign'. It never had the full use of a propaganda van with which at one time all constituencies were supposed to be endowed and there was some grumbling among the party's temporary employees at the non-appearance of other resources. There is no good reason to suppose that really large sums of money ever arrived in the constituency for its campaigning purposes, though there is much reason to suppose that this came as a considerable and disagreeable surprise to many of those concerned. Indeed some senior members of the party were still expecting the arrival of some thousands of pounds in the constituency on the very eve of polling itself. The party's stylish propaganda vans drove through the main towns from time to time, playing the same catchy religious popsongs from their speakers as those favoured by local motorised salesmen of patent medicines, and the party's slogans were duly broadcast at the bystanders. As campaigning it had, as far as it went, a harder, brassier tone than that of its opponents, slicker, more modern and more urban. But as campaigning goes, it cannot be claimed that in quantitative terms it went very far, and the image it left behind it had some of the meretriciousness, the urban untrustworthiness of the patent medicine vendors, besides its protective promises. The yawning gap between this assured and transient public advertisement and the furtive, persistent, 'organisational' efforts of the local party machine, was not reassuring. It suggested the menace at least as much as the blandishments of modernity.

The climax of the N.A.L. campaign, by contrast, was the most dramatic and the most public local event of the entire election campaign: the visit of the party's leader to Goaso, Kukuom and Mim a fortnight before polling day itself. The excitement generated by this event was intense. Whatever may have been its causal weight (and no doubt this should not be exaggerated since the party's total poll barely exceeded the joint attendance at its three meetings), its symbolic significance could hardly be overestimated. As the beautiful Ewe girls in all their finery danced on the hillside in the sunshine, waiting for their leader, the atmosphere in the crowd was sharply expectant. When the party vans at the head of the procession hurtled into town, blaring out the thudding Twi rhythms, 'He is coming: He is coming: He is coming,' a quite different level of political panache had entered the campaign however briefly. The meeting itself in Goaso was a demonstrative exercise in the new political respectability. Gbedemah's former Parliamentary foe and locally prominent current opponent, Mr. Osei, was given a

seat of honour with Gbedemah and his local aides on the steps of the
Goaso Local Council building, while Gbedemah's speech (which took
up the entire meeting) included much stress on the virtues of opposition
in a Parliamentary democracy and the iniquity of political violence and
the one-party state. A tall and powerful-looking man, of extraordinary
self-assurance and striking physical glamour, he formed as he stood up
to speak a stunning incarnation of sheer power and success. If this was
success, then it was easy to see how many might feel that nothing else
could succeed quite like it. The speech itself, although fluent enough and
undeniably forceful in delivery and sentiment, hardly matched the
dazzling quality of the physical presence. Partly this was a matter of
clashing styles. The speech was delivered in a confident Twi, but it kept
lapsing at the more aspirational points into clusters of apparently well-
worn phrases or whole sentences in English.[31] The attentive
cosmopolitan 'liberal' stress on the values of Parliamentary opposition
jostled against a rather cruder presentation of the meaning of
Gbedemah's campaigning presence: the bringing of rain to a parched
Navrongo and of a miraculous draught of fishes to the port of Elmina.
The main theme of the speech was the certainty of his electoral triumph
all over the country: Keta, Dodze, Cape Coast, Sekondi, Bawku, Bolga,
Walewale, Wa, Manya, even Wenchi, and the consequent
rationality—prudential and emotional—of joining in. The whole
speech was an articulation of the party's slogan 'N.A.L. VICTORY'.
The offer was plain and forceful enough and if it was made in English,
rather than, as with the P.P.'s pietistic chant (P.P. Good Party) in Twi,
there is no doubt that it was couched in a dialect which has become per-
vasively understood in Ghana. Shorter versions of the speech were
delivered to smaller crowds in Kukuom (where the cavalcade paid a
brief private call on the chief but the latter did not appear at the public
function); and at Mim where Gbedemah was jeered by a hostile crowd.
One small detail, no doubt a consequence of the strains of the campaigning tour,[32] stood out in retrospect. As the resplendent Gbedemah
towered over the slight, bemused figure of the local N.A.L. candidate,
whose hand he held up in introduction to the people ('if you vote for
him, you will be voting for ME'), he twice, at Goaso and at Kukuom,
forgot the candidate's name and was obliged to ask in an irritable hiss
what it was.

When the electors went to the polls a fortnight later, they voted
overwhelmingly for the Progress Party, as they did in both the other
constituencies along the main road out of the Ahafo forest towards
Sunyani and Kumasi.

Asunafo	A. Badu Nkansah (P.P.)	13039	81 polling stations
	J. K. Osei (N.A.L.)	2715	P.P. wins 79

Asuntifi	I. K. Osei Duah (P.P.)	6026	42 polling stations
	Nana Kojo Bonsu (N.A.L.)	1707	all won by P.P.
	Kwame Anane Obinim (U.N.P.)	124	
Ahafo-Ano	H. M. Adjei-Sarpong (P.P.)	11959	49 polling stations
	G. K. Annin-Adjei (N.A.L.)	2268	all won by P.P.

It was a remarkably peaceful and administratively well-organised poll. Before considering, however, what the electors were voting about, it is necessary to discuss a number of possibly coercive features which would make such a question otiose. If men are compelled to vote in a particular way it cannot usefully be said that they vote *about* anything. They merely do what they are told. Many Ghanaians, for convincing inductive reasons, undoubtedly do expect that electral behaviour will be essentially an exercise in obedience. As one old man whom I interviewed replied testily in an answer to the question of how one should choose a political party: 'I don't know anything about that. But when the time comes I will put the paper into the box into which all the people are putting theirs.'[33] Ghanaian society is in many ways highly authoritarian and it would be naive to expect political parties as composite social realities, if not as formal hierarchies of command, to eschew the use of such dispersed authority as is available to them. But it is not a trivially definitional matter to insist, against Hobbes or possibly Marx, on the crucial significance of the voluntaristic element in electing. Fear is not the same as respect, and force without right as the basis of electoral choice does erase whatever symbolically consensual element might be thought to reside in the act of voting. It is thus a matter of some embarrassment, though one which in prevailing conditions could hardly be otherwise, that it is impossible to pronounce with complete assurance on the degree of random social coercion or malpractice involved in the election. One point which does seem clear is that such coercion as did occur was on this occasion, because of the real secrecy of the ballot, effective at an economic rather than a physical level. The fear of violence may not have been altogether absent. There were a small number of brawls in the course of the campaign—the N.A.L. candidate in the neighbouring constituency, Kojo Bonsu, was even taken to court himself on a rather tendentious assault charge—but the actual incidence of violence was distinctly lower than almost everyone expected. Gbedemah himself did feel it worthwhile to warn in his speech in Goaso that the soldiers in the constituency were not coming to threaten people but to assist the wholly inadequate numbers of the police in supervising the large number of polling stations. But only a small number of soldiers ever appeared and they certainly did not intervene in the electoral process. More graphically, the chief of one town did threaten to beat the passengers if a N.A.L. propaganda van came to his town, but it was reported later that one had done so without injury being incurred.

In general, traditional authority does not appear to have been very active in the campaign even in a non-coercive fashion, though one chief did arrive at the main P.P. rally with a busload of supporters from his town and at least two others publicly declared their support of the P.P. The average age of the chiefs in the area was rather high, most of them having been removed by the C.P.P., and then replaced by the N.L.C. under decree 112. Their formal legitimacy was on the whole impeccable, but it might be doubted whether all could have survived the threat of destoolment for so long in a more open political environment. In any case, whether because of the inertia of age and a sense of subjective fragility in their authority, or because of the strong governmental directives to chiefs to remain neutral in the electoral campaign, most did maintain some public decorum. Furthermore the P.P., which for obvious historical reasons enjoyed the support of the majority of them, was in no position because of is unceasing public commitment to rectitude to make use of these dubiously legitimate political actors for publicly coercive purposes in any general way. Any effort to do so on its part would have risked not only an embarrassing exposure at the hands of its opponents but also, since the ballot was in fact secret, distinctly counterproductive effects when it actually came to the voting.

Perhaps the level at which the notion of coercion is relevant at all is the level of vague menace, characteristic in industrial society on occasion of some aspects of workplace solidarity in which a measure of blackmail is indubitably involved, but in which it is clearly appropriate to see the threats as largely those of moral scorn, rather than of instrumental violence.[34] There was at least one occasion when the Progress Party representatives read out from the electoral registers the names of the inhabitants of a small forest village, and warned them darkly that the election results were going to be known this time, polling station by polling station, and the party would know all too well which way they had voted. There can be no doubt too that Gbedemah, when he emphasised the secrecy of the ballot in his Goaso speech[35] against those who had been threatening share-croppers and cocoa labourers with dispossession or unemployment if they voted the wrong way, was attempting to deal with a real political threat. The reality of the threat was indeed confirmed by the explanation given by a N.A.L. organiser of the small forest wards in which it did prove successful: that the main landholdings in the area were under the control of strong party supporters. The nagging fear, too, that physical violence might ultimately be deployed was not a total fantasy, though it was also not justified in the event. At least one prominent P.P. campaigner suggested in the immediate aftermath of its crushing victory that the party's supporters take the opportunity to repay some of the violence which they had incurred in the past at the hands of their C.P.P. opponents, though the suggestion was indignantly repudiated as atavistic and disgraceful.[36]

It would have been absurd in a society like that of Ghana to expect an election campaign to be uncontaminated by a good deal of more or less discreet bullying. But even where the numbers of electors involved was low enough partially to vitiate the protection conferred by the secrecy of the ballot, it would be easy to misdescribe the implication of the directed quality of the vote. Even if the politics of Asunafo is largely to be described as a politics of patronage, and of integrating clientages for political purposes, it does not follow that such mechanisms—in conditions of genuinely secret balloting and without recourse to state power—can appropriately be envisaged as the rule of terror or as the subjection of a mass of individual wills to the antagonistic will of a single man. After all, one can only vote in an election between the candidates who present themselves, and between the two candidates who did so in this instance it would have required a more than Chinese ideological sensitivity to detect a trace of difference in the character of their class appeal. This is hardly an occasion for wonder in view of the virtually complete absence of class-consciousness as such from the political mind of Asunafo. Such patronal political instruction as was put about under these conditions was certainly less likely to represent the coercive repression of the desires of individual voters to vote in a particular fashion than it was simply the provision to them of reasons for troubling to vote at all. In the particular N.A.L. village in question—a village organised by a long-term resident from the Kusasi area of northern Ghana and peopled largely by Kusasis whom he had settled there—its patronal reliability is as plausibly represented as depending on its ethnic homogeneity and the strength of personal obligations as on its susceptibility to purely economic threats. In general, such solidarism as there was in the constituency seems to have taken an ethnic and not a class form. In a multi-linguistic area of recent, but geographically dispersed, settlement the dimensions of community which are directly relevant to the structure of men's lives necessarily have more to do with the concreteness of cultural affinity than with the abstract dimensions of social stratification. Inter-ethnic trust is a necessary, and as yet unavailable, prerequisite for the experiential salience of a consciousness of class.

It is not a simple matter to capture the meaning of these events. Indeed the problems of analysing the politics of such an area substantially recapitulate the problems of, in the graphic Ghanaian vernacular, 'doing politics' in such an area. Where practice is so intricate and so densely particular, theory is in no condition to leap confidently ahead. The entire election can be aptly seen as an investigation in very practical terms of the social location of moral feelings. But it would have been rash for any participant, and it would be still more rash of an external observer, to claim with confidence that he was certain of just where the boundaries of such feelings do lie for different groups. But if we are to make any serious attempt to delineate the intersection between the national and the local which such an election necessarily represents, and, above all, if we are to move towards determining the terms of trade between the national and the local which is where the internal meaning of the national politics of African states largely resides, it is essential not merely to distinguish in the current American style between symbolic identification and technical economic rationality in electoral choice but also to offer a serious account of the moral character of such identification.

The dimension of technical rationality need not detain us for long. It has been the indubitable achievement, though it may perhaps not have been the aim, of the American economic theorists of democracy to prove conclusively that no actual individual in a western democracy has sufficient egoistic grounds, by their own stringent criteria of egoism, to bother to drag himself to the polling station at all.[37] A possible incidental felicity of the study of African elections might thus be—whether through the offers of money, corned beef or sardines or the threat of blows—to provide belated instances of the vote as an economically rational act. It must indeed have been true during some elections in Ghana under the C.P.P. that electors were on occasion tried by the fearsome ordeals of Downs and Olson and not found wanting in egoistic rationality. But the secrecy of the ballot on this particular occasion, while it may have left some men with reasons upon compulsion to make their way to the polling booths, cannot have given anyone a reason actually to cast a valid vote for anyone once he had got there. It is true that for anyone who did reach the ballot box after extended waiting in the queue, because it had been made clear to him that it was in his interest to do so, the marginal cost of choosing to vote for the side he preferred over making a purely random choice might seem small; and the discrimination of rationality under such circumstances may perhaps prudently be left to those with the requisite mathematical techniques. In any case few electors had a sufficiently complex picture of the political universe, upon which they might have attempted to exert a purchase by their vote, to be in any position to indulge in such complex mathematics.

But if the rationale for voting must have been of a symbolic and not merely an egoistically rational nature, the more traditional understandings of democracy do plausibly regard some forms of symbolic identification as distinctly more symbolic than others. A traditional understanding of egoistic rationality in voting would merely require that in voting men are choosing a state of affairs which they would, in their expectation, prefer to any alternative on offer. Rationality inheres in the preference (or set of preferences) itself, and does not have to be stretched to the willingness to participate in the entire ritual. No doubt in the absence of effective sanctions at the level of expressed preferences (the ballot being clearly secret in *effect*—as it was everywhere in procedure—in all but a few small and isolated polling stations),[38] the electors of Asunafo did on the whole attain this minimal standards of rationality. Agreement on this matter, however, does not greatly sharpen the point at issue because of the virtual unanimity of the parties on what might be politely called policy issues. Not only was there no detectable difference in the class appeals of N.A.L. and P.P., a matter in which Ghanaian rhetoric may well be closer to Ghanaian reality than is true of the politics of many other countries; there were few detectable explicit disagreements on the techniques to be employed in the pursuit of agreed goals. Political rhetoric remained firmly within the bounds of the kingdom of ends, and even there it cannot be said to have taken a very contestatory form. All parties promised economic development, employment, industrialisation, the fostering of agriculture, educational advance. (You want it, we name it). None provided concrete suggestions as to how the cargo could be inveigled down to earth. The P.P. manifesto was perhaps slightly more explicit than that of its main opponents. But whatever significance that fact may have had in Ghanaian politics at large, it cannot have had much in the politics of Asunafo since virtually no one in the constituency had seen a copy by polling day and it is doubtful whether *anyone* in the constituency had read it. Few parties in any country, of course, go to the polls on a platform of bringing about swingeing cuts in the general standard of living, and it is hardly unique to Ghana to regard politicians' public proclamations of their intentions as possessing little or no predictive value. But it is more unusual for a rational preference over social and economic policies to depend exclusively upon the relative credibility of the parties' proclaimed good faith.[39] Since there was nothing about which to choose between the parties, except the degree to which one could contrive to believe what they said, the level of symbolic identification involved in electoral choice was, on this occasion, notably high.

Two types of symbolic identification were in fact marketed by the two parties, and their purveying formed the ideological content of the campaign. The election result itself represented the decisive, if perhaps necessarily temporary, choice of one of these identities by the electors of Asunafo. But there are two other types of symbolic identification with which the election might conceivably have been concerned, but which it in practice evaded. These two require to be discussed independently of the campaign itself. The first may well have been a potentiality only at a purely mythical level, the creature of a story put about by Nkrumah and David Apter: the children of the transformational promise of the

C.P.P., the youthful and pioneering protagonists of modernity. The committed *croyant* in the efficacy of political mobilisation might endeavour to explain its absence by the military government's resonant antipathy to the notion, and by the fact that the N.A.L. was almost as unenthusiastic about it as the N.L.C. itself. Since, however, its earlier appearance in the story derived directly from the even more resonant sympathy of the preceding C.P.P. government, it is not necessary to be over-impressed by the economy of this explanation: 'no political mobilisation without the risk of subsequent political demobilisation'. The state gave and the state hath taken away. Blessed be the name of the state. No one in Asunafo appeared to conceive of himself in terms in any way continuous with these. Fifteen years of submission to the ordeal of political modernisation appeared to have left local identities not merely unreconstructed but virtually unscathed.

The second potential identity which failed to appear in the campaign to any significant extent was almost the obverse of the first. Whereas the C.P.P. had been an instance of political lexical transfer masquerading as political institutional transfer, this second identity was un-challengeably concrete, historical and there. The terms of trade between national and local had been such indeed that, while the C.P.P. supplied the words, Ahafo retained a fairly unremitting control over their meanings. The history of the C.P.P.'s struggle to establish its local power by the manipulation of multitudinous local identities proved, in substance, to have lent its power to their purposes to an even greater extent. Localism is a powerful force in Ahafo and the meaning of the election might well have been purely localist, might have been confined to the reenactment of local factional conflict between town and town or between one consolidated chiefly interest and another. The first eventuality seems never to have occurred. Even such inveterate historical foes as Kenyasi I and Kenyasi II[40] voted firmly for the same candidate. The fact that in the Asutifi constituency N.A.L. did not even win a single polling station, and in Asunafo it won only three out of some 80, disposes conclusively of the possibility that either party contrived on this occasion to turn the election into a simple town squabble. The traditional tensions between Kukuom side and Mim side came out in an etiolated form only in the candidate selection process of the two parties. But as a shadow of its former self it was so pale as to bereft of causal significance. The most impressive result of the election, and the conclusive testimony to N.A.L.'s failure, was the establishment of the unity of Ahafo as a political interest. A necessary condition for such unity, and one which was surprisingly in practice available, was an accepted common front on the problems of the traditional political order of Ahafo.

The difficulty of contriving this requires some little explanation. Most local areas in Ghana are subjected to regular disputes over the location of traditional political legitimacy. Enormous energy is expended on such disputes, and it requires great political sensitivity and skill (sometimes greater than is available) for the local and national administrations to control the dimensions of conflict.[41] Extensive efforts, both financial and coercive, are made by local protagonists to secure the services of the national administration for their purposes, and equally strenuous efforts in much the same currency, are made by national political forces to use local dissensions to consolidate their own national patronage structures. The monopoly of power in the hands of the state now makes it (and has made it for some time in the past) impractical for local actors to offer explicit resistance to the state as such. Biafra may dream of secession. But no such opportunity, transparently, can be open to the Dagomba or the Nzima.[42] Nevertheless, due subservience to state authority does not necessarily imply obedience to its local representatives. The King is always good, but any of his local ministers is plausibly wicked and may at least be subjected to purposeful obstruction on behalf of the King's supposed real will. (Even within the colonial theory of impassive obedience, the impassivity at the receiving end often surpassed the obedience.) This presentation is made easier by the fact that the state has not ceased to advertise the virtuous quality of its will since the time of the British conquest of Ashanti, and there has been general verbal agreement on the criterion for virtue in the adjudication of traditional legitimacy: namely, tradition. Ideologically the transaction has been one between a national near-monopoly of fire-power and a local near-monopoly of legitimacy. It has been a transaction in which each participant has been able to supply real services to the other. Indirect rule provided both agents with cheap, if intrinsically limited, increments of power. But over the years fire-power has proved distinctly easier to concentrate than legitimacy. If this is in some ways deplorable, it should not be in any way surprising. The promise of the integrative revolution is the construction of an ideological or spiritual surrogate for an armoury. But it is increasingly unclear whether in post-colonial states the spiritual component can, for some time, be much more than a legend over the armoury door. Traditional legitimacy in actuality is almost as dispersed locally as charisma. Conceptually it reposes very solidly upon history. Practically, however, history must be seen as being tastefully rearranged around it. Few statements about the history of Ahafo, however innocent in intention, can escape being politically partisan in effect. There are almost as many histories of Ahafo as there are long established settlements in Ahafo.[43] Since, too, they exist orally rather in a written form and since politics goes on, both locally and nationally, their political availability need not be impaired even by the constraints of consistency over time. The Ancient Constitution of

Ahafo has many historiographers and they display what Nkrumah, for instance, would have seen as an altogether excessive measure of feudal legalism.[44] Village Spelmans and Bradys, they are far from mute and they can enjoy their own glories without having to submit to the chastening disciplines of print.

Much of the political dispute in Ahafo is conducted in consequence, just as it was in the seventeenth century England or France,[45] in terms which wear, to the alien modern eye, an air of rather desperate paradox. It is not the historicist oddity of regarding a set of events in the sociologically (and indeed chronologically) distant past as the proper criterion for a set of present political arrangements, but the extraordinary logical contortions (made familiar for English history by John Pocock) which are necessarily involved in the reasoned defence of the set of past events selected to act as the criterion. When these logical conundra have been resolved in the constitutional history of Ahafo they have had to be so more by exercise of the will than of the intelligence. There has been no obvious shortage of wills, however, ready to shoulder the burden, either inside or outside Ahafo. Whatever the origins of the earliest settlers of Ahafo, it is undisputed that the area was at one time thoroughly integrated within the Ashanti empire. Both of the main constitutional traditions in Ahafo acknowledge that the proper context for its political analysis, ever since its incorporation, has been the struggle between centrifugal and centripetal forces inside the empire. The circumstances under which it was integrated, serve to explain the character of its political subordination to Ashanti, while this character in its turn goes some way to account for the enduring strength of local separatism. Its initial incorporation into Ashanti followed on the pursuit, into the virtually uninhabited forest area by a punitive expedition under several of the Kumasi wing chiefs, of an invading force from what is now the Ivory Coast, which had contrived to sack Kumasi. In the aftermath of these events (the Abiri Moro war) the Ashanti leaders left behind them in the forest areas a number of small settlements manned by their followers. These settlements naturally retained their Kumasi traditional allegiances. Consequently, different Ahafo towns owed allegiance within the traditional constitution of Ashanti to different Kumasi chiefs and the Ahafo area as a whole lacked a unitary local political focus. During the last quarter of the nineteenth century, under the impact of British military and diplomatic pressure, the central political control of Ashanti weakened and the possibility of successful local political consolidation against Kumasi became a real one.[46] In 1896 the British signed a treaty of protection with one of the major Ahafo chiefs, the Kukuomhene. Shortly afterwards, with the defeat of the last Ashanti struggle for independence in the Yaa Asantewaa war, the British authorities recognised the Kukuomhene as the Paramount

Chief of an Ahafo division which was rendered formally independent of Ashanti. In the Ashanti understanding of these events, this represented the recognition of a *fait accompli,* but one the status of which was exclusively *de facto* rather than *de jure.* In the separatist understanding, it was merely the recognition of the rights already secured by the Ahafo war of liberation, the Asibi Entwi war, the very occurrence of which is denied by Ashanti.[47] The British colonial authorities at this stage appear to have displayed a fair degree of moral relaxation in their treatment of traditional legitimacy. Their recognition of Ahafo's independence undoubtedly owed more to their sense of prospective administrative convenience than to their regard for the historicity of Asibi Entwi.

Over the next thirty years, the British administration in Ashanti developed, as public bureaucracies and particularly British ones are apt to do, an extremely moral conception of its own rôle. Partly out of guilt at its own initial callowness (evoked largely by the intractable figure of Rattray who enlightened his bemused colleagues on the spiritual meaning of the Ashanti habit of human sacrifice) and partly out of sheer exhaustion at the recalcitrance of local political identities, it acquired a healthy respect for the significance of history. Eventually, in 1935, it chose to expiate its past guilt and enhance its future power by the resuscitation of the Ashanti confederacy in virtually its pristine splendour. (Human sacrifice was omitted). This restoration was a supposedly consensual affair. All Paramount Chiefs affected were consulted and most welcomed the proposal, though Kukuomhene did show apprehension over whether he would be permitted to retain his Paramountcy.[48] In the event, since the restoration was so complete, Ahafo towns returned to their disparate traditional masters in Kumasi and the Kukuomhene became once again merely one among the many other local chiefs. The restoration was undoubtedly effective in that chieftaincy affairs, after slight initial turbulence, remained relatively placid and uncontroversial for the next two decades. But there is no doubt that the interest of Ahafo as such, both in the costly traditional courts of Kumasi[49] and the relatively modernist exploitation of the Ashanti National Levy, were not well protected against those of Kumasi.

There was consequently extensive local separatist sentiment, of a firmly economic character, available for political utilization. In his struggle against the Ashanti-based N.L.M. Nkrumah was consequently able to unite the economic and traditional political components of Ahafo separatism to provide a supplement to the Brong separatism of the Brong-Kyempim Federation. The institutional outcome of his strenuous rewiring of the circuits was the creation of a separate Brong–Ahafo region out of most of what had long before been the Western Province of Ashanti and the restoration of the Paramountcy over a reconstituted Ahafo division to the Kukuomhene. The lines of political division inside Ahafo thus arrayed the traditional political interest of Kukuom and the modern political interest of the C.P.P. (a union symbolised by a number of substantial favours the Kukuom State Council were prepared to do for the former C.P.P. Member of Parliament, B. K. Senkyire) against the traditional political interest of Ashanti and the modern political interest of the United Party. In the aftermath of the 1966 coup however all the chieftaincy arrangements of the C.P.P. were conscientiously undone. The former U.P. chiefs were returned to their stools, the Kukuomhene ceased to be a Paramount, the lines of allegiance to the Kumasi chiefs were restored, and the Kukuomhene in due course was personally, if perhaps rather untraditionally,[50] summoned to pay his allegiance to the Asanthene.

The political situation to which these events gave rise was as murky as it was important. Indeed it is largely the case that it remained so murky precisely because it was so important. The traditional issues were so delicate that they were at no point left in the hands of the Chieftaincy Secretariat,[52] the decorous body set up by the N.L.C. to restore belated impartiality to the State's handling of traditional affairs, but were dealt with throughout directly by the government itself. A government commission, the Bannerman Commission, was set up to consider the question of Ahafo lands, but its proceedings were shortly suspended *sine die*, and nothing more was ever heard of it. In the meantime Ahafo traditional land revenues were frozen, the area being bereft of a State Council. Chiefs failed to receive their salaries and scholarship and other development funds were rendered unusable. There was general local agreement on the imperative need for the restitution of *some* local political order, though the local supporters of Ashanti, headed by the Chief of Mim, and those of Kukuom inevitably continued to differ on the issue of what form this order should appropriately take. As the election campaign began, the Kukuomhene was appearing on a state charge before the High Court at Sunyani for refusing to obey the Asantehene's legal summons to pay his homage in person. He was defended against this charge—the penalty for which, had he been convicted, would have been a substantial jail sentence—by a Sunyani lawyer, Munufie, who duly turned out to be the interim Regional Chairman of the Progress Party and who became a Minister in the government. On 9 June the Circuit Judge found the Kukuomhene not guilty of the offences charged on the ground that the Kukuom stool was not subject to the Golden Stool of Ashanti.[52] The extended historiographical basis of the judgement did not conceal (as in all arguments of a prescriptive character, where argument has become necessary, it inevitably could not conceal), the firm basis of choice on which the verdict rested. There are, plausibly, many legal contexts in which it is not a felicitous analysis to maintain that law is what the courts decide. But this was certainly not one of them. The effort to cement the chief's allegiance persisted until the election itself. Munufie took the opportunity of his acquittal celebrations to hold a Progress Party rally at Kukuom, rather to the chief's annoyance. Gbedemah in his turn duly paid his respects of the occasion of his own visit to Kukuom. The P.P. local organisers worried intermittently over the chief's prospective support and many of the N.A.L. campaigners tended to assume the continuity of his loyalties. Even in Kukuom itself there remained doubt about his sympathies almost up to the day of polling. Given such a level of decorum and discretion, the effect of his sympathies cannot have been very extensive. But whether it remained a decorous prudence or a genuine impartiality, there is no question that it furnished a necessary condition for the exclusion of one potentially salient meaning from the campaign, that of being yet another battle in the long war against Ashanti control of Ahafo. The Progress Party in Ahafo did not need the forceful backing of the chief of Kukuom in order to win the election. N.A.L. undoubtedly did, if it was to present a real political challenge at all. Perhaps such an opportunity was closed to it even before the campaign began, and before the High Court in Sunyani brought in its verdict. After the close of the P.P. inauguration rally in Sunyani, prominent party supporters congregated at Munifie's house on the outskirts of the town. Among them, at one point, in two successive cars of drastically varying elegance, there appeared the Kukuomhene and Victor Owusu, former N.L.C. Attorney General and the only leading politician of long standing to enjoy ministerial responsibility under them. Balancing the political and economic claims of Ashanti and Ahafo had been a tricky political assignment and it must have required all the attentive governmental handling which it could be given. When the voting came, this attentive delicacy was amply repaid. Once again impartiality was to show itself to be the subtlest and most effective form of partiality.

It is possible in this way to dismiss the potential relevance of both the universalist face of the C.P.P. and the purely localist face of Ahafo's faction-torn traditionalism to the meaning of the election by noting the absence of any identifiable groups in the context who conceived it firmly in these terms. The problem of assessing the scope of the two competing meanings which must now be considered, is not that they cannot be shown to be embodied in the persons of any of the contestants, but rather that it is not altogether clear how intimate is the connection between these energetically purveyed identities and the identifications of those whose electoral allegiance they secured. If the two meanings were to be offered as a causal explanation of the voting figures they would plausibly beg the question they purport to answer. Accordingly, a simple if slightly evasive causal explanation is set out as a rational debate between the effort to derive power from authority and that to derive authority from power.

The election was a contest between national élite coalitions for local mass support. In the political history of Ahafo with its extensive cocoa interests and strong, if ambivalent, Ashanti connection, local allegiance had been predominantly, even under conditions of substantial political pressure, to the former United Party. The Progress Party, being led by the former United Party's leader, inherited the allegiance of a political coalition held together by a common history of struggle and to some degree governmental neglect and oppression. In the preceding three years this local élite, with some national assistance, had contrived to begin to undo the ravages of neglect by securing the provision of supplies of clean water[53] and by an increase (claimed specifically in the course of the campaign to be a product of Dr. Busia's advice) in the producer price of cocoa. At the same time, as we have seen, it had contrived to close up some of the historical fissures of localist political conflict[54] which the C.P.P. years had widened alarmingly. Its effectiveness in consolidating this historical inheritance of political support in the event of the campaign was enhanced by the distinctive identity of the party which eventually emerged as the alternative national contender for power. N.A.L. was not referred to commonly in the constituency (as it was for instance among the Legon students) as 'Ewe party'. It would certainly be false to describe the campaign locally in terms of the projective engineering of primordial hostilities. The position of Ewes in Ahafo is not one which subjects them to any obviously greater suspicion than any other stranger groups—and the Ahafo population probably has a higher stranger component than that of any other part of Ghana except the new urban conglomerations. Ewes are particularly prominent in the teaching profession, but unlike the Ibos in Northern Nigeria before 1966, they do not represent a pervasive economic threat in petty retailing or modern craft work. It was true that Busia comes from Wenchi and Gbedemah from Keta and this geographical symbolism did play a part in the campaign.[55] But the way in which it was presented was very secular, and far from atavistic. It is safe to assume that whereas few Ahafos identify themselves with Brongs for any, except crudely political, purposes, all would be likely, other things being equal, to feel strikingly more at ease in political union or social intercourse with a Brong than with an Ewe. Yet in Ghanaian politics other things never remain equal unless they are energetically made so and the achievement of keeping them so was not in practice lightened by any effort to invoke hostility to Ewes as such. As is suggested by the example of the Legon students, ethnic hostility was often much stronger at an élite than at a mass level, and in Ahafo at least the local élite was fortunate that it did not need to draw heavily on ethnic hostility to cement its mass following, since the requisite style of hostility was only dubiously available for it to draw on. Gbedemah's problem in Ahafo turned out to be not that the fact that he was an Ewe counted against him, but that so little but the fact that he was an Ewe counted *for* him, and that in Ahafo, as in general outside the Ewe areas, this alone could hardly count enough. As a non-Ashanti he appealed forcefully to many of the poorer southern (and indeed northern) strangers, and as being at least more C.P.P. than Busia, he appealed to those to whose lives the C.P.P. had rendered substantial and direct services. But when it came to the count these twin appeals turned out to make little inroad into the inherited U.P. political clientages. The causal explanation of the P.P. triumph was locally (as it was nationally) the degree of political skill in its consolidation of élite support, coupled with the fact that it had as a genuinely national competitor only Gbedemah's apparat to compete against. The egoistic basis of the P.P.'s national solidarity in the inter-ethnic élite competition for power and profit may have been rational even in Olson's terms[56] (though I do not believe that its motivation can be accurately and exhaustively analysed in this fashion). And the solidarity of its local electoral clientages may have derived largely from the members doing their betters a prudent favour, rather than from any more intensely moralistic performance. But whether or not this is what it derived from—whether or not public morality is still something which their masters have to do for them[57]—it cannot be the case that this was all it meant.

What men do, the meaning of their actions, cannot be fully known, while resolutely ignoring what they suppose themselves to be doing. To uncover this final layer of meaning it is necessary to brush aside the axiomatic professional cynicism of the political scientist and attend in all simplicity to the stories which actors told themselves. For these were stories which they did tell in private or when exhausted late at night, when gloomy, irritable or excited, not just on the pompous respectability of the public platform. If they were masks at all, they were certainly masks most of the time to the men themselves. If that was not where the action was, it is hard to see where there was left for it to be at all.[58]

The commonest local account of the meaning of a political party was simply men coming together to help to choose a government. The electoral reference is plain enough. The significance of 'coming together' is its fusion of the descriptive content of campaigning (which does tie men from different localities to a common purpose, though it certainly does not dissolve them into a common purpose) with the moral content of the traditional political values of unity and harmony. It is a reflection of traditional culture as much as of recent experience that the commonest reply to the question 'what would you most like to happen in the world' among the ordinary citizens of Goaso was simply 'peace'. Both parties necessarily marketed to individual electors the benefits of uniting

for peace. The dramatic difference between the two lay in their presentation of what peace meant. The essential character of the N.A.L. appeal
was individualistic and pragmatic, that of the P.P. collectivist and
moral. The N.A.L. campaign stressed (as the party slogan implied)
'Victory' and what you could get out of it, the P.P. campaign (again as
its slogan suggested) stressed 'virtue' and what it could mean for you.
This is not to imply that the N.A.L. campaign was self-consciously
diabolist or even amoral nor that the P.P.'s appeal could be aptly
described as ascetic. Asceticism has markedly little appeal in Ghana
and the most flamboyantly corrupt C.P.P. ministers were often
generous to their own (sometimes *very* extended) 'families'. The polarity
remained nevertheless, in these terms, astonishingly sharp.

At the N.A.L. candidate selection meeting a leading member of the
party observed with stunning economy 'If power is being sold, try to sell
your old lady to go and buy the power. After you have got the power
you will be able to go and bring back your old lady.' When asked how
support was acquired politically, all N.A.L. organisers replied in terms
of the expectation of concrete benefits to be received.[59] Electoral
allegiance was seen as being consolidated in whatever currency was
practically available. Morality stopped at the boundaries of the party.
Party unity was a technical prerequisite for party victory which, in turn,
was plainly a technical prerequisite for the many good things which it
would bring with it. Such moral characteristics as it did display were
products of the shared history of struggle, moral artefacts in the
Hegalian manner of the conflict itself,[60] not ends external to it and
helping to constitute its point. Politics was a severely technical activity
with its own toughly Machiavellian rationality.[61] The former C.P.P.
organisers were proud of their own professionalism and scornful of
what they saw as the P.P.'s bumbling amateurism. Indeed in a way this
conception was at least partly accepted by the. P.P. workers too;
amateurs they might be, but they were also in contrast to their opponents, at least arguably, gentlemen.

Holding this unflinchingly egoistic view of political value and lacking,
on this occasion, access to the coercive or incentive resources of the
government, the N.A.L. organisers faced their bleak assignment with
gaiety and a good deal of courage. Indeed they showed some little
political imagination in the degree of symbolic identification which they
did manage to evoke. The core of party organisers entered the N.A.L.
campaign because of their past C.P.P. loyalties, and they entered as a
political *équipe* purchased on the oligopolistic national political market
by Gbedemah. Much of the support which they gathered came from
those with a common history of C.P.P. allegiance or from stranger
elements whose affection focused upon N.A.L. as an anti-Ashanti party.
But the most interesting group of supporters were the local members

(here sometimes Ashanti themselves) of the groups to whom Gbedemah's national campaign rhetoric of inevitable victory was directed.[62] Often young and usually not very well educated, though sometimes highly intelligent, their feelings revolved very much around the image of Gbedemah himself as a conceptually diffuse, but highly cathected symbol of social effectiveness. The reason why he was certain to win the election, they felt, was also the reason why it was desirable for him to win it. He knew all the big men in the country (enjoyed, that is, the support of leading C.P.P. dignitaries) and was well acquainted with and well esteemed in all the big countries abroad, especially the biggest and most exciting of all, the United States. Above all he had extensive *business* contacts, and even more business skills. A high level of structural unemployment and an increasingly steepening pyramid of educational advance threatened most young Ghanaians with a gloomy future. Entrepreneurial skills (which consist subjectively in a heady combination of magic, chicanery, intelligence and sheer efficacy) of a very high order were clearly to be required to make these clouds lift. In the face of this disagreeable and pervasive aura of *necessita,* Gbedemah's supereminent command over *Fortuna* was just what was needed. All this may sound like purely technical rationality, but it was in practice every bit as much a mode of symbolic self-identification, a participatory value, as the P.P.'s preferred virtue.

In strictly political terms it had, too, a rather dense historical rationale in the experience of C.P.P. rule. Where instrumental politics is the politics of patronage systems, the most apparent political value is simply to succeed, to associate yourself with the biggest and best. Gbedemah's appeal was explicitly pitched (apart from the totally unintelligible cosmopolitanism of his party's title) at a level of pure economic egoism. The tactical disadvantage of this was that, since no one was against progress,[63] it only constituted a reason for voting for Gbedemah himself among those whom he could furnish with direct incentives for so doing.[64] Even in the post-electoral fantasy world of the party's triumph, it would be a mistake to suppose that most of its supporters expected with any assurance to derive concrete benefits from it. What they were committed to, symbolically speaking, was a government which took their dreams seriously. Few were still optimistic enough to expect a government to realise their dreams. The value which Gbedemah represented was the value of success and N.A.L. offered, as had the C.P.P. in its later stages, symbolic participation in the most powerful patronage machine. The atmosphere of gleeful and rather naive chicanery which hung over the N.A.L. campaign, reflected the self-image of those whose chance of living well could derive only from their manipulative wits along with plentiful draughts of sheer luck. For these secular and non-ethnic supporters what N.A.L. offered was a belated form of participation in modernity, the consummation of knowingness as a political value (the consummation, too, in an oddly pure form in which knowingness became its own reward). One historical consequence of the C.P.P.'s rule had been to offer a view of politics in which knowingness did become a truly participatory value, not merely one which reflected an axiomatic distrust of all social loyalties.[65] In an area with such a large proportion of relatively recent immigrants, such an offer might have been expected to enjoy a wide appeal. But in a competition between knowingness as its own reward and virtue devoid of costs, the pains of social change and geographical mobility turned out to be insufficiently searing to make knowingness a more attractive offer.

The basis of the Progress Party's success was their capacity to establish a belief, of however fleeting a character, that virtue would turn out to be devoid of costs. This belief, in practical effect, meant a belief in the moral trustworthiness of the official local status system. It is a commonplace of contemporary anthropology that many of the strains of modernisation for traditional communities are carried by individuals whose rôles place them in an interstitial position between traditional village and modern city, and thus enable them to act as cultural brokers between the two. Such men reinterpret the bleak demands of modernity and the unintelligible requirements of public bureaucracies into assignments within the grasp of traditional villagers. They perform these services, on the whole, for extremely concrete rewards.[66] They tend to play a peculiarly critical role in the engineering of rural credit and may at times be well placed to exact a steep price for the indispensability of their services. The demographic history of Ahafo and its intimate connection with the spread of cocoa as a cash crop cast some doubt on the propriety of describing its villages as traditional communities at all, and the sheer frequency of geographical mobility in Ghana, plausibly implies that the market for such cultural brokerage is more competitive than it was for Wolf's Mexican villages. But the demands posed by the extent of illiteracy are common to both countries, the role of mediator is even more heavily culturally approved in Ghana than in Mexico, and the need to have matters fixed is certainly often a pressing one in Ghana too. The entrepreneurial provision of such an unofficial surrogate for the Citizens Advice Bureau may not exemplify the highest standards of market freedom, but it does do the community certain services. Knowingness is the cultural value marketed by such fixers. The fact that the value has to be paid for may even, as perhaps in the case of psychoanalysis, serve retrospectively to enhance its credibility. The initial scarcity of information is such that it is far from simple to be certain in any particular instance what one has obtained in return for one's investment (even if, again like psychoanalysis, it is often apparent that it is certainly not quite what one wanted). Such brokers may not always be trusted—literacy is too great an inequality of power to be compatible with any great trust. The point of education is to avoid being cheated by literates.[67] But however equivocal their trustworthiness, no one would be likely to deny their indispensable role in the social division of labour. The fact that they are indispensable, and that they are paid piece work rates, may also make them subjectively more reliable than their publicly-salaried superiors whose direct services to individual lives are not always intelligible to the naive understanding. Social distance can breed distrust as readily as admiration. It might feel substantially safer to put one's trust in the raffish and knowing fixer than in the respectable incumbent of a social role, the rationale of which may be unintelligible (and on occasion might not even be there). Ghanaians have a sharp nose for hypocrisy, and the course of twentieth century social change has given them extensive practice in its detection.

The political achievement of the P.P. campaign was to tease out these ambivalent characteristics of the experience of modernity and the social roles around which it focused into a sharp polarity. On the one side they set in their public rhetoric (and indeed substantively in their private conception of the campaign) the sly, knowing, undependable tricksters, explicitly hell-bent on Victory, without status to lose in their pursuit of power and with class all too much to gain. On the other side they displayed themselves, perhaps with some complacency, a stage army of the good, but one in which some warriors at least did bear the scars of real and far from forgotten battles, also modern men, men who had indeed to their credit some small achievement in the discipline of modern status and class competition, the educated, the virtuous, the wise, the brave. It is not to be supposed that this glowing transfer was in fact made to adhere in its entirety to the consciousness of most voters. But it does appear to have struck quite deep chords in many. It derived its plausibility from a history of guilt displayed in disunion, and the suffering generated by disunion; and the remedy which it offered was the re-establishment of union, a proposal which assimilated the moral and the practical. Most importantly of all it offered an account of how such a union could be morally credible in terms of the pledged good faith and knowledge of those in the community whose word and judgement men had most reason to trust. What the Progress Party did politically was market the moral self-image of the higher segments of the local status system, modern and traditional.[68] The consumer response suggested a stability in the status dimension of social stratification,[69] which current writings on the sociology of modernisation have totally failed to capture. In Dahrendorf's terms an abstract élite seemed well on the way locally to becoming an established élite.[70]

The moral project offered by this élite was the exorcism of a past shame by the engineering in the present of a collective moral will. Disunion had been brought into Ahafo[71] by thieves and cheats. Ahafo, as a whole, had had to pay the moral price of disunion because of the complicity of some of its citizens in this invasive immorality. It was precisely because members of the community had been ready to demand—or at least to accept—concrete rewards for the allocation of loyalties which should have been allocated on a basis of Kantian purity, that the moral integrity of the community had been violated. The fact that the violation of this integrity occasioned a history of overt and, at times, violent conflict, served both to deepen the moral squalor of the betrayal, and to provide a moral rationalisation of the sufferings in which the betrayal resulted. Having touched pitch, the men of Ahafo had only themselves to blame if they had duly become defiled. A few had done well out of these impure practices, but for the community at large it had spelled nothing but neglect and dangers. In a village a private thief, if apprehended in the act, might risk being beaten to death. Without justice, what could the state be but a great band of public thieves? The people of Ahafo were summoned to endow the state with justice by keeping their own hearts pure.

Two questions are raised by this remarkable rendition. How was it that the P.P. attempted to show that this, in some ways, rather strained story merited the belief of the electors, and why was it that they succeded in some measure in arousing such belief? It is important to separate these issues since the form of authentication which the P.P. in fact strove to provide, while it was the only form of authentication conceptually available, may equally well not have been the cause of its acceptance by the electorate. That the problem of credibility was at the heart of the election no one who listened to the gloomy private responses or the ribald public challenges at the party's rallies could well doubt. As far as promises of improvement went, the long suffering electors had heard it all before and they were not slow to inquire how they were supposed to tell whether it meant anything more on this occasion than it had before. The P.P.'s dialectical response to this challenge was not in detail impressive. (It is hard to see how anyone's response could have been). But it did attempt intuitively to forestall it by one feature of its campaigning. In that representative democracy necessarily implies the choice of a single man by a large number of men, and in that the chosen individual in Ghanaian politics is legally required to be somewhat unrepresentative in a statistical sense[72] (and in all representative politics he is sociologically likely to be highly unrepresentative) the question of what reason electors could have to choose someone to represent them is a very acute one. If democracy is indeed a choice between competing élites, in a country in which the class, status and power gaps between élite and mass are as yawning as they are in Ghana, it is not at all obvious what the point of democracy is supposed to be for the mass of the population; while it is abundantly clear that its point, as far as the élites are concerned, might readily take on the character of a Conspiracy of Unequals. All that could be provided to avert the risk of such conspiratoir betrayal, was a set of character references from those who did not obviously stand to gain too directly from the upward mobility of the successful candidate for inequality. Thus the former United Party M.P., Mr. Osei, spoke eloquently at the Akrodie rally of how he had known Busia since their schooldays together in Kumasi and how he had never known him perform a discreditable act, while at the Progress Party's candidate selection meeting at Sankore, a former school fellow of Badu Nkansah also talked at length of how long he had known him and how sterling had been his conduct throughout this time. The intimacy of the recollections offered a trajectory across the massive social chasm between state and people without submission to mere fantasy. It provided, however evanescently, an image for the unimaginable, how the subjects could also become citizens, the ex-colonial state become a nation. To be a credible representative, their candidate had to be a man with a firm local identity and a man for whom others with firm local identities would stand surety; and the leader of their party, while it certainly helped that he had a geographical identity which was not too distant, also *had* to be vouched for as a man by those with firm local identities. The coalescing of local political élites was not just the mechanism of party integration on the national level; it was also the most eloquent vehicle of party propaganda on the local level. It was on the knowledge of men whom they themselves knew and respected that the rationality of the choice of the majority had necessarily to depend.

The moral credibility (such as it was) of the leaders' presentation of themselves in this role depended, in part, upon adventitious historical factors. The local élites had been rather unusual by prevailing standards in the extent to which they had resisted the blandishments of the C.P.P. government, to say nothing of its less gentle approaches. This meant both that their own hands were comparatively clean, and that the area as a whole had undergone a rather more than average share of governmental neglect. Uniting for peace in this instance, and behind these leaders, could be plausibly presented as uniting against neglect and oppression. Furthermore, the image of the local community as the moral victim of an immoral government was paradoxically strengthened by the extent of local prosperity. Such prosperity was, to be sure, relative; there was continued and vociferous economic discontent. But it was nevertheless indubitably there. The Ahafo production of cocoa and timber remained as high as anywhere in Ghana. Wealth was unquestionably produced in the constituency and it required little political or economic sophistication to grasp just precisely how large a part of the surplus was extracted by the government. The low level of government development expenditure, the high level of local production and the history of extensive governmental taxation on the production of cocoa and timber, served together to confirm a simple physiocratic image of the location of economic virtue. A set of parasitic public thieves had battened on the virtuous and productive forest. The time for justice to be done had come at least. Since the local élites had, however, failed to collaborate with this brigand invasion, it was in fact they who (to sharpen a historical irony) were the 'natural leaders' of the exploited peasants in the effort to secure this belated justice.

All this is very much taking the Progress Party at the value of its own moral face. It had naturally other and less moral faces. Once in possession of state power, no party in Ghana today could well retain such purity of moral outline, let alone out in a neo-colonial setting the simplistic fables of physiocratic economics. If the dreams of Frantz Fanon could not be realised by the Algerian war of National Liberation, they were in no danger of being fulfilled by the electoral triumph of the Ghanaian bourgeoisie. Indeed the constraints of social structure made it all too probable that, while the élite campaigners of the P.P. might derive fairly direct benefits from their share in the marketing of virtue, having voted for virtue would turn out for most voters to have been its own sole reward. It would be unjust to the Progress Party to suggest that the second of these considerations loomed large in their consciousness. But it would be naive to suppose that the first had not occurred to a fair number of them. Discussion of the fruits of electoral victory was often as directly egoistic and as uninhibited in its gusto among them as among the N.A.L. supporters. But these fruits were seen as rewards for having invested in virtue, not simply as returns on having invested in investment. The moral image was closer to that of the spiritual churches than it was to either the unbending principles of Kant or the crude importunities of the National Lottery. Rewards were genuinely rewards, prizes for having been virtuous, not merely adventitious windfalls. Even if the point of being virtuous (in the sense of the sufficient motive) was the prospect of its resulting in concrete gains, it would be an error to imagine that many inhabitants of Ahafo had the poise to conceive their lives unflinchingly as a market enterprise. Early socialisation, however variegated, had certainly served to accentuate for many the subjective probability of rewards accruing to virtue. Whatever history may have done for the inhabitants of eighteenth century Königsberg, it has not left those of Ahafo today in any condition to make sense out of the bleak requirements of Kant. To say that they did not sense the deprivations of altruism in the attachment of political virtue to public goods, is thus only to observe that it remains a psychological possibility in Ahafo to have reason to attempt to live virtuously. Whether it remains a philosophical possibility is not a question which can be answered here.

Even in the extensively studied societies of the industrial west elections cannot plausibly be claimed to be events which are particularly well understood. Their position in the ideology of representative democracy is well established, but their precise character as social events, their social meaning, remains imaginatively opaque. In the thinly studied societies of contemporary Africa it would be remarkable if their meaning was not even more opaque. Along with their abandoned state apparatus, the departing colonialists left behind them the recently introduced formal prerequisites for egalitarian democracy. It could thus be argued that what Africa is stumblingly in search of is not democracy (which at least intermittently and unstably it perhaps enjoys or at least *experiences* already), so much as representation. Elections as a mode of choosing rulers are tied historically not so much to democracy as such as to *representative democracy*, a theory of how democracy could be made a reality in a territorial rather than a city state. In the territorial states of western Europe the practice of representation long preceded the achievement of democracy. Indeed it long preceded the establishment of anything resembling a nationally self-conscious system of social stratification. Representative Assemblies were summoned by existent state power, the monarch and his court, largely in order to enhance his tax-gathering effectiveness. Naturally such local representatives were for the most part men of high status in the local community. Had they not been so, they could hardly have served to bind the other inhabitants of their community by their choice. Despite its origins as a device for increasing the central power of the state, representation did not (where it was permitted by the state power to remain at all) remain restricted to the service of this purpose. Indeed over time, and largely before the advent of democracy, it became the device by which society acquired such control as it has over the state. With the (causally linked) advent of democracy and a self-conscious national system of social stratification, representation became the instrument for securing the level of social equality and individual freedom, such as it is, now characteristic of western societies.

If the account which has been given of the election in Asunafo is to any significant extent veridical, it raises an interesting question. In the current absence of a nationally self-conscious class stratification in Ghana, what authentic forms of representation are possible? The possibility of representation stops at the boundary of the moral community. Socialist theory in nineteenth and twentieth century Europe attempted to stretch these boundaries first to the national and then to the international proletariat. Although it cannot be said that it was very successful, it does seem likely that the electoral transposition of a measure of proletarian solidarism was a necessary condition for such internal political rationality as the political systems of the western world currently display. When it comes to interpreting African politics, however, western observers seem for the most part to have left behind such feeling as they possess for this painfully slow extension of the moral community. Taking their cue from the legalistic universalism of the electoral systems left behind by the colonial powers, they have seen the insistent recurrence of localist values, 'tribalism', as a reversion to primitive barbarism. By insisting on peering irritably at the national level and noting how badly the states have managed to cope with the problems left to them by their former masters, they have failed to perceive most of the extended political achievement involved in beginning to deal with the difficulties which they actually face. 'Tribalism' is undoubtedly a danger from the point of view of the state, but it may also represent the painful construction of a political community. Whilst it was simply a matter of sharing out the contents of the public coffers among the successor élites such a perspective might seem perverse. When it can be shown, however fitfully, at work in the processes of a democratic election campaign, it may be easier to understand the moral substance which, along with its immoral and its dangerous characteristics, it does beyond question display. The Progress Party in Asunafo advanced an image of Ahafo as a moral community. They elected a man from Ahafo who had grappled with modernity but returned to live within Ahafo to stand for them in the national tourney in which community struggles against community for the goods and evils which the government distributes. Under the C.P.P., as the chief of Sankore bitterly observed, a black man had forgotten that he was black, but after the coup 'People who had made themselves white men came to understand that they were black men like us'. The anxious image of the future which the Progress Party campaign attempted to allay, and at the same time the eventuality which it attempted to avert, was that once again black men should think they had become white men. In the election, what the Progress Party offered was an image of virtue predicted on a moral community. The story of how the electors of Asunafo, perhaps rather bemusedly, chose virtue is a story which deserves a share of honour even outside its own country. What else better, in all innocence, could they in fact have done?[73]

Notes

1. Jean-Jacques Rousseau, *Du Contrat Social*, Bk 111, ch. XV, *Political* Writings, ed. C. E. Vaughan Oxford, 1962, II, p. 96.
2. This freedom is, naturally, a very limited matter, limited by scarcity of information

and sheer insecurity. The secrecy of the ballot may still make it in some respects more free than that enjoyed by most eighteenth-century English electors. The scope of the franchise also is vastly wider in Ghana than it was in the England of which Rousseau wrote.

3. This picture emerges equally clearly from the studies conducted in the tradition of Paul Lazersfeld and Bernard Berelson, *The People's Choice* (New York, 1944) and *Voting* (Chicago, 1954), and from the work of the Survey Research Centre, Michigan, A. Campbell *et al.*, *The American Voter*, 1960 and P. Converse, 'The Nature of Belief Systems in Mass Publics', in D. Apter (ed.), *Ideology and Discontent*, (Glencoe, 1964).

4. Brief accounts of the changing structures within which the Ahafo division was administered up to the 1939–45 war can be found in W. Tordoff, *Ashanti under the Prempehs*, Oxford 1965, and K. A. Busia, *The Position of the Chief in the Modern Political System of Ashanti*, 2nd. ed. London, 1968. There are extensive records of the conduct of British administration in the Ahafo division in the Ghana National Archives in Accra, Kumasi and Sunyani.

5. The main road from the administrative capital of Ahafo, Goaso, to the north is the lifeline along which the vast bulk of the area's production of timber and cocoa passes. It was one of the two major roads which the British administration decided to build to Goaso at the time at which the main Ashanti road system was designed. The surviving records of the execution of this plan make it clear that it was a consequence more of administrative accident than of economic or geographical calculation that this road was in fact built and the other road which would have connected Goaso directly with Kumasi was never completed.

6. For the economics of this process see especially R. Szereszewski, *Structural Changes in the Economy of Ghana, 1891–1911*, London 1965.

7. The 1960 population census records the population of the Brong-Ahafo South Local Council Area as 81,590. Of these only 9,030 are recorded as Ahafos. It is plausible that, of the 36,150 recorded as Ashanti, some have been resident for more than two generations. But there are good reasons to believe that the proportion of long-term resident families suggested by these figures is of the right order of magnitude. See *1960 Population Census of Ghana. Special Report E. Tribes in Ghana*, Table S 1.

8. One of the largest landholders in Ahafo, for example, is Bafuor Osei Akoto, a major organiser of the N.L.M. in 1954.

9. B. Fitch and M. Oppenheimer, *Ghana: End of an Illusion*, New York 1966, pp. 38–40, 129–30.

10. F. R. Bray, *Cocoa Development in Ahafo, West Ashanti*, Achimota 1959 has a useful discussion of the process by which land rights (the basis of local citizenship) are acquired, see pp. 17–23. Slightly under a seventh of the recorded population of the Brong-Ahafo South Local Council area was born outside Ghana. (*1960 Population Census*, Vol. 11.)

11. The classic treatment of the development of tenurial systems in cocoa production is in Polly Hill's, *The Gold Coast Cocoa Farmer*, Oxford 1956 and *Migrant Cocoa Farmers of Southern Ghana*, Cambridge 1963.

12. The slow progress of both missions and government schools is recorded in the Ahafo District Record Book, Vols. I and II, *Ghana National Archives*, Kumasi. The *1960 Census* (Vol. II) recorded roughly the same percentage of male children in the 6–14 age group as currently enjoying education as was deprived of it (whereas among those over the age of 15 nearly four times as many males had never had access to education as had enjoyed the opportunity). Today the percentage of children attending school appears to be substantially higher than in 1960.

13. Christian religious affiliation is almost as strongly connected with achieved social status in Ahafo among those over the age of thirty as is educational experience.

Before the Nkrumah government's expansion of education, the link between organised Christianity and educational provision was a very close one.

14. When questioned as to which of three roles they would prefer their child to attain, the majority of those interviewed in Goaso preferred an office in the state bureaucracy (District Commissioner) to that of politician or chief on the grounds that the first enjoyed comparable pickings and far greater security of tenure.

15. He felt it necessary to testify at length (and in essentially the same terms) to his devotion to the ideals of multi-party democracy in his speech in Goaso in August as he had in a speech to the Legon students some months earlier. The similarity of the pronouncements may have testified to the sincerity of his commitment. In Goaso at any rate they certainly did not testify to his political sensitivity. Few had any idea of what he was talking about.

16. The theme was repeated at length in Busia's speech at the party's inauguration rally at Sunyani and again at a speech at Techimentia which the Asunafo party dignitaries contrived to attend. It was also emphasised by R. R. Amponsah on his visit to Akrodie. In a more rough and ready way it featured in many local rallies. The behaviour of the party's organisers in the immediate aftermath of victory provided clear testimony of the sincerity of the commitment of most of them.

17. 'We have got two kinds of people, United Party people and C.P.P. people.' (Interview with N.A.L. constituency official, explaining the basis of political allegiance in the election.)

18. Senkyire 5,400. Osei 1,744. B. D. Addai 579.

19. Osei 7,248. Senkyire 2, 854.

20. See the remarkable speech on the expediency of maintaining diplomatic relationships with South Africa made by Osei on 15 February 1965 (*Hansard* cols 1062–63) and the scornful comment of a C.P.P. member 'A short man with a small sense'. Whatever may be thought of the rationality of Osei's argument it required considerable courage to put it forward in the Ghanaian legislature in 1965.

21. The main road north of Goaso is frequently impassable in the rainy season because it has not been tarred. There was alleged to be a confidential file on this road in the Regional Office with a minute from one of the C.P.P. Regional Commissioners instructing that the road not be tarred any further south because the area to the south was solidly United Party in political allegiance.

22. When asked what individual had done most for the town of Goaso in the last few years virtually all of those whom I interviewed in Goaso named the then District Administrative Officer.

23. He took pains to see that his wife did not make friends among the local Goaso community and his social life was largely confined to the official community resident in Goaso. He did not himself speak to the local populace in Twi, although he understood Twi perfectly and could speak it quite well.

24. Both A. W. Osei and Badu Nkansah in their capacity as members of the Ahafo Youth Society claimed responsibility for its arrival in several speeches.

25. Cf Busia's speech at Tecnimentia in July (translated from the Twi) 'This is the meaning of our name, the Progress ... Everyone likes Progress. If you have one cloth and we help you to get one more, will you not like it? If you have no house and you are provided with a house to buy by instalments, will you not like it? As we are short of drinking water, if a pipe is brought into your town to save you going four or five miles to fetch water, will you not like it? Everyone needs progress.'

26. It was not clear until the day of nomination itself how many parties would in fact contest the seat. On the day in question, the Progress Party District Secretary took the trouble to accumulate a new set of signatures on the nomination form because of the rumour that one of nominators had been nominated himself at the last minute to stand as a candidate for the U.N.P.

27. His initial statement in the Constituent Assembly included a strong attack on the abuses of chieftaincy and an allegation that the Constitution was biased in favour of the chiefs (*Proceedings of the Constituent Assembly*, 23 January 1969, pp. 143–45.) Later his attitude upon this point became considerably less urgent.

28. He was celebrating his acquittal before the High Court in Sunyani of a State Prosecution for not carrying out the summons of his lawful traditional overlord, the Asantehene to go to pay his allegiance. The political significance of this prosecution and of the verdict are discussed below.

29. The campaign outside the major centres of population was a sporadic affair. The voting figures are in general (for reason discussed below) more favourable to the P.P. outside the major centres of population.

30. They were both, for example, members in 1952 of the Ahafo Information Service Panel (*Ghana National Archives, Sunyani*, Sunyani District Files, 515).

31. The contrast between this speech and the eloquence of Busia's speech at Techimentia was noted even by N.A.L. supporters who had listened to both. This comparative linguistic advantage would, of course, have been reversed in the Ewe areas.

32. It should be noted that the strains of the campaigning tour meant that Busia's frequently announced (and genuinely expected) visit to Ahafo never materialised at all.

33. In the last C.P.P. election, that of 1965, there was only one box because there was only one party permitted to contest the election. Earlier there had been separate boxes for the different parties, the choice between the two boxes being at times made simpler by the fact that the poll was directly supervised by representatives of the ruling party,.

34. Stein Rokkan, 'Mass Suffrage, Secret Voting and Political Participation', in L. Coser (ed.), *Political Sociology*, New York 1967, especially pp. 114–19.

35. It is unlikely that he wasted his time insisting on this point in the Ewe areas.

36. Compare, however, the account of what was threatened in Sekyere, p. 309.

37. Anthony Downs, *An Economic Theory of Democracy*, New York 1957, Chapter 14. M. Olson, *The Logic of Collective Action*, Cambridge, Mass., 1965. See the comments of Brian Barry, *Political Argument*, London 1965, p. 281, 328–30, and *Sociologists, Economists and Democracy*, London 1970.

38. If the number of voters was very small (as at the Oseikrom polling station, 17 voters, or the Mintumi No. 1 Cocoa Shed polling station, also 17) the chances of punitive action against the disobedient being directed against the right individual or set of individuals is clearly much higher than at a polling station (e.g. the Mim Roman Catholic Primary School) at which more than 400 cast their vote. The sense of security which is the presumable psychological point of the secrecy of the ballot can hardly be maintained when voting is conducted on the scale of these few isolated polling stations and when the results are made public polling station by polling station.

39. It is possible that the personalised, televisual and consensual politics of western democracies are reverting to a condition in which this is the basis of rational choice in their elections also.

40. These two adjoining villages have a tradition of intermittently violent conflict which reaches back to their initial separation.

41. The present Regional and District administrations appear to devote as substantial a proportion of their efforts to the management of traditional affairs as their colonial predecessors. The fact that they do so is an accurate articulation of real political values of most Ghanaians as well as a technically necessary response to concrete problems of social control. It is the latter *because* it is the former.

42. The post-electoral massacre in September 1969 in which the Yendi skin dispute came to its climax recorded a death toll which modernist social conflict in Ghana in the form of industrial disputes are unlikely to match within the near future.

43. They fall at any one time into two broad constitutional traditions, localist or Ashanti. But since they are expounded on given occasions usually in order to sanction particular political positions it cannot be assumed that the history of any particular settlement will always be found in the same constitutional tradition on different occasions. My understanding of the political basis of Ahafo historiography derives largely from the extensive series of interviews with the chiefs of Ahafo which Dr. Robertson carried out.
44. Cf John Pocock, *The Ancient Constitution and the Feudal Law*, Cambridge 1957.
45. Cf in addition to Pocock's brilliant book, Q. Skinner, 'History and Ideology in the English Revolution', *The Historical Journal*, VIII, 1965. F. Neumann, *The Democratic and the Authoritarian State*, Glencoe 1957, cap. IV., F. L. Ford, *Sword and Robe*, Cambridge, Mass., 1953, cap XII.
46. W. Tordoff, *Ashanti under the Prempehs*, Oxford 1965 gives the clearest account available of the impact of British pressures on the Ashanti political order in this period.
47. The late Asantehene affirmed in an interview with Dr. Robertson that no such person as Asibi Entwi had ever existed.
48. Tordoff, *Ashanti under the Prempehs*, pp. 409–10.
49. Busia, *Position of the Chief*, pp. 189–93 especially.
50. The Circuit Judge in his judgement on 9 June 1969 stated that it was undisputed that no Kukuomhene had *ever* taken the oath of allegiance to the Ashantehene or the Akroponghene. (Transcript p. 19).
51. Personal communication from J. A. Braimah, formerly member of the Chieftaincy Secretariat.
52. The legal specification of the judgement is quite complicated. The key premise, however, is explicitly the historical reality of Asibi Entwi and of either the preservation or the establishment of Ahafo independence which his defeat represented. (Transcript, passim).
53. It was claimed by one former C.P.P. official that the plans for the coming of the water preceded the coup of February 1966. It is, however, clear from the administrative files dealing with the project and from personal communication with the former head of the Ghana Water and Sewarage Corporation, M. K. Apaloo, that local political initiative would probably not have been enough ever to get it beyond the planning stage.
54. Cf at the regional level Dr. Busia's promise in his inauguration speech in Sunyani not to dismantle the Brong Ahafo region and the more local effort to cement the unity of Ahafo as a geographical community.
55. The point was made by several of the less sophisticated party speakers in local rallies in Goaso in terms of the difference between the sheer distances to be traversed if one wished to go to approach one of the two men about some issue. The degree of personalisation in Ghanaian political perception (not to say conduct) makes geographical inaccessibility a natural symbol for political inaccessibility.
56. Cf *Logic of Collective Action*, cap VI, D., pp. 141–48.
57. Cf Staniland's observation that we have at the moment no basis for predicting 'how long it will take before ordinary Ivoiriens want to and can make politics more than a growth industry of élites and political scientists, more something they participate in and less something they have done for them'. (Martin Staniland 'Single-Party Regimes and Political Change: The P.D.C.I. and Ivory Coast Politics', in Colin Leys (ed.) *Politics and Change in Developing Countries*, Cambridge 1969).
58. If action is analysed, as by Erving Goffman, *Where the Action Is*, London 1969, in terms of the enactment of socially specified roles, this was the role most persistently identifiable in the actual behaviour of the agents. The deficiencies of such an analysis on philosophical grounds do not affect the point at issue.

59. Either in terms of direct cash payments or of the potentially remunerative consequences of holding power in a ruling party. ('I think we will get something out of it,' was a formulation produced impartially by one leading N.A.L. organiser to enquiries about the reasons for and about the causes of the party's political support.)

60 Cf G. W. F. Hegel, *Philosophy of Right*, (trans T. M. Knox), Oxford 1942, paras 324, 325, p. 210 and *Political Writings*, (trans Knox and ed Pelczynski), Oxford 1964, pp. 143–44.

61. Cf 'Ce n'est rien de bien partir si l'on ne fournit la carrière: le prix est au bout de la lice, et la fin regle toujours le commencement.' (Gabriel Naudé, *Considerations Politiques sur les Coups d'Estat*, n.p. 1667.)

62. The repetitive and resonant affirmation, 'We are going to *win*' was the keynote of all large N.A.L. rallies and the main theme, for instance, of the editorials in the party newspaper, the *Evening Standard*.

63. Cf Busia speech cited in note 29 above.

64. See note 65 above.

65. Cf Edward C. Banfield, *The Moral Basis of a Backward Society*, Glencoe 1958, a study of a South Italian village in which the value system is described by the author as one of 'amoral familism', in that the *interesse* of any family is regarded by all as totally unrestrained by moral responsibility to any larger social collectivity.

66. The rewards may take the form of direct cash payments or they may (in more politically specific clientages) create fairly stable structures of dependence in which the client provides extensive services, rather than cash. For their character in Mexico see Eric R. Wolf, 'Aspects of Group Relations in a Complex Society: Mexico', *American Anthropologist*, LVIII, No. 6, December 1956, pp. 1065–78.

67. This formulation was one of the commonest responses to the question in interviews in Goaso about what was the point of education.

68. There are close kinship links in Ahafo as elsewhere in Ghana between traditional and modern élites. The relationship between initial wealth, traditional power and inequality of educational access, although intricate in detail, is extremely strong. The key position of educational achievement in Ghanaian status perception is firmly based on the economic returns on educational investment. (P. Foster, *Education and Social Change in Ghana*, London 1965, and for a clear account of an area of Nigeria in which this connection is resulting in the formation of a distinct social class see E. Krapf-Askari, *Yoruba Towns and Cities*, Oxford 1969, cap VI, 'Social Stratification.')

69. The Weberian notion of status as a conceptually irreducible dimension of social stratification—as argued by W. G. Runciman, 'Class, Status and Power', in J. A. Jackson (ed), *Social Stratification*, Cambridge 1968.

70. Ralf Dahrendorf, *Society and Democracy in Germany*, London 1968, p. 230.

71. This moral image did not, of course, correspond to fact. Disunion had always been extremely prevalent in Ahafo.

72. An M.P. has to be able to speak English, most adult Ghanaians cannot.

73. This chapter was completed in May 1970. I have altered a number of tenses where subsequent events have made this necessary. A fuller account of the historical and sociological background of Ahofo is now available in John Dunn and A. F. Robertson, *Dependence and Opportunity: Political Change in Ahofo*, Cambridge, 1973.

CHAPTER 8

POLITICS IN ABUAKWA*

J. A. Peasah

The value of the study of elections in an African context—rare though they may now be —is the way in which elections bring into the open the political claims of the periphery upon the centre, claims which the analyst might otherwise ignore. Thus, disputes over land and allegiance, the difficulties of cocoa farming, and conflict between rival towns, go a long way to explain the clash of party interests prior to 1972, and something needs to be said about each of these areas of controversy in the Abuakwa constituency before looking at the actual details of the election.

The Abuakwa are Twi-speaking Akans who are said to have migrated some time in the 1730s to their present locality in the eastern region of the country from the vicinity of Lake Bosumtwi in Ashanti. In alliance with the Dutch and the Ga, they drove their enemies eastwards to the banks of the Volta river, gaining land too vast for their immediate use but over which they had no desire to abandon legal control. Such tenacity generated a large measure of conflict not only among the Akim themselves but between them and other ethnic groupings. For if one of the cardinal principles of customary land law is that there is no un-owned land, there is also the fact that the traditional process of land acquisition, and the boundaries of acquired land, are not by any means precise. Many years ago Mensah Sarbah noted that:

> according to native ideas there is no land without owners. What is now a forest or unused land will, as years go on, come under cultivation by the subjects of the stool, or members of the village, community or other members of the family.[1]

An equally important principle was the communal ownership of land, as in the statement by Nana Sir Ofori Atta I, Paramount Chief of Akim Abuakwa (1912–1943): 'I conceive that land belongs to a vast family of whom many are dead, a few are living and countless host are still un-born.'[2] But although Sir Ofori's conception contained the bedrock of truth, it was also an exaggeration which ignored the strategic position of the living who exercise the full proprietary rights of use and disposal.

* The constituency is in the Eastern Region of Ghana in the Akim Abuakwa traditional Area. With the other two Akim Areas (Akim Kotoku and Akim Bosome) to which it is territorially contiguous, the traditional area of Abuakwa contained eleven of the one hundred and forty seats in the whole country, and half of the twenty-two seats in the Eastern Region.

214

In general terms, ownership of land is good evidence of jurisdiction over people living on the land; but there is a distinction in customary law between ownership of land and personal law. The alienation of title by subordinate stools to non-Abuakwas may not necessarily affect the Paramount Stool's rights over land, despite the introduction of 'stranger' elements into the territorial area of jurisdiction of the Paramount Stool. The fact remains, however, that from the early 1890s, when cocoa growing started in earnest, a rapid and indiscriminate sale of unoccupied lands (especially by the chiefs of Apapam, Apedwa, Asafo, Maase, Tafo, Kukurantumi, Begoro and Osiem) had the effect of introducing very large 'stranger' communities on to Abuakwa territory. In this way there arose a series of closely related issues which were and, in varying degrees, are still important: for example, who has the authority to sell; what rights do the buyers acquire in respect of their personal status; and in what way does the sale of land affect the original boundaries of the Akim Abuakwa traditional area? Such questions raised a number of contentious local issues, not least because the boundaries of the areas controlled by the subordinate Akim Abuakwa chiefs were ill-defined, and because the stranger buyers—mainly Akwapims and Krobos—came from areas directly contiguous to Akim Abuakwa; the purchase of Akim lands appeared therefore to be an extension of Akwapim and Krobo boundaries at the expense of the Akim Abuakwa Paramount Stool. Such disputes still constitute one of the many strands of rivalries between the Abuakwa towns—rivalries which are given extra point by being shrouded in myth and legend.

Of political significance still, today, is an old controversy over the extent of the interests and rights sold to the stranger buyers. If there were a transfer of absolute ownership, then of course the Paramount Stool had no more interest in the land concerned, and no jurisdiction over the activities of the 'strangers': but the Abuakwa chiefs insisted that no such transfer was possible. Before the end of the first world war, it seems to have been the practice among the Akwapims on Abuakwa lands to appoint their own chiefs (*Adkiro*) who recognised the jurisdiction of the Akwapim Paramount Stool to which they preferred to owe immediate and direct allegiance. On the argument, however, that the sale of land by subordinate stools could not legally take away the allodial or absolute ownership of the Paramount Stool, the Akim Abuakwa chief won a series of legal cases against the Akwapim Stool. Today, the Akwapims own land some twenty to thirty miles deep into the Akim Abuakwa boundary and although they no longer challenge the absolute ownership of the Akim Abuakwa Paramount Stool, the earlier disputes have left traces of suspicion on both sides. Several factors have helped to mitigate the rivalry and to facilitate communication between the two groups. The Akwapim and Akim Abuakwa Paramount Stools are occupied by royal families drawn from the same clan and, indeed, from the same family; the Akwapims are also Twi-speaking Akans, sharing a similar language and culture with the Akims. And in the Akwapim-dominated areas, such as Suhum and its environs, there are inter-town rivalries between the immigrants themselves among whom the pattern of settlement in waves of 'companies' encouraged a sentimental allegiance to rival home-towns in Akwapim.

Of greater relevance for the 1969 election was the conflict over land ownership and jurisdiction between the Abuakwas and the Krobos. The Krobos, like the Akwapims, bought land in groups; but the Krobo groups, or *Huzas,* were more or less complete communities, with a well-defined social structure and a clear hierarchy of authority. (The difference between the Akwapim 'company' and the Krobo *Huza* was not unlike that between Tonnies' *Gesellschaft* and *Gemeinshaft.*) The Krobos were determined to settle on the land as distinct communities—completely autonomous if possible from their Akan-speaking Akwapim and Akim neighbours, and incorporating their own system of customs, laws and institutions. There were times, however, when the various *Huza* groups were given financial aid and other forms of support by the Paramount chiefs from whence they came, thus giving the impression that such chiefs were undisclosed principals and the Huzas their agents. Because of such problems of allegiance, the Krobos tended to resent paying taxes to Abuakwa stools, preferring to establish their own markets, levy their own taxes, and settle their own disputes, without any external interference. These ancient disputes continued, and during the 1969 elections the Krobos and some Abuakwa chiefs in the constituency were still contesting ownership of land around the Buti Falls, although it was almost completely populated by and sold to the Krobos.

Conflict between the Akim and the Krobos might not have had the same impact on the outcome of the elections but for the view held by both sides that political power had a direct relationship with court decisions and the recommendations of Commissions of Enquiry. Moreover, impressed by the Nkrumah regime, both sides entertained the reasonable apprehension that Parliament could pass laws favourable to members of the party in power, even if these related to a civil suit between local groups. During the early decades of party rule, the Krobos were more successful than the Akwapims in claiming autonomy from the Abuakwas. And this was attributed first to the unsuccessful opposition of the Akim Abuakwa chief to the Nkrumah regime, secondly to the influence wielded in the Government by E. H. T. Korbo (a Krobo man) who was the Convention People's Party's Regional Commissioner of the Eastern Region.

The majority of the population in the constituency depend directly or indirectly on the growing of cocoa. The average individual holding is not larger than twenty acres, yielding (on the current price of N₡8.00 per lead of 60 lbs. and after payment of costs of cultivation and other incidentals) only a moderate income, scarcely adequate to sustain a tolerable standard of living for the commonly large family units. Unlike the Akim, the Akwapims and Krobos tend to combine cocoa cultivation with foodstuffs grown for local markets in order to supplement incomes from cocoa, but one may doubt whether their economic position is substantially better than that of their neighbours. Now while it may be generally true that a peasant population of this nature is likely to be conservative, traditionalist, and much averse to a life of continuous change and innovation, the proposition needs serious qualification for Abuakwa. The average person in the constituency is certainly a conservative and a traditionalist who sets much store by the opinions of chiefs, clan leaders and eㄴ 'ers; he is also guided in his daily activity by immemorial usages: but not by any means uncritically so. For the impact of western education, and changes in the economic structure of society, have left the cocoa farmer ambivalent in his attitudes. Strong as his conservative disposition is, he shares a certain radicalism with other cash-crop farmers, especially those whose products are subject to the vagaries of international market prices. Such farmers live in fear of sudden changes in the prices of their products and of unpredictable changes in their standard of living. They tend to be individualist, acquisitive, and interested in political power—a personal acquisitiveness and a dependence on the central government which have undermined traditional authority. The politics of the cocoa farmer is a peculiar type of 'class politics' embedded in a traditionalist matrix, a curious mixture of populism and egalitarianism expressed in hierarchical forms.

So there developed a distinct cocoa-farmer flavour to politics which was further sharpened in the Abuakwa constituency by the 'swollen shoot' disease of cocoa. Ever since the disease was discovered in the Eastern Region in 1936, the only remedy has been the deliberate destruction or 'cutting out' of affected trees:

> During the period under review the malady discovered in 1936–37 known as 'swollen shoot' was found to have affected considerable areas within the lines Koforidua–Tafo–Suhum–Mangoase in the heart of the major producing zone of the Eastern Province. In view of the novelty of the malady it was considered safest to assume that it might be infectious or transferable and a campaign of destruction of dead or obviously affected trees was set in hand.[3]

In 1945 the colonial government had taken a firm decision to cut out diseased trees, bringing home more forcefully than ever the part played by the central government in deciding the economic fate of cocoa farmers; and during the 1948 riots, farmers in the constituency offered violent resistance to the government's cutting out policy. It has been calculated that between 1945, when systematic campaign for the destruction of diseased trees was started, and 1961 a national total of 105 million trees—67 million of which were in the areas of Tafo, Koforidua, Suhum, Kibi, Apedwa, Amanfrom and Asamankese—had been cut out. In one year alone—1967—the Ministry of Agriculture recorded that it had cut out 5,796,296 trees. One result was that the Eastern Region produced barely 21,000 tons out of the 264,000 tons for the whole country. Cocoa farmers in the Abuakwa constituency, therefore, are among the poorest in the country.

We need to complete our attempt to identify some of the local social factors which affected the outcome of the election by assessing the relations between towns in the constituency. The following analysis is kept at the level of inter-town relations, since the significant traditional loyalties at constituency level are based principally on town and village allegiances. And in the previous elections of 1954 and 1956 this fact had been critical. By 1967 the total population of the constituency was estimated at 66,701,[4] of which 16,975 (i.e. about 25 per cent) were registered voters, 11,887 actually voting in August 1969.[5] If towns are defined as having at least 1,000 registered voters, only five are worth attention:[6]

Towns	Registered Voters
New Tafo	2,803
Old Tafo	1,501
Kukurantumi	1,801
Kibi-Panoh	1,585
Apedwa	1,271
Total	8,961

Their importance lay in the fact that any political party which intended to win elections in the constituency had to win, as a minimum requirement, the allegiance of the majority of these towns and their immediate environs.

Kibi is the capital town of the whole of the Akim Abuakwa traditional area where resides the Paramount chief (*Okyenhene*) who, according to custom, as the chief magistrate and highest military officer, occupies the position not only of ruler but judge, law-maker, executive officer and supreme commander. In performing these functions, he is aided and advised by a Council of State comprising the important divisional chiefs. His rank as supreme commander is perhaps the most significant, since military functions in Akim Abuakwa are the basic determinants of status. The Paramount belongs to the *Asona* clan, and following him in rank is the chief of the vanguard (*Adontenhene*) who also belongs to the *Asona* clan and resides at Kukurantumi. After him, in order of precedence, come the chiefs of the Right Wing (*Nifahene*) and the Left Wing (*Benkumhene*) at Asiakwa and Begoro. These wing chiefs, and others of similar status, are divisional chiefs who are autonomous in respect of their own territorial areas of jurisdiction. They have under them a number of sub-chiefs whom they control directly: Tafo and Apapam, for instance, belong to the vanguard, and are under the direct rule of the Kukurantumi chief.

Before independence in 1957, Kukurantumi and Kibi were officially on cordial terms, and there was very little sign of open conflict between them until the Kukurantumi chief, Nana Kena, took the momentous step of making his peace with Nkrumah's Convention People's Party in opposition both to Nana Ofori Atta II, the Paramount chief, and to the United Party. Nana Kena, young, handsome, popular and a London University graduate in Ethics, Government and Law, had become chief of Kukurantumi in 1952. He was one of the most enlightened chiefs of his time, held in high esteem both nationally and in the Akim Abuakwa area, and an important figure in the Akim Abuakwa Traditional Council. He became a member of the Ghana Scholarship Secretariat and, eventually, the country's High Commissioner in India where he died in a car accident. He had initially resisted the temptation of being dragged into party politics, adroitly performing his traditional functions, and paying his expected obeisance to the Paramount chief, without allowing himself to be pulled into open support for the latter's political opposition to Nkrumah. It would have been most unusual, however, for a chief of those qualities, in the circumstances of the all-embracing politics of the period, to maintain for long that kind of adroit political neutrality, and three considerations swayed Nana Kena to the side of the C.P.P. Firstly, he was not a typical chief, in the sense that he was educated enough to assume any office of high responsibility outside the traditional framework: he not only understood the values of the traditional system, and the changes being brought about by wealth, education and western institutions, but realised that he was qualified to play some important part in the changes that were taking place. Secondly, the C.P.P. government did not fail to recognise his qualities and potential. As the second in command in the Akim Abuakwa traditional establishment and well-educated, he was a good asset as a possible counter-weight to the strong opposition faction in Kibi, and the overtures made to him by the government (and the national assignments offered) were a challenge which he was reluctant to resist.

Thirdly, a number of decisions taken by the Akim Abuakwa State

Council between 1954 and 1957 convinced him that he should throw in his lot with the C.P.P. In 1953, under the *Native Court (Colony) Ordinance, 1944,* a Native Court Grade 'A' was established to exercise jurisdiction within the area covered by the Akim Abuakwa District Council. In 1954, the court was empowered to sit not only at Kibi but at New Tafo and any place convenient for the carrying out of its function. The Paramount chief refused however to sit in court at New Tafo, and got the State Council's support against the order. The Kukurantumi chief refused his signature to the protest, on the grounds that he had no traditional authority to do so without first obtaining the consent of his traditional 'elders'. As if that was not enough of a *casus belli* between Kibi and Kukurantumi, two further events in 1955 stoked the fires of hostility between the towns. Against tradition, and in the face of protests by the Adonten Divisional chiefs, the State Council elevated Dr. J. B. Danquah to the status of chief within the Adonten Division. The State Council also decided to enter politics by supporting the National Liberation Movement, despite an earlier Joint Provincial Council resolution barring chiefs from engaging in party politics. It was then that the Adontehene entered the C.P.P. camp, and Kukurantumi began immediately to be a beneficiary of C.P.P. favour. In particular, the town was rewarded with a modern, government-assisted Secondary School, although not without stiff contest from Tafo. By 1960, it had become one of the C.P.P. strongholds in the constituency. When the chief was appointed High Commissioner in New Delhi, A. K. Akuoko, a Kukurantumi barrister, was made legal adviser to the C.P.P. headquarters in Accra, and G. D. Ampaw, another Kukurantumi barrister (later to be the Progress Party candidate in the 1969 elections) was made a member of the Board of Directors of the Ghana Commercial Bank. Meanwhile, Kibi was being punished by the C.P.P. government. The Abuakwa State Secondary School, founded by Sir Ofori Atta I in 1937 at Asafo, and later moved to Kibi, remained in its war-time military huts. The Paramount Chief was destooled, and banished to Accra by the government. Dr. J. B. Danquah, William Ofori Atta (son of Sir Ofori), Ofori Ware (the treasurer of the N.L.M. and later chairman of the Kibi Progress Party), Kwaku Tawia (the jasehene of Kibi and a stalwart of the N.L.M.), and several other Kibi notables, were kept in 'Preventive Detention'. As a result, Kibi remained fundamentally opposed to the C.P.P. regime.

The relationship between Tafo,[7] traditionally subject to the Kukurantumi Stool, and Kukurantumi has been disturbed by a more subtle rivalry. At the base of a number of disputes has been the fact that when the railway from Accra reached New Tafo in 1917, only two miles away from Kukurantumi, the former became a major commercial centre where branches of all the leading firms and companies were es-

tablished. In addition, after the establishment of the West African
Cocoa Research Institute in 1937, New Tafo enjoyed such modern
amenities as electricity, well-laid out streets, and good drinking water,
giving it the status of a 'rural metropolis', overshadowing Kukurantumi.
New Tafo thus acquired a bargaining power denied to its neighbours, an
advantage further reinforced by the fact that, from the very beginning,
the commitment of the Tafos to the cause of the C.P.P. was almost
total. New Tafo became a rich beneficiary of C.P.P. largess. It was en-
dowed with a modest but decent hospital; the Old Tafo chief was
elevated to the position of a divisional chief, thus becoming independent
of Kukurantumi; and the new secondary school for the area would
almost certainly have been located in the town but for the strong, persistent lobbying of Kukurantumi and the government's need to win Nana
Kena's support. To crown its success, Tafo supplied the C.P.P. with
two successful Parliamentary candidates, both of whom became
Cabinet Ministers. Following the triple defeat in the 1954 general election of William Ofori Atta, K. Dua-Sakyi, and Dr. J. B. Danquah, the
earlier dominance of Kibi effectively came to an end, and Tafo
stepped into the vacancy thus created.

Relations between Tafo and Kibi were at best strained. The Tafos
still believe that it was Sir Ofori Atta I who dissuaded the Colonial
Government from making New Tafo the Eastern Regional capital, and
there is some inexplicable belief among them, shrouded in myth and
legend, that it was their town, and not Kibi, which should have been the
capital of the Akim Abuakwa traditional area. This traditional rivalry
between the two towns was made worse by the clash of private interests
between Tafo members at the court of Sir Ofori Atta I. The early es-
pousal of the C.P.P. cause, the victory of that party, and the favours
showered by the Government on Tafo (including the siting of the
District Council Offices in the town) soured still further relations
between the two towns.

The Apedwas also had their axe to grind with Kibi. At the funeral of
Nana Sir Ofori Atta I at Kibi in 1943, the chief of Apedwa, Akyea Mensah, vanished in mysterious circumstances and was found murdered, a
sordid crime which led to deep antipathy between the Apedwas and
Kibi.[8] It was also an additional cause of the strong support for the
C.P.P. by the Apedwas against both Kibi and the National Liberation
Movement during the period of party conflict a little before independence. It is true that time has blunted the edge of these various
rivalries: but they are there still, and they remained important in the
1969 election.

We turn now to the contest itself. Although four political parties—the Progress Party, the National Alliance of Liberals, the All
People's Republican Party, and the United Nationalist Party—stood in

the constituency, the main battle was fought between the P.P. and the N.A.L. As a matter of political prudence both these parties began their organisation and campaign long before the lifting of the ban on party activities by the military regime. And both had would-be candidates active in the field.

On the P.P. side, the earliest was X, a civil servant, who would like to remain anonymous for obvious reasons. A graduate of the University of Ghana, he had been a member of the various main opposition parties to the C.P.P. and, on graduation, worked initially for a foreign company. A little before the coup, he had resigned from business and joined the civil service, ostensibly on the ground that his intimate knowledge of the operations of the firm had opened his eyes to the truth of 'neo-colonialism', and to the fact that foreign companies were employing all manner of ruses to fleece Ghana. 'I found it a disgrace helping those people to exploit my own country.' He never joined the C.P.P. however, remained opposed to that party, and after the coup began to organise branches in support of any party that Busia would form. Not having either the time, because of the demands of his work in Accra, or adequate independent financial resources (a common plight among many a civil servant), he confined his activities to the eastern half of the constituency around Tafo, Kukurantumi and Maase. He made only tentative efforts at Kibi in the belief that the pace-setters and the political nerve centres of the future party would be located in other areas, a neglect of the western half which was later to cost him the nomination for Progress by the constituency organisation.

He was opposed by three other would-be candidates: Y, another (barrister) civil servant; K. Dua-Sakyi, a barrister and former Kibi opposition politician who had become a magistrate and Director of Public Prosecutions under the C.P.P. regime; and G. D. Ampaw, a Kukurantumi barrister, who had also been a member of the C.P.P. Y did very little campaigning, although he collected valuable votes from the western half of the constituency, from where he comes. Dua-Sakyi became a member of the Constituent Assembly, and worked ceaselessly at Kibi; but it was G. D. Ampaw who was finally nominated by the constituency and endorsed by the Progress Central Working Committee. He was a former C.P.P. stalwart, not particularly liked by the old United Party's national and local establishments: he was said to have been one of the persons behind the attempt in 1958 to eject the U.P. leaders from 'Opposition House' in Accra.[9] But by the time of the coup, he was a prosperous lawyer-businessman who at one time had formed a diamond winning company. He made no effort to conceal his former political affiliations; put all his cards before the P.P. Working Committee and the constituency organisation, and won the nomination through one of the most astute political lobbying campaigns in the election. He clearly sensed the impending victory of the P.P., not only in the country but also in the Abuakwa constituency.

While X was campaigning for himself and for the not yet formed Progress Party, A. K. Akuoko, a Kukurantumi barrister-at-law, was also bringing together a local following in anticipation of any political party that K. A. Gbedemah might form. Akuoko was a philosophy graduate of the University of Ghana and for several years a teacher at the Akim Abuakwa Secondary School at Kibi. After leaving the University, he worked with the District Council at Kibi and Tafo, and was widely known throughout the Abuakwa traditional area, above all in the Abuakwa constituency. He then left to study law in Britain, and on his return served as legal adviser to the C.P.P. headquarters up to the time of coup in 1966. He was therefore a leading C.P.P. figure in the country, and a very powerful one within the constituency. After the coup, he settled in his hometown, Kukurantumi, and practised his profession at Koforidua, some thirteen miles away. A very affable person, his life-long close links with the traditional networks of power made him a formidable local force whom no opponent could in any sense comfortably ignore. He was a foundation member of the N.A.L., and when he died suddenly in June 1969, barely a month after the lifting of the ban on party politics, the party lost a candidate of considerable influence. It was he who, with the help of a hotelier, E. C. Agyakwa of New Tafo, began to form branches of the N.A.L. in the constituency.

The blow was even greater because the N.A.L. had confidently refused to groom any other possible successor. Then two suitable candidates, Edward Antwi, a Kukurantumi barrister, and S. C. Abrokwa, a Tafo businessman resident in Accra, eventually presented themselves. There was no open contest between the two, for Antwi was persuaded to stand for N.A.L. in Asiakwa-Kwabeng where the party was experiencing difficulties in finding a suitable candidate. At the end of June, therefore, without any contest at a constituency delegates conference, S. G. Abrokwa was declared N.A.L. candidate for the area.

What kind of candidate was he? A Presbyterian trained teacher, he had taught at his home town, Tafo, and in Begoro and the Kwahu Traditional Area between 1945 and 1949. In 1950, he resigned his teaching appointment, worked in the West African Cocoa Research Institute at Tafo, and ended up in the government service as an Agricultural Survey Officer in the Ministry of Agriculture. Between 1963 and 1965, he was in Germany, training to become a production manager, and a private businessman; but he retained his local contacts particularly through his interests in sport and a number of voluntary associations. He was a member of local football teams, founded branches of the Boys' Scouts Movement, and was for a long time secretary of the Akim Abuakwa Presbyterian Teachers' Association. Between 1961 and 1963, he was also a member of the Kumasi Youngmen's Literary Club, and of the C.P.P. branch of the Ashanti Youth Association.

As a former C.P.P. member, though not by any means a nationally prominent one, he was one of those who saw in the P.P. a re-incarnation of the opposition United Party, and N.A.L. as a reformed C.P.P. shorn of its left-wing elements: he was unable, therefore, to make the ideological about-turn in support of the P.P. which he saw as a 'reactionary' party full of intellectuals, out of touch with local sentiment. But he too was hardly of great populist tendencies. He regarded N.A.L. as a businessman's party which was capable of resuscitating the Ghanaian economy, improving the employment situation in the country, and opening avenues for private business. Business considerations were clearly central to his political affiliations. A former employee in Henry Djabah's Ghana Agricultural Machinery Company, he had joined Solo (Ghana) Ltd., a rival company to the G.A.M.: and, indeed, had given evidence in a court suit that ended in the imprisonment of his former employer, Djabah. The latter had been freed by the Appeal Court after the coup, and was so deeply antagonistic to his former C.P.P. colleagues for deserting him that, in revenge, he decided to support the P.P. This fact too probably weighed heavily in the mind of Abrokwa. For much the same reasons, E. C. Agyakwa, a hotelier at Tafo, a prominent former C.P.P. member, and one time President of the Ghana Hoteliers' Association, also decided to support Abrokwa and the N.A.L.

For the elections, the N.A.L. divided the country into zones, each comprising a number of constituencies, to which party propaganda vans and funds were allocated. Within this arrangement, Zone 2 had its headquarters at New Tafo and comprised the New Juabeng, Begoro, Abuakwa, and Suhum constituencies. Its chairman was E. C. Agyakwa; other officers of the zonal executive were from Old Tafo, Koforidua, Suhum and Osino. In addition, there were regional organisations, whose executives were elected by constituency representatives at a regional conference. For the Eastern Region, an Executive was elected in June with the following membership: Prince Yaw Boateng, a former C.P.P. ambassador to Brazil, chairman; R. K. Dokyi of Kukurantumi, organising secretary; the late A. K. Akuoko, secretary; and E. Ohene Djan, a former Director of Sport under the C.P.P. regime, as 'campaign strategist'; twenty other constituency representatives were also elected. At that same meeting, E. H. Boohene, senior lecturer in accountancy at the University of Ghana and one of the three National Deputy Leaders of the party, was elected to represent the Eastern Region on the National Executive.

The zonal executives were distinguished from the regional executives in the sense that the former were purely campaign and propaganda organisations with no policy-making powers. Parliamentary candidates were excluded in order to free the zonal executive members of any responsibility for a particular constituency: they were expected to operate as 'free' agents who could tour as many as three constituencies a day, thus creating the impression of ubiquity, toughness, resilience and resourcefulness, notwithstanding the poverty or sloth of a particular candidate. It was an ingenious arrangement in the light of the resources available to the N.A.L. and the individual candidates, although it tended to create confusion over lines of communication.

When Abrokwa became the official N.A.L. candidate, he found an organisation on the brink of collapse, confounded by the defection not only of the zonal and constituency propaganda secretaries but of the Susu Biribi Sporting Club—a popular local football club—to the P.P. camp. The Club had originally hoped to reap financial support from E. C. Agyakwa and the N.A.L. until Djabah, a former Patron, succeeded in weaning them into the P.P. camp, a loss which cost the N.A.L. a body of enthusiastic, popular, young campaigners who were very influential. Abrokwa had to rebuild an organisation almost from scratch against great odds, using personal contacts and any harnessable goodwill which, on his own admission, came more readily from the non-Akims. It was, he confessed, an asset as well as a liability since it accentuated the ethnic undertones of the whole campaign. The final outcome was a makeshift machine but by no means an ineffective one.

The constituency executive was selected in such a manner as to satisfy both sectional and personal interests. The chairman, a former U.P. member, was from Apedwa, the secretary from Tafo, and other officers from Kukurantumi and Asafo. In the hectic moments of the campaign, the constituency executive, in co-operation with the thirty-three town, village and ward branches, were very influential; but the most important organisation was the candidate's own entourage of University undergraduates and journalists who constituted a sort of peripatetic machine, organising instant rallies, and recruiting activists wherever there was a response to their appeal. N.A.L., like other parties, relied mainly on membership dues and voluntary contributions either in kind or cash from its supporters. It had three main categories of members: national members, restricted to no more than 320 all told, regional members, and constituency or district members, who contributed N₵50.00, N₵20.00 and N₵0.20 respectively to the national chest for such general expenses as election deposits, petrol costs, posters, salaried employees and drivers. For the whole campaign, cash subventions to the candidate personally amounted to N₵4,000.00 while, on Abrokwa's own estimate, the enterprise cost him

NȻ6,000.00. If one takes into account the expenses of local well-wishers, such as the cocoa-buying agents who were strongly allied to N.A.L., and the running costs of the candidate's own car, the campaign in the constituency may well have cost NȻ10,000.00.

What sort of campaign did the party conduct and to whom did it appeal? Both on the national and local level, attempts were made to project a number of related images. There was, first, that of a 'populist' party which appealed to the 'small' man, the unemployed, the 'unestablished' and those who prided themselves on not being academic intellectuals pursuing the will-o'-the-wisp of theories. But it also tried to convey the impression that its leaders were practical and experienced men who did not waste time on interminable debate but spent both muscle and brain power on action.

> You cannot afford to entrust the destiny of your children into the hands of an 'experimental government' whose members, judging from recent pronouncements are *inexperienced, impractical, unimaginative.* A VOTE FOR N.A.L. will ensure that these risks and any likely miscalculated judgement does not militate against your interests.[10]

Perhaps the most persistent attempt by the leaders was to portray the N.A.L. as a national party, speaking for all the people, not rooted in sectional interests—a charge frequently levelled against it because of its firm base in the Volta region. In practice, however, it was seen throughout the constituency as an anti-Akim party, spearheaded especially by Ewes and Krobos. The N.A.L. certainly exploited the fears of the Krobos, and made good use of traditional disputes—as between the Queen-mother and the chief at Apedwa, and between the *Mankrado* and the chief at Maase; it also drew support from the Tafo Chief who had been brought back to his traditional status, as a subject to Kukurantumi, after the coup.

On the further charge, that it was a re-incarnation of the C.P.P. the leaders were equivocal. When a rally was held at Kibi, Gbedemah found occasion to lay a wreath on the grave of Dr. J. B. Danquah, an inveterate opponent of the C.P.P. When it suited its purposes, however, the party tried to lay claim to the good deeds of the C.P.P., of which they deemed themselves the heirs, while being careful to stress the fact that the N.A.L. leader had left the country to go into exile in 1961. The party undoubtedly had a preponderance of former C.P.P. members at every level in its organisation, the result being that the N.A.L. ambivalently asserted its right to inherit the assets but not the liabilities of the C.P.P. although the Abuakwa voters were to hold it responsible for the former party's defects as well as its virtues.

The organisation of Progress followed the same lines as that of the N.A.L. except in two respects. The country was not 'zoned' for the elections, and the only intermediate level between the National Working

Committee, (which was by no means a democratically elected body, but personally appointed by the leader), and the constituency was the regional organisation. Nevertheless, the Committee gave a large measure of autonomy to the regional as well as the constituency organisations, except for the tight hold it retained on who was or was not to be a candidate. The actual organisation in the constituency was very similar to that of the N.A.L., and needs very little elaboration. Many of the leaders in key positions, especially at the regional level, were of the former United Party including those who were already members of the Constituent Assembly. It was true to expectation, therefore, that the moving force of the party in the Eastern Region should have been William Ofori Atta, a member both of the Constitutional Commission and of the Constituent Assembly, and a former leading member of the United Party. At the constituency level, Progress—like its opponents—had to take into account the different sectional interests of the population at large, but in the Abuakwa constituency, the P.P. looked more like a mass party than the N.A.L. 'mass' here meaning no more than the extent of support and the general social composition of that support rather than the party's actual programmes or beliefs. And as it happened, when nominations were decided at a very democratically conducted meeting, it was the most C.P.P. of the contestants who won, to the chagrin of some of the U.P. old guard. The best known of the former U.P. members—K. Dua-Sakyi—lost the nomination, and promptly decided to stand as an independent. Two interesting aspects of the nomination contest were, firstly, the general desire not to support the candidate from Kibi—a reflection of the traditional tension between the periphery and the centre—and, secondly, the manner in which the constituency officers were appointed in such a way as to satisfy the claims of the various nerve centres of the area. The chairman was from Tafo, the Vice-Chairman from Apedwa, and the secretary from Panoh, a suburb of Kibi. All were well-known former opponents of the C.P.P. regime.

For its finance the party depended on membership dues as well as on voluntary contributions. Again, two categories of membership were instituted: founding members, limited to 2,000 who paid N₵10.00 each, and ordinary members who contributed N₵0.20 per annum into the national coffers of the party. Apart from the deposits of the candidates, the national headquarters made no cash subventions to the constituency; it merely contributed posters and other campaign materials. The total cost of the election, therefore, fell on the shoulders of the activists, especially the candidate himself (a lawyer-businessman), the chairman (a timber contractor and general merchant), and Djabah, all of whom together probably contributed between N₵6,000.00 and N₵10,000.00. In substance, therefore, the P.P.—like the N.A.L.—was also a businessman's party although it made no attempt to advertise the fact.

As to the picture of itself that the P.P. *wanted* to project, there was not much difference between it and the N.A.L. Much like its opponent, Progress proclaimed its national character, its dislike of regionalism and tribalism, its love of liberty and its ability to redeem the country from its economic difficulties—familiar platitudes of both parties. But perhaps the most notable feature of the P.P. was its desire to persuade the electorate of its puritanism and incorruptibility, including its determination to cleanse the nation of graft and to elevate the country and its politics to a new level of decency. To demonstrate its sincerity in these matters, the P.P. stressed that it was not simply the old U.P. resuscitated, and accused its opponents of being the men who ruined the country under Nkrumah. The slogan '*Efaa won nsa ntam*' (it slipped through their fingers) was continually and monotonously on the lips of P.P. propagandists in order to drive home the point that the nation's resources passed through the fingers of their opponents—or, more precisely, that wealth had been frittered away by the men who occupied key positions in the N.A.L.

The P.P. was also helped by the fact that, even when it was identified with the former U.P., the defects of that party's record were so remote in time that they meant very little to the younger electors who grew up in the post-independence period when the opposition was effectively muzzled. The general mood, therefore, was one of a wish to give the P.P. leadership a chance as an alternative to the experience of the former civilian regime. Much of the credibility of P.P. propaganda depended, in no small measure, on this hope of an alternative; and the P.P.'s plea was one of innocence not on the grounds solely of alibi but of non-feasance.

Within the constituency itself, Progress was most convincing when it charged its opponents with responsibility for the C.P.P.'s mishandling of the economy. In practice, whatever the leaders might say, the P.P. was a revived U.P. Yet it would be too simple an analysis to conclude that support for the P.P. was nothing but an anti-C.P.P. phenomenon. Many areas of C.P.P. support swung to the P.P. side; and the P.P. candidate himself was a well-known C.P.P. supporter and member. Two reasons may be held to account for the change. Firstly, many of the former C.P.P. rank-and-file were not at all politically committed to the former party in the sense of finding it difficult—psychologically or practically—to redirect their political allegiance; secondly, they saw the P.P. basically as an Akim party and were very willing to allow themselves to be swayed by ethnic feelings and attachments.

The two minor parties—the A.P.R.P. and the U.N.P.—which, on the past record of their candidates in the constituency, appeared to represent the more left wing and ideological splinter groups of the C.P.P., failed to establish even a rudimentary organisation in the constituency. The independent candidate. K. Dua-Sakyi as a well-known lawyer and former politician had managed at first to persuade supporters in Kibi and its immediate environs to support his bid for the P.P. ticket. He had independent resources, and the name to wage a good campaign. He chose the Bible as his symbol; and he organised his whole campaign on the need for honesty, combined with incessant attacks on the P.P. in such a manner as led one to suppose that he was campaigning primarily in revenge for the loss of the P.P. nomination, since he paid no attention to any other candidate. His defeat was interesting not simply because he lost but because he lost so decisively. Indeed, the fate both of the independent and of the two minor parties, and the success of the P.P. despite its ex-C.P.P. candidate, underlined the fact that, however important local issues might seem, the electorate voted with a keen eye on the national standing of the parties and not solely on the individual candidates.

TABLE 2

Name of Candidate	Party Affiliation	Votes Obtained
G. D. Ampaw	P.P.	8,197
C. Otchere Darko	A.P.R.P.	53
Seth Gilbert Abrokwa	N.A.L.	3,465
Boakye Otchere Darko Acheampong	U.N.P.	44
Kwesi Dua-Sakyi	Independent	128
Total Votes Cast		11,887
Registered Voters		16,975

Out of the 24 wards, the N.A.L. won in 6, polled nearly as many votes as the P.P. (i.e. between 45 per cent and 50 per cent) in four, and less than 20 per cent of the votes cast in five. Taking 20 per cent (i.e. one-fifth) of the votes cast in each of the wards as our yardstick, we can say that the N.A.L. showed an effective presence in 19 of the 24 wards, and the P.P. in all. Except at Kibi, where the independent polled 53 votees, in no other ward did either he or the A.P.R.P. or the U.N.P. candidate poll more than 10 votes.

What factors accounted for these results? The election did not conform to the pattern of the 1954 and '56 contests in the constituency when the C.P.P., despite its wide membership and the variety of its support, deliberately waged on incessant anti-traditional authority campaign. There had been instances then where the C.P.P. even used chiefs in its campaign against traditional authority, while its opponents had been prepared to use non-traditional procedures and methods to prop up the chiefs. That was not true of 1969. There was a remarkable acceptance now by traditional authorities of their subordination to the new political structures. It was only in the strictest of confidence that most of the chiefs in the constituency would divulge their party political preferences: the Paramount chief even went to the extent of making it a point to absent himself from Kibi whenever there was a political rally. In the absence of this 'chief/commoner' or traditional/non-traditional conflict, one could certainly not talk in any way of 'class politics', even in the sense that it might be said to have existed under the C.P.P.

Was the election simply a revival of the old C.P.P./U.P. quarrel, ending in a major victory for the U.P.? It is an attractive proposition, provided the limits on its validity are recognised. At leadership level—except that both candidates in Abuakwa were former C.P.P.—the two parties gave every indication of a revival of the confrontation between the former parties, and many of the voters understood it that way. And to the extent that this image persisted, the N.A.L. was on the defensive, especially when the idea gained currency in the constituency that it was high time for change and that a 'destooled chief does not succeed himself'. But the extent of the swing was too large to be explained simply in terms of former political alignments. There was something new about the two major parties and the bases of their support—something too peculiar to fit neatly into the old models. One of the most striking features of the election was undoubtedly the increased use made of ethnicity to gain political support. Consider, for example, the position of the Krobos. They were finally swung in favour of the N.A.L. by a prominent Krobo leader, E. L. Madjetey, former Commissioner of Police until dismissed and imprisoned by Nkrumah. Madjetey was chosen as a N.A.L. candidate in the nearby constituency, Manya Krobo, and the effect was decisive among the Krobo community in the Akim areas, despite attempts by Progress to act through another Krobo, H. K. Djabah. And underlying the Krobos' decision to vote for N.A.L. was the continuing Akim-Krobo rivalry.

Similarly, relations between the Ewe and the Akim in the constituency were much affected by the significant (if muted) ethnic conflict which we have seen to have been of so much importance at the national level: almost to a man, the Ewe in the constituency rallied to the support of the N.A.L., and the overwhelming majority of the Akim (barring highly localised and deep rivalries) gave their support to the P.P.[12] The situation was not by any means helped by the fact that the first constituency secretary of the N.A.L. was an Ewe civil servant and that (at the national executive level) the Ewe held sway in the party; or that the Akan dominated the P.P. At most N.A.L. and P.P. rallies in the constituency, it was the Ewe and the Akan who, respectively, supplied the festivities and the music.

These observations are confirmed by the geographical distribution of support for the parties in the constituency. Polling booth by booth, the results indicated that, for instance, in New Tafo most of the N.A.L.'s 820 votes came from the Ewe quarters of the town, while the Akim sections voted P. P. Similarly, in the four major akin towns (Old Tafo, Kukuratumi, Kibi and Apedwa) Gbedemah's party barely obtained one-fifth of the votes.[13] In all the six wards where the N.A.L. beat the P.P. scrutiny of the very small turn out of voters showed that the N.A.L. votes came from 'rural' clusters of homesteads inhabited by either Krobo or Ewe farmers—a factor which helped considerably to modify the inter-town rivalries among the Akims.

Three general conclusions, therefore, may be hazarded from the elections. First, they were contested principally on *national* policies, adapted to suit local issues in the constituency. Secondly, Ghanaian politics (in the light of the elections) took on more strongly than ever the colour of élite competition. If populism means not simply a belief in government based on mass consent but a theory implying a validation of the virtues of the 'small' man, and a rejection of an élite leadership, then none of the parties which contested in the constituency was genuinely populist. Yet, thirdly, the results and the campaign confirmed the view that such local issues as land disputes and ethnic feelings are still important factors in the politics of 'mass voting': again to a much greater extent than before. Yet it was all in good humour. For such issues scarcely affected established personal links whether in the workshop, or market place, or on the farms. By all accounts, the elections were among the most peaceful and orderly that were ever conducted in the constituency.

Notes

1. John Mensah Sarbah, *Fanti Customary Laws,* (London, Frank Cass, 1968), p. 66.
2. Quoted in N. A. Ollennu: *Principles of Customary Land Law in Ghana,* (London, Sweet and Maxwell, 1962), p. 4; cf. Edmund Burke, *Works,* Vol. II, p. 368.
3. Gold Coast Colony, *Report of the Department of Agriculture, 1937–38,* (Accra, 1939), pp. 3–4.
4. *Report of the Electoral & Local Government Reform Commission,* Accra, 1967, p. 120.
5. *Ghana Government Gazette No. 91,* 9 September 1969, p. 1051.
6. Figures made available by the Returning Officer, Abuakwa Constituency.
7. Unless otherwise stated, 'Tafo' refers to both New and Old Tafo since, for all practical purposes, they are one town split into two.
8. For an account of the 'Kibi murders' see A. C. Burns *Colonial Civil Servant* London 1949, p. 219.

9. A rented house where the leading members of the opposition lived in the 1950s.
10. *The Evening Standard*, (Accra), 29 August 1969.
11. *Ghana Government Gazette No. 91,* 9 September 1969, p. 1051.
12. The procedure of counting votes on the spot at each polling station facilitated this analysis.
13. But not at Apedwa where a funeral on polling day disrupted voting and made many Akims disinclined to go and vote.

CHAPTER 9

POLITICS IN SWEDRU

Maxwell Owusu

Throughout its history the Convention People's Party was characterised in a most glaring way by a steady and continuous accretion of power. It succeeded in dominating first the political and then the social and economic scene by its control of 'integral organisations', and it purported to give general direction not only to workers, farmers, market women and petty traders but, in a more general sense, to the 'youth'. Overall, it was perhaps what may justly be termed a 'party corporation'. And the legalising of a one-party state in 1964 was simply the granting of *de jure* recognition to a state of affairs that had existed *de facto* since 1958.[1] In Swedru all councillors had, therefore, to be card carrying members of the C.P.P. The spirited opposition headed by Nana Kum and Kojo Essilfie—whom we shall meet later—had been eliminated, and only C.P.P. members could contest local elections. In many instances, there were no genuine and free elections: the nominees of the local C.P.P. executive were always returned unopposed. Council activities and decisions were then controlled by a party-appointed District Commissioner (and his close friends) whose word, as the most senior party man at the local level, was almost always law. In other matters, the party relied for its organisation and finance on a relatively small number of men whose contribution to the party were seen not as personal sacrifices in the national interest, but as investments of time and money in the party corporation. The C.P.P. was expected in time to yield to these party member 'investors' or 'shareholders' not only substantial 'dividends' but assured positions on the political 'board of directors', as Regional and District Commissioners and Chairmen of councils. The President of the state, who was also the Life Chairman of the C.P.P., became (or was seen as) the trustee for the corporate property of the state as a whole and for all the economic resources vested in it. State property became party property. At the very least, the party had almost unlimited power to allocate the resources as it thought fit, and this authority to distribute resources was the primary basis of the party's supreme power.

The C.P.P. had attracted to its ranks in Swedru many who felt strongly that they should improve their economic and social status. For its electoral support the Swedru party (as in many other constituencies) had depended very much on the small-scale, heavily-indebted cocoa farmers in the surrounding countryside who were concerned with fin-

233

ding money to redeem two or more acres of cocoa farms. These small-scale farmers saw the party-controlled Cocoa Purchasing Company as an unfailing source of financial aid, and as the instrument for their economic and social well-being. Accordingly they had voted C.P.P. The party was also popular among minor clerks, salesmen or storekeepers, semi-skilled workers, and lesser municipal functionaries, some of whom provided the party with its leadership at local and regional levels. Their interest in the party was rational, and their commitment instrumental. For a people who had neither the educational qualification to become university graduates in the foreseeable future, nor the financial nor kinship resources to become cocoa magnates, the only possible avenue to power and wealth, and the social standing they brought, was through the party.

Unhappily, however, the government could not forever create employment opportunities for this or any other group of a rapidly expanding party following, nor could it continue to reward materially its many friends of fortune, without a substantial rate of continuous economic growth or at least a high and stable international price of cocoa. Neither happened, and government expenditure on roads, schools, hospitals and other government services, resulted in a monetary expansion which, by the early 1960s, as many people in Swedru attest, began to exert a powerful inflationary impact on the economy. Import restrictions, and anomalies in the issue of import licenses, led to a serious scarcity of consumer goods, including farm implements (cutlasses in particular) and imported food, the demand for which far out-stripped supply. The result, as described in Chapter 2, was further price inflation. In Swedru, trading stores (both African and European) grew emptier; hoarding and black marketing increased.

The situation grew worse until by 1965 it was hurting almost everybody. There was no increase in the daily wage rate in this period; living standards went down, and the C.P.P. began to lose its popularity. As Yaw Twumasi has shown, the introduction in 1961 of compulsory savings as one of the measures to control inflation, led to strikes, and when the world price of cocoa fell drastically, the government took the further unpleasant decision of fixing the producer price at £2 per 60 lb. load compared with the 1951 price of £4 per load and the 1954–58 guaranteed minimum of £3 12s. From this £2 the Swedru farmers were obliged to pay a 'voluntary' contribution to the national development plan at the rate of six shillings, plus a compulsory contribution of four shillings per load of cocoa, making a total contribution of ten shillings. The decision was taken in consultation with representatives of the United Ghana Farmers' Council Co-operative, many of whom were not farmers but party men.[2]

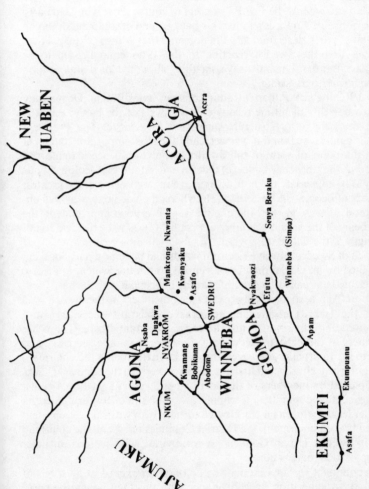

SWEDRU-NYAKROM-NKUM CONSTITUENCY

Note the positions of the towns of SWEDRU,
NYAKROM and NKUM on secondary roads

By 1964 the government had lost many of its supporters. In Swedru a sizeable number of those who had voted for the C.P.P.—clerks in the post office and the Public Works Department, elementary school teachers, semi-skilled workers of the electricity corporation and rediffu sion station, and the small scale habitually-indebted cocoa farmers were now bitterly against the C.P.P.—except of course those who held party office of profit. And it is against this background of a rapidly declining economy, party desertion, and the potential breakdown of the political system, that the Swedru reaction to the 1966 coup needed to be assessed. But first one must say something about the local organisation of the former party-state.

In 1962 the C.P.P. had introduced its new constitution. Democracy was to be at its plenitude throughout *all* levels of the party: this was what the new party structure purported to achieve. The President further emphasised (and it was certainly the most important statement from the point of view of the Swedru population, since it reinforced what was their primary concern) that 'to understand the ideology of our party is to appreciate the need to improve the well-being of the greatest number of people'. In Swedru, as elsewhere, the 'ideology' was well understood. It was, in fact, the one message everyone appreciated: 'the well-being of the greatest number of people'. It was to be the acid test of the right of the C.P.P. to govern.

Each of Swedru's twelve electoral wards had become a party branch, managed by an eleven-member executive committee which, in theory, was elected annually at a general meeting in keeping with the party constitution. Again, theoretically, the leading members at the branch level were the (ward) chairman, secretary, assistant secretary, and treasurer, the chairman being the most important figure. The other members of the branch executive were the propaganda secretary and six others. In practice, however, the executive (including the chairman) was not freely chosen and had little or no power. On the contrary: it was handpicked by members of the next higher level organisation, the district executive committee. Certainly this was true of Swedru where at district level there was a working chairman (who was said to represent all the branch chairmen), the District Commissioner, and the chairman of the Swedru Urban Council—a triumvirate who formed an inner group of local party cadres.

Recruitment by appointment or co-optation existed at all levels of the party organisation. In consonance with this tacit policy the party managed to enforce the participation not only of traditional notables but socially influential leaders and other possible *loci* of opposition in the various wards. It was through such mechanisms that the party hoped to ensure the essential stability and continuity of the party not only in Swedru, but in the region, and the nation as a whole. And although the constitution emphasised an 'inner party democracy', in practice there was virtually one man who held the greatest power and who controlled his executive members. At the district level, he was the District Commissioner: at the regional level, the Regional Commissioner: at the national level, the President. It must be stressed that in practice, since local people were in daily contact with the D. C. and the R.C. and not with the President, it was the former who were associated particularly with 'tyrannical' power and misuse of authority. (It was often said by local Swedru citizens that the President should actually be sympathised with, since he had no effective way of controlling the behaviour of his Ministers, Regional Commissions, and District Commissioners.) The Regional Commissioner for the Central Region, J. E. Hagan, became so powerful, according to the Jiagge Commission, that 'he did things which even the Government he served could *not* do'. He arrogated to himself the powers of judge, jury, politician, administrator, all in one, and controlled the public institutions associated with those roles. Hagan himself admitted before the Jiagge Commission, which inquired into the assets of C.P.P. ministers, that he sat on 'over-3,000 cases and even settled cases which the Courts could not settle'. Although he had no power to award contracts over one thousand pounds, he entered into large scale deals with local businessmen in Swedru and other towns, and like the District Commissioners he used his party position to acquire private property in land until, during the last phase of C.P.P. rule, the party bosses became more and more unresponsive, in face of very harsh economic realities, to the needs of the people they claimed to represent. That alone accounted for the overall popularity in the constituency of the military coup of February, 1966, and the acceptance (at least during the first year of the coup) of the army and political leaders.

The writer has tried to show elsewhere[3] that political relations in Ghana are considered extensions or primary dimensions of economic relations. The very ideas which affect political relationships and maintain these relationships (between leaders and the led) are often—though not of course exclusively—economic in origin. Political power is believed to be a resource and a means, extremely important although not the only one, to the organisation, accumulation and consumption of wealth in order to achieve an improved social status in the community. And the traditionalists, that is the upholders of tradition, are not necessarily against change; they resist only when change threatens to destroy the economic basis of traditional power, privilege and prestige. Thus, tradition is strategically reinterpreted in situations of change by groups and individuals as they compete for political and economic advantage. The evidence for this contention—the economic base of politics in Swedru—can be drawn from a wide range of sources, among them an attitude survey conducted by the writer which is of some interest to the theme.[4]

Eighty-five men and women teachers in seven major elementary schools in Swedru, ranging in age from twenty-one to fifty, and representing all of the major ethnic groups in Swedru, were asked to respond to four questions among others: (1) 'What did you like about the C.P.P.?'; (2) 'What did you not like about the C.P.P.?'; (3) 'Can you tell me anything about the C.P.P.?'; (4) 'In the event of an election tomorrow, would you vote for someone you know who belonged to the C.P.P.?' The evidence from the opinion poll is suggestive if not directly conclusive. Seventy of the eighty-five respondents gave opinions on all four questions. The rest of the group responded with 'Don't know' or 'Nothing'. The responses to questions No. 2 and No. 3 were then grouped under the following headings: (a) Type of regime; (b) Economic policy; (c) Political recruitment. The responses to question No. 3—'Can you tell me anything about the C.P.P.?'—turned out to be elaborations of points raised under either questions No. 1 or No. 2. Out of seventy negative responses to the C.P.P., fifteen were related to 'dictorial' or 'autocratic' ways or the ideology of the party; thirty-seven concerned 'economic' policy of the party; eight had to do with the method of recruiting people for economic and political posts. Ten mentioned all three factors. It may suffice here to give a few examples of each type of response.

(a) 'The party was oppressive. If you had no party card you had no job.' 'My relative was detained for no reason.' 'A man disliked by the people was imposed on us as a chief by a D.C.'s order.'; 'C.P.P. used power arbitrarily.'; '. . . Everybody became afraid and joined the party.'

(b) 'I was once threatened with loss of job because I had refused to organise school children to attend Young Pioneer meeting.'; 'I approached D.C. about acute water shortage in my village in 1965 and nothing was done.'; 'C.P.P. people were selfish and greedy.'; 'Essential commodities were denied to masses.'; 'Councillors strove to satisfy their selfish needs.'; 'C.P.P. was a gang of robbers.'; 'Nepotism, favouritism, bribery and corruption that was C.P.P.'; 'My father's shop broke completely.'; 'I hate the high rate of taxes and compulsory savings.'; 'Nkrumah amassed wealth and impoverished the masses.'; 'My mother, a trader at Axim, could not get cod fish, pig feet, beef and other stock to sell.'; 'Essential commodities, milk, flour, sugar, and clothes were scarce or not available.'; 'Followers of C.P.P. were crude and thought that government affairs were just like chieftaincy affairs where people near the crown are blessed and privileged.'; 'C.P.P. gave help only to C.P.P. members.'

(c) 'C.P.P. gave posts to unqualified people.'; 'Councillors were unqualified and useless.'; 'Councillors were inexperienced and selfish.'

It was clear that local attitudes towards the C.P.P. were dominated by economic considerations. At the same time, almost all agreed that the C.P.P. had made significant contributions to education and welfare. 'Nkrumah tried to give inexpensive education and lucrative employment to all.'; 'Nkrumah brought us pipe borne water, clinics, first class roads, free education for poor farmers' children, free medical care' and so on. One young man considered Nkrumah's lasting contribution to have been 'Putting Europeans and whites in their place'. Yet many also believed that Nkrumah and the C.P.P. could have done better. Some of the responses were mixed. 'The C.P.P. was a dynamic party in early 1950s, became a corrupt party in late 1950s and 1960s; in 1960s semi-literates were swept into key posts that should be held by the educated'; 'C.P.P. achieved independence for Ghana but later became corrupt and tyrannical and led Ghana to economic disaster.'

A minority believed that the particular behaviour of party members—and many names were mentioned, though not that of Nkrumah himself—had brought about the bad state of the economy. On question No. 4, forty-five out of the eighty-five people said that they would not vote for anyone they knew belonged to the C.P.P. because 'they would do the same things'; 'because of their past record'; 'would do worse things because of their ideology'; 'you cannot teach an old dog a new trick'. Six of the eighty-five indicated they might vote for a former member of the C.P.P. because 'almost everybody was C.P.P.'. One respondent was cynical. 'I would not vote at all. I have lost faith in any human being. I don't know what the fellow I would vote for would do after the election.'

It is apparent from such replies that the leaders and the led in Swedru were (and no doubt still are) held together primarily to get what the political system is primarily designed to give—that is, status, jobs, and material benefits. The relationship between leaders and followers tends to be personal, yet significantly utilitarian. Political commitment, therefore, is primarily instrumental. Leaders confer political office and status, and—for their active followers—public employment. Subordinate leaders and their followers who are rewarded by the system make payments in the form of votes and other modes of support for the system. Ghanaian political leaders are thus chiefly accountable to their followers and the general public for private, utilitarian stakes.

The fact, therefore, that many Ghanaians were indifferent to military decrees which impose restrictions on personal freedom is not difficult to understand. The public was less concerned after 1966 about freedom of speech, which was said to have been attained by the overthrow of Nkrumah, than about the scarcity of consumer goods and material well-being. There was a general belief that one must have a full belly to enjoy freedom.

We turn now to the Swedru–Nyakrom–Nkum constituency. The nodal town of Swedru in which the population in 1960 was said to be 20,546 is located in the Central Region; the constituency has an area of seventeen square miles; and, since 1,209 persons occupy each square mile, Swedru is one of the most densely populated towns in the country. Its politics, both local and national, have always proved exciting. The town played a crucial role in, and to some extent shaped the pattern of, the modern political development of Ghana, its particular character being that of a dynamic combination of indigenous and alien elements in a predominantly commercial setting, lending sometimes an accommodationist, sometimes an explosive flavour, to the town's politics.[5] The outlines of its early growth are clear, but the details of its development and the circumstances of the founding of the Agona State, of which Swedru is an important unit, still need painstaking research to unravel. The disentanglement of the knotty and confused history of the area would require a comparative study of the founding of each of the ten chiefdoms making up the traditional Agona State, and of the history of Gomoa Assin which, until the closing years of the nineteenth century, was the overlord of Agona. The following account, however, may be useful as an accompaniment to the story of its present politics.

The original inhabitants of the area, and of much of southern Ghana, are believed to have been the Guan who seem to have been displaced by the Agona in waves of successive migrations from Tekyiman as early as the middle of the seventeenth century.[6] The traditional chiefdom of Agona-Swedru, headed by the Adontenhene of Agona, was (and still is) organised around the principle of matrilineage (*abusua*) common among the Akan peoples of whom the Ashanti are the best known. There was constant rivalry for the hegemony of the state, including inter-chiefdom struggles over seniority and for the control of economic resources. Despite such rivalries, however, the growth of Swedru from a village of largely clan-based subsistence farmers and hunters into a heterogeneous modern centre was remarkably swift. It began with the introduction of cocoa as a cash crop and the building of motorable roads centring on Swedru and connecting it to the then major ports of Winneba and Cape Coast. The town became an important administrative, educational, and commercial centre after the Second World War, not only for the Agona but for the nation as a whole. And it is now poly-ethnic. Apart from the Agona proper, who constitute 19.8 per cent of the local population, there are the Fante (40.5 per cent), Ashanti (2.1 per cent), Kwahu (4.1 per cent), and many others, including the Lebanese, Syrians and Europeans. Commerce and transport are still the two dominant occupations in Swedru: indeed, the basic character of the town derives from these relatively modern occupations.

The retail trade in secondary products is effectively controlled by migrants, particularly the Kwahu, and a number of Fante, and by Indians, Levantines, and Europeans. The Agona are still mostly engaged in primary production, producing both for themselves and for the ever-growing domestic market. Thus the cosmopolitanism of Swedru—such as it is—developed not out of the sophistication of the rural traditions of the leading elements of the local Agona population but, as in other societies,[7] out of the intrusion into the local scene of cosmopolitan groups with entrepreneurial skills. None the less, there is a large element of unity in Swedru based on three factors. One has been a growing economic interdependence through an extensive nation-wide network of production and exchange and a complex system of internal and external credit and indebtedness. A second factor has been that of social integration, based not only on membership of local, regional, and national organisations which are ethnically heterogeneous—football clubs, churches, religious sects and political parties—but on patterns of 'obligatory joking relationships' among different ethnic groups on the basis of the relevant stereotypes available to the local populations. These joking exchanges of abuse are both cause and consequence of the fact that all the diverse groups are aware of their mutual interdependence, and of the fact that there has developed over the years a strong identification of all migrant groups with Swedru.[8] The third factor has been a political unification founded on the administrative, legal, and territorial unity of the area. In addition, the dependence of the Swedru Urban Council on the central government for substantial grants for development projects has created an awareness of the need for a strong national economy and a paternal central government.

These characteristics quickly became apparent after the 1966 coup when an administrative framework of control superceded the former party structure. In a memorandum on 22 March 1966—barely a month after the coup—the Ministry of Local Government informed the clerks of the 158 local and twenty-one Urban Councils that the N.L.C. had approved interim measures for a new administration. All councils were suspended, and Management Committees were appointed in their place. The powers previously vested in Regional Advisory Committees and Regional Commissioners were to be exercised by Administrative Officers. The N.L.C. also directed that elderly and responsible persons of probity, integrity, and maturity should be nominated for the approval of the N.L.C. not later than 1 April 1966 to serve on the new local committees. Thus, in Swedru, as Robert Dowse has argued in the opening chapter, the coup had the effect of transferring power from the C.P.P. to more established persons, very reminiscent of the colonial power structure. There was a new Town Planning Committee, for example, whose composition included members of the Management Committee, the

Senior Lands Officer of Accra, and the Town Planning Officer of Cape Coast who was the secretary. It also had the effect of denying the local population an effective say in decisions that concerned them directly. Yet to the majority of the residents of Swedru, what really mattered was not so much the denial of a civil right, whose exercise had often been a formality, as the taking of decisions (whoever may be responsible for them) beneficial to their material and social well-being. As the Gyasehene of Agona, Nana Yaw Amponsah II bitterly remarked in a personal interview: 'Lawyer, I honestly feel that our most important objective should be the prevention of C.P.P. rascals and thieves from power. To ensure this, I would not mind,' he continued, 'if the N.L.C. and their representatives ruled for ten years.' The chief went on to say that at the end of ten (or at least five) years government should be handed over to civilians, made up of mature Africans and a few Europeans. The inclusion of Europeans was not surprising. The coup was widely interpreted by elderly people of both sexes, illiterate and literate alike, as by many professional men, as ushering in a new era of peace and prosperity, a return to the colonial social order. To these people, the colonial administration represented an economic and political golden age. The Gyasehene emphasised that, in pre-independence days, the chiefs received their allowances regularly and had much authority: Nkrumah had reduced 'chiefs into begging sycophants'. After the coup, therefore, the ratepayers in Swedru were demanding not a representative local government but tangible benefits from the N.L.C.—the reduction or elimination of property rates and taxes, increased employment (through the setting up of small industries in the area), higher cocoa prices, and the revival of the commercial importance of Swedru. In particular, the chiefs wanted the N.L.C. to restore to them their former pre-eminence, destroyed by the C.P.P. These considerations were greatly to influence the outcome of the 1969 general election.

It is in the context of these observations that the particular role of the Swedru Town Committee needs to be assessed. Before the formal establishment of the Committee in July 1967, there was already in existence an interim development committee—in itself an indication of a strong civic responsibility and the close identification of the inhabitants (irrespective of sex, age, education and ethnic background) with the town. In a welcome address on the 14 April 1967 to the District Administrative Officer and the members of the Swedru Management Committee, the Secretary of the Interim Committee, E. E. Owusu-Ansah (a Probation Officer) stated that '. . . following the overthrow of the old regime, we of Agona Swedru have always been conscious of the magnitude of the great responsibilities entrusted to you on behalf of the Swedru community. . . . With this in view, and under the chairmanship of the traditional head of Swedru, a committee made up of represen-

tatives of the various communities (ethnic groups, commercial and
other interests) in Swedru has been formed. Our aim is to assist in finding workable solutions to problems affecting the general welfare,
progress and development of the town.' The secretary then asked that
the interim committee be officially recognised and its functions brought
in line with other town development committees within the framework
of 'your administration'. Owusu Ansah went on to suggest that its
members be invited to serve on the revenue raising body of the Management Committee to facilitate the effective collection of basic and other
rates which must be used, 'in the best interest of the people'; he also
asked that members of the Interim Committee should serve on any
development Projects Committee that might be formed. It should be
noted that the formulation of these requests showed a remarkable
readiness on the part of many people in Swedru to co-operate freely
with the N.L.C. and their local agents, an attitude translated later into
actual voting behaviour.

Local political initiative was thus quickly assumed by traditional
bodies, voluntary groups and civil servants, as would-be agents of the
Central Government. There was also a renewed emphasis on
status—on the respect due to age, independently-acquired wealth,
education and traditional political office, until it began to look as if the
colonial (and even pre-colonial) privilege systems had been fully
restored. The D.A.O., for example, in giving his approval to the Interim
Committee, stressed that its sole purpose was to be town improvement—to enable Swedru to attain municipal status (a comment
which drew wild applause from the audience). Its purpose was declared
to be non-political—not a forum for personal or 'tribal' rivalry, or self-
interest. Yet implicit in the statements of the D.A.O., and the representatives of the Interim Committee, was a commitment to reverse the
order established by the C.P.P.; to begin once again from where the
colonial system left off. On 12 July 1967 the D.A.O. formally inaugurated the newly constituted Town Committee of twelve. Its
membership was the same as that of the Interim Committee it was
superceding. Detailing its functions, the D.A.O. said, 'I need not over-
emphasise the fact that the Government will not hesitate to suspend the
committee if it becomes a liability rather than an asset to the people of
Swedru'. The committee '. . . must seek to provide the right atmosphere
that will keep the people away from litigations, lawlessness, and the use
of force as a means of settling quarrels. It must clear . . . off matters like
enstoolment and destoolment of chiefs. These should best be left to the
traditional elders and those . . . directly concerned.'

From what has been said, one can see that, with the fall of the C.P.P.,
national and local power passed into the hands of the 'old establishment'—chiefs, professional men, wealthy traders, senior civil

servants, and senior army and police officers. Members of this establishment were generally older, and considered 'more responsible' than the
C.P.P. leadership, as a comparison of the Swedru District Executive
Committee of the C.P.P.—most of whose members were either Urban
Councillors or had been councillors—and that of the Town Committee
shows very clearly. The latter were not only older but better educated,
more successful in their occupations, held higher traditional offices, and
were more 'career oriented' as civil servants or public officials. The
C.P.P. members were younger, had a limited education as minor clerks
and storeboys, were less successful in their occupation (other than
politics) and were generally dissatisfied with their jobs. One can easily
understand why the latter had seen politics as their best avenue to an improvement in their social and economic positions. Similarly, in the
course of personal interviews with members of the Town Committee,
their enthusiastic support for the N.L.C. almost equalled their bitterness
with the C.P.P. Some argued that there should be no elections for a
period ranging from three to ten years after which (it was said) the
N.L.C. should simply hand over power to civilians under Busia.

The abolition by decree of party activities did not, of course, mean
the end of politics in Swedru. On the contrary: the coup that overthrew
the C.P.P. established *pari passu* the dominance of the former U.P. opposition just as the N.L.C., in giving a hero's welcome to Busia on his
return from a self-imposed exile, symbolically identified its own interest
with that of the banned U.P. Opposition to the C.P.P. had never been
strong in Swedru, having to endure a good deal of persecution; but it
had been kept alive by the courage of a few supporters led by Nana
Kum and Kojo Essilfie. The former (the son of a wing-chief of Cape
Coast) had come with his mother to Swedru in 1923 where he finished
his Standard VII education at the local Methodist school in 1932. He
then worked as a painter for the Public Works Department until 1949
when, with a small inheritance, he opened business as a money lender
and prospered. By 1966 he was a wealthy man, sixty years old, and a
disappointed politician, having stood for the N.L.M. in 1956 in Swedru,
only to be decisively defeated, and for the United Party in the Urban
Council elections in 1958—the only U.P. member to do so—when he
was again defeated. Then, in November 1961, he was detained without
trial under the Preventive Detention Act and released the following
year. His companion, and comrade in arms against the C.P.P., was
Kojo Essilfie, whose fate was a good deal more grim since he was
detained, without charge, for five years, and then held cruelly in detention once more until the coup. The dark days of the C.P.P. after the
coup were, therefore, a sunny period for the former U.P. Nana Kum
captured the political mood of Swedru when, celebrating the fall of
Nkrumah a few days after the coup, he led a sacrificial cow through the

streets of Swedru, slaughtered it, and shared the meat ceremoniously
with the people of the town. He was to repeat this ritual act of symbolic
sacrifice when the Progress Party, led by Busia, won the 1969 general
election. Like most people in Swedru, Nana Kum was now outspoken
against the C.P.P. and even criticised the N.L.C. for their 'Christian
politics' because he thought that it was too lenient in its treatment of
former C.P.P. officials and members.

Similarly, the submission in 1966–67 of oral and written representations to the Constitutional Commission was seen as an exercise in
pro-N.L.C., pro-U.P. politics. To many in Swedru, the N.L.C. and the
former U.P. were indistinguishable. In an open hearing before the Commission at the Swedru Town Hall on 8 January 1967, a spokesman on
behalf of the Agona Traditional Council read a written memorandum
which included a number of requests quite unrelated to the terms of
reference of the Commission. They included the creation of jobs for 'our
young men who are unemployed', adequate compensation by the
government when acquiring private lands, the restoration of the one-
third traditional representation on local councils (abolished by the
C.P.P. in 1958), and government help to the Agona to recover their
lands which had been lost to the Fante. The demands were rejected
because they were out of order, but most of the people who came to the
meeting believed strongly that it was the primary responsiblity of any
legitimate government to provide its citizens with their economic and
material needs. And the N.L.C. was seen as a legitimate government.

That this was generally accepted in Swedru could be seen in the street
dancing, parties and general merry-making which had greeted the coup.
The Agona State Council vowed that any attempt on the part of
Nkrumah to return to Ghana to re-establish C.P.P. rule would be met
by the force of the Agona Asafo companies. On the first anniversary of
the coup, local employees of the Ghana National Trading Corporation
described Nkrumah on placards as 'Africa's No. 1 Rogue and a Thief,'
and parents encouraged their children to look up to Kotoka, the principal architect of the military intervention, as a national hero. Then on
17 April 1967 the news reached Swedru that there had been a counter-
coup. The former C.P.P. District Commissioner, together with those
who had benefited financially from C.P.P. rule, drank, poured libation,
and drove triumphantly through Swedru clad in white—the symbol of
victory. Even a local ex-serviceman rejoiced because 'the N.L.C. has
neglected the welfare of ex-servicemen'. These anti-N.L.C.
demonstrations were very isolated—although they showed that the
C.P.P. still had some support in Swedru—and in general the counter-
coup reinforced people's resentment against the C.P.P. On the initiative
of Nana Kum, a number of ex-C.P.P. members in Swedru—whether
they had welcomed the counter-coup or not—were arrested by the

police and detained for some time. And the death of Kotoka plunged virtually the whole of Swedru into mourning. Over 10,000 people, including the Swedru Asafo, Boy Scouts, churches and voluntary associations, held mass demonstrations against the C.P.P. and its supporters in the principal streets of the town. The demonstrations of 19 and 20 April were led by over 100 taxis, buses, lorries, and private cars, covered with the customary strips of red mourning cloths. Nana Kum again distinguished himself by holding at his own expense a wake-keeping and funeral ceremony for the murdered Kotoka, to which he invited the whole town. The D.A.O., the Clerk of Council, members of the Town Management Committee, and many prominent men attended, and on 21 April the Omanhene of Agona held a similar funeral at Nyakrom. Kotoka's death resulted, therefore, in a renewal of support for the N.L.C.; people donated freely to the Kotoka Trust Fund, and photographs of the General were sold quickly at the funeral.

Four days after the assassination of Kotoka, rumour reached Swedru that a military coup had taken place in Guinea. It was said that President Sekou Touré and Kwame Nkrumah had been seized and the latter was about to be returned to Ghana. (The rumour was undoubtedly a mis-hearing of the morning's news on the Ghana Broadcasting Service and the B.B.C. of the coup in *Greece*.) Fantasy (and perhaps a wish fulfilment) had it that Nkrumah had been captured either in the Volta Region near Ho, in Lomé in Togoland, or in Takoradi. It was rumoured that he had returned to Ghana to organise and direct the abortive coup of April 1967, and had been seized trying to escape to Guinea. He was now safely incarcerated in the Ussher Fort Prison in Accra where, under the old regime, he had once detained his political opponents. The excitement in Swedru beggared description. People waited anxiously for the 6.00 p.m. and 6.30 p.m. news for confirmation. Eventually, the announcement was made that Nkrumah had not been arrested. Yet one person held on to the rumour. For Nana Kum, whose conduct sometimes came close to that of a paranoid, and who liked to claim that he had access to State secrets, the N.L.C. was withholding the truth from the public, deliberately waiting until passions had died down to break the news.

Until the ban on party political activities was formally lifted, three months before the general election of 29 August 1969, there was a close debate on the question whether or not to deny former C.P.P. members the franchise. In Swedru, Nana Kum and Kojo Essilfie argued for the denial of any political rights including that of voting to all former members of the C.P.P. The majority, however, were inclined to the view that all but former Ministers, Regional Commissioners, District Commissioners, and party secretaries, should enjoy the right to vote in elections or stand for elections, since some in Swedru had supported the

C.P.P. under duress. The debate was somewhat settled after the passage of the Disqualification Decree in January 1968. It meant that former C.P.P. officials like R. K. Appiah, E. S. Quainoo, Yaw Ampadu, S. Y. Annobil, and Yaw Eduful could stand for an election if they so desired: but John Annan, Yaw Ampadu, S. K. Mbroh and E. K. Bensah, a former Minister, were disqualified from holding public office. There is little doubt that to most of the townspeople the decree was seen not simply as banning the C.P.P. but as preparing the way for Busia. It was a foregone conclusion that when Ghana returned to civilian rule it would be Busia's party which would form the government. Indeed, had the N.L.C. decided to hand over power to Busia and his party without a general election, there would probably have been very little criticism in the district.

Registration of voters in the Central Region started on 1 October, 1968; it was to end on 4 November 1968 but was then extended for two weeks. The two Urban Council areas of Nyakrom-Nkum and Agona-Swedru had been delimited as a constituency for the purposes of the election; but, despite the measures taken to ensure substantial registration, not more than half of those qualified to register did so, and the most likely explanation was that former supporters of the C.P.P. believed that there was no point in registering and voting in an election designed to ensure the victory of Busia and his party. Either that or they had been strongly advised by their relatives, wives and friends to forget about party politics. Then on 1 May 1969 the ban on parties was lifted, and in a broadcast to the nation on the eve of the lifting of the ban, J. W. K. Harlley reaffirmed the general stance of the N.L.C. 'We are determined that so long as we continue to have any control over the affairs of this land ... the former regime shall not be allowed to repeat their diabolical acts ... Let them be members of the parties; but by all means let us try other leaders.'

The warning was of particular relevance in the Central Region since the region as a whole, and Swedru in particular, had been a stronghold of the C.P.P. In the 1950s only Nyakrom, of all the Agona towns, had offered substantial opposition to the C.P.P. and even there, as in many other towns throughout Ghana, the resistance offered had been broken by the early 1960s. As described earlier, the U.P. faction, including Nana Kum and Kojo Essilfie, had been detained. In the Agona Traditional area (most of whose towns and villages were within fifteen miles of each other) the presence of four District Commissioners—in Swedru, Kwanyaku, Nyakrom, and Nsaba—out of a total of twenty-one for the Central Region was a clear testimony of the control of the C.P.P. And it was from the Central Region that the highest percentage of 'yes' votes (98 per cent) was recorded in the 1964 referendum on the one-party state and the granting of unlimited discretionary powers to

Nkrumah: in Swedru itself there was not a single 'no' vote recorded. So at least it was publicly announced. Yet by 1968 it was also believed that the economic policy of the C.P.P., and the venality of the local leadership, had had a crippling effect on the commercial basis of the towns in the region. It was in the context of a widespread malaise, therefore, the electorate was being asked in August to decide either to restore to power what was left of the former C.P.P. or to return the only real alternative, the former U.P. So at least it was argued by a majority of the voters in Swedru. The theme song in the town for the majority of the inhabitants—traders, market women, school teachers, Agona and non-Agona—after the coup was very simple: 'Let us give Busia a chance and see what he can do.'

In a personal interview with Nana Kum in 1967 I asked him whether he himself would consider standing for election in the future. 'Oh no!' he said, 'I am too old for that. But no candidate without my support can hope to win an election in Swedru, I promise you that.' It was not a vain boast. Nana Kum had worked hard, spending money, time and energy, for the overthrow of Nkrumah and the C.P.P. As soon as Busia announced in May 1969 that he was leading a party Nana Kum—in consultation with Kojo Essilfie, the chiefs and elders of Swedru and Nyakrom, the Swedru Town Committee, and local notables—converted his pre-existing, informal, yet powerful, pro-Busia propaganda machine into a formal constituency branch of the P.P. Nana Kum was very understandably given the position of constituency chairman. Later, local branches of the party were formed in Swedru, Nyakrom and Nkum. The size of the branch executive was determined in large part by local circumstances and the need to win the election rather than by the requirements of the party constitution. But the immediate and most pressing problem facing the party was the nomination of a candidate for the coming election. Although many voters in Swedru believed, quite realistically, that it was wasteful to vote for a candidate whose party did not have the slightest chance of forming a government, all the five national parties put up candidates to contest the election for the Swedru–Nyakrom–Nkum constituency. Yet in Swedru town, only two—P.P. and N.A.L.—were considered seriously; in Nkum only the P.P.; in Nyakrom, the P.P. and the U.N.P. Each of these parties in the constituency is worth considering separately but, before doing so, something should be said of the problem as a whole.

As in previous elections in the 1950s, the availability of money to a prospective local candidate proved to be crucial. In the campaign for the nomination, and later for the election of a candidate, money was required to buy the customary drinks for local chiefs and elders whose approval or blessing was usually helpful and sometimes necessary. Money was also needed to entertain as many of the electorate as possible—the fact that treating was an electoral offence did not stop candidates from engaging in it openly—and to influence the decision of those responsible for the election of a party candidate. Money was required to pay the N₵200 deposit and the N₵100 nomination fee, for the hiring or purchasing of a propaganda van or car equipped with loudspeakers, and the hiring of drivers and campaign assistants. The credit worthiness of the candidate was indeed a factor with the voting public and the party executive. In the Swedru–Nyakrom–Nkum constituency the question of money was particularly important since the candidates received very little help from the national headquarters of their parties once they had been nominated. Each of the candidates had to rely either on his own resources or those of a wealthy sponsor. An impoverished candidate was not worth serious attention, other considerations notwithstanding.

The primary control of decisions about the nomination of a candidate for the Progress Party in the constituency was in the hands of three men: Nana Kum, the founder of the local branch of the P.P., who was now constituency chairman and regional organiser; Kojo Essilfie, constituency propaganda secretary (both of Swedru); and Ninson, an executive member of Nyakrom. And the first choice of the constituency executive was Dr. Kuta-Danquah, a native of Nyakrom who expressed an interest in standing shortly before the ban on politics was lifted. A highly successful medical practitioner living in Accra, Dr. Kuta-Danquah had contested and lost the 1951 general election against the C.P.P. candidate, E. K. Bensah, an Ewe, and a dispensing chemist. The chiefs and elders of the constituency now supported his candidature. But when he was invited by the constituency to attend the formal inauguration by Busia of the Central Regional organisation of the P.P. on 14 June 1969, an occasion used for the introduction of constituency candidates to the public, he failed to come. A second invitation to him, to attend the party's inauguration in the Western Region at Sekondi-Takoradi, met with the same response. The chiefs and elders of the constituency then requested that he visit Nyakrom to discuss his candidature and the election with them. Again he did not come. Meanwhile, J. G. Amamoo, who had been wavering between leading his own party and joining the A.P.R.P., discussed the matter with Busia and some members of the national executive committee; and, after weighing carefully the probable fortunes of each of the parties, he decided to seek the P.P. nomination for the constituency.

The decision was still not final. When it became reasonably clear that Dr. Kuta-Danquah was not in the race, some of the Swedru elders approached his kinsman, E. Y. Eduful, a former C.P.P. public official (the elders at least were prepared to make an individual exception to their dislike of the former regime) and suggested that he consider standing for the election as a P.P. candidate. Eduful flatly rejected the tentative offer, having already made up his mind to stand as the N.A.L. candidate. Eduful's decision was perhaps understandable since he had been investigated and found guilty by a Commission of Enquiry set up by the N.L.C. which he equated with the P.P. It was, therefore, Dr. Kuta-Danquah's failure to meet with the chiefs and elders, and E. Y. Eduful's anti-P.P. attitude, which helped Amamoo, since the P.P. appeared to be in danger of not finding a suitable candidate.

Amamoo had hesitated in declaring his support for the P.P. since he feared that Nana Kum would reject him outright because of his past connections with the C.P.P. But knowledge of the difficulty and ambiguity surrounding Dr. Kuta-Danquah's candidature encouraged him to try and secure the necessary approval of the elders and the constituency executive. He met with the Agona elders at the Swedru *Ahenfie* (palace of the Chief), gave them the customary drinks, and managed to bring them to his side. His next problem was to win over the constituency executive, a difficult task at first since Nana Kum and Opanyin Ninson, in particular, were against him, and the elders of Nyakrom and Nkum still strongly favoured Dr. Kuta-Danquah. Eventually it was decided by the constituency executive that each of the three towns—Swedru, Nyakrom and Nkum—should send twelve representatives to a delegates' conference to settle the issue. The delegation was made up of the executive officers and members of the local branches of the P.P., some of whom were elders of the three towns. The first three meetings of the body ended in confusion. The Nyakrom delegation, headed by Ninson, argued vehemently that the party's candidate should come from Nyakrom because of its historic position as the traditional capital of Agona and as the seat of the Omanhene. It was certainly reasonable to campaign for the nomination of a candidate from one's own town, since there were considerable personal and communal benefits to be gained from a resident M.P., and the particular town gains prestige in the constituency. In the past, the Nyakrom delegation pointed out, the M.P. had been a resident of Swedru; it would only be fair to have someone this time from Nyakrom.

Most of the delegates from Swedru, as well as from Nkum, turned to Amamoo. They argued that it would be wrong to have both the M.P. and the Omanhene associated with the same town: the M.P. should continue therefore to be a person from Swedru, the 'commercial capital' of Agona. The Nkum delegation, influenced by K. Ofori a young and wealthy local timber contractor and a personal friend of Amamoo, also threw its weight behind Amamoo. It is worth noting that Ofori had been financial secretary for the Agona C.P.P. West Constituency in 1954 and that both he and Amamoo had jointly provided, not very long ago, cement and money for the construction of a school block and a public latrine for Nkum. But it was only when it became clear to the delegates that Dr. Kuta-Danquah, apparently on the strong advice of his English wife, had decided not to run for election that the fullest support was given to Amamoo. The elders of Nyakrom along with Ninson, Nana Kum, Kojo Essilfie and other supporters of Dr. Kuta-Danquah now had little choice but to back Amamoo. In filing his nomination paper in July 1969 Amamoo was officially proposed by Nana Kum and seconded by A. A. Quarshie. Others in favour were Kojo Essilfie, S. Y. Annobil and Yeboah Coomson. The nomination of Amamoo had brought together in co-operative teamwork—almost by default—some of the leading local members of the former U.P. (including Nana Kum) and the former C.P.P. (including S. Y. Annobil), thus destroying any direct equation of P.P. and U.P., or of N.A.L. and C.P.P.

The selection of candidates for the other four parties—N.A.L., P.A.P., U.N.P., A.P.R.P.—posed a very different problem. The P.P. had to choose between two rival contestants. The others were parties in search of candidates. The U.N.P. had nobody until John Alex Hamah merged his party, the Ghana Democratic Party, with the U.N.P. and stood in Swedru. The P.A.P. candidate, Alhaji Seidu Ben Alhasan, was unknown to most of the constituents. W. Y. Eduful, a government pensioner, had difficulty at first convincing his sponsors to support his candidature. The A.P.R.P. candidate, Edward Ferguson, was self-selected and unopposed.

Only the P.P. had a relatively formal and viable organisation. That of the other parties was either non-existent, informal or chaotic, not surprisingly perhaps since the parties had less than a month in which to organise. Many of the executive officers and organisers of the smaller parties were inexperienced, and relied heavily on equally inefficient 'field-workers' who were unfamiliar with canvassing. Many of the local agents for N.A.L. and P.A.P. were 'bookmen' and drivers whom chronic unemployment had reduced to near alcoholics. They were prepared to campaign for a glass of local gin, and their campaign speeches consisted largely of drunken vilifications of opposing candidates and their parties. The meetings of the N.A.L. members which the writer attended were casual, sloppy, discouraging; they were held in the dance hall of the Happy Corner Bar where the customers and N.A.L. members and supporters mixed almost indistinguishably. The meetings of the P.P., on the other hand, held usually in one of the houses belonging to Nana Kum at Dwinho, were spirited and confident, knowing very well that the outcome of the election would depend as much on the organisational structure of the parties as on the personality of the candidates.

J. G. Amamoo, the thirty-eightyear-old P.P. candidate, was the most formidable. He had worked for the C.P.P. government-controlled newspaper, the *Ghanaian Times,* in London in the late 1950s before becoming Public Relations advisor to the High Commissioner. He was then appointed Ghana's Ambassador to Hungary in December 1961 and served there for some years, leaving the foreign service in 1965 to read law in London where he wrote a number of critical articles against Nkrumah. From August 1967, on his return to Ghana, until a few weeks after the lifting of the ban on political activities, he was the editor of his old newspaper, the *Ghanaian Times*. Few people in Swedru knew him as a lawyer before his campaign, although his success in a minor court case concerning tax payment in Swedru during the last week in August 1969 introduced him to some as a redoubtable candidate. He was the N.L.C. nominee to the Constituent Assembly, where he consistently argued the case for the freedom of the press, and lived in Accra (with an Irish wife) where he was better known than in Swedru. His younger brother, a medical doctor, was (at the time of the election) a professor of medicine in West Berlin, and his still younger sister was a lawyer: but Amamoo's main electoral strength derived from his mother, a successful trader in Swedru, the chief town of the constituency, for many years. Amamoo's father was a cocoa farmer who had moved north to Ashanti Mampong (where Amamoo was born) and then to Bekwai where he died. That Amamoo had written a book in 1958, *The New Ghana*, which was somewhat favourable to Nkrumah was now almost forgotten.

Amamoo was a shrewd politician. A little pedantic at times, over-confident and ambitious, he was an admirer of President Nixon and liked to compare his own campaign with that of Nixon's 'Let the People Decide': he was not only the richest of the candidates, he also worked harder than the others. For the campaign he had a Mercedez Benz, and a couple of other cars, one belonging to Nana Kum, both equipped with loud-speaker equipment which was quite adequate for a compact constituency fifteen miles across with only thirteen thousand registered voters. Amamoo's slogan was simple enough: 'He is Your own Man.' He was indefatigable in distributing suitably inscribed ballpoint pens and women's head scarves to leading persons and school children in the constituency; at a mammoth P.P. pre-election rally on 27 July 1969, he flew gaily coloured balloons (reminiscent, he said, of the Republican Party Conference at Miami). Throughout the campaign, he was aided by the fact that he was popularly described as a possible 'shadow' Minister of Information for Busia, although immediately after the election results were known a number of his elderly supporters came to his mother's house where he stayed and advised him not to accept a job involving 'looking after files and papers' but to ask for a better appointment as Minister of Trade, or Labour or Industry, so that he could use his position to bring employment and factories to Swedru. In the event, he was appointed Parliamentary Secretary to the Mininster of Health.

Amamoo's principal opponent was the N.A.L. candidate W. Y. Eduful, forty-eight-year-old, who was also an Agona from Swedru. He was similarly spoken of as the 'shadow' Minister of Information for Gbedemah. Mr. Eduful is described (*Report of the Commission of Enquiry on the Commercial Activities of the Erstwhile Publicity Secretariat,* Chapter 4) as having been 'born of humble parentage of Agona–Swedru in 1922'; he passed standard seven at his primary school in 1936, became a temporary clerk of the Post and Telegraph Department, and from there was transferred to the Information Department in 1942 as a Second Division Clerk. He worked for a time as Information Officer at Tamale in northern Ghana, and then in 1961 became head of the Information Service at the Ghana Embassy in Washington. Later again, he was appointed head of Nkrumah's Publicity Secretariat. He was portrayed as having 'an urgent and deliberate plan to live big'; until the coup, it was said that he held 'the highest paid post in the civil service'. Despite this he was chronically in debt; the total amount he owed (admitted by him in the Commission of Enquiry sittings) came to over £8,000, a fact consistently used by his opponents against him in their campaigns.

Eduful was well known to be one of the few candidates who stood under the shadow of article 71, despite the fact that he had left the civil service on full pension. Certainly there was a good deal of evidence that his past connections with the C.P.P. worked against him, especially in Nyakrom. He appeared unenthusiastic and not quite sure of himself, very likely apprehensive—as many people were aware—that just before the election the N.L.C. might use article 71 against him, as was true of Gbedemah. He spent much of his time at the Happy Corner Bar in Swedru drinking with his sponsor and supporters, many of whom were unemployed Fante drivers, 'bookmen', minor cocoa clerks, and a few elementary school teachers, most of whom were ex-C.P.P. supporters. Since the Commission of Enquiry had impounded his Rover car, he appeared to have no car of his own for electioneering. The district N.A.L. propaganda van, equipped with loudspeakers, was for use also in a number of nearby constituencies, and therefore not available most of the time for campaigning in Swedru–Nyakrom–Nkum. Eduful's canvassing concentrated, therefore, on Swedru, where his fieldworkers could walk from door-to-door and from compound to compound.

Unlike Eduful, John Alex Hamah the U.N.P. candidate had a small Volkswagen sports car for his vigorous election campaign which was centred very much on Nyakrom where he was Amamoo's chief opponent. An elegant and energetic young man in his middle thirties, Hamah was a former educational secretary of the C.P.P.-controlled T.U.C. who had left the party before the coup to become one of the leaders of the exiled opposition. The Exemptions Commission freed him in 1968 from the provisions of the decree banning the C.P.P. from public office. An active trade unionist, he had opposed the candidacy of B. A. Bentum, Secretary-General of the Ghana T.U.C., at the second biennial congress in Tamale in July 1968.[9] Then in April 1969, by now editor of the *Comet,* he announced his intention to lead a political party when the ban on politics was lifted. The decision arose, he said, from a belief that it was 'the youth of Ghana' who must hold the mantle of political leadership in the Second Republic: what the country needed was a change in leadership, ideology, mentality, and a new approach to national issues. When the ban on parties was lifted, he formed the Ghana Democratic Party until financial difficulties forced a merger with the U.N.P. sometime after the middle of July 1969. Hamah's rich uncle, J. B. Essandoh, a cocoa farmer, timber contractor, and former chairman of the Swedru C.P.P., was his principal sponsor. He was an attractive candidate in many ways, yet it was difficult to see how he could muster much support outside Nyakrom where his father was born and where he went to school.

Edward Ferguson, a youthful forty-one, was born in the Western Region. He had been the local C.P.P. branch secretary, and had taught in an elementary school in Nyakrom for thirteen years before resigning a little before the election. He lacked the essential car or van for canvassing, and did very little campaigning, being forced to rely almost completely on local connections in Nyakrom, Swedru and Nkum. The P.A.P. candidate was Alhaji Seidu Ben Alhassan, a Moslem who had been to Mecca on a pilgrimage: a successful 'Hausa' cattle-dealer, who had been a prominent supporter of the C.P.P., he was ardent in his propaganda among the leading Malams, chiefs and other important Moslems in the local Zongos, whose support was mistakenly considered adequate. His local agents—Frank Siriboo, the P.A.P.'s central regional secretary, who as a freelance cartoonist had been employed in Flagstaff House under Nkrumah, and a local field-worker who was infrequently sober—generated a great deal of wasted energy. The P.A.P. propaganda van, which had to cover practically the whole of the Central Region, did little good, and the Alhaji remained hardly known outside the Zongos.

The three manifestos issued before the election by P.A.P., P.P. and N.A.L., in that order, were strikingly similar. All of them concentrated on agricultural development; all referred to the massive problem of unemployment, the question of debt repayments, and the need to give emphasis to rural welfare. Of the five parties which contested the Swedru–Nyakrom–Nkum constituency, only the N.A.L. manifesto was distributed for sale in the constituency. The electorate was mostly illiterate, and those who could read did not take them seriously. Certainly the electorate could not have based their choice on the policies laid down in the manifestos since they were essentially the same. What, then, did one need to win?

Ethnicity, local identity, the personality of the candidate, money, party image, and past experience were all important determinants. The strength of each, or combinations of one or more of these factors, depended very much on the primary values and beliefs of the voter—on his initial commitment. Fortunately we have the detailed results of the election for the Swedru–Nyakrom–Nkum constituency as a whole, and it is there—in the electoral wards of Swedru in particular—that we can see the relative importance of these attitudes.

Was the sweeping victory of the P.P. the result of 'tribalism'—that is, was there an overwhelming Akan vote? In the Central Region (a predominantly Akan area) the P.P. won all of the fifteen seats. And to the electorate in the Swedru–Nyakrom–Nkum constituency, as elsewhere, N.A.L. was an Ewe party, the U.N.P. a Ga party, and the P.A.P. a 'Pepe' (Hausa, Dagomba, Mamprusi) party. In Swedru the P.A.P. was made to stand derisively for 'Pepeni Atew Party' meaning a 'Pepe man has founded a party'; and the fact that, in Swedru, P.A.P. attracted mainly the Zongo vote reinforced this identification. The N.A.L. executive officers often gave the impression, no doubt inadvertently, that the party was Ewe-based. In a pre-election interview, the writer asked Okyere Kwaku, branch chairman, in which of the twelve wards of Swedru he thought the N.A.L. had the greatest support. After mentioning half of the wards, he explained to me: 'The Ewe vote is secured. We have to share the Pepe and the Akan vote with the P.P.' Amamoo also argued with satisfaction that 'N.A.L.'s Ewe "tribalism" will work in favour of P.P. The Ewe are a minority. The Akan speakers are in a majority. P.P. will win nearly all the seats in the Akan area.' And Amamoo was right despite, or because of the fact that the former C.P.P. member of parliament had been an Ewe. An elderly Ashanti man in Swedru was equally emphatic: 'Have you heard of an Ewe chief ruling over Ashanti? No. Busia is our man.' In his campaign speeches Kojo Essilfie, P.P. organiser, deliberately manipulated the ethnic stereotypes of the electorate. In an early morning electioneering address on 23 July 1969 he warned the Swedru market women against N.A.L., thus: 'N.A.L. members are murderers. They have just killed a number of people at Winneba. The public is warned against going near the N.A.L. propaganda van. Do not vote N.A.L. because the members are murderers.' Essilfie was deliberately playing on the stereotype in the Swedru area that the Ewe are 'murderers', and was associating a number of recent killings in the district, believed to have been carried out by some Ewe, with N.A.L.

Nevertheless, four of the five candidates for the Swedru–

Nyakrom–Nkum constituency were Akan, three of them from
the constituency: Amamoo and Eduful from Swedru, and Hamah
from Nyakrom. All three, until recently, had had important C.P.P. connections. (Indeed it is an interesting comment not only on the election
but on the former party regime that every one of the candidates had
been C.P.P. officials.) It was a choice therefore among candidates of the
same community but—by 1969—different political persuasion. Other
factors, more important than 'tribalism', must therefore have accounted
for the distribution of the actual votes cast. Let us turn to the results:

TOTAL VOTES CAST

	P.P.	N.A.L.	U.N.P.
	J. G. Amamoo	*W. Y. Eduful*	*J. A. Hamah*
Swedru	3,992	1,025	48
Nyakrom	1,384	244	1,050
Nkum	525	50	50
Police/Army	40	17	—

The number of voters in Swedru was 7,472, including 61 registered
special voters (Police and Army); there were 4,536 registered voters in
Nyakrom, 964 in Nkum. Looking at the distribution of votes it is clear
that each of the three candidates received the greatest number of his
votes in his home town. Local identity was therefore extremely
significant.

A ward-by-ward analysis of the poll in Swedru also lessens the importance of 'tribalism'. After all, both the P.P. and N.A.L. candidates
were Akan—despite the identification of N.A.L. with the Ewe—and
both received nearly as many votes in the non-Agona Pepe wards of the
Zongo as in the predominantly Agona (Akan) wards. P.A.P., identified
with the Pepe, did badly in all wards, including the Zongo.

Number of Votes in Each Ward (Swedru)

Ward	P.P.	N.A.L.	P.A.P.
Assesim	314	107	9
Owane	298	79	17
Ankyease	363	31	5
Kubease	308	77	7
Zongo	236	33	10

The 'Pepe' rejected their 'tribesman', A. S. B. Alhassan, in favour of an Akan, J. G. Amamoo.

In Nyakrom where Hamah grew up, and where the older women described him as 'our own son', Amamoo's majority was only 334. Many of Hamah's votes very likely came from many of the young women, among whom he was very popular. Similarly, Amamoo did well in Nkum because, as he himself readily admits, the voters saw him as their material benefactor, and because of the local patronage of Amamoo's close friend, the wealthy Ofori. The Ewe living there were locally threatened with ejection unless they voted P.P., the only party (it was argued) which could bring material and economic progress to Nkum.

The voting picture in Swedru town was particularly interesting. There the contest was essentially between two local men related by kinship, Amamoo and Eduful. A number of factors combined to give Amamoo a sweeping victory: his majority was 2,772. It has been seen how Nana Kum converted his well-established pro-Busia, pro-U.P. campaign into a P.P. electoral machine. The writer remembers an evening in May 1967 when he went to Nana Kum's house to watch the television which he made freely available for public viewing, with benches for the watchers. Gbedemah was then before the Jiagge Assets Commission, and he appeared on the television screen that evening, having to account to the Commission for state money he had allegedly misappropriated. As soon as Gbedemah appeared, Nana Kum asked all the viewers, numbering about forty, to boo, which they did with great satisfaction. Through tactics like this Nana Kum managed to mobilise popular support against Gbedemah and later against the party which Gbedemah led. Nana Kum stressed in his propaganda that 'Gbedemah and the C.P.P. destroyed the commerical prosperity of Swedru' and that 'the C.P.P. brought hunger to the people'.

Nana Kum also convinced an electorate eager for economic improvement that the close ties Busia had with Europe and America would bring investment and business to the country. Only Busia could help revive the commercial prosperity of the town. 'Busia will return the country to pre-independence economic prosperity; the cost of living will be lowered: corned beef will cost two shillings, sugar sixpence, and sardines threepence.' It is significant that the other parties, N.A.L., U.N.P., P.P. and A.P.R.P., made themselves unpopular by asserting that Busia and the P.P. would sell Ghana to Europeans: Alex Hamah stressed that 'N.A.L. and P.P. will both sell Ghana to foreigners' if they were returned. But that rubbed the wrong way. And in the end it was the mobilisation of a pre-coup sentiment against the former C.P.P., plus the overwhelming esteem accorded the 'Prof', which were decisive.

Amamoo's mother was also an important local factor. As a

successful trader and creditor she wielded tremendous influence among the market women's organisations; she was also a leading member of the local Methodist church, and an honorary member of the Swedru Brass Band. Her mother's funeral in 1967 was attended (if attendance is any indication of popularity) by most of the elders and local notables, including representatives of all ethnic groups. In return for past favours, most of the market women and their friends voted for 'their own son'; and Amamoo, aided by his mother, entertained liberally his supporters who streamed into her house. She bought them drinks (or supplied the money to buy them) and fed them, whereas Eduful and the other candidates lacked the money to compete with Amamoo on this scale. After Amamoo had won the elections, his mother's house was packed with ostensible well-wishers and at one point, distressed by the demands of an importunate supporter, the good lady exclaimed: 'If all the thousands of people who voted for my son were to come here to demand money and gifts in return where would I get the resources to meet their demands?'.

But if many voted for Amamoo because of his prominent and influential mother, the image of the P.P. also added to his victory. Everywhere in town the popular slogan was 'Pro-Pro-sure' pronounced 'shoo-wa' or 'Party Papa, eye shoo-wa', meaning 'the good party is sure to win'. The popular belief that the P.P. would win generated its own victory: a 'band-wagon' effect was created, and a fear of being on the losing side pushed many to vote P.P. The belief that the Progress Party would sweep the polls was so strong that it led a N.A.L. executive officer to remark sadly that 'If Eduful were a P.P. candidate he would win easily'. A similar comment was made about Hamah by his supporters. In a door-to-door random survey of political attitudes among some fifty Fante, Kwahu and Guan petty traders, their wives and adult children, all except one Kwahu and two Fante said that they would vote for the P.P. And the typical reason they gave ran like this; 'There is nothing against Busia. Busia has not squandered our money and has not made us go hungry. Europeans like him and they will help the country if Busia is the head of government. Busia is honest and God fearing.' It was equally clear that those traders who were against Busia had had important C.P.P. connections and flourishing businesses before the coup eliminated them. They tried to argue, in essence, that Gbedemah was the only man in Ghana with the necessary business and financial experience to put the country back on its feet economically. But it was an argument that could not easily be demonstrated and it was certainly not generally accepted.

In conclusion, we can emphasise a number of points. First, that in the Swedru–Nyakrom–Nkum constituency, the votes were clearly cast in relation to past experience and future hopes. After three and a half years of anti-Nkrumah purges, and of the anti-C.P.P. propaganda of Nana

Kum and others, the pre-1966 party regime was decisively rejected. In voting against N.A.L., many believed that they were voting against the C.P.P. It did not matter that a number of former C.P.P. executives actually supported P.P. or U.N.P.—people *believed* in the C.P.P.–N.A.L. equation, and beliefs and values do not have to be true to influence behaviour. When, therefore, local traders, teachers, transport workers, farmers, motor mechanics, and market women voted for the Progress Party, they considered that they were condemning the C.P.P. Similarly, among the minority which voted for N.A.L.—drivers' mates, 'bookmen', unemployed school leavers, and minor clerks of cocoa and farmers' co-operatives—there were those who (rather like the early supporters of the C.P.P. in former years, were rejecting the élitism and intellectualism of the U.P.) believing that, if the Progress Party won the election, people without superior qualifications would be denied jobs. The party 'image' on each side was therefore very important.

One may add to this equation a second, related belief. The constituency can be labelled (and was certainly seen to be) a 'depressed area'. It was commonly believed that the whole of the Central Region—the 'cradle of education and trade'—had been neglected by the C.P.P. government, despite the overwhelming support once given to the former regime. In voting the way it did, therefore, the region was again demonstrating, belatedly, its strong dissatisfaction with the C.P.P.—a condemnation of the failure of the economic policies of the former regime which contributed greatly to turning people against N.A.L. whose leader was identified with their implementation. The change of government in February 1966 was seen not only as necessary but overdue. Using a traditional analogy, it was frequently pointed out that a chief who worked against the welfare of his subjects was destooled: Nkrumah's overthrow amounted to his destoolment. And the only successor to Nkrumah worth considering, it was argued, was Busia who had been his rival prior to 1966. To many in the constituency, there was no question but that Busia should succeed Nkrumah.

Thirdly, there was the 'Akan-ness' of the Progress Party, in the sense that, at the national level, for a predominantly Akan population, it was thought historically realistic and logical to have an Akan man as the national leader. As one old, illiterate, fairly prosperous Ashanti Kente weaver remarked: 'If the British had not come, the Ashanti would have taken over the whole country.' Except for the A.P.R.P. whose leader was *Fante* (and, therefore, also an Akan) each of the parties (as we noted earlier) was identified with a particular linguistic–cultural group, depending on the ethnic background of the party leader. The P.P. was Akan, N.A.L. was Ewe, U.N.P. was Ga (*ababa se*), and P.A.P. was 'Hausa', the people of northern Ghana being mistakenly perceived as Hausa. It was not a *determining* factor, but it was an added national bonus to the local appeal of Progress over N.A.L. or P.A.P. or U.N.P.

Fourthly, however, although the ethnic background and education of the candidate were important, it is plain that a majority of the electorate, as elsewhere in the country, voted for the party or candidate they perceived as the most likely to bring about economic progress for the constituency, town, and individual voter. The identification of people with their towns, either where they were born or where they live, seems to have grown stronger than ever in Ghana. In Swedru, where immigrants—the Fante in particular—are in the majority, and where there exists an impressive co-operation between ethnic groups, political cleavages are rarely on the basis of ethnic affiliations. Even the Agona themselves can hardly be described as a homogeneous political group: inter-town and inter-lineage disputes of long standing have always characterised their politics. And very likely everyone in Agona, and certainly in Swedru, would agree that, because of the neglect associated with Nkrumah's regime, there had developed a new sense of local identity based on a joint aspiration for economic and social development. There is a sense of trans-ethnic identity that is easily deployable—that of 'Akan-ness'—but the common concern of the area for economic advance binds the majority of the people together not as 'tribes' but as administrative units based on a district or a constituency.

Lastly, we must note that the electorate in the Swedru–Nyakrom–Nkum constituency wanted tangible things. They wanted a hospital in the constituency: the clinic at Swedru is not well-equipped nor well-staffed, and the Winneba hospital (fifteen to thirty miles away) is too far in emergency cases. They wanted the dusty, rugged road from Swedru to Nyakrom and on to Nkum, a fifteen mile stretch, to be re-built and tarred. The condition of the road had made it almost impossible in the past for the corporation omnibuses to serve Nyakrom, the traditional capital, regularly. The electors were also demanding that the supply of electricity in Swedru should be extended to Nyakrom and Nkum. Above all, they wanted some form of industry in the constituency to absorb the unemployed youth—a demand particularly strong in Swedru—and for Swedru's past commercial importance to be revived. In all these respects, the people of Agona were not essentially different from their neighbours: the concern of most communities in Ghana has been for local or regional improvements. Everywhere people have wanted jobs and more money, and have asked for the raising of rural standards of living or the elimination of urban unemployment.

Miss Grace Asamoah was quoted in the *Ghanaian Times* a little after the election[10] as saying: 'This is how we rejoiced with Nkrumah and suffered in the end. I hope Busia will not make us go hungry any more.' And there, alas, was the rub.

Notes

1. See: Maxwell Owusu, *Uses and Abuses of Political Power*. Chicago: The University of Chicago Press 1970, for a discussion of the concept of 'party corporations'.
2. In *The Ghana Coup* (London: Frank Cass, 1966). Afrifa talks about the opposition of farmers to a government under whose rule their 'money was being squandered by so-called Secretaries, chief farmers and a host of brigands who had never held a hoe in their lives'.
3. In *Uses and Abuses of Political Power*.
4. Carried out in Swedru in the summer of 1967.
5. See: Maxwell Owusu, *op. cit.*
6. Ellis notes that, although the Agona are now considered a distinct group, they are linguistically Fante, who were once subjected by the Goma (after the Sasabor War of the 1690s), and that part of the Agona lands was at one time occupied by the neighbouring Efutu of the Winneba area. See, too, J. B. Christensen, *Double Descent Among the Fanti*. New Haven, H.R.A.F., 1954.
7. See: C. Geertz, *Pedlars and Princes*. Chicago: The University of Chicago Press, 1963.
8. This sense of local identification, certainly found in many West African towns, is usually expressed by the claim 'we are Swedrufo'—'citizens' of Swedru—heard from all ethnic groups. In many social situations this sense of Swedru-ness overrides that of ethnic and primordial attachments.
9. Bentum won by 88 votes to nil.
10. 2 September 1969. See: Maxwell Owusu, *The Search for Solvency: Background to the Fall of Ghana's Second Republic, 1969–1972*, in *Africa Today*, Vol. 19, No. 1, Winter 1972; 52–60, for an account of the causes of the 1972 Ghana coup.

APPENDIX

MEMBERS OF THE SWEDRU TOWN COMMITTEE

Biographical Sketches

1. *Dr. R. A. A. Quarshie*   for the GA/ADANGBE Community
   Age: 50 years old
   Education: Edinburgh University
   Occupation: A Private Medical Practitioner
   Residence: Has lived in Swedru since 1952.

2. *Mr. E. E. Owusu-Ansah*   Secretary, Department of Social Welfare and Community Development
   Age: 33 years old
   School Certificate: Left Form V in 1956
   Occupation: A trained social worker in the Department of Social W/C.D.
   Residence: Has stayed in Swedru since 1964.

3. *Mr. M. K. A. Awittey*   for the Ewe Community
   Age: 43 years old
   Education: Left Primary standard 7 in 1945
   Occupation: A sales storekeeper—U.A.C. Motors
   Residence: Has lived in Swedru since 1960.

4. *Mr. Yaw Frempong-Manso*   for the Ashanti-Akim Community
   Age: 44 years old
   Education: Left Primary standard 7 in 1940
   Occupation: a druggist
   Residence: Has lived in Swedru since 1956.

5. *Mr. Ankamah-Asamoah*   for the Akwapim Community
   Age: 51 years old
   Education: Left standard 7 in 1931
   Occupation: A storekeeper
   Residence: Has stayed in Swedru since 1959.

6. *Mr. R. A. Chahal*   for the Lebanese Community
   Age: 50 years old
   Education: Standard reached equivalent to standard 7.
   Occupation: Motor Dealer
   Residence: Has lived in Swedru since 1952 (1942?)
   Made Asafo Supi.

7. *Madam Esi Tawiah*   for Market Women Association
   Age: 56 years old
   Education: Had no formal education
   Occupation: Trader, fishseller
   Residence: Has lived in Swedru since 1937.

8. *Mr. K. A. Hagan*   for Agona/Fante
   Age: 50 years old
   Education: Left Primary standard 7 in 1936
   Occupation: Secretary to the Central Regional Distilleries Co-operative Union
   Residence: Lived in Swedru, his home since birth.

9. *Nana Kweku Adjei IV*   alias H. A. Okyere, Chairman for Traditional Members
   Age: 55 years old.
   Education: Left primary standard 7 in 1930
   Occupation: Retired from the Civil Service. Now building contractor—accepted
                contract for the Swedru Stadium. Head of the Adonten Stool Family
                of the Agona State
   Residence: Comes from Swedru.

10. *Mr. G. N. Moore*   for the Commercial Firms
    Age: 64 years old
    Education: Left standard 7 in 1921
    Occupation: U.A.C. Pensioner, where he was Manager. Now serving on contract
                 as District Manager of the G.N.T.C.
    Residence: has stayed in Swedru off and on for many years.

11. *Mr. C. K. Ansong*   for the Kwahu Community
    Age: 42 years old
    Education: Standard 7
    Occupation: Storekeeper trading mostly in provisions
    Residence: Has lived in Swedru since 1950.

12. *Zerikin Isifu Darfi II*   for Zongo
    Age: 49 years old.
    Education: Arabic
    Occupation: Former wage-labourer of G. B. Ollivant and Co. Ltd., since 1952 Chief
                 of Zongo and Malam.
    Residence: Has lived in Swedru since 1928.

CHAPTER 10

POLITICS IN SEKYERE*

Mark Graesser

Nowhere was the first *coup d'etat* more welcome than in Ashanti, where the election was seen by many as an opportunity for the former United Party and its leader to even the score, and where it was held to be particularly appropriate that Afrifa (an Ashanti) should be among the leaders of the N.L.C. Few observers were surprised, therefore, when Progress secured every seat in the region, winning 78 per cent of the vote against 17 per cent for Gbedemah's National Alliance of Liberals—a party identified not only with the former C.P.P. but with the minority Ewe community. Our particular focus, however, is the three north-eastern Ashanti constituencies, Mampong North, Mampong South and Sekyere, comprising the sub-region traditionally referred to as 'Sekyere'.[1] The area takes in more than one-fourth of Ashanti, but two-thirds consist of the largely uninhabited Afram Plains extending north and east from the high extension of the Kwahu Scarp which forms the backbone of the district. Most of the estimated 200,000 people[2] occupy the heavily-forested, mountainous south-west portion which lies within 35 miles of Kumasi. Making their homes in the towns and villages beneath these dramatic cliffs, or on the hilly plateau, most of the Sekyere people are farmers producing foodstuffs—plantain, cocoyam, yams and other staples—for consumption and marketing. Cocoa has brought significant surplus wealth, as evidenced by the numerous two and three-storey cement buildings in most of the larger towns, but Sekyere itself was never a major cocoa-growing area. Its more enterprising farmers have established farms in the frontier areas of the Brong-Ahafo Region, from which they annually bring home the harvest proceeds.[3] Wealth, prosperity, and the advantages they bring, are compelling goals for Sekyere citizens, whether measured in personal, family or community terms, and within a generation after the introduction of mission schools in 1896, education was recognised as the

* The research on which this chapter is based was conducted under the auspices of the Massachusetts Institute of Technology and the Institute of African Studies, University of Ghana. Financial assistance was provided by the National Science Foundation Graduate Fellowship Programme and the Department of Political Science, M.I.T. The writer lived in Mampong Ashanti, district headquarters of the Sekyere area, from October 1968 to September 1969. Most of the material was gathered from first-hand observation or from discussions with local citizens. To these many helpful individuals, he wishes to record his deep appreciation. He also received generous co-operation from Mr. G. A. K. Bonsu, Secretary to the Interim Electoral Commissioner, and his staff of registration and election officials.

sine qua non of material progress. It is true that in 1960 only 20 per cent of all Sekyere District adults (over the age of 15) had ever attended a school; but the situation was changing fast, and a primary school is now to be found in almost every village.

Although its northern reaches are on the frontier of the Brong area, Sekyere is very much an Ashanti district.[4] Its towns trace their origins to migrations from the Adansi area, south of Kumasi, before the formation of the Ashanti Confederacy at the end of the seventeenth century, and the chiefs and people recite with pride their ancestors' part in the rise of Ashanti. Each town and village is traditionally organised within the well-articulated political–territorial system formulated by the great Asantehene, Osei Tutu, and his successors on the Golden Stool. Within the Sekyere area, three semi-autonomous divisions (*aman*) owe allegiance only to the Asantehene: Mampong, Nsuta and Kumawu. Commanded by an *omanhene* (paramount chief) each of these traditional areas comprises subdivisions and villages. In addition, the district contains smaller towns—Kwamang, Beposo, Oyoko and others—which also owe allegiance directly to Kumasi; and although the chiefs have been stripped of nearly all the substantive functions of their office, they remain symbols of the strong attachments which most Ashanti have to their village and division of origin.

In Sekyere, as throughout most of Ghana, there was open jubilation on the day the coup was announced, and local C.P.P. leaders were beaten and abused before being taken into 'protective custody' by the police. The four C.P.P. Commissioners were replaced by a single District Administrative Officer from the civil service, whose local rule was on the pattern of pre-party Commissioners. The C.P.P. local councillors were dismissed, and their functions taken over first by committees of civil servants, then (early in 1968) by Management Committees appointed from the local community by the government. The party-dominated Development Committees at the village level were also reconstituted. Such formal changes in local leadership tended to bring to the fore either old U.P. supporters, or non-partisan 'respectable' citizens; but former C.P.P. adherents were by no means completely purged. After the banning of the C.P.P., strident party activities ceased, and the pre-coup climate of fear and malaise gave way to a period of respite. Temporarily, at least, people were content to demand little more of the government than that it leave them alone, and the N.L.C. made few calls on the people beyond acquiescence in its programme of control and retrenchment.

Although few people wanted the N.L.C. to rule indefinitely, they seemed satisfied with the measured progress towards civilian rule. The registration of voters in October and November 1968 met with a mixed response. Many registered their names without question, and some even

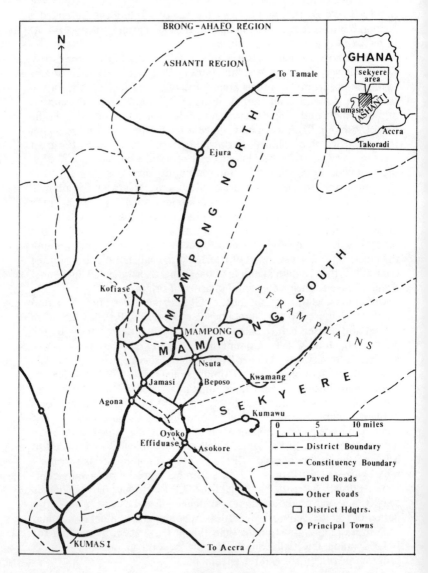

SEKYERE

complained when registration officers failed to appear at their villages; but others were apathetic or cynical or hostile. Procedural abuses in earlier elections, and a neglect of constituents by those elected, had bred disenchantment, while a good many asked—'Whom are we to vote for?'—in the absence of parties or an immediate election.[5] After two extensions of time and strenuous publicity, however, between 60 and 70 per cent of those eligible registered in the (Sekyere) area, a result comparing favourably with that achieved in previous campaigns. And yet the constitution-making in Accra was little noticed, and still less understood, by the rural population. The local intelligentsia—schoolteachers, and the like—were aware of the Akufo-Addo Commission's efforts to draft a document capable of thwarting attempts at a Nkrumah-like dictatorship, and when the time came to form the Constituent Assembly, an electoral college composed of Management Committees of six Local Councils gathered to elect a delegate from Mampong District (somewhat larger than the 'Sekyere area'). R. R. Amponsah, the former U.P. M.P. who had been imprisoned by the Nkrumah regime in 1958, was elected by 35 votes to 16 over J. E. K. Osaffo, a young Kumasi lawyer who was thought to have the covert backing of former C.P.P. leaders. But few of Amponsah's newly-acquired constituents knew of his election and its purpose.[6]

The quickening interest in the return to civilian rule, at least among a vocal minority, was better indicated by the widespread speculation as to when the N.L.C. would lift the ban on political party activity so that those who were so inclined could start campaigning for the elections. Late in 1968 and early 1969, Ashanti became alive with such surrogate political groups as a revived Asante Youth Association and a Current Affairs Club. Both of these organisations aroused interest in Mampong, chiefly among a few would-be leaders of a revived U.P. (Former C.P.P. members remained more discreet in political matters.) Two years earlier, these local politicians had been thwarted by the military Government in their efforts to organise a Ratepayers' Association, which was regarded as a contravention of the ban on 'political activities'. Now, the authorities—accepting the inevitability of a return to open politics in the near future—were more tolerant, and local leaders began to engage in the oratory and scheming which were foreshadowed the actual contest.

It was difficult to gauge how strongly the general run of local people felt about an early return to civilian rule. Was the relative tranquility of military rule, albeit economically austere, preferable to a return to the party disputes which had brought tension and uncertainty to life in the past? And had not the lesson of Nkrumah's era been that *all* politics and politicians were bad? Some of these issues were put to a representative sample of Mampong townspeople and surrounding villagers in an opinion survey conducted at the end of 1968. When asked to compare the performance of the N.L.C. regime with that of the C.P.P., 73 per cent declared that they preferred the N.L.C., against a bare 2 per cent who ventured openly to regret the coup.[7] But, despite this amiable expression of satisfaction with the N.L.C. (which corresponded to similar claims by the national media), 63 per cent called for a return to civilian rule within the year 1969, and only 18 per cent wanted the army and police to stay on. The reason cited most often for favouring the army's withdrawal was that it was 'not proper' for soldiers to govern: they were neither lawful nor qualified. A 74-year-old illiterate farmer, who had expressed appreciation of the N.L.C.'s raising the cocoa price and lowering the cost of cloth, put it succinctly: 'We want a "president", not a "soldier".' The prospective politicians who champed at the bit thus reflected a broader, more disinterested belief that the soldiers had done their work in turning out the old regime, and should now go back to the barracks to make way for a new civilian government.

Although well aware of the connection, many of those interviewed were considerably less enthusiastic about the politics which such a transition would probably entail. To the question, 'How do you feel about lifting the ban on political parties now?' 36 per cent approved, whereas 36 per cent thought it 'a bad idea', and 28 per cent declined to express an opinion. Many of those who wanted the ban lifted said that it would have the effect of promoting open debate of key issues and a competitive selection of representatives; but the most common counter-argument was that lifting the ban would bring back the turmoil (*basabasa*) which characterised party politics in the past. Most could recite bitter personal experience of violence and intimidation during 'the tension' of the mid-1950s, and in the period of C.P.P. consolidation which followed. Yet, despite such misgivings, 94 per cent of those eligible claimed they would vote if an election were held in 1969 (64 per cent of those registered in the towns which were surveyed actually did so eight months later), and 48 per cent said they would join a political party if given the opportunity.

While public opinion in the Mampong area was equivocal about returning to the partisan fray, local would-be leaders, mostly with 'U.P.' connections or aspirations, were less diffident. There was rejoicing in the bars and around the wireless sets on 7 April 1969 as they listened to the newly-installed Chairman of the N.L.C., Afrifa, when he announced that the ban on party activity would be rescinded from 1 May. Already pre-party manoeuvring had been increasing in tempo and moving closer to the local level for many months—generally to the advantage of Dr. Busia and his supporters. The reconstitution of Village Development Committees and Local Council Management Committees had seen the elevation of many former U.P. figures to positions of official authority.

The registration of voters was not popularly understood as offering any opportunity for a C.P.P. return—and the only alternative in most minds was Busia's old United Party. Those who were aware of Amponsah's election to the Constituent Assembly also knew him to be one of Busia's right-hand men in U.P. times. Thus these N.L.C.-sanctioned activities and rituals had the anticipatory effect of endowing any party which Busia might form with an aura of legitimacy by identifying it with the objectives of the popular February 'Revolution' and the post-coup 'establishment' both nationally and locally.

Of particular interest in any attempt to measure the impact of this pre-party period on the ensuing election campaign was the role of the Centre for Civic Education. It undoubtedly provided Busia with a well-financed national organisation from which to project himself as the virtuous leader and to confirm his judgements on the C.P.P. era—essentially the message which was to become the focus of his party's campaign propaganda. Busia's appearance at numerous C.C.E. events enhanced his personal stature and increased his following. In February 1969 he came to Mampong, with Brigadier Afrifa—a native of the town—at his side, to inaugurate the local C.C.E. branch. An enormous crowd, including the Mamponghene, turned out to pay homage and to hear Busia talk of the need to restore the nation after the bad government of Nkrumah. Afrifa, for his part, urged his listeners to 'forgive' former C.P.P. members if they regretted their misdeeds and came back as 'true prodigal sons'. Themes such as these provided large numbers of potential voters with a preview of the message Busia's P.P. was to bring them a few months later.[8]

Another form of proto-politics, more explicitly partisan, was the 'underground' canvassing by individuals who hoped to raise the Busia flag in particular constituencies once the elections were officially announced. Busia privately gave these activities his sanction shortly after his return to Ghana,[9] and in both Mampong South and Sekyere constituencies contenders for the party's support quietly approached locally influential notables up and down the bush roads in order to establish a claim for support. Later, as open candidates, these early-comers boldly proclaimed that they had 'brought Busia's party here'. In Mampong North, R. R. Amponsah was the obvious Busia candidate. Although he scrupulously avoided campaigning until the ban was lifted; self-appointed supporters promoted Amponsah, and he had been persuaded to stand election for the Constituent Assembly in 1968 as the only figure around whom all U.P. forces would consolidate without equivocation.

After the ban was lifted, it was an easy matter for the district leaders to summon their village contacts to meetings at which the formation of a 'Busia party' was formally announced; interim executive committees were confirmed, and the outlines of party doctrine delineated. The message was a simple one: now that the soldiers and police were giving the country back to the people, Busia was forming a new party to embrace all the people in Ghana. The old C.P.P. and U.P. parties were 'dead', and everyone would now come together and 'go forward' in the Progress Party leaving the bad politics of the past behind. Supplied with party membership forms for the people already clamouring to 'write their names for Busia', the village representatives carried these words home and set up branch committees to proselytise their neighbours, friends, and kinsmen. Most of those approached were identifiable as old opponents of the C.P.P., but on occasion former C.P.P. activists joined the Busia fold.[10]

As the parties took shape, national and regional leaders became familiar to observers in the cities through the mass media, yet it was in the villages that most of the votes were obtained. Linking these two levels of the mass party were the district (constituency) leaders who interpreted nationally-determined issues and symbols to the villagers, and then co-ordinated the extensive campaigns in each constituency. The table opposite presents a profile of the P.P. leadership in Mampong North constituency.

Notable characteristics of the group were its predictable U.P. complexion[11] and its relatively venerable (median) age of 50 years. The older members were all men of substance—Mampong town businessmen, or elders in outlying villages—and the younger men were of superior education of whom the dominant figure was J. K. Dwomoh, a 37-year-old Mampong storekeeper whose staunch anti-C.P.P. credentials dated back to 1950, confirmed by nine months in prison as a political detainee in 1961. Dwomoh's career had been ascending since the coup, when he was appointed to the Mampong Urban Council Management Committee and the C.C.E. Regional Advisory Committee. Progress Party plans were made in his store, where he contributed long political experience and a passionate dedication to the management of Amponsah's campaign for Mampong North.

In neighbouring constituencies, the pattern of U.P. revival was not quite so clear or explicit. At Nsuta, headquarters of Mampong South, half the Executive were deliberately selected from former C.P.P. ranks to symbolise the all-inclusiveness of the P.P., although leading positions were reserved for former U.P. stalwarts. In the Sekyere constituency, it would have been impossible to find prominent U.P. men in former C.P.P. areas such as Kumawu, once the stronghold of the former C.P.P. minister, Krobo Edusei.[12] The constituency committee eventually formed was unified less by previous party ties than by its support for a favourite local son'—Kingsley Abiyie—who (as will be seen) succeeded in gaining the Progress Party nomination.

The party's head-start in the May-to-August race for votes was never

Mampong North P.P. (Interim) Constituency Executive

Office	Occupation	Age	Education	Past Party
Chairman	Building contractor	37	Standard 7	C.P.P. supporter
Vice Chairman	Retired Govt. painter	(57)	None	U.P. supporter
Treasurer	Retired cocoa broker	79	Standard 7	U.P. Chairman
Member	Storekeeper	65	None	U.P. Chairman
	Storekeeper	37	Standard 7	U.P. Secretary
	Council tax collector	58	Standard 7	U.P. Executive
	Farmer/weaver	(50)	None	U.P.
	Farmer	56	None	U.P.*
Secretary	Teacher	30	Secondary	U.P.
Propaganda Secretary	Research Assistant	39	Standard 7	None
Publicity Secretary	Teacher	29	Secondary	None

( ) : estimated or assumed
* : subsequently joined C.P.P.

seriously challenged The former C.P.P. network of organisation and
influence failed to re-emerge in anything like its old form; and, in the
absence of any national or local issue to compete with the new party's
opposition to the former regime, there was no basis for any other effective coalition. Dr. John Bilson's 'Third Force' appealed locally to a
handful of dissidents, mostly of C.P.P. background, who found it
difficult to respond to Busia's leadership, and felt rebuffed by his local
agents; but the Third Force remained an intellectual ideal at a time
when organisational support—cars, money, and candidates—was
needed in the constituencies. It was these which K. A. Gbedemah
offered when the N.A.L. appeared belatedly in Ashanti. It was not until
late in June that S. A. Kwaku-Bonsu, Mampong's former C.P.P.
member of parliament, arrived from Accra to chair a meeting at which a
Mampong N.A.L. Executive Committee was elected: see opposite page.

The composition of this body was indicative of the very marginal appeal
the party was to have among voters. Unlike the all-Ashanti Progress
Executive, 4 of the 17 N.A.L. leaders were non-Ashanti, and whereas
all the Progress Executive members were natives of the Mampong area,
only half the N.A.L. executive could claim local roots. With a median
age of 36, they included no prosperous businessmen, or men who could
be broadly termed 'elders', with the sole exception of a former chief of
the *zongo* (the strangers' quarter). All but he had been C.P.P. officers,
members, or supporters.[13] But notably absent from the local N.A.L.
ranks were the most important figures of the former C.P.P. establishment, the local men of ability, substance, and influence, who had
brought the nationalist party to Mampong twenty years before and had
risen with it to such positions as District Commissioner, National
Executive Member and Local Council Chairman. These men, wise in
political ways, for the most part carefully avoided participation in the
1969 contest, acknowledging, in the words of one:

> There is only one party in Mampong—Progress. We have decided to
> unite and support that party because, it is very strong and can do the most
> to help the [Mampong] state. Besides, we have seen that the C.P.P. did little
> for us, while the Brigadier [Afrifa] has already brought electricity, a hospital,
> and water.[14]

Little wonder that the N.A.L., organised relatively late and led locally by
a marginal C.P.P. rump, was able to take few votes from the firmly rooted
P.P.

Of the other parties, Joe Appiah's U.N.P. placed a propaganda van
in Mampong South, which they considered to be a 'stronghold'; but
they polled less than 1 per cent of the vote there. So it was with the
P.A.P. and the A.P.R.P. except—as we shall see—in the Sekyere constituency which was bitterly divided between rival towns. But even there

N.A.L. Mampong Area Executive

Office	Occupation	Age	Education	Past Party
Chairman	Taxi owner/driver	42	Standard 4	C.P.P. Branch Treasurer
Vice-chairman	Ex-zongo chief	65	*	U.P.
Secretary	Poultry farmer	28	Standard 7	C.P.P.
Treasurer	Public Letterwriter	(45)	Secondary	C.P.P.
Vice-secretary	Teacher	(30)	T.T.C.	n.a.
Vice-treasurer	Teacher	(30)	T.T.C.	n.a.
Overseer	Akpeteshie bar owner	38	None	C.P.P. Dist. Executive
Ward leader	Taxi owner/driver	33	None	C.P.P.
	Food contractor	46	Standard 7.	C.P.P. Branch Executive
	Farmer	n.a.	n.a.	C.P.P. Branch Chairman
	Government worker	36	Standard 7	C.P.P. Branch Secretary
Brigade leader	Worker's Brigade	n.a.	(Lit.)	C.P.P.
Dagomba leader	Dagomba chief	(40)	n.a.	C.P.P. Branch Executive
Ewe leader	Government worker	n.a.	(Lit.)	n.a.
Women leader	Akpeteshie seller	34	None	C.P.P.
Vice Women leader	Hawker	26	None	C.P.P.

* Muslim *malaam* (reads Arabic): English-speaking
T.T.C. Teacher Training College

( ):estimated
n.a.: not available

the dissident vote went to a pro-Busia independent rather than to any opposing party.

We turn now to the question of nominations, which was very often a more important hurdle for the would-be Progress candidate than the actual election.

Since the party was little more than a pro-Busia popular sentiment during the early weeks of its existence, it was without any established procedures by which the struggle for nomination could be decided. Local leaders understood only that each choice should be 'democratic', expressing the will of the party's adherents within the constituency as determined by the Constituency Executive. When this vague aspiration failed to yield candidates in many districts, the national leadership vacillated between persuasion and compulsion, and then fell back on the 'democratic' permissiveness which it favoured as the approach least likely to check the groundswell of diffuse enthusiasm for the party. This inconsistency in party policy allowed local issues and individuals to express themselves more fully at the nomination stage than in the election itself, when the tendency in Ashanti was to unite behind the P.P. Thus strikingly different patterns in the selection process and its aftermath were displayed in the three Sekyere-area constituencies. On the other hand, while the dominant party was contending with the problem of eliminating contestants, others in the three constituencies were hard put to find a candidate who was willing to stand on a non-Progress ticket. The N.A.L. had emerged by July as the leading opponent of Progress, but few of the former C.P.P. leaders were willing to provide the party with such influence and organisational skill as they retained from the old days. The U.N.P. put up token candidates in all three constituencies, as did the P.A.P. in Mampong North, and the A.P.R.P. in Mampong South: but among these minor parties, only the P.A.P. exceeded 1 per cent of the vote in the subsequent election.

Mampong North epitomised the ideal nomination pattern: R. R. Amponsah's claim was virtually undisputed, and his final selection did not even require a formal decision by the Constituency Executive. Amponsah had been born locally (an unofficial but important requirement) in 1923, and brought up by a progressive Christian family.[15] He attended Achimota School, and stayed on to study industrial art in the Achimota-based West African Institute of Art, Industries, and Social Science, a pioneering institution devoted to training an educated élite with a 'practical' bent. After teaching for a year in the small Western Region town of Enchi, Amponsah went to London, where from 1947 till 1951 he studied industrial design and education at the Royal College of Art. When he returned to Ghana as a qualified ceramist, he spent a year as an Education Officer in Ashanti, and then took charge of the Cocoa Marketing Board's new Scholarship programme in Germany.

Amponsah had been one of the most politically-inclined among his conservative, civil-service-destined classmates at Achimota. He was aroused by the early stirrings of the Ghana nationalist movement in 1947, and participated eagerly in student politics in London as a pro-Nkrumah militant. Later, as a civil servant, he held no formal C.P.P. position but he was in close and sympathetic touch with the party leaders. It was thus a significant blow to the party's stature in February 1955 when he and two other Ashanti C.P.P. intellectuals, Joe Appiah and Victor Owusu, publicly denounced the C.P.P. and joined the N.L.M., Amponsah becoming General Secretary of the movement.[16] As the elections of 1956 approached, he was able to wrest the nomination in Sekyere West from Kwasi Agyarko, an unsuccessful anti-C.P.P. independent in 1954; and he unseated the C.P.P. incumbent Osei Bonsu. In 1958 however he was implicated, on ambiguous evidence, in a plot to overthrow Nkrumah by a *coup d'etat,* imprisoned under the Preventive Detention Act, and held without trial until the 1966 coup opened the prison doors.[17]

His re-entry into public life was quiet. He became Managing Director of a sawmilling company in Kumasi, and then chairman of Ghana Airways. Although fully intent on going into politics when the opportunity arose, he resisted the temptation, to which many others of like mind succumbed, to gain publicity through the C.C.E. and other agencies, claiming that nothing which was said during the pre-party period could be taken at face value. He consented to his election to the Constituent Assembly only at the last moment, but once there he participated actively in its deliberations, and it was clear to his old constituents at Mampong that their former M.P., now bearing the aura of an 'ex-detainee', would be seeking their support again when elections were announced. His considerable personal popularity in his home district was enhanced by the belief that, as a leader of the old opposition, 'R.R.' was sure to receive a high position in a future Busia regime, thereby underwriting Mampong's political well-being. This view was confirmed when the ban was lifted and he was seen to be among the inner circle of Busia's party counsellors in Accra. The only suggestion of a contest came from M. Y. Agyei, a Mampong businessman in Kumasi, who was easily persuaded to withdraw his challenge, and to turn such influence as he possessed to Amponsah's cause. When a committee of national party officials appeared in Mampong on 21 June, naively expecting to conduct a 'democratic election' among Mampong North delegates, they were quietly told by several local leaders that here, at least, no voting was required: Mampong had its candidate, and all were happy with him.

The Mampong North N.A.L. toyed hopefully with the idea of getting a candidate from Ejura who could take advantage of the town's rivalry with Mampong. But Ejura had no university graduate willing to engage in politics, and the candidacy of a former Ejurahene, Standard VII educated, was rebuffed by local N.A.L. members. The party turned instead to Dr. D. K. Poku-Amanfo of Mampong, a lawyer recently returned to Kumasi after fourteen years in Britain, who had worked his way from middle school through a long series of degrees and certificates, including a London University Ph.D. He had acquired a taste for politics as an active participant in Ghanaian student activities in England, but although critical of Nkrumah's regime in its latter years, he did not find Busia's leadership an attractive alternative. He now sought the N.A.L. nomination in his home town, where he was virtually unknown, but he was sufficiently well educated to gain acceptance by local party leaders almost right unseen.

In the short time available to him, Poku-Amanfo campaigned actively; but this was to little avail against the well-established Amponsah and the general popularity of Progress in Ashanti. The results of the polling in Mampong North were:

R. R. Amponsah	P.P.	8,728	79 per cent
D. K. Poku-Amanfo	N.A.L.	1,941	18 per cent
Suhani Nantogha	P.A.P.	228	2 per cent
J. K. Fosuhene	U.N.P.	79	1 per cent

Whereas Mampong North was unusually free of intra-party dissension, and the Sekyere constituency (discussed below) represented an opposite extreme of factionalism among Busia supporters, Mampong South fell between these poles. Three men contended seriously, including an 'old guard' U.P. stalwart and a young intellectual; but all three were party loyalists who were willing to abide by the choice of a delegates' conference. The eventual nominee, Yaw Manu, fitted neither the old guard nor the intellectual image, although he could lay some claim to both credentials. He was 47 years old, brought up by an uncle who was a Chief Clerk in the former colonial administration. Manu served as an Executive Officer for ten years after completing secondary school at Adisadel College in Cape Coast but although a civil servant, he admitted to having actively assisted candidates opposing the C.P.P. at his northern posts in Wa in 1954 and Tumu in 1956. In the latter town, Imoro Egala, a leading C.P.P. figure in the North, was unseated in 1956, and Manu was obliged to resign for his part in this electoral defeat. For the next three years, he operated a store in Nandom, in the extreme northwest of Ghana, before the police banished him from the area on the grounds that he had used his vantage point near the border to spirit political fugitives from the country.[18] As a storekeeper in Kumasi during the time of active suppression of the opposition, Manu continued to support the U.P. He provided a jeep for Kwasi Agyarko's unsuccessful campaign to hold Amponsah's Sekyere West seat in the violent by-election of July 1959. Two years later he fled to exile in the Ivory Coast with Agyarko, and stayed with the Ivory Coast opposition group until he was captured on his way to Lome to meet Busia in 1963. Convicted on treason charges arising from the bomb attack on Nkrumah at Kulungugu in 1962, he was sentenced to death but was held in prison until the N.L.C. released him in April 1966.

It was for this 'death sentence' martyrdom that Manu was best known as the 1969 election approached.[19] Around this emotional appeal, and his claims of close personal ties to Busia, Manu started to organise a popular following in 1966 in his home area, Nsuta, in anticipation of a re-definition of constituencies which would remove this southern half of Sekyere West from Amponsah's Mampong stronghold. A 'tough', large, and handsome man, a prospering poultry farmer and transport owner, Manu had both the energy and the money to travel the difficult bush roads and make the necessary traditional overtures to chiefs and village elders, a humble suppliant for their support when the time came. In 1968 he was appointed by the N.L.C. to the Local Council Management Committee in Nsuta, and in that capacity he actively promoted Amponsah's election to the Constituent Assembly from the district electoral college.

Although Yaw Manu had established a strong emotional and organisational base of support well before May 1969, his claim lacked the stature of Amponsah's. And a similar disadvantage clung to Kwasi Agyarko, who had opposed the C.P.P. unsuccessfully in 1954 and 1959 (and who had lost the N.L.M. nomination to Amponsah in 1956) but who was also determined to try again now that Amponsah had a separate constituency. Although he was approaching sixty years of age, Agyarko relished political life and hoped that the coup and the transition to a civilian regime would at last give him the opportunity to enter the inner circles of national power. His career had been one of vigorous striving, in many ways similar to that of Ashanti's leading C.P.P. figures. Overcoming opposition from his illiterate father, Agyarko obtained his Standard VII certificate at the age of 21, and worked his way up from a rural cocoa buyer to become the owner of a large Kumasi store by 1942. The (British) Chief Commissioner of Ashanti had appointed him to the Kumasi City Council in 1951. And being interested in both local and national politics, he had joined the C.P.P. for a short time, but was then active in the formation of the N.L.M. He continued as an Ashanti U.P. leader until fleeing the country in 1961 to serve as an agent for Busia in Abidjan and Lomé. After the coup, he returned to Kumasi to rebuild his trading business, and was appointed a Director of the Cocoa Marketing Board. But it was a parliamentary seat that he yearned for and some time before the ban on politics was lifted, he had approached potential supporters in Mampong South. His chief hope lay in the old strategem of converting local territorial rivalries into a winning formula. He calculated that he had the support of Jamase and its villages, since it was his 'home town' (the town of his mother), and that the large village of Kofiase would come to him because the chief there was 'brother' to the Agonahene, to whom Agyarko was paternally related. Nsuta was conceded to Manu. But the remaining two large towns in the constituency, Kwamang and Beposo, were expected to oppose Manu (and thus support Agyarko) because for some years they had been grouped in a local council which had been based, to what they believed was their detriment, in Nsuta.

Agyarko's age was something of a liability. In the 1950s it had been the 'young men' who participated most successfully in the political game, and although the term often referred simply to 'commoners', the popular image of an attractive candidate was still that of a dynamic young man. J. Oppong-Agyare, a philosophy graduate of the University of Ghana and editor of the *Ashanti Pioneer* from 1966 to 1968, also offered himself to the Mampong South Progress Party, both as a young man and one who was enlightened not only by his education but by non-involvement in the tainted politics of the past. Like Manu, he came from Nsuta. And he had supporters both there and elsewhere in the constituency among the younger village literati who supported Oppong-Agyare as a 'better qualified' candidate, and enjoyed his discursive articles on politics in the *Ashanti Pioneer.*

By mid-June the Progress leadership had become impatient with the spectacle of prospective candidates carrying their rivalries to the people, jealously spreading insinuations against the character and qualifications of one another. Busia was able to arrange behind-the-scenes accommodations in some instances; but to resolve struggles like that in Mampong South it was announced that representative electoral colleges would be called together to name the party's candidate. A body of delegates was actually assembled in Nsuta on Saturday, 21 June, and those who had been chosen by party supporters in the constituency on three or four days' notice arrived early in the morning to drink in the Atomic Nite Club at the expense of candidates' lobbying for their support. Voting took place later in an open court house under the supervision of national party officials and within hearing of several hundred intensely interested spectators. Would Manu win, to bring Nsuta electricity, or would it go to Agyarko so that he could supply Jamase with water? Could Oppong overcome Manu's support among the old men who thought more of money than education? These were issues which provoked discussion, songs and prayers among the crowd of men, women and children who gathered to witness the nomination.

Interrupted only by minor disputes over the seating of delegates and the voting procedure, the polling was completed by midday: Manu—with money, organisation and personal popularity—received 84 of the 120 votes. Agyarko was given votes only from his Jamase bailiwick, and Oppong-Agyare collected even fewer from a dissident minority in Nsuta. Although greatly disappointed, and privately resentful of what they considered to be a victory of money over ability, the losers congratulated Manu and publicly affirmed their loyalty to the party.

The closing of P.P. ranks in Mampong South left other parties in a predicament similar to that which they faced in Mampong North. The N.A.L. had the support of Osei Bonsu of Nsuta who, after losing his C.P.P. Assembly seat to Amponsah in 1956, had become a businessman and Ambassador to Italy. Now disqualified from standing, Osei Bonsu backed A. K. Bomodu (a young village schoolteacher) with funds and a propaganda van. But neither the party nor the candidate was a match for the now united P.P.:

Joseph Yaw Manu	P.P.	10,748	82 per cent
Andrew K. Bomodu	N.A.L.	2,170	16 per cent
Charles Gyimah	U.N.P.	123	1 per cent
B. K. Ofori	A.P.R.P.	115	1 per cent

The territorial rivalries which had been diminished by strong candidates and party loyalty in Mampong North and Mampong South nearly proved to be the undoing of the Progress Party in the Sekyere Constituency. Bitter and longstanding jealousies among traditional areas combined with personal differences between the two contenders to become a great embarrassment to the party leaders. The constituency was roughly equivalent to the Sekyere East constituency of previous elections, and contained some of the strongholds of the former C.P.P. The Omanhene of Kumawu, the most important chief in the area, was a young ex-serviceman, active in nationalist politics when he was enstooled in 1950. He had exerted a powerful influence on both subchiefs and the volatile Kumawu young men, and quickly saw to the establishment of the C.P.P. throughout his traditional domain. A mutually beneficial alliance was forged with Krobo Edusei, who represented Sekyere East in Parliament from 1954 to 1966, and the constituency had resisted the siren call of the N.L.M. In the 1956 election, when most of rural Ashanti followed the Asantehene and his divisional chiefs into opposition, the Kumawuhene, smarting from a humiliating adverse judgement in land litigation before the Asantehene's court, defiantly upheld the C.P.P. Pragmatism as well as pride was involved, for over the years the small, isolated town of Kumawu benefited handsomely from its loyalty to the party in power, receiving water, electricity, paved streets, a secondary school, and numerous government sinecures for its citizens.

By 1969, however, Krobo Edusei was in prison on a perjury conviction arising from the post-coup investigation of his assets. It was clear to most people in Kumawu, including the Kumawuhene, that Busia was now the man to follow for exactly the same reason that the realists had stuck by the C.P.P. in the 1950s. The question in Kumawu, and elsewhere in the Sekyere constituency, was what man to elect on Busia's ticket. Because the C.P.P. and Krobo Edusei had dominated the area in the past, there was now no obvious claimant. In this void, the primordial consideration of territorial allegiance overrode all others: Kumawu insisted that the constituency be represented by a Kumawu man; but the town and its surrounding villages encompassed only one-third of the constituency, and the other sections were equally determined that the Assemblyman should *not* come from Kumawu to heap more blessings on the Kumawu chiefdom. In particular, the people of Effiduase, the second largest town, which was on the tarred Kumasi road and of greater commercial importance than Kumawu, argued that the representative this time should be an Effiduase man. Traditionally, however, Effiduase was inferior to and, on occasions in the pre-colonial past, actually at war with Kumawu.

Upon this scene appeared two claimants to Busia's favours, closely matched in attributes of youth, overseas education, and non-complicity in C.P.P. rule, the one identified with Kumawu, the other with Effiduase. Kingsley Abeyie, from Kumawu, was an enterprising young barrister in Kumasi. He had become interested in politics as a schoolteacher in Accra in the early 1950s, but was critical of the C.P.P. Government, although he had discreetly concealed his views lest his university education be obstructed. A wealthy uncle had sent him to England, where he read law and politics at Manchester University, and was called to the bar in 1961. Rather than return to Ghana, he obtained a teaching position near London, and immersed himself in Labour Party activities. His uncle finally called him home in 1963, and Abeyie quietly began law practice in Kumasi, while entertaining an ambition for political office contingent on the C.P.P.'s being displaced. When the 1966 coup heralded the coming of a new order, he busied himself with preparations: frequent visits to Kumawu to attend funerals, to settle disputes, and to show that, despite his lofty status, he was not above 'moving with the people'. In addition he founded the Kumasi Current Affairs Club, and worked for Busia by laying plans for the future party's organisation. All seemed in readiness by May 1969 to bring together these local, regional and national political connections to secure for Abeyie the Progress Party nomination and his election to the Assembly.

Such was the view from Kumawu and from Abeyie's Kumasi legal chambers. But Thomas Oduru-Kwarten, from an Effiduase village, had also been in the field since the coup. As an engineering student in a number of American universities he had led an association of Ghanaian students in North America opposed to Nkrumah. His connections with Busia, on the basis of his opposition to the C.P.P., led him, once back in Ghana after the coup, to start 'grooming a constituency' in anticipation of Busia's forming a party. As Editor of the *Sporting News,* and operator of an import–export business in Accra, he had less frequent contact than Abeyie with his Ashanti home base. None the less, by 1969 he was able to extend a village-level organisation into a popular base in the Effiduase territory which was the match of Abeyie's in Kumawu.

When the ban was lifted, Abeyie and Oduru-Kwarten took it upon themselves separately to 'introduce' the Progress Party in the constituency, watching over the formation of village committees and opening offices in the larger towns. Rival 'Progress Party' offices actually faced one another across the main street of Effiduase, the official constituency headquarters. Abeyie, well financed by his uncle B. S. Mensah (a prominent businessman in Accra) provided his canvassers with three 'Progress Party' propaganda vans. From their home base, both candidates branched out to seek support in 'neutral' villages—constituting one-third of the constituency—and sought to make incursions into rival territory. A prime hope of Abeyie's Kumawu supporters, for example, was to forge an alliance with Asokore, a large town adjacent to—and often at odds with—Effiduase. All such calculations were based on the assumption by each would-be candidate that he was the more popular with 'the masses', and that if the party nominee were chosen democratically he would win. Neither, therefore, would accede to the private pleadings of Busia and other leaders to withdraw voluntarily. Similarly, the significance of the outcome for Kumawu and Effiduase was greatly exaggerated in the popular mind. All hopes for the future prosperity of each area seemed to its inhabitants to hinge on its local choice being elected.

On 23 June 1969 P.P. officials attempted to hold an election on the lines of that held in Mampong South. The effort failed miserably, as both contestants disputed the 'representativeness' of delegates from certain areas, particularly Asokore, where Oduru-Kwarten alleged that Abeyie had intrigued with the chief to substitute names at the last minute for those 'democratically' chosen by Oduru's local committees. The officials then rashly proposed to settle the matter once and for all in two days time with a 'direct primary' election in which every P.P. member in the constituency was to vote at the neutral village of Oyoko. This unprecedented decision became a debacle. During the preceding day, Abeyie and Oduru-Kwarten travelled the muddy roads from dawn until well after dark imploring their supporters to come to Oyoko next morning to vote, while their agents saw to the registration of hundreds of new party members. Many saw the contest as the official election, although they were hard put to understand why they must all travel many miles to vote in one place. By 6.00 a.m. on 25 June scores of buses and lorries (hired at a cost of hundreds of pounds) were ferrying rival supporters from the far corners of the constituency to the cross-roads village of Oyoko. Their numbers swelled into thousands, and emotions rose under the influence of a hot sun, quantities of high-proof *akpeteshie*, and virulent preliminary campaigning. Huge cocoa lorries, laden with youthful singers of Ashanti war songs, thundered through the village, narrowly avoiding frenzied, sweat-drenched groups shouting the praises of their respective hero. Party officials from Accra and Kumasi were aghast at this spectacle when they finally arrived at midday. Having made no preparations for efficient polling, and having exhausted the patience of the emotional crowd, the officials managed to process only a few dozen of the estimated 5,000 voters present before rowdy elements disrupted the procedure. Officials and candidates alike fled the scene. Fighting then broke out among the frustrated mass of people, resulting in several injuries and damaged vehicles—the worst instance of political violence in the country prior to the election.

Nothing had been resolved. It was clear that the Progress Party had overwhelming support in Sekyere, but who was to claim that support? After Oyoko, the division proved too deep to heal in the short time remaining to the party to choose a candidate. A three-man committee was dispatched from Accra to investigate; its recommendation was that, since the Kumawu people were implacable, and since Abeyie seemed to have established the broader organisation, the nomination should be given to him. Oduru-Kwarten was persuaded in Accra to accede to this ruling, and not to stand as an independent or on another party ticket. But Abeyie had so estranged the Effiduase people that they put up a last-minute independent candidate, Kwakye Akyeampong, who had been Oduru's campaign organiser. Campaigning as a P.P. supporter, opposed only to the 'unpopular and arrogant' candidacy of Abeyie and against 'Kumawu domination', the comparatively unknown Akyeampong held Abeyie to the poorest P.P. performance in Ashanti:

Kingsley Abeyie	P.P.	6,369	57.5 per cent
Kwakye Akyeampong	Ind. (P.P.)	3,759	34.0 per cent
P. K. Boateng	N.A.L.	885	8.0 per cent
P. L. K. Boateng	U.N.P.	53	0.5 per cent

The basis of the voting in the constituency became clearer when these results were divided into their territorial components:

Traditional Area	Total Vote	P.P. Vote	%	Indep. Vote	%	N.A.L. Vote	%
Kumawu	3,940	3,510	89	83	2	347	9
Effiduase	3,140	199	6	2,725	87	216	7
Asokore	2,477	1,611	65	685	28	181	7
Sekyere 'Islands'	1,425	1,027	72	266	19	132	9
Total	10,982*	6,347	58	3,759	34	876	8

*'Special voters' (31) and U.N.P. votes (53) excluded.

Kumawu and Effiduase each voted as a bloc for its own man, Abeyie receiving more than half his total vote from Kumawu; the rest of the constituency voted for Progress in proportions somewhat below the Ashanti average. It was, in its way, another victory for the Progress Party. Had the roles been reversed, Akyeampong would probably have won with the P.P. vote in the two 'neutral' areas plus his own Effiduase vote. N.A.L. fielded a candidate from Asokore who drew only scattered support, and he failed completely to take advantage of the dominant local issue—which town, Kumawu or Effiduase, would elect the Progress Party Assembly member?

In this fashion did the candidates of Progress dominate the August election in the three constituencies. What was the basis of this massive and peaceful victory in the Sekyere area?[20] Expressed briefly: Busia and his party seemed the obvious alternative to the defunct C.P.P.; they bore the 'party in power' image; and opposing parties were identified with non-Akan ethnic groups. By looking at the form and content of the campaign at a local constituency level we can gain some sense of how these factors were understood by the rural population.

As was stressed earlier, in so far as the election was intended to choose among individuals seeking office, the decisive stage was that at which the Progress Party nominees were selected. Thereafter, the P.P. needed only to gather a latent support for Busia's party into a firm identification with its candidates. Other parties, and N.A.L. in particular, had the far more difficult task of converting sizeable numbers of voters to their side or of trying to revive the old C.P.P. 'propaganda machine' which was decimated by the demise of its national leaders and the loss of government backing. It was the N.L.C. and Busia which were now well established, not the C.P.P. and Nkrumah. Seen in this light, the

Progress Party campaign served only a limited function in bringing about a majority at the polls. All that was needed was to instruct voters in how to express their party support at the polls. In all three constituencies the Progress candidates were widely known. Yaw Manu and Kingsley Abeyie campaigned personally and actively in their constituencies; Amponsah, pre-occupied throughout the pre-election weeks with Constituent Assembly and national campaign responsibilities, came to his constituency to appear at rallies in Mampong and Ejura, to contact key influential men in those towns, and to bring instructions and campaign materials to his local campaign organisers. It was perhaps typical of Ashanti's upper political echelon, that all three candidates resided in Kumasi rather than in their 'home' areas.

Since the energy and money expended on campaigning, especially by Progress supporters, were out of proportion to the minimal effort needed to marshal a majority at the polls, a secondary explanation was needed, and it was there, in the need felt by many leading party members and their supporters to express openly and emotionally their identity with a party—and particularly with the party now in the ascendant. Former U.P. leaders could savour the change in their fortunes while seated prominently at P.P. rallies. Those who were too young to have been identified as U.P. or C.P.P. in the old days could assume prominent local positions in the P.P., and hope to rise with the party —just as many earlier ambitious young men had grown with the C.P.P. a political generation earlier. A number of former C.P.P. adherents made public displays of 'repentance' with vows to follow, henceforth, the righteous path of Busia,[21] and the women and children who cheered passing Progress vehicles and shouted down N.A.L. members made it quite clear that community and party political beliefs were not to be sharply distinguished.

A final function of the campaign, in the eyes of both national and local party leaders, was to muster a broad and active support. There was a clear commitment among all parties to the importance of a mandate at the polls for the new civilian government. To show that they had this mass support, each party encouraged its supporters to turn out for meetings and rallies; and a major expense incurred in the constituency campaigns was the cost of ferrying members to party events. In theory, the N.L.C. could have handed over to a civilian government—probably very similar to the one produced by the elections—without going through the election process, or it could have held the elections but prohibited the formation of parties to contest them. Such limitations have not been uncommon in the few instances in which military regimes have given way to civilians. But most Ghanaians had come to assume that the transition would involve the full panoply of democratic devices introduced in the transition to self-government twenty years before, including parliamentary elections contested by mass-based parties. The importance of voting was stressed in the language of classical participant democracy: '*tumi ne krata!*' (Your vote is your power!). But how was the message conveyed? Most local leaders conformed to patterns shaped by the past. Perhaps the foremost means of effective persuasion was the 'house-to-house campaign' which all party workers were expected to undertake. In such situations, it was crucial that the conveyor of the message be well-regarded, and the Progress organisers set up auxiliary branches for women, youth, and the *zongo* community, whose members and officers were expected to have a special influence among their equals, leaving the district and branch executive committees free to speak to the whole community. When asked what her work as Progress Party Women's Chairman consisted of, a woman who was respected for her age (65), her occupation (successful cloth trader), and her traditional status (head of the local women in her clan) replied:

> I go to my friends and others, mostly women, and ask them to join the Progress Party. I tell them that during past elections Dr. Busia told people that Nkrumah was wicked and not God-fearing. But people did not heed him [Busia] and when he [Nkrumah] went to power he detained people, even those with small children [motions to a grandson with her] to care for. Some even died in prison. So Busia has shown he has foresight . . .

She went on to recount how, under the old regime, her elderly husband, a U.P. leader, had been beaten by local C.P.P. officials . . .

> That is what the C.P.P. was like, I tell people. You can see that [my husband] is one of our most respected citizens, yet he was beaten by them.

The implication, which needed no articulation, was that a vote for N.A.L. was a vote for the reprehensible C.P.P.

The Secretary of the same women's auxiliary, a young schoolteacher and a leader in the Centre for Civic Education, said that she would convey essentially the same sentiment to her friends, but in the more sophisticated language typical of younger party supporters:

> I saw that the C.P.P. was doing extremely well at first, but getting to early 1960, things changed rapidly for the worse. When the N.L.C. came, things got better. I saw then that Busia should be our leader, as he was the Opposition leader before. I personally heard him at a rally in Mampong say so many things which came true. So I am in the P.P. because I feel my leader is the best person to rule this country. He is a very great man.

Branches of 'Operation Youth Decency' were formed in the larger towns for student supporters of Progress. Members were instructed to explain 'respectfully' to their uneducated elders the meaning of the party symbol and the procedure for voting, and to stress that the party youth would promote obedience to parents and teachers, unlike the C.P.P. Young Pioneers. The youngsters were assured that their names would go on record at National Party Headquarters (to some, a vital concern in times of high unemployment, although no specific promises of jobs were made), and they were conveyed *en masse* to party rallies where they provided a lusty, colourful accompaniment to the main speakers.

The dominant theme was a repudiation of the C.P.P. era as a time of 'detention and torture', 'bribery and corruption'. Rescued from this morass by the army and police, Ghanaians should learn from '15 years in Kwame's school' to follow Nkrumah's old opponent, the 'honest' Dr. Busia, to a glorious future. Indeed, the term 'Busia-party' was widely used until the name 'Progress' became familiar:[22]

> Busia has already won: his campaign was finished fifteen years ago. They tried to destroy him for fifteen years, but he is too strong. And so now, look, it is his turn!
>
> Let us leave that [the C.P.P. era] behind now and look for a man who is honest and will not bring back the troubles of the past.
>
> Dr. Busia is very brilliant. He is a black man but white men fear [respect] him . . . When Kwame Nkrumah's government was overthrown, there was not even a pesewa in the country. The soldiers had to seek loans for the country. How could the soldiers do this? They did not know anybody, so they said: Let us call Dr. Busia to come and help us. (Applause) When he met the people overseas he said: We need loans to build the country. They said: Take some. When he reached America, they gathered many things and sent them to us. So it is not only Ghanaians who support Busia, but people all over the world support him. And if he goes to power you will all see the profit which will come into the country, and will go to all parts of the country.
>
> Master (*Owura*) Busia will come to Mampong in two weeks: Everyone must come so that he may bless you.

K. A. Gbedemah, Busia's opponent, was regularly villified:

> I say that Kwame Nkrumah alone was not responsible for the destruction of the nation . . . Gbedemah was a Minister and helped to make the Preventive Detention Act. When he was Finance Minister he stole £17,000, and I am not afraid to say it—it is in the *Annie Jiagge Report*. Gbedemah speaks of his 'experience' all the time, but you can see that he has experience in stealing and not the experience to build a nation!

Gbebemah's support was characterised as tribal:

> But our tribal feelings tend to dominate our better sense in politics. An Ewe man will say that because I am an Ewe I must follow my brother Ewe who leads a party. Whether the leader is good or bad, he will follow him because they are of the same tribe. When I have a brother who is a hooligan, who drinks and fights in the street and beer bars, I will not help him in a fight just because he is my brother. But now look, the Ewes say that they will follow

N.A.L. because Gbedemah is an Ewe. They don't care whether he is honest or dishonest.[23]

Secondly, Progress was identified as the party favoured by the N.L.C.

> The soldiers and the policemen saw that the people of this country were suffering and so they overthrew the C.P.P. government. Now the soldiers and the policemen want to give the government back to civilians. They have asked us to give government to honest people who would make good government.
> But we see that there are some people who were formerly C.P.P., who have decided to come up again to destroy the country. When these former C.P.P. people get the government we shall be put under perpetual slavery. These C.P.P. people cannot make a good government, in which the country will be free from oppression. Dr. Busia is the only man who can continue the good work done by the N.L.C.

In Mampong, the home of the N.L.C. Chairman, Afrifa, the implied sanction of the N.L.C. was of course of great significance. Afrifa visited his home town regularly during the campaign, and although he scrupulously avoided any activities smacking of partisanship after his February C.C.E. appearance with Busia, it was well-known that his sympathies were with the P.P. One month before the election, speaking to the national conference of chiefs in Kumasi, he

> wondered why Ghanaians, who barely three years ago jubilated at the overthrow of a corrupt and tyrannical government, should rejoice and receive the same people who came back in another disguise . . . 'I will not accept defeat easily,' he said.[24]

A few days later, Busia appeared at a 'monster rally' in Mampong, and was introduced by a local party spokesman:

> Afrifa now occupies the throne in the N.L.C. kingdom, but soon he will vacate it. Out of the five 'princes' who are now struggling for the stool, some are selfish and some are wise; some are thieves and some fear God. Tell me the prince you want to inherit from Afrifa? (Crowd: 'Busiaaaa') . . . That is all I have to say. Master Busia, we have given the throne to you to inherit from Afrifa.

Busia responded effectively with a paean to Afrifa's valour and achievements:

> Afrifa was a little child who shot a gun and redeemed the country . . . But now he says that governing the country is not his work; he says: 'It is true, Mampong, I want to show you some signs—I have given you lights, I have given you water, I have given you a hospital. But this is not my work. I, for one, I only know how to shoot. So today take me away and let other people come and continue the work and judge me right.' Mampong State, what answer do you have today? Are you going to desert him? (Applause). If you are going to desert him, then in Mampong here I need not speak any more.

Progress was also the party of reconciliation, the only truly national party:

> The U.P. is dead; the C.P.P. is dead: Now all must come together to form the Progress Party. It is a new party, and all Ghanaians may join.

It was also the party of 'progress', a term no less euphemistic in its simple Twi translation than in its usage in popular Ghanaian English:

> 'Progress' means '*nkosoo*' (progress, success, furtherance, prosperity, edification). There is not a town or village in Ghana where a branch of the Progress Party has not been established. [This] shows that the Progress Party is a 'progressive' party. Everyone knows that it is the Progress Party which will build the country . . . *Prooo-gress!*
> Response: '*Sure!*')

Although they promised to 'build the country', the party's spokesmen seldom made specific promises of local benefits to be derived from supporting the party, nor was the national manifesto much discussed except in the vaguest terms:

> We are like the rising sun: give us the country and we shall wipe out the poverty and the crimes of the past which trouble the country.

After telling an Ejura audience that the Party would specifically promise no money or gifts for this poorly developed town, only 'good government', a Muslim Hausa spokesman went on:

> When you pray, do you not do so for the blessing of Allah? So let's forget about money and seek our more general goodness by voting for Amponsah to help Busia. Then look to see whether at Ejura you will not get light, water and farm land. I know, with the help of God, you shall get these things.

Finally, as we have seen, voters were repeatedly reminded that Busia's Progress Party was sure to win. In a society in which, for many, government means simply the capricious power to oppress and the capacity to bestow scarce benefits, this was perhaps the most important factor in the P.P.'s favour. No specific commitments were made, but the local significance of backing the winner was not lost on voters in the Sekyere area:

> Nothing is more shameful than to vote and lose.
> Today all of us have seen that the Progress Party is moving ahead, so if you want to get some of the profits to eat, then come and tie the edge of your cloth to the edge of Busia's cloth, so that when the profit comes, you will get some also. Do you want a tarred road? Do you want light and water from Mampong? Then tie your cloth to Busia's cloth . . . I just want to help you by telling you that throughout all of Ghana the Progress Party has already won . . . and later they will see how (this village) also voted before they decide to share some of the profit here . . . What is sorrowful in the country is when some people are eating and others are weeping.

The following speaker was more explicit:

> You all say now you are for the Progress Party. But if you are just saying it for fun, we shall know. 'By all means', whatever happens, the Progress Party has been blessed by God already and it shall go to 'power'. So after the voting, we shall count the papers here. There are 336 voters, and if about 40 vote for the other party, we will know who they are. (Applause). We do not want that![25]

When the National Alliance of Liberals emerged as the only significant local opponent, the Progress Party in Mampong North sought to discredit it as a powerless C.P.P. revival:

> If anyone comes from Mampong to tell you that they have formed another party, judge their claims wisely. Ask them how many people have you got in Mampong? How many elders support you? Go to Mampong and see for yourself—they only have about six taxi drivers, so ignore them.
> When they come to tell you they have formed a kind of Kwame Nkrumah group, ask them where is Kwame Nkrumah now? When someone speaks his name, shake your head in disapproval. It is shameful that they should show such ungratefulness [to the N.L.C.].

The N.A.L. response was necessarily equivocal. Admittedly (it said) Nkrumah had been corrupt and sought absolute power, but the C.P.P. era had not been all bad, for jobs and money had been in greater abundance then. By the same token, the coup was laudable for restoring freedom in Ghana, but the N.L.C. economic programmes had brought unemployment and much suffering to the young people. The P.P. was a party of intellectuals who would favour only the well-educated, yet the N.A.L. candidate Dr. Poku-Amanfo was also to be respected for his many degrees, whereas Amponsah had gone overseas only to learn 'plate-making'. Although tribal considerations were only rarely mentioned in public by Progress, it was apparent from frequent N.A.L. rejoinders that popular opinion in Ashanti had widely identified them as supporters of an 'Ewe party':

> Those people [the P.P.] are tribalistic. They say we should not follow an Ewe, but General Kotoka was an Ewe, and they all mourned his death. And Busia is not truly an Ashanti—he is a Brong. Furthermore, our National Chairman [John Cobbina] is the Asantehene's nephew, and he will be President when N.A.L. goes to power.

As election day approached N.A.L.'s ambivalence reflected an awareness that the contest was lost and that dire consequences might lie in store for those few who had openly espoused Gbedemah's cause. 'Do not be afraid . . . your vote is secret . . . We are brave, and they will never catch us.' Such refrains in the waning days of the campaign were not likely to bring wavering voters into the N.A.L. column. It was also somewhat ironic to note that the N.A.L., at least in Ashanti, proved a poor challenge to Progress even in its campaign organisation and style. Despite the highly touted reputation for mass propaganda skill attributed to former C.P.P. leaders from Gbedemah on down, the N.A.L.—with substantial financial resources and fleets of shiny cars—proved to be top-heavy in organisation and rhetoric. In Ashanti, most of the full-time party functionaries were based at the large and bustling regional headquarters in Kumasi, whereas Progress relied primarily on constituency organisations (financed by the candidates) which were closer to the majority of voters.[26]

The writer has suggested that there was a popular demand for active party campaigning, and indeed virtually every villager in the three constituencies was reached by some form of overt propaganda. In response, some remained passive; but a great many, especially in the larger towns, were moved to active expressions of partisanship. In Mampong North, for example, at least one-third of the 15,000 voters probably took part in the twenty public rallies staged by the P.P. alone, some attending several events. On two occasions, virtually the whole populace of Mampong town was mobilised: to welcome Busia on 4 August, and later to celebrate the P.P. election victory. Gbedemah also visited the area, and received a smaller but genuinely enthusiastic response in Mampong and other towns. As the long campaign developed, individuals became inescapably identified with one party or another, whether by personal choice or not; neutrality was difficult to sustain amid party vans, uniforms and shouted salutes which served as constant reminders of the overriding political contest. Social and business intercourse between P.P. and N.A.L. partisans (or between towns divided by the election, such as Kumawu and Effiduase) was reduced to a minimum; quarrels led to petty court cases. An atmosphere of rancour and suspicion strained the normally affable rural Ashanti society although not, fortunately, to the degree reached during the party struggles of 1955 to 1959. It was clear that the population was widely involved. Yet sporadic occurrences of mass political activism were not unusual in the Sekyere area well before the era of national politics: hundreds, even thousands, of citizens were actively engaged in chieftaincy contests throughout and, no doubt, before the colonial era. There were, therefore, traditional impulses and behaviour patterns which did not in themselves imply any lasting commitment to the national symbols and values to which the party supporters responded.[27]

In the small towns and villages a second source of enthusiasm for the campaign was its simple entertainment value to the many youthful, unemployed, and semi-employed individuals who complain constantly of the 'boredom' of their rural existence. Yet whatever their motives for cheering party cars, donning party clothing, and attending party rallies, the people of Sekyere took the voting act itself very seriously. The turnout on polling day was high: 71 per cent of those registered in the three constituencies, and the figure would have been higher had the cumbersome new procedures (introduced to preclude election offences so common in the past) been less time-consuming. The Electoral Commission provided too few polling stations to cope with all the voters under a polling procedure which required up to five minutes per voter, and many were turned away in disappointment at the end of the day.[28] There was also a widespread belief in the importance and credibility of the election, and on polling day voters displayed a mood that was in marked contrast with the raucous campaign just ended. In their best attire, they formed long queues at the polling stations, and there they quietly waited, some the whole day, for the chance to put their symbol in the ballot box. There was an air of irrelevance about the special army and police patrols which patrolled the roads, weapons at the ready, to guarantee security.

The spell was broken in each town and village as the polls closed and the results were announced, massively in favour of the P.P. Public rejoicing in Mampong, Nsuta and Jamase lasted long into the night and through the next day, Saturday, to a climax on Sunday, when the magnitude of the national P.P. victory became known. The outcome was exceedingly popular in most of Sekyere, and those who did not share in the ecstasy of its celebration were wisest to remain in seclusion.

Against this strong trend, non-P.P. voting (mainly for N.A.L.) was by no means uniform, ranging from 0 to 51 per cent in wards of Mampong North and Mampong South (and up to 99 per cent in Oduru-Kwarten's home village in the Sekyere constituency). But only in rare instances did the non-P.P. vote exceed 30 per cent, although the pattern of marginal variation in the opposition support provided interesting evidence about the basis of dissent in the three constituencies.

It seemed reasonably clear, for example, that it was a continuing allegiance to the former C.P.P. which moved a number of voters to support Gbedemah's N.A.L. or at least to vote against Busia and his local 'U.P.' followers. We have already noted that local party leaders in 1969, especially in Mampong North, were sharply divided along old C.P.P.–U.P. lines. Comparison of 1969 ward voting figures with those for the 1956 Sekyere West election indicated a similar relationship: those wards which ranked highest in N.L.M. voting in 1956 tended to rank highest in the Progress vote in 1969, and those which were strongly C.P.P. in 1956 ranked highest for N.A.L. in 1969.

Two caveats must be applied to this finding. In 1956, N.L.M. voting ranged from 4 to 94 per cent in the wards considered, the median being 75 per cent; whereas the 1969 Progress vote never fell lower than 61 per cent, with a median of 89 per cent. Thus, a 'low' Progress percentage in 1969 would have placed a village relatively 'high' for the N.L.M. in the

1956 and 1969 Party Voting Compared [29]
(Sekyere West Area Wards)

1956: per cent N.L.M.	1969: per cent P.P. Above 89	Below 89	Total
Above 75	12	5	17
Below 75	5	12	17
Total	17	17	34 wards

more competitive 1956 election. Secondly, one or two old C.P.P. strongholds were among the villages giving Progress its highest vote. In the Sekyere area, the most striking and significant example of such a reversal was Kumawu, which stood firmly with the C.P.P. throughout the 1950s, yet voted almost 90 per cent for Progress in 1969. At most, then, the evidence supports the conservative proposition that while N.A.L. probably drew much of its modest support from among former C.P.P. adherents, the majority of the old C.P.P. joined their one-time U.P. opponents in support of Busia.

A second hypothesis suggested by the election data was that Progress was relatively stronger in small villages, while N.A.L. and other parties drew a disproportionate amount of their support from the larger towns. The 94 wards in Mampong North and Mampong South are grouped below according to town size, indicated roughly by the number of voters and the proportion of their vote for Progress. Quite clearly, the party performed least well in the larger towns:

Town Size and P.P. Voting in Mampong North and Mampong South Wards (1969)

Voters in town†	Per cent voting P.P.* 49–69	70–89	90–100	Total
Under 500	2	27	34	63
Over 500	13	14	4	31
	15	41	38	94 wards

* Median: 85 per cent.
† Number who actually voted. For wards which were sub-divisions of larger towns, the total number voting in *all* wards in that town is used to categorize *each* ward in the town. For wards which include several smaller towns, voters are regarded as being in a single town; had it been possible to divide such wards into true villages, the relationship between P.P. voting and small town size would have appeared somewhat stronger.

Two inter-related factors may explain the phenomenon of non-Progress strength in the larger communities.[30] One is the greater pressure for consensus in the smaller villages, where traditional social ties are stronger and 'anonymity' is less tenable in political matters. If the prevailing trend was in support of Busia, deviation from this pattern was socially less acceptable in a community with a few hundred voters than, for example, in Mampong town with more than 3,000. Secondly, if parties opposing Busia were indeed supported disproportionately by non-Ashanti—as the Progress leaders claimed—such support would tend to be concentrated in the larger towns. There are few 'strangers' in the Sekyere area as a whole (78 per cent of the 1960 population were Akan-speaking, 75 per cent spoke *Asante*); moreover, most of the non-Akans are Northern Ghanaian or foreign labourers scattered on farms in the village areas, and they are unlikely to vote in large numbers. But immigrant concentrations do exist in Ejura, Mampong and other larger towns with *zongo* quarters, and among the employees of various government departments and institutions. The wards occupied by non-Ashanti—both from the North and the South—did give marginally weaker majorities to Progress, contributing to the lower overall proportions in these towns. This is not direct proof of 'tribal' voting for N.A.L. or other parties. It would be safer simply to conclude that parties opposing the Progress Party in the rural constituencies of Ashanti were most successful among relatively heterogeneous and less traditional communities.

More important than ethnicity as a factor uniting and dividing rural Ashanti in the past has been 'local territoriality': loyalty to the home town or village in its rivalries with neighbouring areas. This parochial sentiment has frequently been more salient than 'national' issues in the matter of party alignment. In 1969, Effiduase became totally alienated from the official Progress candidate from Kumawu: it found the pull of the party as a whole too strong to turn to a rival organisation, so it voted instead for an independent candidate. Elsewhere, there were less extreme instances of voters deserting Progress, apparently out of similar feelings of communal jealousy. In Mampong North, the town of Ejura voted 61 per cent for the party—almost 20 points below the figure for the constituency as a whole. The comparatively low figure may be attributed partly to the former C.P.P. and 'stranger' factors discussed above, since both were more prevalent in Ejura than in Mampong. Yet the Progress vote in the two predominantly Ashanti wards in Ejura was also down to 60 per cent, and it is probable that at least part of the anti-progress sentiment was the result of the town's longstanding dislike of being a 'poor cousin' to Mampong. Ejura is traditionally subordinate to Mampong, but it rivals Mampong in size and commercial importance, and its inhabitants have always resented the disproportionate amount of public improvements with which Mampong has been blessed while Ejura remains without an adequate water supply, electricity, a secondary school and so forth. Political logic suggests that a principal reason for this was that Ejura had never sent an M.P. to Accra. If the Mampong-based P.P. sent a Mampong man (Amponsah) to Parliament, Ejura's 'backwardness' would continue. Playing on this jealousy, the N.A.L. courted Ejura by locating its constituency headquarters there, and by electing its district chairman, secretary, and half its executives from Ejura. The results indicated that these calculations were not entirely without results. Aware of his potential weakness in this sector, Amponsah lavished attention on Ejura in his campaign and, after the election, presented the branch executive members with a new propaganda van in appreciation of their efforts on his behalf.

In Mampong South, the turnout in the large town of Kwamang was a similarly low 62 per cent for Progress, despite concerted local efforts by Yaw Manu. Kwamang was a C.P.P. stronghold in previous elections; but its relatively high vote for N.A.L. may also have arisen from the town's active resentment both of the Nsuta-dominated local council, which it felt had neglected Kwamang, and of the national government, which had failed to improve the nearly impassable Kwamang road. Since Progress was locally identified with Nsuta and the Accra government, such feelings may well have produced the relatively high vote for N.A.L.

In conclusion, we may note that the transition to civilian rule in Mampong—perhaps more than in any other town in Ghana—was seen as a triumph for the local community in a series of auspicious developments which began with Afrifa's participation in the successful coup, and continued with his elevation to the Chairmanship of the N.L.C. After 1 October 1969 the Brigadier became Chairman of the Presidential Commission, and R. R. Amponsah was appointed Minister of Lands and Mineral Resources. The general feeling was expressed simply by a local leader at a post-election victory rally:

> Mampong now has three 'ministers'—Amponsah, Bonsu [K. G. Osei-Bonsu, a junior minister, elected from a Kumasi constituency, was claimed by Mampong as Amponsah's nephew], and Afrifa, who has been crowned head of Ghana! No other town can boast three ministers. We can get whatever we want from the government now, and I am happy about it!

Mampong South, too, was happy, for Yaw Manu was appointed Parliamentary Secretary to the Minister of Transport and Communications. But in the Sekyere constituency, Effiduase was bitter that the Kumawu man had won; and Kumawu was greatly concerned that Abeyie had received no post. The Asokorehene, who had supported

Abeyie, began to construct a new road from his town to the Kumasi road so that his people would no longer have to pass through Effiduase.

On balance, however, the election probably served more to unite than to divide the Ashanti Region. It had involved most of the people in the locality more fully and willingly in national political affairs than had any other event since the 1956 election. And the issues which had aroused them were essentially national, the rejection of the old regime and confirmation of the new. Busia and his Progress Party Government had received an undeniable stamp of popular support; those opposing the new Government were apparently without a leg to stand on. National 'Opposition' movements had succeeded previously in the area as harbingers of a new order (the C.P.P.) or as a quasi-tribal movement (the N.L.M.); but Busia's party seemed now to monopolise both the 'new dawn' and the 'Ashanti' images. Indeed, the local Progress Party settled quickly into its role as a governing party, instead of being merely an electioneering instrument. The Mampong party leader, Dwomoh, told the public that henceforth they should bring their problems with the government to him for mediation, and he was appointed Chairman of a new all-Progress Management Committee to take charge of the Mampong Urban Council until elections could be held. In this vein, the above-quoted spokesman remarked:

> I tell you today that Kwame Nkrumah and his murderers ruled us for 15 years, but we will rule over them for 1,000 years . . . All N.A.L. men must resign and join us, for they will not get even one local councillor.

Similar words had been used and put to ill effect by the C.P.P. ten years earlier, but now in 1969–70 as in 1959–60 they made insufficient allowance for the frailty of politics in Accra. For by 1972 Sekyere was again under military control and the Progress Party, together with all its rivals, had been decreed unlawful.

Notes.

1. The Sekyere area (*Sekyereman* in Twi) refers to several traditional divisions sharing a vague sense of unity, strengthened by administrative and electoral boundaries first imposed by the colonial regime in 1902. The people of Sekyere, however, have never owed allegiance in common to any traditional authority other than the Asantehene. In the present context, the terms 'Sekyere' and 'Sekyere area' refer to the larger area, as distinguished from 'Sekyere Constituency', an electoral sub-unit.
2. This figure is a projection from the 1960 Sekyere Local Council (equivalent to 'Sekyere area') population of 136,416 reported in the 1960 population *Census of Ghana, Vol. 1* (Accra: Census Office, 1962) on the assumption of 4 per cent annual increase. (The annual increase for this area from 1948 to 1960 was about 6 per cent, probably exaggerated by undercounting in the 1948 census.)

3. The *1960 Census* gives the following occupational distribution for employed adults in Sekyere

Farmers (total)	70%
Farmers (Cocoa)	21%
Craftsmen	14%
Traders	9%
Others	7%

4. *1960 Census* tribal composition of Sekyere (per cent)

Asante	75%
Other Akan	3%
Mole Dagbani	11%
Others	11%

Most of the non-Ashanti are migrant farmers and farm labourers from Northern Ghana, Upper Volta and Togo.

5. In particular, it was said that those who were still inclined to support the C.P.P. saw little point in registering, since the N.L.C. Disqualification Decrees indicated that no former C.P.P. office-holders would be allowed to participate in future elections. This theory was advanced by some Registration Assistants to explain the reluctance of people in certain 'C.P.P.' villages to register. There was no substantial evidence, however, to indicate a bias among those who registered.

6. In a sample opinion survey in the Mampong area (see Note 7) at the time of the formation of the Constituent Assembly (see below), when it was receiving maximum press and radio publicity, only 27 per cent of the respondents were able to identify the 'Constituent Assembly', and only 18 per cent could name Amponsah—a well-know figure—as the Mampong District delegate. No doubt these figures would have been lower in samplings in sections of the district farther from Mampong. For Amponsah's political career as a former C.P.P. member, N.L.M. General Secretary and U.P. member. See Austin *op. cit.* Ch. VI.

7. 280 adults (aged 18 and over) were selected for interviews on a quota basis to reflect the age, sex, literacy and tribal composition of the district estimated from the *1960 Census.* Twenty-five per cent responded 'no difference' or 'don't know'.

8. This is not to say that the P.P. built its local organisational network on the basis of the C.C.E. structure. The Mampong C.C.E. Branch Advisory Committee never met after its formal inauguration—nor did the half-dozen others formed within the district—and certainly never worked directly to promote Busia's party before all such committees were dissolved in June 1969. Three of the Mampong committee later became P.P. executive members; the other seven remained inactive. But the single and spectacular inaugural ceremony had the effect of identifying Busia and his followers with political virtue, the established regime, and the popular Brigadier Afrifa.

9. Allusions to Busia's personal sanction were made openly by Yaw Manu in Mampong South and Oduru-Kwarten in Sekyere constituency.

10. For example, an energetic young man, who had been C.P.P. secretary for his village before the coup, was recruited into a similar role in the P.P. with the promise of 'something better' than village farming 'when Busia goes to power'.

11. The chairmanship, a largely honorary position, was given to a popular young man 'with money', whose past C.P.P. tendencies bespoke a willingness of the P.P. to set aside some of the old differences. The chairman reciprocated the honour done him by constructing a P.P. office at his personal expense.

12. Austin, *op. cit.,* p. 24.

13. Due to differences in local organisational patterns, the Progress and N.A.L. committees described here are not strictly comparable. The Progress Executive claimed

to represent the entire Mampong North constituency, although it included only one member from the large Ejura area. *Subordinate* branch committees were formed in Ejura and the Mampong *zongo* thus tending to give the party a 'Mampong town, Ashanti tribe' image locally. On the other hand, the N.A.L. Executive represented only the Mampong sector of the constituency, the *zongo* and other non-Ashanti representatives being explicitly included. When N.A.L. later formed a constituency-wide organisation, 8 of 15 executives were from Ejura and 9 were non-Ashanti.

14. In fact, Mampong's excellent water-supply had been opened in 1961 by the C.P.P. Government. It was indicative of the prevailing temper that a local leader who had had much to do with this development now attributed it to Afrifa, along with post-coup improvements—electricity and a NȻ1.5 million hospital—in which the Brigadier may have been instrumental.

15. Amponsah's uncle, who had been Mampong's first Presbyter when the Basel (Presbyterian) Mission was introduced in 1896, saw to it that almost all of his nephews received that vital concomitant of Christianity, an education, in an era when schooling was rare in Ashanti. Several of Amponsah's brothers and cousins have made distinguished careers in business, government service and politics. A nephew, K. G. Osei-Bonsu, was elected to Parliament in 1969 from Asukwa (Kumasi), and an elder brother, R. B. Kwakwa, had stood unsuccessfully in Sekyere West in 1954.

16. Dennis Austin *op. cit.*, pp. 267–68.

17. The Granville Sharp Commission found that Amponsah and M. K. Apaloo (a fellow Opposition leader) '. . . were engaged in a conspiracy to carry out at some future date in Ghana an act for an unlawful purpose, revolutionary in character'. The Commission was divided on the exact nature of the 'act', and on whether the 'conspiracy' remained active. It included Major Awhaitey of the Ghana Army. The finding was alarming to the Government, but the evidence was hardly sufficient to gain a conviction in court. (See Austin, pp. 380–83 and 424–9.)

18. Manu was popularly thought to have aided Busia's escape by this northern route in June 1959; he had, however, left Nandom for Kumasi in January that year.

19. Sympathy for Manu was enhanced by the fact that his death sentence had remained in force while similar sentences on Tawia Adamafio and Ako Adjei, who were Ga, were commuted to prison sentences. Manu thereby symbolised for many Ashanti, even in 1969, the 'victimisation' of their people by Nkrumah's regime.

20. The violence, coercion and bribery with which many associated past politics were almost wholly avoided in 1969. Also absent in Ashanti was the overt exercise of chiefly influence: the majority of Ashanti chiefs found it prudent to exercise their much diminished persuasive powers privately, if at all.

21. The religious cast of these conversions was epitomised by the old C.P.P. stalwart in Mampong who attended Progress rallies with bible in hand. As a local council employee, he had a clear stake in being on the winning side, but as a prominent funeral-goer and participant in traditional music groups, his feeling for communal solidarity was perhaps a more powerful motive for sensing and responding to the changing tide.

22. The remarks quoted here are extracted from public campaign speeches at several rallies in Mampong North constituency. In most cases the quotations are direct and literal translations from tape recordings of the original Twi (or Hausa) words used by the speaker. In a few cases, the relatively rambling and circuitous vernacular is compressed by paraphrase. The painstaking translation of many hours of repetitive oratory was ably performed by Mr. J. Agyapong-Mensah.

23. The attribution of 'tribalism' to opposing parties was a reminder to local Ashanti that victory by any other party would mean 'domination' of Ashanti by a non-Akan government. The tribal issue—never a prominent one in the Sekyere area during the 1969 campaign—became more overt during the final weeks before the

election when P.P. leaders began complaining that the local police superintendent and court magistrate were favouring the N.A.L. 'because they are Ewes'. (The police officer in question was in fact a Fanti.) In fact, most local troubles with the police and courts were a result of over-enthusiastic and aggressive partisanship on the part of the dominant party. Paradoxically, as victory loomed closer, a sort of paranoia seized local Progress leaders, and this was most easily expressed in tribal terms.

25. One can only speculate as to what illiterate villagers inferred from such comments. The speaker simply meant that in a small community, it would be common knowledge who the dissident voters were; but the reference to the esoteric ballot-counting procedures might have left the impression that voting would not be strictly secret. N.A.L. agents, on the other hand, were at great pains to stress that no one could know how any individual had voted.

26. Unlike the name 'Progress', the 'National Alliance of Liberals' was not easily translated into vernacular languages. The P.P. salute, an aggressively projected clenched fist, had more appeal than the N.A.L. 'V-for-Victory', which was ridiculed as indicating how easily 'Ghana's money slipped through the C.P.P. fingers'. Such matters of form and style were not trivial in rural Ashanti and they tended to reverse the old image of the C.P.P. leaders as being more attuned to the thinking of the masses than the 'Westernised' U.P. men.

27. In 1931 when the colonial government sanctioned the election of a Mamponghene by the fourteen constitutional elders or 'kingmakers', despite opposition among the majority of Mampong's 'young men', the leaders of the 'malcontents'—who, in the eyes of the British District Commissioner, had 'no important positions in the body politic'—persuaded 2,000 followers (according to the official report) to desert Mampong and settle in the Kwahu area forty miles away. After four years of petitions, mass demonstrations, and appearances before commissions of enquiry, these nascent politicians led their people back home, and the unpopular chief was soon destooled. His successor, the 'young men's choice' in 1931, met a similar fate in 1951 when the commoners found his administration detrimental to the development of Mampong state. They skilfully rallied thousands of townsmen and villagers in a show of opposition sufficient to effect the destoolment of the chief by the Chief Commissioner.

   The above episodes are documented in *Mampong District Record Book*, Vols. 1 and 2. Ghana National Archives (Accra) A.D.M. 52/5/3–4; Ashanti Chief Commissioner Case No. E.P. 34/1932 ('Mampong Native Affairs'), G.N.A. (Kumasi) No. D. 306; and Mampong District Office File 0164/v.1–2 ('Mampong/Gyase State Council Affairs'), in Mampong District Office Archives.

28. In Ejura many voters remained in line when the polls closed; and in Mampong South, at least two villages, Appaa and Yonso, reported as many as 100 voters turned away. Polling at many stations in Sekyere constituency did not begin until 1.00 p.m. because of delays in dispatching proper ballot papers from Accra. Although voting continued as late as midnight in one village many wanted the polls to be re-opened the following morning. Under severe election-day pressure, however, most local polling officers were conscientious and efficient.

29. 1956 voting figures for 55 polling stations comprising Sekyere West were compared with 1969 data from the same area, now consisting of 72 polling stations in parts of Mampong North and Mampong South constituencies. To permit direct comparison, it was necessary to create 34 'analytical wards', each representing the smallest combination of villages for which discreet results were reported each year. Ranking the 34 'wards' according to the respective proportions of N.L.M. and P.P. support in the two years revealed considerable consistency at both the upper and lower ends of the distribution:

Ward	1956 N.L.M. %	Rank	1969 P.P. %	Rank
Asuafo/Jansa	95	1	91	11
Dewu/Tabre	94	2	91	4
Jamase North	93	3	83	21
Anansu	92	4	97	3
Atwea	92	5	94	2
Jediako/Drobonso/etc.	17	30	74	30
Daaho/Bosofuor	15	31	81	26
Yonso	14	32	72	32
Sabuso/Nkaneku/etc.	8	33	93	7
Atonsu/Abodiase	4	34	64	33

30. The relationship of town size to 1969 party voting seems to be independent of the previously mentioned factor—1956 party tendencies. That is, the Sekyere West data for 1956 indicate that the N.L.M. received support in roughly the same proportions in towns and villages of all sizes:

Town Size and N.L.M. Voting in 1956
(Sekyere West)

Voters in town	Per cent N.L.M. Vote		
	Under 65	Over 65	
Under 273	15	12	27
Over 273	12	16	28
	27	28	55 wards total

The above relationships can be summarized statistically:

		Correlation coefficient (Pearson's r)
1969 % P.P.	with 1956 % N.L.M.	.505
1969 % P.P.	with 1960 population	−.337
1956 % N.L.M.	with 1960 population	.010
1969 % P.P.	with 1960 population	−.451

controlling for 1956 % N.L.M.
by partial correlation

These statistics were calculated from data for the 34 matching synthetic 'wards' described above, with 'population' being the average for communities within a given ward as reported in the *1960 Census*.

EPILOGUE

MALCONTENTS IN UNIFORM— THE 1972 COUP D'ÉTAT

Valerie Plave Bennett

Why did the military intervene again in 1972? The withdrawal from politics in 1969 had been very competently done, and there seemed good ground for believing that the armed forces would keep aloof from politics. Yet on 13 January 1972 there was the second coup. Why did it happen? The most salient factors were probably the Progress government's refusal to exclude the military and police forces from the general cut-back in government expenditure, the personal ambitions of a small group of officers, and—reinforcing these two motives—a third element, namely, what was seen as an anti-Ewe stance of the Busia administration and the effect it had on the senior command of the army. We need to begin, therefore, with the effect of the July 1971 budget on the armed forces.

An earlier chapter by John Esseks has described how the cost of imports and falling cocoa prices brought the economy in 1971, as in 1961, to a point of crisis, and how they led once again to an 'austerity budget'. Its purpose was two-fold—as a signal to Ghanaians of the need for retrenchment, and as an indication to international financiers that the government was dealing realistically with its problems. The budget not only prohibited a wide range of imports, it also abolished a number of allowances for civil servants and army officers; and it reduced expenditure on the armed forces. The vote for the Ministry of Defence went down from the N₵45m. of the 1970 Budget (in itself a reduction from the previous year's figure of 49.1m.,) to N₵40.4m., of which N₵31.4m. was for recurrent and N₵9m. for capital expenditure. When J. H. Mensah introduced the budget, he reminded the party-dominated Assembly that the government had been faced 'with the problem of what to do about a level of defence expenditure which was clearly onerous for a small country such as ours'.[1] The most severe cuts were experienced by the Air Force and Navy—both of relative unimportance to Ghana's limited defence requirements—but all three services were affected.

The Navy, for example, had not been expanded for several years. Its ships were in need of refitting but money had been unavailable, and they were reported to be in such poor shape that they could not put to sea:—the 'Achimota', the old Flag Ship of the Naval Chief of Staff, had been decommissioned and was being offered for scrap. In addition, part of the Sekondi Naval Base was turned into a fishing harbour. The Air Force was similarly placed—no new planes had been bought for many years, very little flying time was logged because of the high cost of fuel, and foreign exchange was unavailable for spare parts or for the overseas training of pilots and mechanics. The Army, too, experienced its share of cuts. The parachute battalion at Tamale was first disbanded, then reformed as the Seventh Battalion at Takoradi in an attempt to keep some airborne capability, but was still found to be too costly, whereupon the entire battalion was absorbed into other units. The armed services as a whole were also expected to pay taxes on items ordered from overseas, making repair and replacement a great deal more expensive than previously. The net result was that there was very little money for exercises, training and ammunition, while the restrictions on imports led to problems of supply, since many vehicles were not locally repairable.[2]

A related problem was that of the role of the armed services which, after almost fifteen years of independence, was still unclear. The Army saw its main (and possibly sole) function as that of guarding the nation against its foreign enemies. But to the Progress Government such a role was not easily justified and they sought new ways to make use of the armed forces as a whole. Since April 1970 the military had been supporting the police in an anti-smuggling campaign on the borders, and in September joint police–military operations against crime were started. The Army Medical Corps was active in the anti-cholera drive, and the Air Force provided flood relief aid in the north. But, despite these activities, many Ghanaians were left with the feeling that the military could be more useful. When in the summer of 1970 the National Union of Students suggested that the technical branch of the army should be used in agricultural and constructional work, the Minister of Defence, Kwesi Lamptey, said that soldiers would only be used for defence purposes; but a year later, after B. K. Adama had become Defence Minister, and when the general financial position of the country had deteriorated, the government's attitude towards reconstruction work changed. In the July Budget, Mensah announced that:

> ... it is possible to combine ... training with substantial contributions to national development. Therefore during this financial year, it has been arranged that whenever units ... go out on training exercises they will seek to leave behind them some positive development project ... by way of roads or sanitary buildings.[3]

The corporate indignities of the new Budget did not hurt the officers as much as the personal losses they suffered. (The abolition of a car maintenance allowance was particularly resented.) A major who was taking home N₵215 a month prior to July, received only N₵125 under the new budget.[4] The government also put an end to the free supply of water and electricity, reduced the telephone allowance, and increased rent payments from $7\frac{1}{2}$ per cent to 15 per cent of officers' salaries. An actual cut in pay was also rumoured,[5] but the final blow to the officers' well-being came at the end of December, when the government announced that the Cedi would be devalued by 44 per cent. For those living in the quasi-European style of many of the Ghanaian élite, a 44 per cent devaluation represented a loss of as much as 25 per cent of purchasing power. It was on these grounds of retrenchment and reform of the armed forces that Busia was to explain the January intervention as 'an officers' amenities coup arising from their grievances at my efforts to save money'.[6] And, as is often the case, the Progress government were well aware that the financial grievances of the officers corps heightened the danger that the army would act to remedy them. It was in an attempt to forestall such a calamity that numerous shifts were made in senior military appointments. The effect, however, was to precipitate the disaster it was designed to prevent.

There had already been a serious disruption of the armed forces at command level. It had happened in three stages. There was, first, the retirement of the officers associated with the Nkrumah regime, including General Aferi, Col. Hassan, Col. Ashitey, Col. Zanlerigu, Col. Kuti and Col. Assassie. Later, there was the semi-retirement of officers whose loyalties at the time of the 1967 abortive coup were unclear: Brig. Gabbe, Gen. Bruce, Admiral Hansen and several younger officers—Major Acquah, Major Achaab and Major Asante. Then in 1969, when the National Liberation Council handed over power to the Busia government, all the military members of the N.L.C. left the army—Afrifa, Ankrah and Ocran, as did some of the Regional Commissioners, including Col. Laryea and Col. Lartey. In addition, two officers were killed in the 1966 and 1967 coups—General Barwah in February 1966 and General Kotoka in the unsuccessful attempt in April, 1967. Other officers lost to the army included those seconded to run public bodies—Col. Ewa, the Director in charge of Administration for the Ghana Industrial Handling Corporation; Major Cobbina, the Chief Transport Officer; Col. C. K. Yarboi, Deputy General Manager for the Ashanti Goldfields Corporation; and Col. Sanni-Thomas, in charge of the State Protocol Section of the President's Office. Col. Quaye, an Ewe, was transferred out of the army to become Head of the Navy, and four officers out of favour with the N.L.C. government became Military Attachés abroad. The result of these shifts was that one-half of those who held ranks of Lieutenant-Colonel or above at the time of the 1966 coup were not there in 1970. The command structure was therefore weak and inexperienced. The retirement of the senior men brought rapid promotion for middle-grade officers in the good graces of the N.L.C. or the Busia government, but it did not remove the promotion blockages which faced the junior officers, particularly since the size of the military establishment remained constant. The Ghana Military Academy, which took as many as 120 men a year in the early 1960s, had cut back its intake to twenty-five cadets per annum by the end of the decade.

Shortly before the 1969 Election, the N.L.C. again made important changes in the High Command. The previous year, Air Marshall Otu had become Chief of Defence Staff, and Brigadier Amenu—an Ewe—had been appointed Deputy Chief of Staff in order that someone with command authority could look after the armed forces since Otu was busy with N.L.C. duties; but, when Otu was arrested in November 1968, Brigadier Addo, rather than Amenu, was made Acting Chief of Staff. Then, in August 1969, Addo became Commander of the Army; Brigadier Kattah, an Ewe protegé of the late General Kotoka and Commander of the First Brigade in Accra, was appointed Military Attaché in Washington; Lt. Col. Twum-Barima, a supporter of Busia (and in charge of the Third Battalion) was appointed in his place; and Lt. Col. Acquah, Director of Military Intelligence, became Commander of the Second Brigade. Thus the N.L.C. removed the two senior Ewes—Amenu and Kattah—from troop command.

Such was the position in October 1969 at the beginning of the second Republic. By the summer of 1971, the Busia government was already in economic difficulties. The import boom had ended, and declining cocoa prices, coupled with rising short-term debts, were leading the government towards the policies described in Chapter 2. In addition, as noted in the Introduction, the Progress government succeeded in offending a remarkably wide array of its former supporters. We can do no more than list them here. They included trade-unionists who led a number of strikes in 1971 in the mines, on the railways, among harbour workers and in the construction industry, not only in protest against the cost of living and rising unemployment, but against particular policies of the Busia government. The ten day stoppage at the Samreboi African Timber and Plywood factory in the Western Region in March was violent, three of the strikers being killed when the police opened fire. As industrial unrest grew, the government reacted sharply. It froze the assets of the union and, under a Certificate of Urgency, enacted a new Industrial Relations Bill, the effect of which was to dismantle the existing T.U.C. in an effort (it was said) to encourage the autonomy of its constituent unions. The civil servants were upset and the judiciary was divided over the Sallah case.[7] The students were indignant over the government's intention to impose a loans scheme (interest-free and repayable over 12 years) on the universersities. And there was widespread criticism of the sharp contrast between the private affluence, conspicuously displayed, of the party leaders and the general exhortation by the government of the need for economy. The nervousness of the regime, despite its massive parliamentary majority, was seen at the end of August 1971 when a bill was rushed through the Assembly, again under a Certificate of Urgency, which made the sale of portraits of the former president, and the advocacy of his return, a criminal offence.[8] Such were the circumstances in which discontent began to grow.

Among those who felt particularly aggrieved, were the police. It was actually said that Busia had received a letter which threatened a further coup if conditions within the police force did not improve.[9] The following week, B. A. Yakubu retired as head of the police, the last member of the former N.L.C. to hold an army or police position. But instead of appointing a new Inspector-General from within the ranks of the police, Busia brought in a lawyer civil servant, R. D. Ampaw, to succeed Yakubu. The introduction of the July Budget led to further changes. Lt. General Otu (Air Force ranks had been changed to Army titles) was said to have strongly opposed the cuts in military expenditure and accepted retirement; Amenu was then next in line but was moved sideways to become Director of the National Service Corps, and Major-General Addo (the former Army Commander) was appointed Acting Chief of Defence Staff after agreeing to the reductions in the Defence Budget. Brigadier Acquah, the former Commander of the Second Brigade became Acting Army Commander, and Brig. Osei-Owusu filled Acquah's former position. Meanwhile, Brigadier Ashley-Lassen, the Ewe Commander of the Air Force, was hurriedly assigned to a one-year course at the Indian Defence College, and Lt. Col. Kattah (also an Ewe), having been posted as Military Attaché in the Indian capital, was brought back to face charges of theft arising after the 1966 coup, and put before a civilian court.[10] By 1972 there was only one Ewe—Col. Tevie—in any position of senior army rank. None the less, in mid-November 1971 another re-organisation began. Brigadier Acquah was asked to resign immediately, having informed the government that he planned to retire early in 1972 in order to enter the building industry 'while he was still young'—and, because of the earlier retirement date, he lost a number of benefits. He was replaced by Brigadier Twum-Barima whose position at First Infantry Brigade Headquarters—and here was the fateful appointment—was filled by Lt. Col. Acheampong.

At about 2 a.m. on 13 January, troops of the first Brigade began to move on key installations in the capital, including the radio station, airport, the cable office and the Castle. Logistically the coup was relatively simple; all these installations were guarded by the Fifth Infantry Battalion which had been under Acheampong's command in 1970. It was said later that Acheampong had thought of staging a coup that year, and had already begun to plan what he would do if he were given control of the First Infantry Brigade;[11] but that was impossible as long as Brig. Twum-Barima, Commander of the First Brigade, remained loyal to Busia since he would have been able to mobilise the First Battalion against any attempt at a coup on the part of the Fifth Battalion.[12] Acheampong simply bided his time, as Afrifa had admitted he had done in similar circumstances in November, 1964 when he was Acting Brigade Major at Second Brigade Headquarters.[13] Acheampong's sudden posting to Trinidad to serve on the court martial of officers who had mutinied against the government of Dr. Eric Williams interrupted his planning. Then, in November 1971 he was given command of the First Brigade, and the period between November and January was sufficient to prepare the coup.

Up until this point, Acheampong's career had not been unusual. Born in Kumasi in September 1931 he had taken his General Certificate of Education and worked as a teacher, secretary, and school principal. In 1958, when he was twenty-seven, he joined the army and passed out of the Mons Officer Cadet School in March 1959. In 1962–63 he served with the Ghana forces in the Congo, and then returned to Ghana before leaving for the United States to attend Staff College at Ft. Leavenworth, Kansas in 1968, and a senior officer maintenance course at Ft. Knox, Kentucky, the same year. Before taking over the Fifth Battalion in Accra he had been Commanding Officer of the Sixth Battalion at Tamale; he had not held a staff position under the Busia government, although he had served as Chairman of the Administrative Commission of the Western Region under the N.L.C.

Acheampong belonged to a class of officers whose careers had suffered because they were not affiliated with the group that brought off the 1966 coup against Nkrumah. As he plaintively explained, Afrifa had been a Company Commander under him, and was now a retired Lt. General.[14] Men such as Twum-Barima who, like Acheampong, had been Lt. Colonels in 1967 were Brigadiers, while the latter remained only a Colonel. (Acheampong was promoted full Colonel two days before the January coup.) Others, such as Col. Osei-Owusu, in charge of the Second Brigade, had been only a Major in 1967. After the January coup, Col. Bernasko, one of the Regional Commissioners under the National Redemption Council, assured a group of students that the 'escalating promotions' which had characterised the N.L.C. period were 'unlikely to be heard of this time'.[15] In this sense, Acheampong and the few Majors whom he trusted with his plans might best be described as the 'non-politicians' of the army, officers of the line rather than the staff. The small group responsible for the coup included Major Baah, Second in Command of the Fifth Infantry Battalion in Accra, and Acheampong's former deputy; Major K. G. Agbo, Second in Command of the First Infantry Battalion at Tema; and Major A. Selormey, Second in Command of the Cavalry Regiment. All these men were junior to Acheampong, thus assuring his leadership of the conspiratorial group. Acheampong is an Ashanti, Baah a Brong, and Selormey and Agbo are Ewe. Friendships based on career patterns were more important (at least in 1972) then ethnic considerations, but it is also true that many Ewe officers felt that they had been badly treated by the Busia government.

Major Baah's career had not been particularly distinguished. Although he had joined the army only a year after Acheampong, he was still a Major in January 1972. (He had been commissioned in India in 1960.) In 1966–67 he was promoted to Acting Major and assigned to the staff of the Ghanaian Defence Attaché in London and later to Washington. It was not until the spring of 1970 that he was promoted to the rank of substantive Major. After his promotion, Baah asked to attend Staff College but the request was denied and he saw his contemporaries, who had been to Staff College, promoted ahead of him. Major A. K. Agbo, like Baah, had joined the army in 1959 after attending Achimota School. He, too, had been appointed substantive Major in 1970, and had not been allowed to go abroad for further training. Major Anthony Selormey joined the army in 1961 and graduated from the Ghanaian Military Academy in 1962. He received a period of training abroad at the Royal Armoured Corps School in Wareham in the United Kindom and then at the Armour School at Ft. Knox (1967–68) in America. Selormey was a personal friend and neighbour of Acheampong, and a particularly valued ally since, as an Ewe, he too was likely to be a candidate for a rival Ewe conspiracy that was rumoured to be in train late in 1971 and early 1972. Selormey was also considered to be particularly sensitive to, and incensed by, what many (Ewe) officers considered to be Busia's mistreatment of Kattah.

Busia was in London, undergoing medical treatment, at the time of the coup—as Nkrumah had been away in Peking at the time of the first coup. The Progress cabinet Ministers and the President were easily arrested. So too were officers about whom the conspirators were unsure—Addo the Chief of Staff, Twum-Barima the Army Commander, Ampaw the Inspector General of Police and Hamidu, the Head of Military Intelligence. The most pressing problem was whether the Second Infantry Brigade Group in Kumasi would accept the coup. The Chief Regional Executive in Ashanti, Maxwell Owusu, announced on the radio that the coup had failed, but was contradicted by Captain David Weir who was then third in command of the fourth Battalion. The same day, Lt. General Afrifa called upon Acheampong, and declared that he was in agreement with what had happened, but he was arrested on the morning of the fifteenth and accused of conspiring with Col. Osei-Owusu, the commander of the Second Brigade, to overthrow

the new government.[16] A remarkable aspect to the arrest of a number
of senior officers in the first days of the coup—Afrifa, Addo, Twum-
Barima, Hamidu, and Osei-Owusu—is that they were all Sandhurst
men; they were loyal supporters of the Busia government and, for that
loyalty, had been rewarded with promotion.

Immediately after the coup, Acheampong was faced with the difficulty of naming a ruling council. After several annoucements over the
radio, the N.R.C. emerged as:

Colonel Acheampong	Major A. Selormey
Major Kwame Baah	Lt. Col. Barnor
Commander Boham	Lt. Col. Benni
Major Agbo	Mr. E. N. Moore (Attorney General)

Lt. Col. Benni, a Dagarti and Commander of the Third Battalion,
had studied in India 1960–62 and at Ft. Leavenworth 1969–70. E. N.
Moore, a lawyer not previously identified with any of the major parties,
was a man of ability and independence, widely respected as President of
the Bar Association at the time of the coup, who had been one of the
counsels for the accused in the 1963 treason trial. Nine Regional Commissioners were also named on 23 January as:

	Region	Origin	Date of Birth
Col. Acquaye-Nortey	Greater Accra	Ga	?
Col. Nyante	Eastern	Akwapim	1929
Col. Agyekum	Western	Fanti	1923
Lt. Col. Baidoo	Ashanti	Fanti	1933
Major Habadah	Volta	Ewe	1928
Cmdr. Kyeremah	Brong/Ahafo	Brong	1940
Lt. Col. Idissah	Northern	Gonja	1936
Lt. Col. Minyila	Upper	?	?
Col. Bernasko	Central	Fanti	1931

There was no single career pattern uniting these new Commissioners.
Five had received their military education in Great Britain; Idissah and
Minyila at Sandhurst, Baidoo at Mons, Kyeremah at Dartmouth Naval
College, Nyante at Eaton Hall. Two of the Commissioners had held administrative posts under the N.L.C.; two had held staff appointments
before the coup, one was a university graduate, and two had served in
the pre-independence army as enlisted men. They were a mixed bag of
those willing to accept appointment.

At 6 a.m. on the day of the coup, Acheampong broadcast his reasons
for the intervention. The corruption, economic mismanagement, and

other malpractices that had characterised the Nkrumah government were (he claimed) equally in evidence under the Busia administration. He then cited what were very likely the essential factors:

> The first people which Busia put his eye on were the armed forces and police. Some army and police officers were dismissed under the pretext of retirement. Some officers were put in certain positions to suit the whims of Busia and his colleagues. Then he started taking from us the few amenities and facilities which we in the armed forces and the police enjoyed even under the Nkrumah regime. Having lowered morale in the armed forces and the police to the extent that officers could not exert any meaningful influence over their men, so that by this strategy coming together to overthrow his government was to him impossible, he turned his eyes on the civilians.[17]

As leader of a group composed of a small number of military malcontents, Acheampong had no precise political objective other than that of a reversal of many of the decisions taken by the Busia government which now shared the earlier fate of the C.P.P. and Nkrumah. Nor had he any instruments of control through which to govern. There was a good deal of jockeying for position, therefore, among army, naval and air force officers to try and secure a place on the N.R.C. and in any new administration that might be formed. The day after the coup the composition of the N.R.C. was substantially altered. Only Acheampong and the three Majors remained from the first list, and the new members included—in addition to Acheampong, Baah, Agbo and Selormey—Brigadier Ashley-Lassen, Colonel E. A. Erskine, Commodore Quaye, Brigadier Beausoleil and Mr. J. H. Cobbina.[18] Then on 22 January, a further list added Major Felli of the Signals Regiment, Colonel Adjeitey, who had been appointed Regional Commissioner for Greater Accra, and the new Attorney-General E. N. Moore.

At the end of January, Ministerial portfolios were assigned to nine of the thirteen members of the N.R.C. That the new government was essentially a coalition of the 'outs' of the N.L.C. and Busia period was indicated by the appointment to office under the N.R.C. of a number of soldiers who had been serving abroad, including Nathan Aferi and Coker-Appiah. It is true that the appointment of General Addo as the new Minister for Agriculture was cause for surprise, since he had been Busia's Chief of Staff, but it is also the case that the General had succeeded in remaining on good terms with Nkrumah as well as Busia, as well as with several members of the anti-Busia opposition. And one may reasonably see the new military junta as being supported primarily by officers whose careers had either languished or been prematurely ended under Busia. They were relatively young at the time of the coup; the average age was forty (including Acheampong who was then forty-one) despite the inclusion, as a gesture to military rank, of the more senior officers—Addo, Aferi, Ashley-Lassen, Beausoleil and Quaye.

They were also few in number and diverse by ethnic origin (with an over-representation numerically from among the Ewe). At first sight their ability to govern the country, faced with the serious economic problems of January 1972, was very much open to doubt, although the Council members were sufficiently prudent to appoint Major Baah and Major Agbo as Battalion Commanders to safeguard their military position. There had been nothing in the military career of the N.R.C. members to suggest that they would succeed not simply in staging a coup but in retaining control after they were in power. And yet, despite these difficulties, they acted purposefully.

As described in Chapter 2, the Cedi was revalued, and part of the debts repudiated. At the end of February 1972, a 'Mini-budget' was introduced for the January to June period, and it showed clearly that the new government was determined to reverse many of Busia's policies:

> The political frame of reference which has guided . . . actions and . . . advice in the past two years must be cast into the rubbish heap of history. This means a departure from the laissez-faire so-called free market economy and the institution of effective planning in the allocation and utilisation of resources.[19]

The Progress Party Government, said Acheampong, had 'preferred a doctrinaire attachment to a free market economy which meant that we had to leave our fate in the hands of market forces whose operations are beyond our control'.[20] The military intended 'to control rather than be controlled' by the economy. These were the days when it seemed almost as if the new military had turned for inspiration to the heroic days of the former Convention People's Party, although what Nkrumaism might look like without Nkrumah was not easy to see. There was also a renewed emphasis on the need for state intervention in the foreign sectors of the economy—mining, banking, insurance—and a much tighter control of external trade, particularly at the ports and frontiers, than the Progress government had been willing to impose. But the most likely explanation of such policies was not simply an undoing of what the Busia government had tried to achieve—there was no professed desire to return to the 1950s—but a stumbling forward of necessity towards a greater degree of self-reliance, helped considerably by a very sharp rise in both cocoa and gold prices.[21]

Much the same pattern of change could be seen in the N.R.C.'s external relations. Shortly after seizing control, Acheampong announced that his foreign policy would be based on 'non-alignment' and 'positive neutralism'—evocative phrases in Ghana. The notion of a dialogue with South Africa was finally abandoned, and diplomatic relations (severed by the N.L.C.) were resumed with the People's Republic of China. The N.R.C. also announced that it intended to resume full diplomatic relations with Guinea, despite the non-payment by Sékou Touré of the £6 million still owed to Ghana. But the government ran into difficulties following Nkrumah's death in Bucharest on 27 April 1972. A delegation led by Col. Benni, and including Joe Appiah and Imoru Ayarna, went to Conakry to bring the body (which had been flown from Romania) back to Accra, but were refused permission to do so by Sekou Touré until four conditions had been met: Nkrumah's rehabilitation in the public's esteem in Ghana, the release of any C.P.P. members still detained in Ghana, the lifting of the ban on those individuals who had shared Nkrumah's exile, and the burial of Nkrumah's body with the honours due a Head of State. The N.R.C. was offended by these demands. According to Acheampong, 'in effect Sekou Touré wanted us to negate the coup of 1966'. Moreover, compliance would have meant dishonouring Kotoka, who was as much a hero for the Ghana military as Nkrumah was for his former party followers. Sekou Touré then held a funeral for Nkrumah in Guinea, in conjunction with the fourteenth anniversary of the country's independence, while the N.R.C. simply held a memorial service. It was the intercession of General Gowon of Nigeria which ultimately effected a settlement, and the body was returned to Ghana on 7 July where it lay in state in Accra for ten hours before burial at Nkrumah's birthplace in the small village of Nkroful. The Eulogy was read by Colonel Agyekum, the Western Regional Commissioner, on behalf of Acheampong, who praised Nkrumah for waging:

> a relentless war against colonialism and racism . . . Today we mourn . . . a great leader . . . But like all of us, Dr. Nkrumah had his shortcomings. Perhaps the problems of Africa and the world looked so large in his horizon that he overlooked certain serious difficulties and irregularities at home.[22]

It was possible to note in such remarks, as in the general stance of the N.R.C., a certain distancing of the new regime from the politics of the pre- and post-independence years. The former politicians were all but gone, and such leaders as might emerge were likely to be military or civilian spokesmen of a different generation. Of course, familiar problems remained. The N.R.C. looked initially for allies in familiar places. It even turned momentarily to an Advisory Council of former civil servants and businessmen—among them A. L. Adu, J. V. L. Philips and Robert Gardiner—which met at a week-end, and then disbanded; it turned to surviving politicians, including Gbedemah and Joe Appiah; and to former C.P.P. advisors like Appiah Danquah, Amoaka Atta and Ayeh Kumi. There were familiar rumours of plots and strategems against the government. In July 1972 it was announced that a conspiracy had been uncovered, and a military trial was held of army N.C.O.'s and former Progress party members who were found guilty of plotting with Busia (in exile in Oxford) to stage a counter-coup in which (it was said) the intention was not only to remove the N.R.C. but to kill all officers above the rank of Captain.[23] There were rumours also of quarrels between the police and army, between rival factions within the T.U.C., and between Akan and non-Akan, Ewe and non-Ewe, within the administration. Within two years, there were further plots hatched (it was said) by members of the former C.C.P.—including Kojo Botsio and John Tettegah. Such reports were familiar indeed! But there was no talk this time of an early return to civilian rule. Instead, there was Acheampong's statement that: 'We of the N.R.C. will only hand over power when we are satisfied that a firm foundation has been laid both economically and socially.[24] The old politics, it seemed, were over and it was time to begin anew. That being so, neither judgement nor prophecy about what might lie ahead was possible.

Notes

1. *The Daily Times,* 29 July 1971, p. 7.
2. General Ocran had noted that in 1965, on the eve of the first coup, only 40 per cent of the armoured vehicles were roadworthy and only 30 per cent of the general purposes vehicles could be used. A. K. Ocran, *A Myth is Broken,* (Essex: Longmans, Green & Co., 1968), p. 46.
3. *The Daily Times*, 29 July 1971.
4. *West Africa*, 25 February 1972.
5. Maxwell Owusu, 'Ghana's Search for Solvency', *Africa Today*. These problems are reminiscent of Ocran's description of the army in the 1964–65 period. 'One day they (the officers) were to pay for their electricity; the next day they were to lose their training allowances; the following day, they were to lose their travelling facilities ... The salaries introduced in 1957 meant little in 1965; they were worth only a third of their value.' Ocran *op. cit.*, p. 43.
6. *New York Times*, 22 January 1972.
7. See above, p. 80.
8. The Act followed the bringing together in Kumasi in January 1971 of a People's Popular Party under Mr. Johny Hansen.
9. *West Africa* 25 July 1971. Busia's reaction (if the reports are true) was both realistic and uncharacteristic: he is said to have remarked that, if a coup took place, he would offer no resistance.
10. The N.R.C. dropped the prosecution of Kattah in January, 1972.
11. *Times 18 Jan. 1972.* Interview with Michael Wolfers. Col. Acheampong 'told me that he had been considering a military takeover since the middle of 1970.... He said that almost from the beginning, Dr. Kofi Busia's civilian government had not followed the spirit of the constitution. Col. Acheampong said that he had not wanted to judge hastily what he regarded as constitutional infringements, and on return from duty overseas he had begun to sound out opinion. He had waited until Dr. Busia appeared fully committed to actions that justified a change.'
12. *Command Structure: November 1970.*

First Brigade H.Q. (Accra)—Brigadier H. O. Twum-Barima
First Battalion (Tema) (Vacant)

Second Battalion (Takoradi)—A/Lt. Col. E. K. Utaka
Fifth Battalion (Accra)—Lt. Col. I. K. Acheampong
Second Brigade H.Q.—(Kumasi)—Brigadier J. R. Acquah
Third Battalion (Sunyani)—Lt. Col. C. D. Benni
Fourth Battalion (Kumasi)—Lt. Col. E. M. Osei-Owusu
Sixth Battalion (Tamale)—Lt. Col. F. W. K. Akuffo

13. It had been the dismissal of Otu and Ankrah by Nkrumah in 1965 which had led to the appointment of Col. Kotoka as Commander of the Second Brigade and of Major Afrifa as his Brigade Major. See Chapter 1.
14. *Washington Post*, 26 January 1972.
15. *West Africa*, 4 February 1972.
16. Troops could have been brought down from Kumasi to challenge the troops in control of Accra—following the 1966 plan.
17. *West Africa*, January 1972.
18. Ashley-Lassen (who had returned from India before the coup) was appointed Chief of Defence Staff; Erskine became the new Army Commander; J. H. Cobbina, the new Inspector-General of Police. The new N.R.C. was almost half Ewe, although it was also *broadened*, in a different sense, by the inclusion of representatives from each of the services and the police. Two days later Lt. Col. Benni was reinstated.
19. *The January–June Budget*, Government Printer, Accra, 1972.
20. Ibid.
21. For a brief analysis of early N.R.C. economic policies see the writer's article 'Ghana's search for a New Economic Policy' in *West Africa*, 25 November 1972.
22. *West Africa*, 21 July 1972.
23. See the report in *West Africa*, 25 August 1972 and footnote 4 *Introduction*.
24. *ibid.*, 8 September 1972.

SELECTED BIBLIOGRAPHY

Afrifa, A. A. *The Ghana Coup,* London, Frank Cass, 1966.

Alexander, H. T. *African Tightrope: My Two Years as Nkrumah's Chief of Staff,* Boston, F. Praeger, 1966.

Apter, David. *Ghana in Transition,* New York, Atheneum, 1963.

Austin, Dennis. *Politics in Ghana, 1946–60,* London, O.U.P., 1964.

Barker, Peter. *Operation Cold Chop,* Ghana Pub. Corp., 1969.

Birmingham, W., Neustadt, I., Omaboe, E. M. (Eds.) *A Study of Contemporary Ghana,* Vol. I and II, London, Allen and Unwin, 1966.

Bretton, Henry, L. *The Rise and Fall of Kwame Nkrumah,* London, Pall Mall, 1966.

Brokensha, D. W. *Social Change at Larteh, Ghana,* London, O.U.P., 1966.

Busia, K. A. *Africa in Search of Democracy,* London, Routledge & Kegan Paul, 1967.

Busia, K. A. *Position of the Chief in the Modern Political System of Ashanti,* London, O.U.P., 1951.

Caldwell, J. C. *African Rural-Urban Migration: The Movement to Ghana's Towns,* London, A.N.U., 1969.

Davidson, Basil. *Black Star, A View of the Life and Times of Kwame Nkrumah,* London, Allen Lane, 1973.

Dunn, J. and Robertson, A. F. *Dependence and Opportunity: Political Change in Ahajo,* Cambridge, C.U.P., 1973.

Fitch, B. and Oppenheimer, M. *Ghana: End of an Illusion,* London, Monthly Review Press, 1966.

Foster, Philip. *Education and Social Change in Ghana,* Chicago, Univ. of Chicago Press, 1965.

Foster, P. and Zolberg, A. R. *Ghana and the Ivory Coast,* Chicago, Univ. of Chicago Press, 1971.

Hill, Polly. *The Gold Coast Cocoa Farmer,* London, O.U.P., 1956.

Hill, Polly. *Migrant Cocoa Farmers of Southern Ghana,* Cambridge, C.U.P., 1963.

Ikoku, S. G. *Le Ghana de Nkrumah,* Paris, Francois Maspero, 1971.

Kay, G. B. (ed.). *The Political Economy of Colonialism in Ghana,* Cambridge, C.U.P., 1970.

Kimble, David. *Political History of Ghana, 1850–1928,* Oxford, Clarendon Press, 1963.

Nkrumah, Kwame. *Autobiography,* London, Nelson, 1957.

Nkrumah, Kwame. *Dark Days in Ghana,* London, Lawrence & Wishart, 1968.

Ocran, A. K. *The Myth is Broken,* London, Longmans, 1968.

Omari, Peter. *Kwame Nkrumah: The Anatomy of an African Dictator,* London, Hurst, 1970.

Owusu, Maxwell. *Uses and Abuses of Power,* Chicago, Univ. of Chicago Press, 1970.

Peil, M. *The Ghanaian Factory Worker,* Cambridge, C.U.P., 1972.

Pinkey, Robert. *Ghana Under Military Rule, 1966–69,* London, Methuen, 1972.

Thompson, W. Scott. *Ghana's Foreign Policy 1957–66,* Princeton, Princeton University Press, 1969.

Tordoff, W. *Ashanti Under the Prempehs,* London, O.U.P., 1965.

INDEX